LANGUAGE PROCESSING IN CHINESE

ADVANCES IN PSYCHOLOGY

90

Editors:

G. E. STELMACH

P. A. VROON

NORTH-HOLLAND
AMSTERDAM • LONDON • NEW YORK • TOKYO

LANGUAGE PROCESSING IN CHINESE

Edited by

Hsuan-Chih CHEN
Department of Psychology
The Chinese University of Hong Kong
Shatin, NT, Hong Kong

Ovid J.L. TZENG
Department of Psychology
University of California
Riverside, CA, U.S.A.

1992

NORTH-HOLLAND
AMSTERDAM • LONDON • NEW YORK • TOKYO

NORTH-HOLLAND
ELSEVIER SCIENCE PUBLISHERS B.V.
Sara Burgerhartstraat 25
P.O. Box 211, 1000 AE Amsterdam, The Netherlands

ISBN: 0 444 89139 0

©1992 ELSEVIER SCIENCE PUBLISHERS B.V. All rights reserved.

No part of this publication may be reproduced, stored in a retrieval system or transmitted, in any form or by any means, electronic, mechanical, photocopying, recording or otherwise, without the prior written permission of the publisher, Elsevier Science Publishers B.V., Permissions Department, P.O. Box 521, 1000 AM Amsterdam, The Netherlands.

Special regulations for readers in the U.S.A. - This publication has been registered with the Copyright Clearance Center Inc. (CCC), Salem, Massachusetts. Information can be obtained from the CCC about conditions under which photocopies of parts of this publication may be made in the U.S.A. All other copyright questions, including photocopying outside of the U.S.A., should be referred to the copyright owner, Elsevier Science Publishers B.V., unless otherwise specified.

No responsibility is assumed by the publisher for any injury and/or damage to persons or property as a matter of products liability, negligence or otherwise, or from any use or operation of any methods, products, instructions or ideas contained in the material herein.

pp. 367 - 382 : Copyright not transferred.

This book is printed on acid-free paper.

Printed in The Netherlands

Preface

Chinese is perhaps the most widely used language in the world. Its popularity and many specific features makes it a unique language. The Chinese language differs from many Indo-European languages in important ways. For example, Chinese words generally do not have inflections to indicate grammatical attributes such as the number, gender, and case for nouns or the tense and aspect for verbs. Words in the Indo-European languages, on the other hand, generally have inflectional markings. Moreover, Chinese words usually have no inherently marked lexical categories, while words in the Indo-European languages normally do. In addition, the Chinese adopted a writing system which is logographic in nature. Unlike the alphabetic principle, its script/speech relationship is highly opaque. The characters, as they are commonly called, represent lexical morphemes, whereas alphabetic symbols, as in common Indo-European languages, represent phonemes. Undoubtedly, knowledge about how people process this specific language, Chinese, is indispensable to the general understanding of human language processing.

The aim of this book is to integrate the most recent research investigating cognitive aspects of the Chinese language into a single academic reference for researchers interested in Chinese language processing and related fields. In fact, in putting together this book, it was our goal to invite contributions from specialists working in major areas of Chinese language processing. We did succeed in assembling an excellent group of researchers, from different parts of the world (i.e., Hong Kong, Taiwan, Mainland China, America, Australia, and Europe), representing a great diversity of research topics and perspectives.

In this book, we have organized 14 papers that deal with several aspects of language processing in Chinese; some review one or several major issues and summarize the related evidence, and others present new research on specific issues. These papers have been grouped into five sections of the book. Part One includes four papers on visual perception and processing of characters. Huang and Wang focus primarily on the role of structural properties of Chinese characters in visual perception. Next, Flores d'Arcais examines the activation processes of graphemic, phonological, and semantic information in character recognition. After this, Cheng looks at the phonological processes in lexical access. In the final chapter, Hue reports the findings of three experiments examining the recognition processes underlying character naming.

Part Two contains three papers which focus more explicitly on lexical representation than on process. Hoosain discusses the concept of the word and the nature of the Chinese lexicon, whereas Zhang and Peng present the results of three experiments investigating the structure of the lexicon. Taft and Chen turn their attention to tonal and phonemic representations in the lexicon and to the use of tonal information in making homophonic judgments.

Part Three comprises two papers on sentence and text comprehension. Chen looks at the comprehension processes in reading Chinese text, while Li, Bates, Liu, and MacWhinney examine the functional roles of several cues (e.g., word order and animacy) in sentence interpretation.

Part Four includes three papers on language acquisition. Miao and Zhu summarize the results to date from the studies conducted in China on language development. Chang surveys the recent studies on the acquisition of Chinese syntax. Chien concerns more specifically on the theoretical implications of Chomsky's "Principles and Parameters" model for language acquisition.

Finally, there are two papers in Part Five: Yin and Butterworth present the results of their work with deep and surface dyslexia and Au looks at the methodological issues in cross-linguistic research on language and cognition.

The volume presents an exciting sample of the current work in Chinese language processing. It reveals both the potential of this relatively new research area and also many intriguing questions that studying language processing in Chinese has raised, thus pointing out a number of possible directions for future research. It will, we hope, provide stimulating reading to anyone interested in the cognitive aspects of the Chinese language, human cognition, and any of the disciplines related to the psychology of language.

Acknowledgments

The idea of putting together a book of this sort was developed and the first stage of planning was completed while the first editor was spending a sabbatical year at the Institute for Perception Research (IPO) in Eindhoven and the Eindhoven University of Technology, The Netherlands. The main part of this project was carried out at the Chinese University of Hong Kong with support from a UPGC Direct Grant for Research provided by the Social Science and Education Panel of the University. The support and resources of these institutions are gratefully acknowledged.

We would like to thank all the contributors for their cooperation through the preparation of this book. We are especially grateful to Rumjahn Hoosain, Marcus Taft, Thomas Lee, and Yun Yang Zee, who helped to review one or more of the chapters in the book. Our colleagues, In-Mao Liu, Norman Freeman, Marcus Taft, and Michael Bond, were generous in their advice and encouragement. We are also grateful to K. Michielsen of Elsevier and George Stelmach, the editor of the *Advances in Psychology* series, for having faith in the project, and to Mary McAdam for her technical editing.

Our special thanks go to Connie Ho, Kit Kan Tang, Candy Leung, Agnes Kwan, Karen Ma, Christine Lo, and Irene Liem for their assistance in preparing the indices and the camera-ready copy for this book, to Tze-Chau Chiu and Yau-Man Fung for their technical assistance, and to Robert Phay and Siu Lung for their help in checking and correcting the English of various chapters in this book. And best thanks, finally, to Yin-Gin and Sen-Lay for their constant support of the first editor.

Hsuan-Chih Chen
Ovid J.L. Tzeng

List of Contributors

Terry Kit-fong Au, Department of Psychology, University of California, Los Angeles, California 90024-1563, U.S.A.

Elizabeth Bates, Department of Psychology, University of California, San Diego, La Jolla, California 92093, U.S.A.

Brian Butterworth, Department of Psychology, University College London, WC1E 6BT, London, U.K.

Hsing-Wu Chang, Department of Psychology, National Taiwan University, Taipei 10764, Taiwan

Hsuan-Chih Chen, Department of Psychology, Chinese University of Hong Kong, Shatin, N.T., Hong Kong

Chao-Ming Cheng, Department of Psychology, National Taiwan University, Taipei 10764, Taiwan

Yu-Chin Chien, Department of Psychology, California State University, San Bernardino, California 92407, U.S.A.

Givoanni B. Flores d'Arcais, Max-Planck-Institute für Psycholinguistik, Postbus 310, NL-6500 Nijmegen, The Netherlands

Rumjahn Hoosain, Department of Psychology, University of Hong Kong, Hong Kong

Jong-Tsun Huang, Department of Psychology, National Taiwan University, Taipei 10764, Taiwan

Chih-Wei Hue, Department of Psychology, National Taiwan University, Taipei 10764, Taiwan

Ping Li, Center for Research in Language, University of California, San Diego, La Jolla, California 92093, U.S.A.

Hua Liu, Department of Cognitive Science, University of California, San Diego, La Jolla, California 92093, U.S.A.

Brian MacWhinney, Department of Psychology, Carnegie Mellon University, Pittsburgh, Pennsylvania 15213, U.S.A.

Xiaochun Miao, Department of Psychology, East China Normal University, Shanghai 20062, China

Danling Peng, Department of Psychology, Beijing Normal University, Beijing 100875, China

Marcus Taft, School of Psychology, University of New South Wales, Kensington, New South Wales 2033, Australia

Man-Ying Wang, Department of Psychology, National Taiwan University, Taipei 10764, Taiwan

Wengang Yin, Department of Psychology, University of College London, WC1E 6BT, London, U.K.

Biyin Zhang, Department of Psychology, Beijing Normal University, Beijing 100875, China

Manshu Zhu, Department of Psychology, East China Normal University, Shanghai 200062, China

Contents

Preface v

Acknowledgments vii

List of Contributors ix

PART I. Character Recognition and Naming

From Unit to Gestalt: Perceptual Dynamics in Recognizing
Chinese Characters 3
Jong-Tsun Huang and Man-Ying Wang

Graphemic, Phonological, and Semantic Activation Processes
during the Recognition of Chinese Characters 37
Giovanni B. Flores d'Arcais

Lexical Access in Chinese: Evidence from Automatic Activation
of Phonological Information 67
Chao-Ming Cheng

Recognition Processes in Character Naming 93
Chih-Wei Hue

PART II. Lexical Structure and Word Processing

Psychological Reality of the Word in Chinese 111
Rumjahn Hoosain

Decomposed Storage in the Chinese Lexicon 131
Biyin Zhang and Danling Peng

Judging Homophony in Chinese: The Influence of Tones 151
Marcus Taft and Hsuan-Chih Chen

PART III. Sentence and Text Comprehension

Reading Comprehension in Chinese: Implications from Character
Reading Times 175
Hsuan-Chih Chen

Cues as Functional Constraints on Sentence Processing in Chinese   207
Ping Li, Elizabeth Bates, Hua Liu, and Brian MacWhinney

PART IV. Language Acquisition

Language Development in Chinese Children 237
Xiaochun Miao and Manshu Zhu

The Acquisition of Chinese Syntax 277
Hsing-Wu Chang

Theoretical Implications of the Principles and Parameters
Model for Language Acquisition in Chinese 313
Yu-Chin Chien

PART V. Neuropsychological and Methodological Issues

Deep and Surface Dyslexia in Chinese 349
Wengang Yin and Brian Butterworth

Cross-Linguistic Research on Language and Cognition:
Methodological Challenges 367
Terry Kit-fong Au

Author Index 383

Subject Index 391

Part I

CHARACTER RECOGNITION AND NAMING

From Unit to Gestalt: Perceptual Dynamics in Recognizing Chinese Characters

Jong-Tsun Huang and Man-Ying Wang
National Taiwan University

The present article discusses the role of geometrical and structural properties in the recognition of Chinese characters. A stage model for Chinese character recognition is proposed that non-accidental properties are first searched within the character, and character regions are parsed. Then, character components and their relations are activated. The activation of the word model finally triggers the identification of the intended character. Under this analytical framework the literature is reviewed on the effects of stroke inter-section, order and number of strokes, character decomposability, component/character relationship, and corner information in character recognition. We critically evaluate the plausibility of perceptual/non-perceptual dichotomy, horse-racing models, and other general issues in the hope that this may facilitate the proper investigation of the perceptual dynamics in recognizing Chinese characters.

Supposing that Chinese characters are functionally equivalent to English words and that visual information processing mechanisms are universal in human perception, one would suspect that the principles derived from English letter perception and word recognition experiments could apply as well to Chinese character recognition. However, there are several ways one might challenge this argument. Hung and Tzeng (1981) examined possible processing differences between alphabetic and logographic scripts. They focused on the facets of phonological recoding, lexical access, and cerebral lateralization, among others. In this article, we will emphasize the geometrical and structural variables to provide a view of orthographic variations which might contribute differentially to Chinese character recognition.

Geometrical and Structural Properties of Chinese Characters

Liu, Chuang, and Wang (1975) identified a total of 40,032 Chinese words from a base of nearly one million printed words. The words are varied from one to six characters with different frequency counts. Two-character words occupy the largest proportion with 65.15% of the entire group (Huang & Liu, 1978). Each two-character word has its unique meanings, but the constituent characters also have separate independent meanings. English nominal compounds are similar; however, they account for a much smaller proportion in the English language. Although two-character Chinese words are often equated in function as English words, one might suspect that the prevailing incidence of two-character words in Chinese will signify different perceptual consequences. However, Tzeng, Hung, Cotton, and Wang (1979) showed a similar pattern in comparison with lateralization studies using English materials. They found that the naming response of a single Chinese character manifested a left-visual-field (LVF) superiority effect, whereas naming or lexical decision time for two-character words showed a right-visual-field (RVF) superiority effect. It might be argued that a single character is processed in a holistic-gestalt manner, while a two-character word is analyzed sequentially and analytically. Suppose that the sequential order between characters must be processed so that a two-character word could be correctly recognized, then a RVF superiority effect in the two-character word recognition might be attributable to the finer temporal resolving power in the left hemisphere. Such a finer cerebral function will, in turn, provide the opportunity for better sequential coding (Tzeng & Wang, 1984). We should therefore be very careful in presenting arguments concerning functional differences between different writing systems.

Even if two-character words are the most frequent semantic units in natural reading, it is inevitable to focus on single characters for establishing a context-free character recognition model. The majority of Chinese single characters are compound characters consisting of one radical component (214 possible radicals in total) and one stem component. In most cases, the stem by itself can serve as a single character, whereas the radical is derived from a simple character but is not commonly used in isolation. In some cases, the stem component of a compound character is itself a compound character. That is to say, a radical-stem compound = radical + stem = radical + (radical + stem) = radical + (radical-stem compound). It is reminiscent of a recursive function. A recursively defined function is one in which the function is defined in terms of itself. This function f might be defined by indirect recursion through a "stem" function g, while g is in turn defined in terms of f (radical-stem). Such a mathematical structure possesses abundant computational properties (Arbib, Kfoury, & Moll, 1981; Hopcroft & Ullman, 1979). Recursive structure is seldom found in English words.

For most alphabetic scripts, the word is composed of left-to-right letters (Taylor & Taylor, 1983). Word reading follows a unidirectional or one-dimensional scanning path. Although horizontal (AB structure) and vertical ($\frac{A}{B}$) configurations account for the largest proportion in Chinese, there are more than 15 identified configurations such as A, ABC, $_B^A C$, and $A_C B$, among others. Figure 1 presents some selected configurations with exemplars. Character reading is therefore performed through a multi-directional or 2-D scanning path.

Besides their possible recursive structure and 2-D scanning configuration, Chinese single characters are confined in a fixed region, irrespective of the number of strokes in a character. Therefore, simple and complex characters all occupy the same prescribed area in regular printed materials. The same does not hold for alphabetic scripts. The greater the number of letters, the longer the string. It is thus possible in Chinese to manipulate the degree of complexity while holding the occupying space constant. In alphabetic scripts, complexity level and string length are confounded.

With the same complexity level or number of strokes in a prescribed region, we can also compute the degree of spatial compactness. The index of spatial compactness can distinguish some patterns composed of the same number of pieces. This is the square-root-area-over-perimeter measure that Podgorny and Shepard (1983) adapted from Attneave and Arnoult (1956). They showed that probes of less compact figures required more time to classify correctly. Subjects were more successful in confining their attention to sets of mutually proximal items (Podgorny & Shepard, 1983). Bethell--Fox and Shepard (1988) also noticed that mental rotation time became independent of stimulus compactness after continued practice. They found that stimulus representation is rotated piece by piece if it is unfamiliar; however, it is rotated as an integrated whole if it is sufficiently well known. There exist no studies directly applicable to the role of spatial compactness in character recognition; however, it might be expected from the above arguments that no effects should be found since Chinese characters are over-learned semantic units.

Structural Category	Exemplar
AB	好　暗　封　獻
A B	否　音　異　幫
A	日　正　兩　為
ABC	測　假　辨　謝
A B C	森　嵌　箱　露
A B C	替　照　整　雙

Figure 1. Selected Chinese orthographic configurations with exemplars.

With these geometrical and structural properties in mind, it might be observed that frequency counts, association values, and imagery ratings of characters could be influenced by these idiosyncrasies. Let us take frequency counts as an example. Frequency count in English is in most cases simply an enumeration for the words appearing in isolation on a computational base, for example, the frequency of occurrence in one-million words. However, two additional categories are quite important in Chinese character recognition. The first is that of unit frequency. *Unit frequency* refers to the total frequency count of an item either by itself or as part of another character (e.g., a syllable in a word in English or embedded in a larger radical-stem compound character in Chinese) (Fang & Wu, 1989; Kucera & Francis, 1967). The second is that of marginal frequency (Cheng, 1982; Huang, 1979). *Marginal frequency* refers to the total frequency count of an item either by itself or in other two- to six-character words. Simply stated, a character not only appears in isolation with unique meaning but also combines with other character(s) to form a word with a different meaning. Marginal frequency comprises all the frequency counts of a single character, no matter how it appears. Selective usage of different frequency count measures will entail different perceptual consequences.

The present article deals mainly with how a Chinese character might be perceptually decomposed into its components and how its components are combined to form an integral character. We investigated the character recognition mechanisms which were responsible for the path of a character from unit to gestalt, and vice versa. The mechanisms should be reassessed on a structural rather than on a cross-cultural language usage level.

Realizing that the Chinese character is more like a 2-D familiar pattern rather than a left-to-right string, we adopted a modified version of Biederman's (1987, 1990) recognition-by-components (RBC) model as our analytical framework (See Figure 2 for reference). We assumed that the basic principles behind character recognition and object recognition were largely similar. Although characters differ from objects in their direct and easy pronounceability, natural object recognition usually involves a naming response.

A modified model shown in Figure 2 indicates that the character components are first parsed at regions of curvature minima or deep concavity. Nonaccidental properties like collinearity, curvilinearity, symmetry, parallelism, and cotermination are found. Properties are called non-accidental if they are only slightly affected by accidental alignments of viewpoints and object features. After non-accidental properties are detected and character components parsed, they serve as precursors to trigger the activation of character components and their relations. Activation of the character model is followed by character identification after completion of a chain of interactive processes.

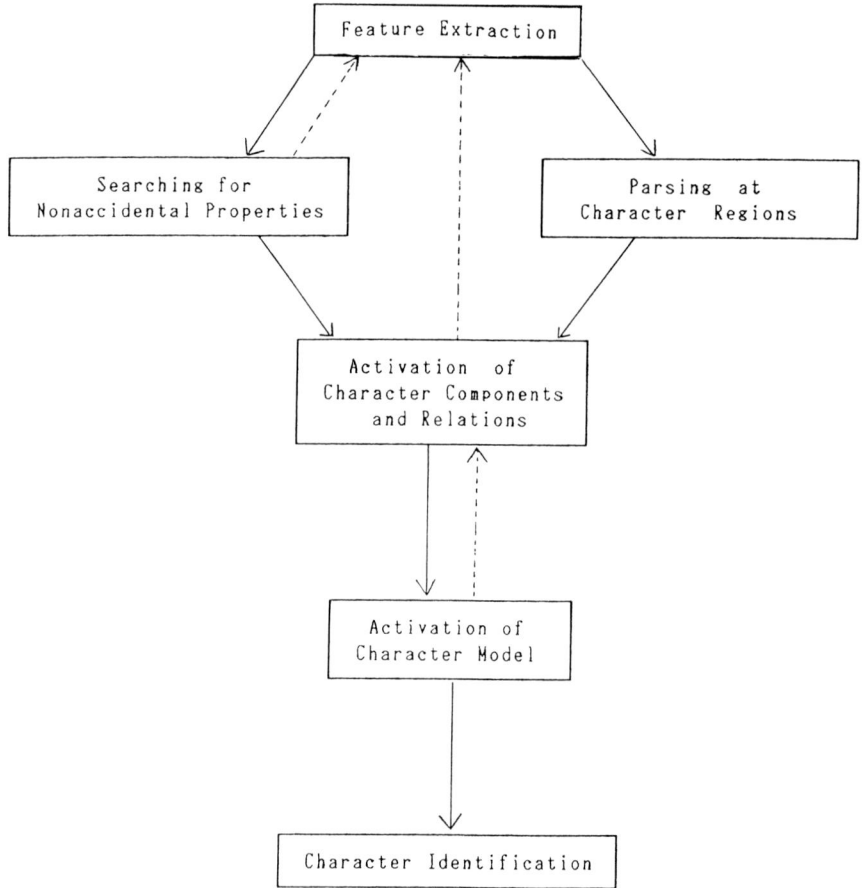

Figure 2. A stage model for chinese character recognition. Possible top-down routes are shown with dashed lines. (Modified from Biederman, 1990.)

It is important to note that our modified stage model differs significantly from Biederman's (1987) at its very early stage. We adopted the concept of feature extraction into the model. Biederman (1990) claimed the notion of "feature" was inapplicable in constructing a stage model for recognizing natural objects. Instead, he proposed "geon" (geometrical ions) as a basic perceptual unit. Although we fully agree with his arguments in the context of natural object recognition, we decided to replace his "edge extraction" stage with "feature extraction". The reason is that the operation of feature extraction at the very early stage in word recognition has been well documented (e.g., Gibson & Levin, 1975; McClelland & Rumelhart, 1981). This departure is not serious. We will not go any further on the mechanism of this feature extraction stage.

Searching for Non-accidental Properties within a Character

Biederman (1987) found that the deletion of non-accidental properties in the line-drawn contour hampers the object recovery and, henceforth, the recognition of natural objects. The deletion of accidental properties by the same amount, however, is inconsequential to a satisfactory recognition. It is believed that the filling-in process will be effectively undertaken along the once-intact contour if accidental instead of non-accidental properties are deleted. Chinese characters are structurally 2-D, and non-accidental properties are found abundantly in the intersections among strokes, inflections of strokes, and coterminations. Huang, Sun, and Tsou (1990) compared the effects of deleting accidental or non-accidental properties within a Chinese character and found that a deletion of non-accidental properties to the extent of 25% of the whole character would significantly hamper recognition accuracy of less complex characters under brief presentation. However, no differences were found between the deletion of non-accidental and accidental properties on different complexity levels when the deletion was increased up to 40%. It might be argued that more complex characters do have more non-accidental properties due to their abundant structural contacts among a greater number of strokes. Non-accidental properties might be preserved to a great extent than those in less complex characters when the deletion is made up to 25%. The insignificant differences for 40% deletion might be due to a ceiling effect.

Let's look at this problem from another angle. Suppose that an object picture is cut into pieces: under what conditions can these pieces be successfully put together to achieve a satisfactory object recovery? If an object or a character has become unrecognizable due to the deletion of non-accidental properties, then it is probable that unrecognizable but intrinsically correlated pieces could be chunked together to identify the non-accidental properties existing among these pieces. To simplify the case, two unrecognizable halves of a character can be put together to see if they could be made recognizable. Huang and Sakurai (1987) decomposed a character into 64 pieces. Two non-overlapping and complementary halves were then constructed from the 64 pieces under the constraint that a subunit for each eye should not trigger any obvious phonetic or semantic possibilities. They were then dichoptically presented to the subject. Table 1 summarizes the result of our experiment. High incidence of successful binocular identification occurred even if monocular cues were completely eliminated.

The results do not support a prediction generated from a cooperative algorithm. To account for human early visual information processing under stereoscopic conditions, Marr and Poggio (1976) and Marr (1982) have developed, with a certain degree of success, a cooperative algorithm with three operational constraints among perceived surface patches. There are three matching constraints embodied in this cooperative algorithm. (a) Uniqueness: in almost all cases a dot from one retinal image can match no more than one black dot from the other image. (b) Compatibility: black dots (or surface patches) can match only black dots (or similar patches). (c) Continuity: the disparity of the matches varies smoothly almost everywhere over the image. In Huang and Sakurai's study, they use a 2-D planar dichoptic matching task. The continuity requirement is fulfilled by noting that zero disparity dominates everywhere over the image. The uniqueness constraint is not violated in matching two non-overlapping and complementary halves to a meaningful character. However, the compatibility constraint is not operated in this case since a black patch matches a white one in reconstructing the character recovery. According to the cooperative algorithm, it is impossible to obtain a result as shown in the lowest row in Table 1. It is therefore highly probable that an alignment procedure between two retinal images was conducted before a compatibility mechanism was initiated. In the process of alignment, many chaotic contacts between parts can occur, followed by the emergence of some useful non-accidental properties. A sufficient set of non-accidental properties with their connected neighborhood might in turn activate an awareness of character occurrence, then redirect the subject's controlled alignment to some other properties. This alignment procedure is supposed to be interactive in nature.

Table 1
Correct Identification Rates (%) of Chinese Characters under Dichoptic Presentations (N=14).

		High-Frequency Words		Low-Frequency Words	
		Whole-Word Display	Non-overlapping and Complementary Display	Whole-Word Display	Non-overlapping and Complementary Display
Monocular Cues Still Effective	Left-Eye Recognition	100	42	100	44
	Right-Eye Recognition	100	50	100	11
	Successful Binocular Recognition	100	67	100	78
Monocular Cues Completely Eliminated	Left-Eye Recognition	--	0	--	0
	Right-Eye Recognition	--	0	--	0
	Successful Binocular Recognition	--	17	--	44

The same task was also performed on 24-corner random polygons. Experimental results showed that the performance with random polygons can not match that with Chinese characters. The superiority might be due to an unconscious but sophisticated grouping mechanism which has been firmly developed through over-learned character recognition. The detection of intersections, coterminations, local symmetry, parallelism through the alignment procedure is then put together by this grouping mechanism. It is then possible to trigger useful chunks to facilitate recognition of meaningful components and, henceforth, character recognition.

In the case of non-zero disparity, Chen (1991) prepared a stereo pair composed of two non-overlapping and complementary but unrecognizable halves of a character. Two unrecognizable halves were observed to lie on different depth planes through dichoptic presentation. However, they could be integrated for a successful character recovery through different planes. Consistent with Huang and Sakurai's (1987) result, the rate of successful binocular identification of Chinese characters was found to be greater than that of geometrical figures in this study. The above argument might also hold for this result.

Parsing at Character Regions

Although global precedence is sometimes suggested to be at least as effective as local processing, parsing at character regions is surely a prerequisite for efficient character recognition. It is not easy to study how character regions are parsed in a natural reading situation. Responsible mechanisms are therefore explored under a brief or blurred presentation. Sentence or word context is also provided to compare with the isolated presentation of the target character.

Components Parsing and Perceptual Separability

Single-character words have their unique meanings. For some single characters, their constituent components also have independent meanings. With this property in mind, Huang (1984) selected some radical-stem compounds which are horizontally structured (AB configuration) to demonstrate component separability in single character recognition. He arranged these target characters to appear in isolation, in two-character combinations, or in short sentences (around 6 characters). In order to facilitate the occurrence of perceptual separability of target characters in a speed-reading experiment and to examine the effect of varied semantic context length, the left and right constituent components of the target characters were spaced somewhat apart. The magnitude of spacing between two components for the target characters was on average 2.45 mm, compared with 0.16 mm for non-target characters. It was shown that the incidence of perceptual separability (i.e., to consider components in the target character as two legitimate reading items), is highest for the target characters presented in isolation. The incidence is about four times greater than those appearing in two-character combinations or in short sentences. The same study also explored how blurring of the target character in a two-character combination might affect the incidence of component separation. The difference was remarkable. About 90% of the subjects separated components in blurred target character presentations. The separation frequency was nine times that for reading non-blurred target characters.

Wu (1986) performed a subitizing task to enumerate the stroke (or line) difference between two comparison items. The comparison was made between pairs of single Chinese characters, geometrical figures, or random-line constellations. In the character comparison condition, subjects were asked to compute the stroke difference between two presented characters. For geometrical figures or random-line constellations, subjects responded to line-segment differences between the presented items. A stimulus pair was designed in such a way that two items were related in a hierarchical, embedded, or independent way. If they were related hierarchically, one item was a distinctive component of the other item. The embedding relationship required the elements of one item to intersect with those of the other one. The inclusion property was also assured in the embedding situation. If two items were structurally independent, no relationships might be easily found. Between-strokes (or between-lines) differences and the number of combined strokes (or lines) were also manipulated. If one item has 4 strokes and the other has 8, the between-strokes difference is 4. The number of combined strokes (or lines) was calculated by counting the strokes (or lines) of both items within a stimulus pair. The above example gives a total number of 12. Figure 3 illustrates the selection and preparation of materials.

Subjects were asked to quickly compute the between-strokes (or between-lines) difference within the stimulus pair. Figure 4 depicts the performance for character pairs. Results for geometrical figures or random-line constellations followed a similar pattern. Statistical analysis showed that hierarchically structured materials were computed the fastest, followed by the embedding relationship, and independent pairs, the slowest.

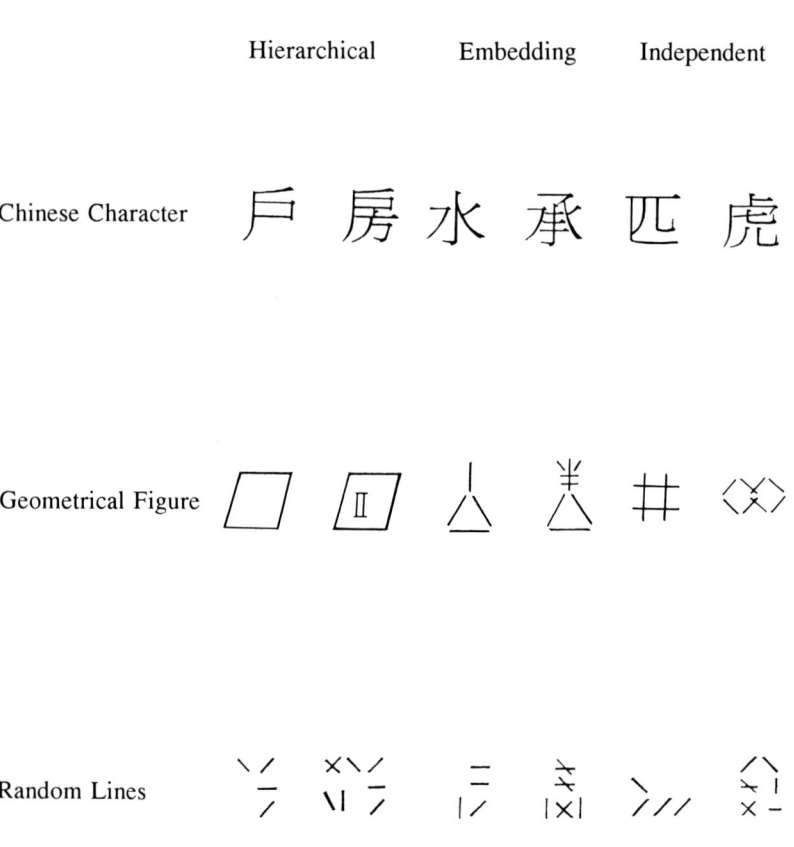

Figure 3. Sample pairs for calculating strokes (or line segments) difference. Items in a stimulus pair are matched in such a way that both items are hierarchically structured, embedded, or independent. Strokes (or line segments) difference between the left and the right items in the stimulus pair is equal to 4. Total number of combined strokes is 12 for every stimulus pair. (From Wu, 1986. Reprinted with permission.)

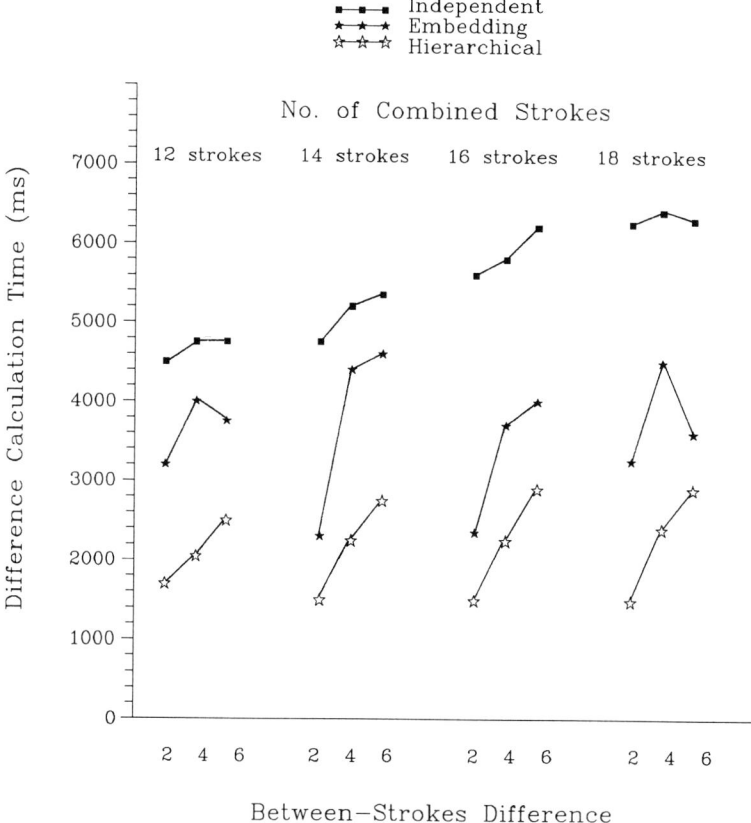

Figure 4. Mean correct calculation time for finding strokes difference between two items. One item is hierarchically structured, embedded, or independent with the other one in the character pair. (From Wu, 1986. Reprinted with permission.)

It seems that subjects learned how to adopt an optimal strategy to perceptually separate components in the stimulus pair so that the common part could be blocked out before the difference counting. Subjects could therefore benefit from this cancellation process to improve their counting speed in the remaining segments. This strategy was most obvious in character pairs (Wu, 1986). This result might have arisen from the fact that the deleted common character part which did not enter into the counting process was also an independent semantic unit, and henceforth perceptually more separatably.

It is obvious from Huang (1984) and Wu (1986) that components can be separated from the single character and parsed under various experimental arrangements. Semantic context, if provided, helps prevent perceptual separability and strengthens the cohesiveness of components in a single character. In our study, we were also concerned with the effect of some structural variables on perceptual separability. To cite the simplest case: Given a horizontally- and vertically-structured two-component characters, which one is perceptually more cohesive?

Yu, Feng, Cao, and Li (1990a) and Yu, Cao, Feng, and Li (1990b) found that the character component was named more quickly when it belonged to one part of the horizontally-structured single character in both natural reading and brief exposure conditions. This result might be an indication that vertically-structured characters are perceptually more compact. However, this direction of difference exists only when character components are read in a normal sequence, i.e., reading from left to right or top to bottom. They also found no differences in the latencies for naming between left and right components in horizontally-structured characters. The same did not hold for vertically-structured characters; bottom components were named faster than top ones. Although their studies did not focus directly on perceptual separability in a Chinese character, the studies might indicate that horizontally-structured characters are more vulnerable to perceptual separability, and that bottom components are perceptually more separable from vertically-structured characters.

A separability phenomenon also occurs in Chinese bigrams. Huang (1979) found that the correlation of word frequency with word association in two-character Chinese words was quite low, which contradicts what had been documented with English materials. Giving a lenient time restriction, he allowed subjects 60 seconds to perform free association on a two-character word. Data from every 20 seconds were examined. The results showed that the subjects produced associations by first responding to a two-character word and its first constituent character. As time passed, the subjects responded to the second constituent. Thus, when subjects are required to associate as many words as possible in response to a presented word without a stringent time restriction, they may first generate words as response to the whole stimulus word. If they run out of associations, they may generate words by considering each constituent as a stimulus. Therefore, perceptual separability might also occur in reading Chinese bigrams.

Free-Floating Components and Perceptual Cohesiveness

When attention is overloaded or diverted, simple features which are extracted from early visual information processing in the scene should be free-floating with respect to one another. In the absence of focused attention and effective constraints from a top-down processing, the features should therefore at times be incorrectly recombined to form "illusory conjunctions" (Treisman & Gelade, 1980). In natural reading, we are seldom aware of the conjunction problem. It might be that letters in words and words in sentences are highly redundant. Subjects may supplement the missing location information by top-down constraints from the lexical nodes or from orthographic structure. However, illusory recombination of letters, i.e., illusory words, can be seen when some words are presented too briefly to allow focused attention on each item in turn (McClelland & Mozer, 1986; Mozer, 1983; Prinzmetal & Millis-Wright, 1984; Treisman & Souther, 1986).

When applying the illusory conjunction paradigm to the study of Chinese character perception, illusory characters were also found (Fang & Wu, 1989; Lai & Huang, 1988; Wu & Fang, 1988). Factors affecting the emergence of illusory characters were partly identified as unit frequency (Fang & Wu, 1989) or conceptual distinctiveness (Wu & Fang, 1988). Unit frequency refers to the total frequency counts of a character either by itself or as part of a larger unit. By keeping character frequencies (i.e., frequency counts of characters appearing in isolation) equal, stem compounds have a higher unit frequency than that of unique compounds. A stem compound refers to a character that can be combined with various stroke patterns to form new characters. Not all compound characters can form parts of more complex compounds. Some cannot join any radical to form new compounds. They represent a unique stem-radical pairing within the repertoire of Chinese characters. They are called unique compounds. Fang and Wu (1989) found that stem compounds indeed give rise to fewer illusory conjunctions than unique compounds when character frequencies were matched closely. Lower unit frequency consistently resulted in a higher rate of illusory conjunctions. It seems that stem compounds are more "compact" and resistant to decomposition into smaller components.

In the feature-integration theory of attention (Treisman & Gelade, 1980), it is not only simple features from an item that should be free-floating; location information specific to those features should also be floating. However, Lai and Huang (1988) found that location-specific information was still preserved in the formation of illusory characters. They briefly presented a horizontally-structured character pair AB and CD by providing a context character CB to facilitate the occurrence of illusory conjunctions. It was designed in such a way that AB, CD, CB, AD, and DA were all legitimate Chinese characters. The result was that the percentage of illusory characters in the form of AD was significantly higher than that of DA.

Let's return to the notion of perceptual cohesiveness again. Chen (1984, 1986) observed a Chinese character inferiority effect by adopting a component detection task. He asked subjects to detect a target component which is embedded in the Chinese characters of a text. If the display size was controlled to let a series of characters (e.g. 10) be seen at one exposure, the character inferiority effect was found. The detection was more difficult for targets embedded in high-frequency than in low-frequency characters. This inferiority effect was significantly reduced if the display size was one character for each exposure. The finding is consistent with that of Healy, Oliver, and McNamara (1987), in which English materials were adopted. Both findings can be interpreted by the utilization model suggested by Drewnowski and Healy (1977). By assuming an independent processing mechanism between character (or word) and component (or letter) levels, character identification could be completed solely on the basis of character-level information. For high-frequency characters, the speed of processing character-level information might be very rapid. Processing of the character components might be underway upon the completion of character recognition. The error rate will thus be higher for component detection task among high-frequency characters, if compared with that among low-frequency ones. Such a character inferiority effect seems to emerge more often in a natural reading arrangement. Under such circumstances, the subject has to scan the characters in a text rapidly so that component detection can be made in a limited exposure time. The large display size in Chen's (1984, 1986) studies resembles that in natural reading conditions, whereas a reduced display size for one single character in one exposure does not conform to the conditions of natural reading.

It is also interesting to note that Wu and Fang (1988) actually provide a different interpretation. They claim that high-frequency target characters in Chen's (1984) study are also high unit frequency characters. These characters, like stem compounds, are more compact and resistant to decomposition into components. Therefore, component detection of a high unit frequency character should be more difficult than that of a low unit frequency character or a pseudo-character. This interpretation reflects Wu and Fang's basic assumption about the formation of perceptual unit, "that frequently encountered patterns are most likely to be adopted by the perceptual system as an integral unit ....." (Fang & Wu, 1989, p.440). However, their interpretation cannot explain satisfactorily the effect of display size in Chen's (1984, 1986) studies. Some additional processing mechanisms, like resource allocation, may need to be incorporated for a better explanation. Healy, Conboy, and Drewnowski (1987) have indicated such a possibility. It still awaits further experimentation.

The final point concerning us here is the unit of processing in forming an illusory character. No definite conclusions can be drawn now. It might be tempting to postulate that character components are free-floating, thus illusory recombinations are performed on these floating components. This argument could be wrong. The occurrence of illusory characters demonstrates only the perceptual consequence under an illusory conjunction paradigm. It does not necessarily imply that the basic free-floating elements are character components. According to the feature-integration theory of attention, it may be that simple features of a character float freely. Under a task requirement which determines if a probe character is present or not in the original display, the correlated features are possibly selected to form a chunk or a character component through some grouping mechanism. Task requirements thus play an important role in the formation of character components and, henceforth, illusory characters. Therefore, it would be an unwarranted assertion to believe that free-floating units are character components. The formation of illusory characters with a possible recombination of character components might be due to a post-perceptual consequence under task requirements.

Activation of Character Components and Relations

The activation of character components and relations between components could provide the clues for character models in the representational system. Activated character models will, in turn, redirect attention to the continued search for needed components and relations. The concept of "relations" is in many respects different from that of non-accidental properties. Non-accidental properties deal primarily with crossings, parallelism, coterminations, and other properties within a character component. The notion of relations stresses instead what happens between components. Relations can be composed of these properties like top-of, left-of, larger-than, side-connected, inclination, and orientation. We suspect that the detection of relations may be mediated by processing the conventional order of strokes in a character.

Huang (1986) conducted a visual gluing experiment to demonstrate the effect of stroke order in recognizing characters from fragmentary information. A Chinese character with measurable structural complexity (i.e., the number of strokes), was split up into the corresponding spatial parts (Ci). The parts (Ci's) were then presented sequentially in the correct relative portion of the pages, such that if the pages were aligned and held up to the light, the entire character would be seen. The subject's task was simply to mentally "glue" them together into a single image and pronounce the target character as soon as possible. A visual analogue of this kind is considered a first-order, i-degree approximation to a sequential tactile processing. Local region Ci is processed simultaneously, but i distributed parts are integrated sequentially. Some samples of segmenting Chinese characters into one, two, four, and eight pieces are shown in Figure 5.

Five experimental conditions were tested in separate experiments. In the One-Unit condition, the target character was kept in its intact form and glued on a cardboard. In the Two-Unit condition, each character was segmented into two symmetric parts (from AB or $\frac{A}{B}$ to A and B) and glued firmly on the correct relative portions of two separate pieces of cardboard. Each part in the Two-Unit condition was further divided into two subunits resulting in four parts to form a Four-Unit condition. The order of presentation of these parts was randomized prior to the beginning of each experimental session. For the Eight-Unit (8a) condition, the same procedure was adopted to cut the character into eight meaningless and unpronounceable pieces. These eight pieces of cardboard were shuffled and handed to the subject before he/she was asked to run the experiment proper. When these pages were aligned and held up to the light, the entire character would be seen. One additional condition 8b was created by using the same materials as in the 8a condition, except that the order of presentation was rearranged to conform to the conventional order of stroke writing. If the order of presentation was arranged in such a way, subjects should have been able to integrate the first four pieces to form the component A, then integrate the second four to B. The third step was to combine A and B to

or AB. For the random sequence presentation (8a), the subject had to gather all parts allocated on separate pages to form a single character AB. For the structured presentation (8b), the subject might identify A and B in serial order then integrate A and B to form AB.

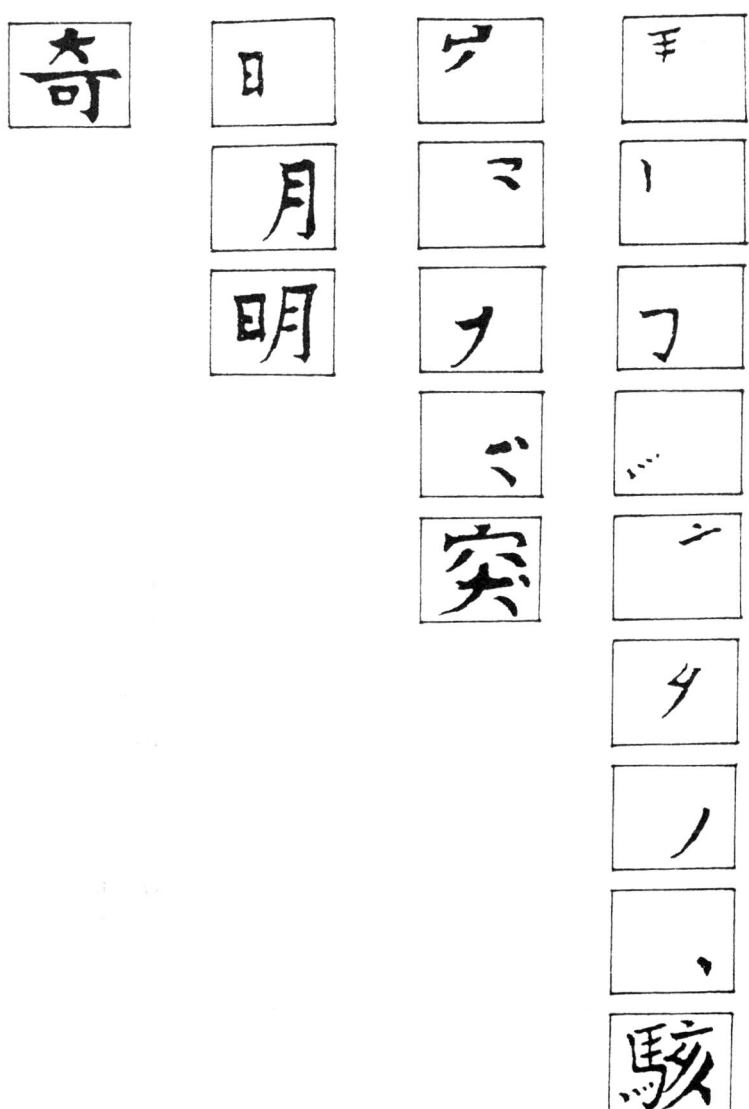

Figure 5. A sample of segmenting Chinese characters into one, two, four, and eight pieces. (From Huang, 1986. Reprinted with permission.)

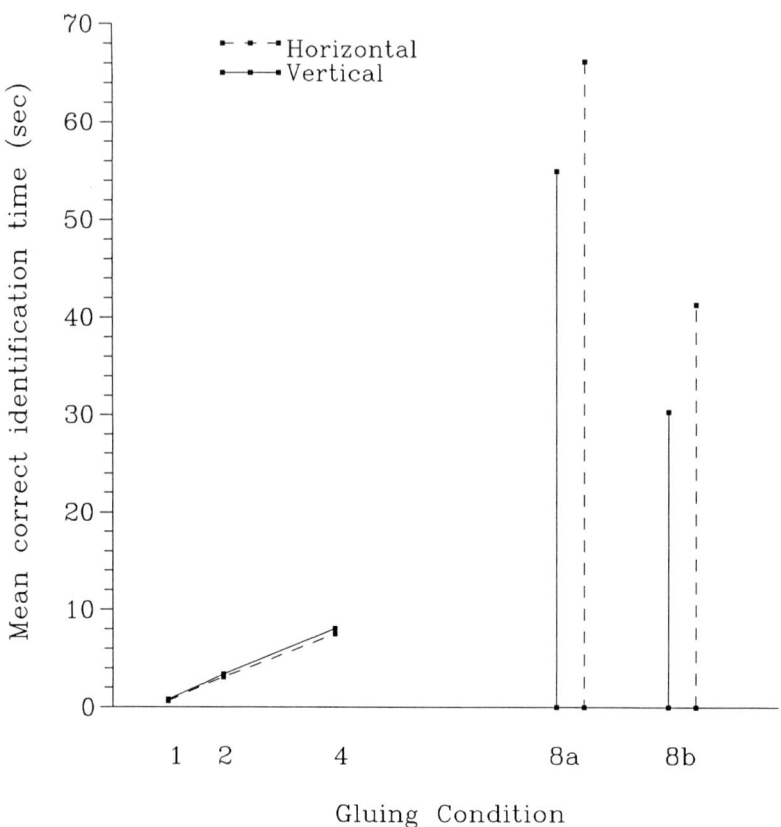

Figure 6. Mean correct identification time for the characters broken into one, two, four, and eight pieces. Presentation order of these pieces were randomized. 8b denotes a presentation mode conforming to the conventional order of stroke writing. (From Huang, 1986. Reprinted with permission.)

Figure 6 depicts the mean integration times for performing these five experimental conditions. An abrupt jump between Four-Unit and 8a groups is evident. The introduction of conventional stroke-writing sequence in 8b improved the integration speed to quite a significant degree. Error rates showed a similar pattern from 0%, 4.7%, 11%, 30.6%, to 11.5% for 1, 2, 4, 8a, and 8b groups, respectively.

By adopting a similar visual gluing procedure, Ji and Luo (1989) also found that a significant integration advantage could be obtained by presenting character parts in a conventional order of stroke writing.
Random serial presentation of character parts hampered the integration speed in character recognition.

A somewhat different experiment conducted by Tsou (1986) demonstrated a consistent tendency. Three major conditions were designed in the following manner: (1) The strokes of a character were consecutively presented according to their conventional order in character writing. (2) The strokes were partitioned into four components and the strokes were conventionally ordered in each component. Four components were randomly presented to subjects. (3) The character was partitioned into four quadrants. These evenly partitioned parts were randomly presented to subjects. All of the materials were shown on a CRT. The subjects could pace their frame-viewing within a time limit. Error rates were 29%, 30%, 47% and mean correct recognition times were 12.74, 38.24, 33.34 seconds for the respective three conditions.

One unexpected finding showed that some characters could be recognized only after a mimic finger writing of what had been presented on the CRT. There were 3, 8, and 6 such cases in a total of 90 trials for the above conditions, respectively. The difference would have be even greater were the stimuli presented in a haptic mode (Tsou, 1986). This indicates that the character could not be well recognized even if every constituent with its item-position information had been perceived. The importance of the order of stroke writing is once again confirmed. If the subjects are not provided with stroke-writing experience, they might have difficulty detecting the relations between components. The result will be a failure to integrate the separated fragments into a character at their early disposal.

Activation of Character Model

The central issue in developing a process model for word recognition is how memory representation is accessed. As interesting as it may be, the issue is a difficult one. We will try to approach it by exploring the role of cue-effectiveness and complexity effects in memory access.

Cueing Function of Local Components

A Chinese character is composed of strokes. Anterior strokes refer to the beginning strokes in writing a character; posterior strokes are the ending ones. Suppose that subjects are asked to reconstruct the removed strokes of a character in which some proportion of strokes have been deleted. Tseng, Chang, and Wang (1965) compared reconstructional performance by deleting the anterior or posterior strokes. They showed that no differences could be found if the amount of stroke deletion was less than 40% of the total number of strokes in a character. However, if the amount of stroke deletion exceeded 50%, the error rate of the anterior-deletion group was significantly higher than that of the posterior-deletion group.

Liu (1983) asked the subject to read stories and random word lists both of 120-character length, with each character being kept intact or one quadrant missing. The result was that more reading errors were found by consistently deleting a top quarter of each character than those by omitting a bottom quarter. Similar results were also obtained on single and two-character Chinese words (Liu, 1984).

A logical consequence could be derived from the findings of Tseng et al. (1965) and Liu (1983, 1984). It might be predicted that the left-top part of a character is most essential for reading accuracy. Peng (1982) did find such results. No matter how a character is structured, horizontally or vertically, stroke writing begins from the left-top corner in most cases. According to Peng (1982), the left-top corner has many junctions and contains a large amount of radical information. Beginning strokes may therefore be more important than ending strokes in providing discriminative information (Liu, 1984).

Further statistical analysis on character structure is needed to show that the left-top corner of a character, compared with other corners, will trigger a smallest set of character models. If this is indeed the case, the formidable matching demand between set members and the presented target character could be largely reduced to assure a better speed and accuracy in character recognition.

Complexity Effect and Memory Access

How does structural complexity affect the access to memory representations in natural object recognition? It was claimed by the recognition-by-components (RBC) model that additional components in complex objects afford a redundancy gain from more diagnostic matches to memory representation. That is the way Biederman (1987) explained why there was a slight reaction time advantage for a complex object (though not statistically reliable). The notion of redundancy gain (Garner, 1962) might also correlate with the concept of emergent features (Pomerantz, 1981). A large number of components might generate functionally distinctive emergent features which could in turn increase the number of diagnostic access paths to memory representations.

Huang, Wang, and Liou (1991) revisited object complexity effects in terms of object naming latencies by manipulating the range of the object geons from 2 to 15. A U-shaped complexity effect was found. The bottom part of this U-shaped curve spans through 4 to 9 geons. Biederman's (1987) result is consistent with the first half of this curve. Huang et al (1991) proposed that the interaction of structural complexity and difficulty level of sampling a minimal effective set of distinctive components determines such a U-shaped curve in object recognition. Supposing that both object and character recognition do share some common mechanisms, the complexity effect might be one of these common properties. We would then expect that a more complex character would generate more distinctive emergent features which in turn would create more access paths to memory representations. The result will be a faster naming response for more complex characters. However, if the number of strokes exceeds a critical value, the naming latency will be increased due to the difficulty of sampling a minimal effective set of distinctive components in an increasingly more complex character.

There exist no consistent findings in the study of character complexity effect. Two factors might be responsible for determining the form of complexity effect. One is the depth of processing in relation to the memory access. The other is the range of the number of manipulated strokes. If task requirements and stroke range differ in one or two above-mentioned aspects, inconsistent conclusions might be drawn accordingly.

Cheng (1981) adopted a forced-choice procedure to ask the subject to select one of the two response items ($\frac{A}{B}$ or $\frac{A}{C}$) to match a briefly-presented character ($\frac{A}{B}$). In the procedure there exists a common part among these three items. The subject may notice only the difference between B and C in the two response items without attending to the whole configurations, resulting in a quick response. Task requirements of this sort may not need a deeper processing for memory access. Cheng's results showed that less complex characters were matched with higher accuracy than more complex characters. However, this result only applied to characters with low frequency counts. Referring back to Figure 4, Wu (1986) found that less complex characters underwent a faster stroke-

-difference computation. Although the tendency is not clear in the Hierarchical group, complexity effects were significant for both the Embedding and the Independent groups. It seems that less complex characters will be processed faster and more accurately if the task requirements do not need a deeper processing for memory access.

To obtain the curve of the complexity effect, it is natural to manipulate the range of the number of strokes. However, the decision as to the cut-off point for complexity categories is rather arbitrary. Therefore, one's complex characters might be another's simple characters. Yeh and Liu (1972) found that recognition threshold would be elevated as the number of strokes increased. In other words, simple characters were more distinctive. Their manipulated range of complexity spanned from 7.33 to 18.88 strokes. Hue and Erickson (1988) obtained an "unexpected" result of better recall for complex high-frequency radicals. The mean number of strokes for simple and complex radicals chosen was 2.62 and 6.92, respectively. High-frequency radicals appear frequently as individual characters in the language. In explaining why complex high-frequency Chinese linguistic units (e.g., radicals) were recalled better, Hue and Erickson suggested that emergent features might be more easily to be generated to make the complex unit more distinctive or contain redundant components. These two seemingly inconsistent results can be reconciled in a U-shaped curve of complexity effect. Hue and Erickson's (1988) result falls into the first half and Yeh and Liu's (1972) into the second half of this U-shaped curve. This explanation is made more plausible by noting that the mean number of strokes for cutting off these two halves is located around 7, which coincides with the minimum area of the U-shaped curve (Huang, Wang, & Liou, 1991).

Concluding Remarks

Sparse but relevant experimental reports are integrated according to an analytical framework for Chinese character recognition. The present article deals mainly with how a Chinese character might be perceptually decomposed into units and how these units effectively activate character models. Several points are addressed in the sequel to provide a psychological bird's-eye view on Chinese character recognition. It is by no means a complete resolution on this difficult and important issue. There still exist many unresolved and difficult problems to be tackled with.

Units of Processing and Horse-Racing Models

Although people have no trouble in naming and recognizing a Chinese character, we are still uncertain of its basic structural units. Compared with 36 geons in object recognition (Biederman, 1987), strokes, stroke groups, character components (such as 214 possible radicals, stems), or some distinctive feature groups remain to be determined as basic structural units in Chinese characters. If there does exist an ideal set of structural units with componential relations derived from the gamut of Chinese characters, most common characters could then be represented by a limited number of units from this set with their componential relations. We could therefore establish the psychological reality of this set of structural units in Chinese character recognition. Unfortunately, no successful attempts have ever been made.

The same situation seems to exist in defining the processing units in character recognition. No research efforts have ever directly addressed this issue. Considering that many Chinese characters are compounds composed of radical and stem components, and that a radical or a stem may serve independently as a character or be a part of other compound characters, it is therefore easier to identify processing units than to construct a minimal set of structural units by which most characters should be generated. A number of studies have been devoted to such endeavours. One of the particularly important ideas from these studies is that frequently encountered patterns are most likely to be treated as integral units by our perceptual systems (Fang & Wu, 1989). Components of a character compound with high unit frequency are perceptually less separable and less likely to be erroneously conjoined with other character components to form an illusory character. Such findings are consistent with the rationale behind some recent horse-racing models of word recognition (e.g., Allen & Madden, 1990; Drewnowski & Healy, 1977; Johnson, Allen, & Strand, 1989).

Horse-racing models suggest a simultaneous encoding of feature, letter, and word-level information. The encoding speed of different levels of information will be affected by their corresponding frequency of occurrences. The encoding process that wins a processing race will take priority as a processing unit. Perceptual separability phenomena in Chinese character recognition could be reinterpreted following this line of reasoning. A character component with high unit frequency might be perceptually detached if the target character loses the race with it, when the target character is relatively less frequent. Perceptual separability will instead be inhibited if the target character occurs more frequently in the language than its character component. It would be interesting to reconsider the character component relationship in the context of horse-racing models.

Structural Complexity Enhances Memory Access?

Memory access occurs in the process of matching activated components and their relations with memory representations. The description seems to be straightforward; the exploitation is nevertheless difficult. Even though a set of 36 geons was constructed with great generative power, the RBC model could only be conceived as a structural rather than a processing model for natural object recognition. In the description of Chinese characters, we still lack a minimal set of structural units to generate most characters. It is therefore premature to draw any definite conclusion on memory access in character recognition.

Emergent features might be generated in complex characters. Character diagnosticity could thus be enhanced. The result would be an increase of redundancy gain so that access paths to memory representations might be increased. Recognition speed will thus be accelerated due to growing structural complexity. However, the above-mentioned U-shaped complexity effect complicates the matter. Besides, we do not know very much about how Chinese characters are represented in memory. The supposition that mental lexicons could be effectively accessed is at best speculative, since units of processing and effective cueing process are largely unknown. It is thus safe to conclude that the relationship between structural complexity and memory access is still largely undetermined.

Perceptual/Post-Perceptual Dichotomy

Suppose that some kind of semantic context was provided in character recognition. It will in most cases facilitate speed and accuracy for recognizing the target character. The problem is whether this context effect is perceptual or post-perceptual in origin. In Huang's (1984) study, perceptual separation of character components could be reduced by providing semantic context. Recognition speed of the target character could also be enhanced if this character was embedded in a sentence. We might consider the possibility that the semantic context directly involves the recognition and cohesion of character components. If this is indeed the case, semantic context is said to be involved perceptually. This assertion is then compatible with what McClelland and Rumelhart (1981) claimed in their interactive activation model.

On the other hand, subjects may still perceive those detached components as separated characters, but they would decide afterwards to integrate two items into one character in order to be consistent with the provided context. Thus, it is through a cognitive rather than a perceptual operation that the whole situation is reconciled. In this scenario, a context effect is better conceived as a post-perceptual consequence. This argument is also supported by a modified race model, i.e., parallel input serial analysis (PISA), suggested by Allen and Madden (1990). We still need to develop a methodology, like the demarcation of sensitivity and response bias in the theory of signal detectability, to conduct perceptual/post-perceptual dichotomy in character recognition.

Contextual Effects and Hypothesis Testing

Word-superiority effect has entertained a long-respected history due to its direct relevance to the notion of contextual effects. Letter identification is performed better when the letter is embedded in a word rather than in a non-word or in isolation. Cheng (1981) also found such a superiority effect by adopting the forced-choice procedure on Chinese materials. Letter activation might be facilitated by the context effect which is supposed to be generated by the embedding word. Therefore, a faster letter identification would then be followed.

A stage model which has been suggested in Figure 2 of the present article might be applied to explain the Chinese character-superiority effect. The model assumes some processing mechanisms which resemble those of an interactive activation model (IAM) suggested by McClelland and Rumelhart (1981). Although the IAM has been critically evaluated by Allen and Emerson (1991), we still find some useful properties of the IAM for our purpose. The stage model of Figure 2 supposes that characters or their components are activated in parallel within that level and interactive information flow is conducted in cascades between the component- and the character-level. Therefore, partial information generated from the components will elevate the activation of likely character models. Following the same vein, this candidate set of characters, after being activated, will send excitatory and inhibitory feedback back to the component level. If the component is embedded in a word instead of a non-word, the net amount of feedback by subtracting inhibitory feedback from excitatory feedback will be positive. The result will be a higher activation level of the component which is intentionally embedded in a character and, henceforth, a faster component identification will be entailed. Next, we will focus on how the contextual effect which is generated from a larger unit might facilitate character recognition.

Although the deletion of the beginning strokes of a character might prevent effective cueing to activate character models, the remaining strokes might be sufficient for character recovery. By providing extra semantic context like phrases or sentences nearby, speed and accuracy for recognizing this incomplete target character would surely be enhanced to a large extent. To understand how the contextual effect may be involved perceptually or post-perceptually in character recognition requires a better methodology. However, it might be reasonable to propose that extensive hypothesis testing is performed by the subject in single character recognition or in natural reading. The scope of generated hypotheses will certainly be constrained by the provided context. We are still uncertain about how far hypothesis testing should go so that effective recognition can be achieved.

Yang (1982) found that the eye-voice span (EVS) for Chinese prose reading always ended at the semantic boundary or on a completed proposition. The result implies that, in natural reading, Chinese characters could be retained in short-term memory only if the meaning of complete semantic units (e.g., a character with its connected semantic neighbors) has been processed. It also indicates the insufficiency of a single character to activate character models since the presented character might not be interconnected in memory. It is possible that this presented character is located at the last reading item but does not possess an independent meaning or cannot be integrated to the most recent proposition. Such observations reflect a different situation that those experiments with brief exposure of single characters. It is therefore imperative to reconsider the mechanism of character recognition in a natural reading situation.

Word Recognition Studies, for What?

Chinese word recognition studies are mostly conducted on characters in isolation or in context. Despite so many diversified research paradigms, a central question is only sporadically raised. Where are these studies headed?

The researchers may have a recognition machine in mind. Machine recognition of printed and hand-written Chinese characters is more than a simple application of human recognition mechanisms. We are not sure if this goal had been unanimously set in researchers' mind. If so, what others? Chang (1991) cogently pointed out that word recognition studies should indicate their potential to answer such questions like how a beginner learns to recognize Chinese characters. We fully agree with this point of view. A beginning Chinese language user may develop a perceptual strategy to discriminate characters. Later on, the learner could grasp syntactic regularity and their referents efficiently through extensive linguistic exposures. How this process of expertise develops should be one of the keys in exploring basic mechanisms in character recognition.

The same situation seems to apply for object and face recognition. Basic principles governing character recognition might be isomorphic to those in object or face recognition. Discriminative power is especially enormous for face recognition within a familiar environment or society. Although Chinese characters are in most cases easy to pronounce, face recognition is also frequently accompanied with quick naming responses. In these respects, we believe that the study of character and face recognition could meet someday with consensus.

Common principles governing context effect might also apply equally well to character, object, and face recognition. A word in a sentence is similar to the object in a scene or the face of a person. It is then understandable why Biederman (1987, 1990) sporadically referred back to McClelland and Rumelhart's (1981) interactive activation model of word recognition in his treatment of human image understanding.

With such relevance in mind, we think that Chinese character recognition studies belong to and can provide crucial resolution clues for general pattern recognition issues.

References

Allen, P.A., & Emerson, P.L. (1991). Holism revisited: Evidence for parallel independent word-level and letter-level processors during word recognition. *Journal of Experimental Psychology: Human Perception and Performance, 17,* 489-511.

Allen, P.A., & Madden, D.J. (1990). Evidence for a parallel input serial analysis model of word processing. *Journal of Experimental Psychology: Human Perception and Performance, 16,* 48-64.

Arbib, M.A., Kfoury, A.J., & Moll, R.N. (1981). *A basis for theoretical computer science.* New York: Springer-Verlag.

Attneave, F., & Arnoult, M.D. (1956). The quantitative study of shape and pattern perception. *Psychological Bulletin, 53,* 452-471.

Bethell-Fox, C.E., & Shepard, R.N. (1988). Mental rotation: Effect of stimulus complexity and familiarity. *Journal of Experimental Psychology: Human Perception and Performance, 14,* 12-23.

Biederman, I. (1987). Recognition-by-Components: A theory of human image understanding. *Psychological Review, 94,* 115-147.

Biederman, I. (1990). Higher-level vision. In D.N. Osherson, S.M. Kosslyn, & J.M. Hollerbach (Eds.), *Visual cognition and action: An invitation to cognitive science, Vol. 2* (pp. 41-72). Cambridge, MA: MIT Press.

Chang, S.W. (1991). Personal communication.

Chen, H.C. (1984). Detecting radical component of Chinese characters in visual reading. *Chinese Journal of Psychology, 26,* 29-34.

Chen, H.C. (1986). Component detection in reading Chinese characters. In H.S.R. Kao & R. Hoosain (Eds.), *Linguistics, psychology, and the Chinese language,* pp. 1-10. Hong Kong: The University of Hong Kong.

Chen, J. W.(1991). *Emerging mechanism of illusory contour in stereoscopic processing.* Unpublished master thesis, National Taiwan University, Taipei, Taiwan.

Cheng, C.M. (1981). Perception of Chinese characters. *Acta Psychologica Taiwanica, 23,* 137-153.

Cheng, C.M. (1982). Computational analysis of present-day Mandarin. *Journal of Chinese Linguistics, 10,* 281-358.

Drewnowski, A., & Healy, A.F. (1977). Detection errors on the and and: Evidence for reading units larger than the word. *Memory & Cognition, 5,* 636-647.

Fang, S.P., & Wu, P. (1989). Illusory conjunctions in the perception of Chinese characters. *Journal of Experimental Psychology: Human Perception and Performance, 15,* 434-447.

Garner, W.R. (1962). *Uncertainty and structure as psychological concepts.* New York: Wiley.

Gibson, E.J., & Levin, H. (1975). *The psychology of reading.* Cambridge, MA: MIT Press.

Healy, A.F., Conboy, G.L., & Drewnowski, A. (1987). Characterizing the processing units of reading: Effects of intra- and inter-word spaces in a letter detection task. In B. Britton & S. Glynn (Eds.), *Executive control processes*

in reading, pp 279-296. Hillsdale, NJ: Erlbaum.
Healy, A.F., Oliver, W., & McNamara, T.P. (1987). Detecting letters in continuous text: Effects of display size. *Journal of Experimental Psychology: Human Perception and Performance, 13,* 279-290.
Hopcroft, J.E., & Ullman, J.D. (1979). *Introduction to automata theory, languages, and computation.* Reading, MA: Addison-Wesley.
Huang, J.T. (1979). Time-dependent separability hypothesis of Chinese words association. *Acta Psychologica Taiwanica, 21,* 41-48.
Huang, J.T. (1984). Perceptual separability and cohesive processes in reading Chinese words. In H.S.R. Kao & R. Hoosain (Eds.), *Psychological studies of the Chinese language* (pp. 57-74). Hong Kong: Chinese Language Society of Hong Kong.
Huang, J.T. (1986). Visual integration process in recognizing fragmented Chinese characters. In H.S.R. Kao & R. Hoosain (Eds.), *Linguistics, psychology, and the Chinese language* (pp. 45-54). Hong Kong: Hong Kong University Press.
Huang, J.T., & Liu, I.M. (1978). Paired-associate learning proficiency as a function of frequency count, meaningfulness, and imagery value in Chinese two-character ideograms. *Acta Psychologica Taiwanica, 20,* 5-17.
Huang, J.T., & Sakurai, S. (1987). *The plausibility of cooperative algorithm in human stereoscopic processing.* Proceedings of the 1987 Workshop on Computer Vision, Graphics and Image Processing, Ch.22. Taipei: Academia Sinica.
Huang, J.T., Sun, C.W., & Tsou, S.L. (1990). *Chinese character recognition by the Carpenter/Grossberg classifier.* Paper presented to the Fifth International symposium on Cognitive Aspects of Chinese Language, Beijing.
Huang, J.T., Wang, M.Y., & Liou, S.N. (1991). *Component diagnosticity and pattern complexity in object recognition.* Unpublished manuscript.
Hue, C.W., & Erickson, J.R. (1988). Short-term memory for Chinese characters and radicals. *Memory & Cognition, 16,* 196-205.
Hung, D.L., & Tzeng, O.J.L. (1981). Orthographic variations and visual information processing. *Psychological Bulletin, 90,* 377-414.
Ji, G.P., & Luo, C.R. (1989). Capacity limitation and strategy of image processing. *Acta Psychologica Sinica, 21,* 18-23.
Johnson, N.F., Allen, P.A., & Strand, T.L. (1989). On the role of word frequency in the detection of component letters. *Memory & Cognition, 17,* 474-482.
Kucera, H., & Francis, W. (1967). *Computational analysis of present-day American English.* Providence, RI: Brown University Press.
Lai, C., & Huang, J.T. (1988). Component migration in Chinese characters: Effects of priming and context on illusory conjunction. In I.M. Liu, H.C. Chen, &

M.J. Chen (Eds.), *Cognitive aspects of the Chinese language, Vol.1*, (pp. 57-67). Hong Kong: Asian Research Service.

Liu, I.M. (1983). Cueing function of fragments of Chinese characters in reading. *Acta Psychologica Taiwanica, 25*, 85-90.

Liu, I.M. (1984). Recognition of fragment-deleted characters and words. *Computer Processing of Chinese & Oriental Languages, 1*, 276-287.

Liu, I.M., Chuang, C.J., & Wang, S.C. (1975). *Frequency count of 40,000 Chinese words*. Taipei: Lucky Books.

Marr, D. (1982). *Vision*. San Francisco: W.H. Freeman.

Marr, D., & Poggio, T. (1976). Cooperative computation of stereo disparity. *Science, 194*, 283-287.

McClelland, J.L., & Mozer, M.C. (1986). Perceptual interactions in two-word displays: Familiarity and similarity effects. *Journal of Experimental Psychology: Human Perception and Performance, 12*, 18-35.

McClelland, J.L., & Rumelhart, D.E. (1981). An interactive activation model of context effect in letter perception: Part I. An account of basic findings. *Psychological Review, 88*, 375-407.

Mozer, M.C. (1983). Letter migration in word perception. *Journal of Experimental Psychology: Human Perception and Performance, 9*, 531-546.

Peng, R.X. (1982). A preliminary report on statistical analysis of the structure of Chinese characters. *Acta Psychologica Sinica, 14*, 385-390.

Podgorny, P., & Shepard, R.N. (1983). Distribution of visual attention over space. *Journal of Experimental Psychology: Human Perception and Performance, 9*, 380-393.

Pomerantz, J. (1981). Perceptual organization in information processing. In M. Kubovy & J.R. Pomerantz (Eds.), *Perceptual organization* (pp. 141-180). Hillsdale, NJ: Erlbaum.

Prinzmetal, W., & Millis-Wright, M. (1984). Cognitive and linguistic factors affect visual feature integration. *Cognitive Psychology, 16*, 305-340.

Taylor, I., & Taylor, M.M. (1983). *The psychology of reading*. New York: Academic Press.

Treisman, A., & Gelade, G. (1980). A feature integration theory of attention. *Cognitive Psychology, 12*, 97-136.

Treisman, A., & Souther, J. (1986). Illusory words: The roles of attention and of top-down constraints in conjoining letters to form words. *Journal of Experimental Psychology: Human Perception and Performance, 12*, 3-17.

Tseng, S.C., Chang, L.H., & Wang, C.C. (1965). An informational analysis of the Chinese language: I. The reconstruction of the removed strokes of the ideograms in printed sentence-texts. *Acta Psychologica Sinica, 9*, 281-290.

Tsou, S.L. (1986). *Contour detection mechanism in touch and serial vision.* Unpublished master thesis, National Taiwan University, Taipei, Taiwan.

Tzeng, O.J.L., Hung, D.L., Cotton, B., & Wang, S.Y. (1979). Visual lateralization effect in reading Chinese characters. *Nature, 282,* 499-501.

Tzeng, O.J.L., & Wang, S.Y. (1984). Search for a common neurocognitive mechanism for language and movements. *American Journal of Physiology, 246,* 904-911.

Wu, C.J. (1986). *Figural structure and subitizing process.* Unpublished master thesis, National Taiwan University, Taipei, Taiwan.

Wu, P., & Fang, S.P. (1988). Conceptual distinctiveness in Chinese characters. *Chinese Journal of Psychology, 30,* 9-19.

Yang, W.C. (1982). *Perceptual strategy and Chinese eye-voice span.* Unpublished master thesis, National Taiwan University Taipei, Taiwan.

Yeh, J.S., & Liu, I.M. (1972). Factors affecting recognition thresholds of Chinese characters. *Acta Psychologica Taiwanica, 14,* 113-117.

Yu, B., Feng, L., Cao, H., & Li, W. (1990a). Visual perception of Chinese characters: Effect of perceptual task and Chinese character attributes. *Acta Psychologica Sinica, 22,* 141-148.

Yu, B., Cao, H., Feng, L., & Li, W. (1990b). Effect of morphological and phonetic whole perception of Chinese characters on the perception of components. *Acta Psychologica Sinica, 22,* 232-239.

Graphemic, Phonological, and Semantic Activation Processes during the Recognition of Chinese Characters

Giovanni B. Flores d'Arcais
Max-Planck-Institut für Psycholinguistik

This chapter consists of two parts. The first is dedicated to a brief review of a selected number of studies on the processes of recognizing a word written in Chinese characters in Chinese and Japanese readers. The work reported consists of studies on lateralization, reports on aphasia and developmental dyslexia, and experimental studies on the Stroop effect with Chinese characters. The main conclusion proposed here is that there is not clear evidence supporting the hypothesis that reading a word written in a logographic writing system involves processes different from those involved in reading a word in an alphabetic system. The second part reports on some experimental evidence on the process of naming logographically written words. The first experiment investigated lexical decomposition in the recognition of complex characters, and showed that during the process of recognizing these characters the meaning of the component radicals can be retrieved, even when they are not semantically related to the meaning of the whole character. The second and the third studies were concerned with the processes of the activation of graphemic, phonological and semantic information when reading Chinese characters, and offered some evidence on the time course of the activation of this information during word recognition.

The present chapter deals with the processes of recognizing a word written in a logographic system, such as Chinese, for Chinese and Japanese readers. In particular, it will try to highlight some of the processes which access the pronunciation and meaning of the word during reading, be the word presented in isolation, or, as most frequently cases, in a connected text.

The chapter is organized in two parts. In the first I will present a brief overview of available evidence concerning the processes of recognizing a Chinese character. This survey will be very selective, since broad and excellent reviews are available (see e.g. Tzeng & Hung, 1980, 1981; Hung & Tzeng, 1981; Henderson, 1982; Paradis, Hagiwara, & Hildebrandt, 1985; Hoosain, 1991), and will concentrate on some of the critical issues concerning recognition of a word written in a logographic system. The second part reports on three of my own studies on the process of recognizing a Chinese character in Chinese and Japanese. These studies have tried to answer specific questions concerning: a) lexical decomposition in the recognition of Chinese characters; b) the activation of graphemic, phonological and semantic information during the recognition of a character; and c) the time course of these activation processes.

The Processes of Written Word Recognition

What does it mean to recognize a word? During recent years, word recognition has been one of the most actively investigated areas within psycholinguistics and cognitive psychology at large.

Much of this work has been concerned with the function and the structure of the mental lexicon, conceived in a typical metaphor as a kind of storage where word forms and information related with them is kept. Problems concerning storage, retrieval and access of information in and from this storage have been investigated. By far, the largest part of work on the mental lexicon during the last fifteen years has dealt with the notion of how a single unit is accessed, the main interest concerning problems such as facilitation of access, effects of context and the like. In general present research on word recognition is concerned with the following issues: a) the form of the mental representations; b) the process of accessing the mental units; c) the access code involved in getting to the appropriate unit in the mental lexicon; d) the time course of the processes; e) the relations between the work of the different components of the recognition system.

Present questions about the mental lexicon from the psycholinguistic point of view include: 1) What kind of information in the signal is used to contact the word units in the mental lexicon? 2) What are the actual units of access to the mental lexicon: full words, stems, roots? 3) What kind of information is "stored" in the lexical entries? The list would include phonological, orthographic, articulatory, morphological, and syntactic information, and probably also information about pragmatics and thematic roles. 4) What is the role of the lexicon in language production? How are lexical entries triggered by knowledge systems in order to produce a linguistic utterance?

In this chapter I will concentrate mainly on the processes through which the different types of information become available to the recognition system when a word written in a non-alphabetic, logographic system is named, or other tasks are performed which presumably require the recognition of the meaning of the word, such as semantic categorization and (probably) lexical decision. Thus, the issues which will be focused upon are the following. The first deals with the access code to the mental lexicon - is it graphemic, or phonological (or phonetic)? Is phonological and phonetic-acoustic or articulatory information accessed during the reading of a character? Which route is taken by the recognition system to access phonological information? The second question concerns the activation processes of the various components involved in the recognition of a character, namely graphemic, phonological, syntactic and semantic ones. The third question concerns the time course of the activation of these components. I will review some evidence specifically devoted to these issues and then report on my own studies related to these questions.

Many recent papers (e.g. Balota, 1990) have challenged notions such as "lexical access". According to these discussions, it is questionable whether it is empirically sound and theoretically appropriate to think of a kind of "magic moment" in which the word is recognized. In the present chapter I will not enter this debate. I will assume that from the moment in time at which a visual object such as a written character is put in front of the visual system of a literate native speaker of a language, a number of processes take place. This stimulus information has to spark some knowledge in the reader, which normally includes the pronunciation of the word, its meaning, etc. When this contact has taken place, we can say that the word is recognized. Thus, when a character has been recognized, presumably the reader has available the following information: a) information dealing with the figural structure of the character: the acquisition of this information is reached through processes dealing with the discrimination and identification of the appropriate character. With many thousands different characters, the task is not trivial; b) information concerning the pronunciation of the character, that is, its phonological code; c) information about the grammatical class; d) information concerning meaning.

Many of the processes which enable to this end result are very likely to be common and identical, or very similar, across the different orthographies, independent of the features of the writing system which characterizes the particular language of the reader. On the other hand, there might be processes which are specifically related to certain properties of a given writing system. In this chapter I will try to highlight the latter.

A Comparison between the reading processes in alphabetic and non-alphabetic systems

Several studies have tried to compare the different processes involved in reading alphabetic and non-alphabetic systems. The largest number of studies concerns a comparison between Chinese and English or Japanese and English, but there are also studies comparing Chinese and French, etc. Some studies have tried to compare the reading processes involved with a syllabic and a logographic system within the same language, namely Japanese. As mentioned above, a number of excellent reviews on these studies is available in the literature.

Among the questions asked about character recognition the following have been investigated. Are there different representation systems for alphabetic and non-alphabetic systems? For example, it has been proposed that the latter ones are global, holistic, as compared to the former ones, analytic. What are the access codes for the two systems? Are the differences only input differences? Do logographic systems involve more picture-like processing? We will discuss the last question in the following section.

Is character recognition similar to picture recognition?

There are several differences in the processing of words and pictures, and these could be paralleled by differences in the reading process for words written with an alphabetic or with a logographic system. For example, the following properties distinguish picture recognition as compared to word recognition: a) picture naming in literate adults is slower than word naming; b) picture categorization is faster than word categorization; c) words interfere with picture naming more than pictures interfere with word naming (see, e.g. Flores d'Arcais & Schreuder, 1987).

Although So, Potter, and Friedmann (1976) have convincingly shown that Chinese characters are not processed like pictures, the picture-like character of the Chinese orthography has prompted investigators to examine differences in processing between alphabetic and logographic systems. There is by now a considerable body of experimental material which has attempted to show that reading logographic systems is different from processing alphabetically printed words. One of the basic notions underlying these studies was the hypothesis of a direct and more efficient access to meaning in logographic orthographies.

The evidence available comes mainly from the following four types of studies: a) studies on lateralization; b) studies and clinical observations on aphasic patients; c) developmental dyslexia and d) Stroop-type experiments.

Lateralization studies

For words written in an alphabetic systems, one typically finds a left hemisphere processing advantage (e.g. Geschwind, 1972). If characters are processed like pictures, then the opposite should hold for Chinese characters, and we should expect some right hemisphere processing superiority. Japanese offers in this respect a particular interesting characteristic, because its writing system is a combination of the Chinese hanzji and a syllabic system, the kana (I will ignore here the distinction between the two kana systems used by the Japanese), which should be processed more efficiently in the left hemisphere. So, a few investigators set themselves the task of testing the hypothesis of right hemisphere superiority for processing hanzji in Chinese and Japanese, and the specific hypothesis that Japanese readers would display a right hemisphere advantage for kanji and a left hemisphere superiority for kana. Evidence about lateralization comes from normal as well as neurological patients. In this section I will refer to a few studies with normal subjects.

The initial evidence seemed to support these hypotheses. Left hemisphere superiority was found for kana (Hirata & Osaka, 1967; Hatta, 1977c; Sasanuma, Itoh, Mori, & Kobayashi, 1977), while right hemisphere superiority was found for kanji (Hatta, 1977a, c; 1978). However, right hemisphere superiority seems to hold only for kanji representing concrete nouns (Elman, Takahashi, & Tohsaku, 1981; also Hatta, 1977b; and Ohnishi & Hatta, 1980). No difference among hemispheres was found in the recognition of *simple* kanji (Endo, Shimizu, & Hakamura, 1981). Right hemisphere is superior for shape recognition compared to left hemisphere superiority for nonsense words written in kana (Endo, Shimizu, & Hori, 1978).

Right hemisphere superiority was found also for Chinese by Tzeng, Hung, Cotton, and Wang (1979); Hardyck, Tzeng, and Wang (1977). They obtained less Stroop interference in the left visual field (right hemisphere), both for "pictograms" and for "phonograms" types of characters, that is, for characters having an iconic aspect reflecting the shape of the object referred to, and characters completely lacking this property. On the other hand, with tasks requiring either a) lexical decision or b) phonological recording (matching a character to an acoustically presented word) or c) semantic categorization, no differences in processing latencies were found between the hemispheres. With two character words, Tzeng, Hung, Cotton, and Wang (1979) found left hemisphere superiority. Semantic categorization tasks are performed better under left hemisphere processing (Tzeng et al., 1979). Left hemisphere superiority in processing accuracy for phonological and semantic tasks to be performed on Chinese characters also emerged in a study by Leong, Wong, Wong, and Hiscock (1985). Significant left hemisphere superiority for processing Chinese characters was also obtained by Kershner and Jerg (1972) and by Hardyck, Tzeng, and Wang (1977).

Recent attempts with Event Related Potentials (Hatta, Honjon, & Mito, 1983) didn't reveal any hemispheric differences in the potentials recorded during behavioral tasks.

Could possible dominance differences be related not to the type of orthography but be a function of figural complexity or form? In German subjects, not readers of Chinese, simple kanji were easier to recognize than kana and both of these were easier than complex kanji (Hartje, Hannen, & Willems, 1986). No laterality effect emerged for these subjects.

The main conclusions based on the earlier studies on reading Japanese, (e.g. Hatta, 1977a, c; 1978), were that kana are "processed" by the left hemisphere and kanji are "processed" by right hemisphere. As a corollary, it was assumed that kana are read phonologically, while kanji are read "directly". The two characters would therefore be processed along two different routes. However, as we have seen, recent work has shown the limits of these conclusions. The various results here reviewed, together with several others (e.g. the review in Tzeng, Hung, Chen, Wu, & Hsi, 1986) allow the conclusion that words written as Chinese characters are processed normally in the left hemisphere in the same way as words written in alphabetic orthographies. Probably the differences found in some of the studies are much a function of task and of selection of material. Cerebral lateralization, thus, does not seem to depend so much on orthography but is likely to be related to the type of task in which the reader is involved. When the material is processed as linguistic material, then left hemisphere superiority seems to emerge, independently of the orthography involved.

As to the alleged difference in lateralization between kana and kanji in Japanese, moreover, there are a number of confounding factors which have hardly been taken into account, some of which will be discussed in the following section.

Studies on dyslexia

Several studies in Japanese have looked for dissociation between reading kana and kanji characters in aphasic patients. A typical pattern found in the literature is the following: surface dyslexia with kana and deep dyslexia with kanji. Sasanuma (1974, 1975, 1984, 1985) studied a number of cases and found a majority of patients with equal impairment both for kana and for kanji and a number of cases with impairment only for kana and not for kanji. The opposite pattern seems rather rare. This has been taken as an indication of an impairment at the phonological level, and in turn, this was taken as evidence supporting the hypothesis of phonological recording for kana and direct access to the lexicon for kanji.

Other evidence from aphasia research showed a larger number of errors in recognizing words written in kana and fewer errors with kanji, such as in a case of so called Gogi aphasia (Sasanuma & Monoi, 1975), which would indicate kanji superiority in reading.

In general, the evidence from aphasia research is ambiguous. The data available from reports from patients show different impairment syndromes which cannot easily be interpreted in a consistent way (see, e.g., the extensive review by Paradis, Hagiwara, & Hildebrandt, 1985). Many of the differences can be explained in terms of different characteristics associated with the two orthographic subsystems, kanji and kana.

There are a number of differences between kanji and kana besides the mere orthographic properties, and they concern the grammatical class involved and the age of acquisition. Kana is used to write function words, grammatical formatives, affixes, etc. Nouns, adjectives and content words in general, except foreign loan words, are normally not written in kana but with kanji. Thus, a major difference between kanji and kana consists in the grammatical class for which the two systems are used. Second, there is a dramatic difference in the age of acquisition of the two writing systems in the Japanese child. Kana are acquired earlier, usually before the beginning of the formal school program, while kanji are learned gradually and in a fixed sequence which is planned over the whole range of the first eight years of formal school, with a total of some 900 kanji learned by the end of this period, when the child is already 14 years of age. Of course, it should make an enormous difference in ease of lexical access whether a kanji is acquired at 6 or at 12 or 14 years of age!

Evidence from developmental dyslexia

For a long time a claim was commonly accepted, that the frequency of developmental dyslexia in Japan (Makita, 1968) vs. about 6-7% of the children learning to read alphabetic systems. Similarly, developmental dyslexia is reportedly almost unknown in Taiwan (Kuo, 1978).

If these claims were true, we would have a dramatic difference in the reading acquisition process between alphabetic and logographic systems. In absence of a very unlikely genetic predisposition for reading acquisition in the Chinese and Japanese population, this difference could either be based on properties in the teaching procedure or in the learning processes, or could only be explained as due to the properties of the two orthographic systems. Let us consider this last hypothesis. We know from various studies on developmental dyslexia that phonological awareness, and in general phonological skills, are among the best predictors for successful reading acquisition with alphabetic orthographies (see, e.g., Perfetti, 1985). Thus, it could be true fact that Chinese characters can be read "directly" via the lexical route, which would facilitate children weaker in phonological skills. This hypothesis received support in the classic experiment by Rozin, Ponitzky, and Sotsky (1971) showing that American dyslectic children didn't have substantial problems learning to read Chinese characters. As for the Japanese, one of the explanations proposed by Makita (1968) was the perfectly shallow characteristics of Japanese kana, which would minimize efforts in learning and in using complex grapheme to phoneme conversion rules.

Do we have to conclude, on the basis of the older claims of absence of developmental dyslexia in Japanese and Chinese children, and of the Rozin et al. (1971) results, that learning to read a logographic system is easier and minimizes failures in the literacy acquisition process? Before accepting the conclusion that this alleged difference in the incidence of dyslexia between learners of alphabetic systems and learners of logographes is due to the orthographic properties of the two writing systems, one should look carefully for alternative possible explanations. There may be different criteria for defining dyslexia (e.g. in Oriental cultures, failure in achieving a skill such as reading may be considered due to lack of motivation or sufficient work; in other words, children would not be dyslectic, they would simply be lazy). Second, recent work (e.g. Stevenson, Stigler, Lee, Lucker, Kitamura, & Hsu, 1985) has again shown clear differences in reading proficiency in Japanese, Chinese and American children matched in age, social class, type of school and so forth, and the main factor involved here seemed to be the achievement aspiration of the children and their families and the amount of time spent in home work. Thus, on the one hand we are not sure whether the data on the incidence of dyslexia in the population can be taken as reliable. More recent counts seem to indicate that the original claims by Makita (1968) are not very reliable. On the other hand, clear differences in the teaching and learning patterns, in the amount of time invested in the literacy process and, finally, in the motivation and in the aspiration for achievement displayed by the pupils and by their social environment make a comparison between the process of reading acquisition in the Western and in the Oriental culture rather problematic. As a final point, if for Japanese children, as Makita (1968) proposed, the completely shallow kana orthography could favour reading acquisition, the same low incidence should be found for Serbo-Croatian or, almost to the same extent, in Italian or Spanish, and this is not the case. To summarize the points made in this section, we can conclude that the evidence available is not clear and strong enough to support the notion of a real advantage of logographic systems in reducing the risk of developmental dyslexia.

Stroop interference studies

A number of studies with Chinese characters in Chinese and Japanese has used interference paradigm with the Stroop color-word task.

Biederman and Tsao (1979) found greater Stroop the interference with Chinese characters than with English orthography. Their explanation was that in Chinese the two representations for the color and for the words would be more strongly associated in the same representation system and therefore would more strongly compete for perceptual resources.

Results consistent with Biederman and Tsao (1979) were obtained by Tsao, Wu, and Feustel (1981) and by Hatta (1981): Stroop interference is larger when Chinese characters are presented to the right hemisphere than when they involve the left hemisphere. Various other attempts to obtain Stroop interference with two different orthographic systems yielded consistent results. With bilingual subjects, Fang, Tzeng, and Alva (1981) found a stronger interference with kanji than in English. Shimamura (1987) obtained stronger interference with kanji than with kana. However, altogether, the initial evidence by Biederman and Tsao (1979) has not received strong and unequivocal support. Incongruent evidence is also available. Fang et al. (1981), Smith and Kirsner (1982) found more Stroop interference with English than with Chinese. The amount of interference seems to vary with the different writing systems, with logographic orthographies showing, in certain conditions, but not consistently, more Stroop-like interference.

More recently, Chen and Tsoi (1990) used a picture or symbol word interference task, in which both the interfering items and the targets were English alphabetic words, Chinese characters or arithmetic symbols in appropriate combinations. The targets had to be named by English, Chinese and Chinese-English bilingual subjects. The results were rather interesting. For Chinese speakers, Chinese distracters produced the largest interference in word naming, and symbol distracters the largest interference in symbol naming. For English speakers, symbol naming was slower than word naming, and English words created the most interference. No interference was found, on the other hand, for word naming. Thus, English words and logographic items seem to activate different processes.

In conclusion, the available results offer some, not unequivocal evidence, for a stronger Stroop effect with Chinese characters. On the other hand, the existence and size of the effect does not seem to depend only on the use of logographic characters. The amount of interference seems to vary across the different orthographies even within alphabetic systems, and is very sensitive to the specific color words used, their similarity across the languages involved, etc.

Phonological coding of Chinese characters during reading

The "standard" model of word recognition in reading for alphabetic systems (e.g. Coltheart, 1978) envisages two routes: a direct route, which accesses a logogen type of unit; and a grapheme-to-phoneme conversion route. Reading a word can, in principle, take place on the basis of either route. The first makes word naming contingent upon retrieval of the information stored in the mental lexicon, and is therefore a post-lexical process, while the second does not, in principle, require access to the mental lexicon and could take place in the absence of the knowledge of the word.

What kind of processes are involved in reading words in a logographic system? A reader might arrive at the pronunciation of the character either as a result of the access of the phonological information associated with the word corresponding to the character - thus essentially post-lexically, once the mental unit corresponding to the character has been identified - or by using the phonological information, which in most Chinese characters is specified by the "phonetic" radical. Thus, the process would be equivalent to reading a word written in an alphabetic system, which can be read by either route.

The question - whether phonological recording is necessary for reading - is an old and much-debated issue. Several questions have been asked concerning phonological coding in reading. The first concerns the access code to the mental lexicon - is it visual, or phonological (or phonetic)? Second, is phonological and phonetic/acoustic or articulatory information always activated during reading? Third, which route is taken by the recognition system to access phonological information? The theoretical positions with respect to phonological recording range from the most radical claim, that phonological coding is an obligatory way to the lexicon, to the position that phonological recording of words is an obligatory byproduct of lexical access or only an optional byproduct of lexical access.

What is the function of phonological coding for reading? This question has been widely been investigated in the literature. Phonological coding is not necessary for lexical access, but it might be useful nevertheless. For beginning readers the story can be different from that of skilled readers. Phonetic/articulatory and phonological skills seem strongly associated with successfully learning to read, and might be necessary for it. In various models of memory, especially in the sixties, e.g. Atkinson and

Shiffrin (1968), an articulatory loop was taken to be an essential processing component for recording information in long term memory. Phonological coding could help keeping information in working memory and therefore would allow comprehension of connected text. Efficient parsing is helped by a phonetic loop (e.g. the first level of analysis in a sentence in many models of reading and language comprehension, like the "Preliminary Phrase Package" of Frazier and Fodor's Sausage Machine, (1978).

Evidence for obligatory phonetic/articulatory recording during reading of words written in alphabetic systems comes from a number of classic studies, such as Conrad (1964), Krueger (1970), Rubenstein, Lewis, and Rubenstein (1971), and Gough (1972), to name a few. On the other hand, a number of studies provides evidence against obligatory phonological recording for reading. For example, Baron (1973) found that the time necessary to determine whether a phrase makes sense is not affected by phonological recording (e.g. "my new car" vs "my knew car": if the second was recorded phonologically it would sound meaningful and it could take longer to decide that it is meaningless).

The issue is still debated, and even a short review of the main contribution would require discussion of several dozen papers. At this moment, what can safely be concluded is that: a) lexical access is possible without phonological recording; b) phonological recording is likely to take place when a word is read; c) probably there are differences between familiar and unfamiliar words.

Since Chinese characters are not translated into a phonological code "one phoneme at a time" as, at least in principle, is possible with alphabetic writing systems, and since, at least in principle, they can be read "globally", it has become an obvious hypothesis that reading Chinese characters might completely bypass a stage of phonological encoding, and require essentially the direct, lexical route. The meaning of the characters would obviously be extracted lexically, and if the task required reading aloud, the phonological and phonetic information necessary for pronunciation would also be retrieved from the lexicon. This hypothesis is supported by some evidence. For example, neurological reports seem to indicate the absence of phonological mediation in the recognition of kanji (Sasanuma & Fujimura, 1971). In a patient, Sasanuma reports about phonological coding of a kanji written word as seeming to be a post lexical phenomenon.

With Japanese, Kimura (1984) used semantic categorization judgements about pairs of words or pairs of pictures and words. With *kana*, concurrent articulatory activity impaired performance, while with *kanji* performance was barely affected. According to an older study by Erickson, Mattingly, and Turvey (1977), performance in a probed recall task with lists of words was much more impaired by phonetic confusability in the character list than by visual or semantic confusability.

Much of the evidence available indicates, on the other hand, that for logographic writing (Chinese), phonological recording is also likely to take place (e.g. Hung & Tzeng, 1981; Tzeng, Hung, & Wang, 1977). Lam, Perfetti, and Bell (1991) obtained interference effects from the Cantonese pronunciation when readers having Cantonese as their first language and Mandarin as second language were asked to decide whether two characters had the same pronunciation (or the same rhyme) in Mandarin Chinese: apparently they could not suppress the Cantonese pronunciation when reading the characters. Of course, the interference effect could be related to the demands of the task (rhyme decision).

Does phonological activation take place in a reader of a Chinese character even when the task does not demand it? With a backward masking procedure, Perfetti and Zhang (1991) didn't obtain evidence for pre-lexical phonological effects in reading Chinese characters, while such effects emerged in priming experiments with character identification and naming. Thus, according to these results, character identification does not seem to be mediated by phonological coding, but once a character is recognized, the phonological code is automatically activated. Independently of the orthography used, then, printed words seem to automatically evoke a phonological representation as part of their identification .

In an interesting and important study, Seidenberg (1985) has shown that in both English and Chinese high frequency words are recognized visually, without phonological mediation, while phonological coding enters only into processing of low frequency words, for both orthographies. According to the Seidenberg study, thus, in both English and Chinese high frequency words would be read "logographically" via the direct route, while low frequency words would be read "analytically" via a phonological route.

In conclusion, the available evidence doesn't seem to indicate dramatic processing differences for words written in alphabetic or in logographic orthographies.

An additional point should be made here. An interesting feature of the Chinese characters, with respect to the study of the routes which might be responsible for word identification, is the fact that semantic and phonological information are in many cases displayed, as we will discuss further on in this chapter, by two physically separate parts of the character which represents the word. Although both of these parts are taken in by the recognition system simultaneously, both being read together in a single fixation, the contribution of the two parts to the recognition process are, at least in terms of the input information, separate.

Conclusions

The present selective review of some experimental and clinical evidence on the processing of logographic characters allows the conclusion that in general there seem not to be very substantial differences in the way Chinese and Japanese readers process a word written in hanzji as compared to the processes involved in reading a word in an alphabetic system. Although the mental lexicon might be the obligatory route from the character to the pronunciation of the word, at least high familiar characters may well be read in a similar way in logographic and in syllabic or alphabetic systems.

Although there is some evidence from Stroop-type experiments and some, less clear, from clinical data and from lateralization experiments, indicating some differences in the processing of Chinese characters as compared to alphabetically printed words, the conclusion that Chinese characters are processed more "like pictures" than like words can hardly be maintained.

In conclusion, it seems possible to conclude that reading words written in a logographic system such as Chinese and Japanese kanji does not involve processes substantially different from those involved in reading words written in alphabetic systems.

The Activation Processes during the Recognition of a Chinese Character

The second part of the chapter is devoted to the presentation and discussion of some experimental data from studies carried out in Chinese and Japanese with the goal of highlighting some of the processes which underlie the recognition of a Chinese character. All studies reported dealt with *complex* Chinese characters, that is, single characters composed by two or more radicals (simple characters) or by a radical or two with additional strokes (such as the ones exemplified in Figure 1).

The experimental evidence to be reported concerns the activation of graphemic, phonological and semantic information during character recognition. I will report on three studies. The first is concerned with the processes of activation of the components of a complex character. The second and the third deal specifically with the activation of graphemic, phonological and semantic information during the reading of complex characters and with the time course of this activation.

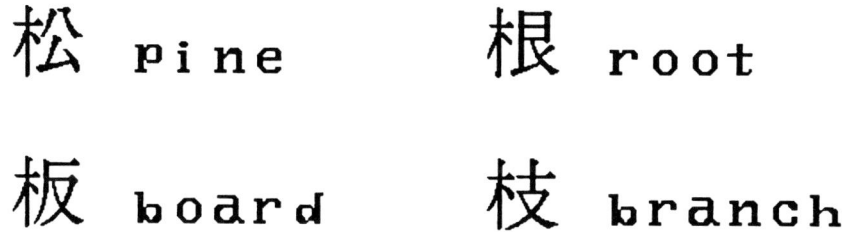

Figure 1. A set of complex Kanji characters including, as a component, the radical TREE.

Lexical decomposition in the recognition of a complex Chinese character

In this section I will report on a study which tried to investigate the question of whether of not lexical decomposition is likely to take place during the recognition of a Chinese character.

In Chinese and Japanese kanji, many complex characters share the same radical. For example, (Fig. 1), the radical TREE is part of the character ROOT, PINE etc. etc.. In several cases the meaning of the complex character is related to the meaning of the radical, as for PINE, while in other cases the meaningful complex character is completely unrelated to the meaning of the component. In the first case, the meaning relation between the radical and the complex character is transparent, while in the second it is opaque.

The purpose of the study was to find out if a single component of a complex character is activated when the character is recognized, even when the relation between the complex character and the single component is completely opaque. When the complex character is read, does the semantic information becoming available include the semantic representation of the components, even when these are opaquely "hidden" in the complex character? For example, will the meaning of *mouth* become available when the character STONE is recognized? This question has been investigated in a series of studies with both Chinese and Japanese readers, using a variety of techniques. In one study with Japanese subjects, for example (Flores d'Arcais & Saito, 1989; Flores d'Arcais & Saito, 1992) we used an interference paradigm with a semantic categorization task. In such a task, readers were requested to make speeded judgments of semantic relatedness on a pair of characters: that is, to decide as quickly as possible if two words belonged to the same semantic category. If the two words A and B were related in meaning, such as EYE and MOUTH, then the subject should have quickly said *yes*. When the words have not related in meaning, the appropriate response was *no*. If one of the two characters, say A, included a component whose meaning was related to the meaning of the other character B, then it was somewhat more difficult to decide that the two words were not related (that is to say *no*) than when A and B were completely unrelated. This was because the availability of the semantic information of the component of A, which was related to B, could have induced a *yes* response, and this could have interfered with the execution of the correct *no* response. Thus, to decide that STONE (which includes the radical MOUTH) and EYE do *not* belong to the same semantic category would take longer, or result in more errors, than to say *no* to the question of whether STONE and HOUSE belong to the same category. Indeed, if during the recognition of STONE the meaning of the "hidden" radical MOUTH is also activated to some extent, this should have tended to produce a *yes* response, because "mouth" and "eye" are obviously two related concepts.

Thus, in one of the studies (Flores d'Arcais & Saito, 1992) a number of subjects, Japanese readers, were presented with pairs of characters and had to decide as fast as possible whether the two characters were related in meaning or not. The results, average latencies and percentage of errors, are reported in Table 1.

Table 1

Experiment 1 - Semantic categorization average response latencies (in msec) and error rates for the critical conditions (correct response: No). (Data from Flores d'Arcais & Saito, 1992.)

Relation in the stimulus pairs semantic relatedness

	Unrelated STONE-HOUSE	Graphically similar LEATHER-GRASS	Component to whole STONE-EYE	Part to whole STONE-MOUTH
Response latencies	857	910	882	872
Error rates	2.78	7.92	6.01	8.09

The differences reported are significant (see Flores d'Arcais & Saito, 1992) and were interpreted to be due to interference in the decision of semantic relatedness for the pairs consisting of a complex character and of a character related in meaning to the opaque component of the first (such as EYE and STONE, which contains as an opaque component the radical MOUTH), showing that it is more difficult to decide that two words or concepts are unrelated when the character of the first contains a "hidden" component whose word is related in meaning to the word of the second character. Corresponding, and even more clear-cut, results were obtained with Chinese material and Chinese subjects (Flores d'Arcais, in preparation).

The simplest way to interpret these results is to assume that the subjects were led to some tendency to a *yes* response which interfered with the execution of the correct response *no*. This tendency would have been based on the availability of the meaning of the critical component of the complex character, related to the meaning of the other character of the pair. Put differently, the presentation of the character STONE would activate not only the corresponding representation in the mental lexicon, but also, at least to some extent, that of the component *mouth*. In the search for semantic relatedness demanded by the task, this meaning would have been incorrectly related to the meaning of the other character of the pair, EYE. According to the interpretation given, this tendency to a positive response interfered with the process of executing the correct response *no*, hence the longer latency. Thus, it might be possible to conclude that at some level of processing, presumably the one involved in the semantic judgment task, the semantic information corresponding to a component character becomes available and is functionally effective when the complex character is recognized.

This indicates the possibility that in the process of recognizing a word written with a complex character, opaque and semantically unrelated components are likely to activated, either as a result of the recognition of the complex character, or as a process accompanying it. This activation would affect a semantic task, such as the one required in the judgment of semantic relatedness. The data thus support the notion of some form of lexical decomposition process in the recognition of complex characters in adult readers.

Graphemic and semantic activation processes in the recognition of Chinese characters

In this study, as well as in the following one, subjects were presented with complex characters to be named as quickly as possible. The presentation was characterized by an onset asynchrony between part of the character and the whole, in such a way that a fragment, often either the left or the right radical is presented before the whole character, the remaining part being withheld for some interval. The method used in the present and in the following experiment here reported was first used for the study of word recognition by Eriksen and Eriksen (1974). By momentarily withholding part of the information given by the character, we tried to exercise some control on the moment at which the information carried by the different parts of the character could become available for processing.

Thus, a typical trial involved the presentation, on a display, of one radical or of a fragment of the whole character, mostly the left or the right radical alone, followed, at a very short interval, by the rest of the character, with the previously presented part still on the display in the same position. Depending on the onset asynchrony, either the difference in presentation rate remains subliminal, or the subject sees a kind of "expansion" of the part into the whole character. The stimulus onset asymmetries used in the present experiments were of 60 and 180 msec respectively.

The technique thus allows pre-exposing, by a short time, the cues which give to the reader the possibilities of extracting graphemic or semantic information. By pre-exposing a radical by a small interval we should obtain preactivation of the whole domain of characters which share that radical, be they related in meaning to the radical or not. On the other hand, by pre-exposing a radical which is congruent in form and in meaning with the total character, we should obtain a preactivation of the meaning of the character which is congruent in meaning, and inhibition of the characters which are incongruent in meaning with the radical.

The present study was carried out with Chinese characters with a total of 64 Chinese subjects, speaker of Mandarin (for a full report, see Flores d'Arcais, in preparation). The basic material consisted of 20 pairs of characters; in each of them there was an identical radical: in the first member of the pair the radical was related in meaning to the total character, while in the second the radical was not related in meaning to the total character, as exemplified in Figure 2. Each character was presented in isolation and had to be named as quickly as possible. The different onset times between the pre-exposed fragment (radical) and the whole character were 60 and 180 msec.

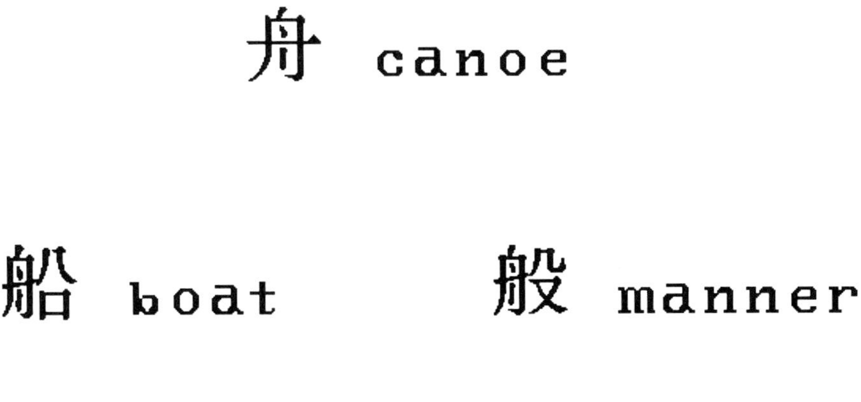

舟 canoe

船 boat   般 manner

Figure 2. An example of a stimulus pair used in study 2. The left radical, CANOE, was presented prior to the whole character, BOAT or MANNER. In the control condition, fragments of the strokes were presented.

Table 2

Average naming latencies (in msec) for complex Chinese characters with pre-exposure of a fragment, a congruent radical, or an incongruent 60- and 180-msec SOAs. (Data from Flores d'Arcais, in preparation.)

Pre-exposed material	SOA	
	60	180
Fragments	540	541
Congruent radical (form and meaning)	514	549
Incongruent radical (only form)	515	569
No pre-exposure	530	

The results of this study are reported in Table 2, and in the following (for a full statistical analysis, see Flores d'Arcais, in preparation). With short SOA between the onset of the first radical and the whole character the radical has a facilitatory effect *both* for a congruent meaning (the radical is part of the complex character and its meaning is related to it) and for the incongruent meaning (the radical is part of the complex character but is not related in meaning to it). This indicates that earlier exposure of a part of a character which is congruent in form with the whole item does have facilitatory effects, independently of the semantic relation. At longer SOA, the semantically congruent radical facilitates the naming of the whole character which is related in meaning to the radical but, when the pre-exposed radical is incongruent in meaning with the name of the character, there is some inhibitory effect.

The results have been interpreted as indicating an early, initial activation of graphemic information concerning the form of the radical. This produces facilitation of the recognition of all characters which share that form, independent of the meaning relation. Subsequently, with a longer SOA, there is an effect of activation of the semantic information. The pre-exposed radical has a given meaning, and all, or perhaps the most frequent, characters which have a related meaning are preactivated. When the target item is inconsistent in meaning with this cohort, inhibition may result.

Activation of phonological and semantic information during the recognition of a Chinese character

In both the original Chinese form, and in the Japanese writing system, a large number of the complex hanzji (sometimes called *phonograms*) are characterized by a combination of a radical which gives information about the meaning, and another radical which gives information about the pronunciation of the character. The first is sometimes called the *signific*, while the second is sometimes called the *phonetic*. An alternative terminology calls the first the *radical* and the second the *stem*. The signific is not always uniquely related to a specific meaning, but is an indication of the category of the character. For example (Fig. 1), a number of complex character include as signific the radical for TREE, (or WOOD) the characters standing respectively for PINE, BOARD, etc. Also, the phonetic does not always necessarily correspond to a unique phonological word, but it gives important cues for the pronunciation. It is the combination of signific and phonetic that is uniquely defined phonologically. However, the distinction made is rather important. The phonetic radical contains information for the phonological structure of the word to be read, and the signific offers at least some basis for the meaning of the word. Almost 90% of all complex characters are of this type (Tsao & Wang, 1983).

The same radical can be, in one character, the signific, and, in another, the phonetic. The positions vary. The phonetic can be the radical which is in the top position or in the bottom, or to the left or to the right. However, in the large majority of this type of character, the *signific* is on the *left* and the *phonetic* is on the *right*. Thus, if we look at the distribution of the properties of the characters which might be relevant for the process of word recognition, the left radical is a likely cue for meaning and the right radical is a likely cue for pronunciation. If these have become valid cues for the reader, one would expect the left radical to be used by the reader to get information as to the meaning of the character, and the radical on the right to obtain phonological information. Thus, although both radicals are taken in within a single fixation, the contribution of the two parts to the recognition process can, at least in terms of input information, be taken as separate.

The existence of this feature, and the fact that, although far from being perfect, at least statistically there is a distinction between the information carried by the two radicals, allows testing a number of interesting questions concerning phonological activation during word recognition. The fact that semantic and phonological information are stored in two different parts of many characters, namely the left and right radical, respectively, allows independent manipulation of the moment at which access to semantic and to phonological information is possible, thus offering the possibility of careful investigation of the rate at which information concerning the meaning and the pronunciation of a character becomes available to the recognition system. Thus, the properties of the types of complex characters which we have just illustrated allow us to answer questions concerning the time course of the activation of the phonological and semantic information associated with the mental representation of the words corresponding to the characters.

In the present experiment we have again used the same technique as in the previous experiment, pre-exposing one of the two radicals - in this case the semantic or the phonetic one - with an onset asynchrony with respect to the whole character. Thus, a typical trial involved the presentation on a display of the left or the right radical alone, followed, at a very short interval, by the rest of the character with the previously presented part still on the display in the same position.

The technique allows withholding for a very short time the cues which give the reader the possibility of extracting phonological or semantic information. By withholding the phonetic radical, the subject would first see only the semantic radical, and therefore would be able to know something about the meaning of the character, but, in most cases, would still be unable to know its pronunciation. Alternatively, by presenting first the phonetic radical followed by the semantic one, we would put the subject in the condition of knowing or at least giving a good guess about the pronunciation of the character without knowing its meaning. With earlier presentation of the left radical, the reader knows at least something about the meaning of the character without knowing how to pronounce it (in fact, the reader is momentarily precipitated in an artificial situation of deep

dyslexia). On the other hand, following earlier presentation of the right radical, the reader knows something about the pronunciation of the word, but doesn't yet know its meaning. By appropriate manipulation of the onset asynchrony between the initial radical and the whole character, we are able to learn something about the time course of the activation of the phonological information as compared to the semantic one. The experimental material of this experiment consisted of four sets of 10 complex kanji based on the orthogonal combinations of the semantic and phonological relation of the radical to the whole. In condition A, the left radical was related in meaning to the meaning of the whole character,
and the right radical had an identical pronunciation as the whole character. In condition B, the left radical was related in meaning to the whole character, but the right radical had a different pronunciation from the whole character. In condition C, the left radical was unrelated in meaning to the whole character, and the pronunciation of the right radical was identical

Condition	Character	Meaning/(Pronunciation)		
		Whole character	Left radical	Right radical
S+ P+	粉	powder (fun)	rice (bei)	minute (fun)
S+ P-	粒	grain (ryu)	rice (bei)	stand (ritsu)
S- P+	粧	makeup (syo)	rice (bei)	farm village (syo)
S- P-	粋	pure (sui)	rice (bei)	graduate (sotsu)

Figure 3. An example of a full set of characters presented for naming. The left or the right radical was pre-exposed with a SOA of 60 or 180 msec.

Table 3

Average naming latencies (in msec) for complex characters with pre-exposure of the left or right radical (differences with corresponding fragment display conditions in parentheses) for two pre-exposure intervals (60- and 180-msec SOAs). (Data from Flores d'Arcais, Saito, & Kawakami, 1992.)

SOA = 60 msec

TYPE OF CHARACTER	SEGMENT PRESENTED FIRST		
	Semantic radical	Phonetic radical	Fragment
Sem+ Phon+	588 (29)	589 (28)	617
Sem+ Phon-	565 (29)	591 (3)	594
Sem- Phon+	582 (-1)	560 (21)	581
Sem- Phon-	606 (-1)	610 (5)	605

SOA = 180 msec

TYPE OF CHARACTER	SEGMENT PRESENTED FIRST		
	Semantic radical	Phonetic radical	Fragment
Sem+ Phon+	575 (18)	540 (52)	592
Sem+ Phon-	582 (-21)	557 (6)	563
Sem- Phon+	594 (-17)	513 (64)	577
Sem- Phon-	580 (-2)	561 (17)	578

to that of the whole character, and finally, in condition D the whole character was different in meaning from the meaning of the left radical and in pronunciation from the pronunciation of the right radical. An example of the experimental material is given in Figure 3.

The task of our subjects, 24 Japanese students, was to name the character as fast as possible. The results are reported in Table 3, and can briefly be summarized as follows. At a short SOA (60 msec) between the onset of the radical and the onset of the total character, previous exposure of the semantic radical facilitates access of the name, and so does anticipation of the phonetic radical. At 180 SOA, there is a significant effect from the previous exposure of the phonetic radical. This has a strong facilitatory effect on the naming of the character. On the other hand, at this SOA the previous exposure of the semantic radical seems to have some inhibitory effect on naming speed. We interpreted this to be due to a possible activation of competitors within a given domain. Inspection of individual items reveals stronger inhibitory effects for the characters in which the domain defined by the semantic radical is large (i.e., when there are many complex characters sharing the left, semantic radical). For more details on this study see Flores d'Arcais, Saito, and Kawakami (1992).

General Conclusions

The conclusions of the studies reported here can be summarized as follows. First, there seems to be an indication that during the recognition of a complex character the meaning of the components of the complex character are likely to be activated, even when they are hidden in the character. This indication supports the notion of an automatic process of exhaustive access to the semantic information supported by the character.

The results of second and the third experiment here reported allow some conclusions concerning the activation processes of three components of the information which I assumed to be stored in lexical-semantic memory about complex characters, namely graphemic, phonological and semantic information. This, when accessed, allows the reader to perform the pronunciation response and to know the meaning of the word. The studies here summarized have provided some initial evidence as to the time course of these activation processes, and to the way the various components involved in a lexical unit are interrelated in the recognition process. At an early moment following onset of the character, graphemic information is available and a number of word candidates are likely to be activated. Subsequently, phonological and semantic information also become available. At least when the task requires pronunciation of the character, phonological information seems to become available prior to the full availability of semantic information. Thus, at least in a naming task, we have been able to obtain some initial evidence concerning the time course of the activation of the three components here investigated.

The conclusions of the last two experiments here reported are limited to the type of task used, namely naming. For tasks requiring the obligatory use of semantic information, but not necessarily the use of phonological information, such as semantic categorization, it is not clear whether the same type of processes here outlined would take place. In other words, it is perfectly possible that the early availability of phonological information in reading hanzji is contingent upon the type of task here used.

The experimental work summarized here represents a contribution to our knowledge of the processing of recognizing and naming a word written in the Chinese orthography. The features of this orthography allow testing a number of issues in word recognition, thus contributing towards a more valid theory on the processing of written words.

Acknowledgements

Part of the work reported here has been supported by a Grant by NWO, the Dutch Organization for Pure Research, and by a SAP Fellowship granted by the Japanese-German Centre of Berlin.

References

Atkinson, R.C., & Shiffrin, R.M. (1968). Human memory: A proposed system and its control processes. In K.W. Spence and J.T. Spence (Eds.), *The psychology of learning and motivation*, Vol. II. New York: Academic Press.

Balota, D.A. (1990). The role of meaning in word recognition. In D.A. Balota, G.B. Flores d'Arcais and K. Rayner (Eds.), *Comprehension processes in reading*. Hillsdale, N.J.: Lawrence Erlbaum Associates.

Baron, J. (1973). Phonemic stage not necessary for reading. *Quarterly Journal of Experimental Psychology, 25*, 241-246.
Biederman, I., & Tsao, Y-C. (1979). On processing Chinese ideographs and English words: Some implications from Stroop-test results. *Cognitive Psychology, 11*, 125-132.
Chen, H.C., & Tsoi, K.C. (1990). Symbol-word interference in Chinese and English. *Acta Psychologica, 75*, 123-138.
Coltheart, M. (1978). Lexical access in simple reading tasks. In G. Underwood (Ed.), *Strategies of information processing*. London: Academic Press.
Conrad, R. (1964). Acoustic confusions in immediate memory. *British Journal of Psychology, 55*, 75-84.
Elman, J.L., Takahashi, K., & Tohsaku, Y.H. (1981). Lateral asymmetries for the identification of concrete and abstract Kanji. *Neuropsychologia, 19*, 407-412.
Endo, M., Shimizu, A., & Hori, T. (1978). Functional asymmetry of visual fields for Japanese words in Kana (syllable-based) writing and random shape-recognition in Japanese subjects. *Neuropsychologia, 16*, 291-297.
Endo, M., Shimizu, A., & Hakamura, I. (1981). Laterality differences in recognition of Japanese and Hangul words by monolinguals and bilinguals. *Cortex, 17*, 391-400.
Erickson, D., Mattingly, I.G., & Turvey, N.T. (1977). Phonetic activity and reading: An experiment with Kanji. *Language and Speech, 20*, 384-403.
Eriksen, B.A., & Eriksen, C.W. (1974). Reading in a non alphabetic system. Some experimental studies. In L. Henderson (Ed.), *Orthographies and reading*. Hillsdale, N.J.: Lawrence Erlbaum.
Fang, S-P., Tzeng, O., & Alva, L. (1981). Intralanguage vs. interlanguage Stroop effects in two types of writing systems. *Memory & Cognition, 9*, 609-617.
Flores d'Arcais, G.B. (in preparation). *Graphemic and semantic activation in naming Chinese characters*.
Flores d'Arcais, G.B., & Saito, H. (1992). *Lexical decomposition of complex Kanji characters in Japanese readers*.
Flores d'Arcais, G.B., & Saito, H. (1989). Semantic activation and lexical decomposition in the recognition of complex Kanji characters. In A.F. Bennett and K.M. McC8onckey (Eds.), *Cognition in individual and social contexts*. Amsterdam: Elsevier.
Flores d'Arcais, G.B., & Schreuder, R. (1987). Semantic activation during object naming. *Psychological Research, 49*, 153-159.
Flores d'Arcais, G.B., Saito, H., & Kawakami, M. (1992). *Phonological and semantic activation in reading Kanji characters*.
Frazier, L., & Fodor, J.D. (1978). The Sausage Machine: A new two-stage parsing model. *Cognition, 6*, 291-325.
Geschwind, H. (1972). Language and the brain. *Scientific American, 226*, 76-83.
Gough, P. (1972). One second of reading. In J.P. Kavanagh and I.G. Mattingly (Eds.), *Language by eye and by ear*. Cambridge, Mass.: M.I.T. Press.
Hardyck, C., Tzeng, O.J.L., & Wang, W.S-Y. (1977). Cerebral lateralization effects in visual half-field experiments. *Nature, 269*, 705-707.
Hartje, W., Hannen, P., & Willems, K. (1986). Effect of visual complexity in

tachistoscopic recognition of Kanji and Kana symbols by German subjects. *Neuropsychologia, 24*, 297-300.
Hatta, T. (1977a). Hemispheric differences in a categorization matching task. *Japanese Journal of Psychology, 48*, 141-147.
Hatta, T. (1977b). Lateral recognition of abstract and concrete Kanji in Japanese. *Perceptual and Motor Skills, 45*, 731-734.
Hatta, T. (1977c). Recognition of Japanese Kanji in the left and the right visual fields. *Neuropsychologia, 15*, 685-688.
Hatta, T. (1978). Recognition of Japanese Kanji and Hirakana in the left and right visual fields. *Japanese Psychological Research, 20*, 51-59.
Hatta, T.(1981). Differential processing of Kanji and Kana stimuli in Japanese people: Some implications from Stroop-test results. *Neuropsychologia, 19*, 87-93.
Hatta, T., Honjon, Y., & Mito, H. (1983). Event-related potentials and reaction times as measures of hemispheric differences for physical and semantic Kanji matching. *Cortex, 19*, 517-528.
Henderson, L. (1982). *Orthography and word recognition in reading.* London: Academic Press.
Hirata, K., & Osaka, R. (1967). Tachistocopic recognition of Japanese letter materials in left and right visual fields. *Psychologia, 10*, 437-445.
Hoosain, R. (1991). *Psycholinguistic implications for linguistic relativity. A case study of Chinese.* Hillsdale, N.J.: Lawrence Erlbaum Associates.
Hung, D.L., & Tzeng, O.J.L. (1981). Orthographic variations and visual information processing. *Psychological Bulletin, 90*, 377-414.
Kershner, J.R., & Jerg, A.G-J. (1972). Dual functional hemispheric asymmetry in visual perception: Effects of ocular dominance and post-exposural processes. *Neuropsychologia, 10*, 437-445.
Kimura, Y. (1984). Concurrent vocal interference: Its effects on Kana and Kanji. *Quarterly Journal of Experimental Psychology, 36*, 117-131.
Krueger, L.E. (1970). Search time in a redundant visual display. *Journal of Experimental Psychology, 83*, 391-399.
Kuo, W.F. (1978). A preliminary study of reading disabilities in the Republic of China. *Collected papers, 20*, 57-78. Taiwan: National Taiwan Normal University.
Lam, A., Perfetti, C.A., & Bell, L. (1991). Automatic phonetic transfer bidialectal reading. *Applied Psycholinguistics, 12*, 299-312.
Leong, C.K., Wong, S., Wong, A., & Hiscock, M. (1985). Differential cerebral involvement in perceiving Chinese characters: Levels of processing approach. *Brain and Language, 26*, 131-145.
Makita, K. (1968). The rarity of reading disability in Japanese children. *American Journal of Orthopsychiatry, 38*, 599-614.
Ohnishi, H., & Hatta, T. (1980). Lateral differences in tachistoscopic recognition of Kanji pairs with mixed image valves. *Psychology, 23*, 233-239.
Paradis, H., Hagiwara, H., & Hildebrandt, N. (1985). *Neurolinguistic aspects of the Japanese writing system.* New York: Academic Press.
Perfetti, C.A. (1985). *Reading ability.* New York: Oxford University Press.
Perfetti, C.A., & Zhang, S. (1991). Phonological processes in reading Chinese

characters. *Journal of Experimental Psychology: Learning, Memory and Cognition, 17,* 633-643.
Rozin, P., Ponitzky, S., & Sotsky, R. (1971). American children with reading problems can easily learn to read English represented by Chinese characters. *Science, 171,* 1264-1267.
Rubenstein, H.R., Lewis S.S., & Rubenstein, N.A. (1971). Evidence for phonemic recoding in visual word recognition. *Journal of Verbal Learning and Verbal Behavior, 10,* 645-657.
Sasanuma, S., & Fujimura, O. (1971). Selective impairment of phonetic and nonphonetic transcription of words in Japanese aphasic patients: Kana vs. Kanji visual recognition and writing. *Cortex, 7,* 1-18.
Sasanuma, S. (1974). Impairment of written language in Japanese aphasics: Kana versus Kanji processing. *Journal of Chinese linguistics, 2,* 141-158.
Sasanuma, S. (1975). Kana and Kanji processing in Japanese aphasics. *Brain and Language, 2,* 369-383.
Sasanuma, S., & Monoi, H. (1975). The syndrome of Gogi (word-meaning) aphasia. *Neurology, 25,* 627-632.
Sasanuma, S., Itoh, M., Mori, K., & Kobayashi, Y. (1977). Tachistoscopic recognition of Kana and Kanji words. *Neuropsychologia, 15,* 547-553.
Sasanuma, S. (1984). Can surface dyslexia occur in Japanese? In L. Henderson (Ed.), *Orthographies and reading,* (pp. 43-56). London: Lawrence Erlbaum.
Sasanuma, S. (1985). Surface dyslexia and dysgraphia: How are they manifested in Japanese? In K.E. Patterson, J.C. Marshall, & M. Coltheart (Eds.), *Surface dyslexia. Neuropsychological and cognitive studies of phonological reading.* London: Lawrence Erlbaum.
Seidenberg, M. (1985). The time course of phonological word activation in two writing systems. *Cognition, 19,* 1-30.
Shimamura, A.P. (1987). Word comprehension and naming: An analysis of English and Japanese orthographics. *American Journal of Psychology, 100,* 15-40.
Smith, M.C. and Kirsner, K. (1982). Language and orthography as irrelevant features in colour-word and picture-word Stroop interference. *Quarterly Journal of Experimental Psychology, 24,* 153-170.
So, K.F., Potter, M.C., & Friedmann, R.B. (1976). Reading in Chinese and English: Naming versus understanding. Unpublished manuscript, University of Massachusetts, Amherst.
Stevenson, H.W., Stigler, J.W., Lee, S-Y., Lucker, G.W., Kitamura, S., and Hsu, C-C. (1985). Cognitive performance and academic achievement of Japanese, Chinese and American children. *Child Development, 56,* 718-734.
Tsao, Y-C, Wu, M.F., & Feustel, T. (1981). Stroop interference: Hemispheric difference in Chinese speakers. *Brain and Language, 13,* 372-378.
Tsao, Y-C, & Wang, W.S-L. (1983). Information distribution in Chinese characters. *Visible Language, 17,* 357-364.
Tzeng, O.J.L., Hung, D.L., Cotton, B., & Wang, W.S-Y. (1979). Visual lateralisation effect in reading Chinese characters. *Nature, 282,* 499-501.
Tzeng, O.J.L., & Hung, D.L. (1980). Reading in a nonalphabetic writing system. In J.F. Kavanagh and R.L. Venezky. *Orthography, reading and dyslexia.*

Baltimore: University Park Press.
Tzeng, O.J.L., & Hung, D.L. (1981). Linguistic determinism: A written language perspective. In O.J.L. Tzeng and H. Singers (Eds.), *Perception of print: Reading research in experimental psychology*. Hillsdale, N.J.: Lawrence Erlbaum Associates.
Tzeng, O.J.L., Hung, D.L., Chen, S., Wu, J., & Hsi, M.S. (1986). Processing Chinese logographs by Chinese brain damaged patients. In H.S.R. Kao, G.P. Galen and R. Hoosain (Eds.), *Graphonomics: Contemporary research in handwriting*. Amsterdam: North Holland.
Tzeng, O.J.L., Hung, D.L., & Wang, S-Y. (1977). Speech recoding in reading Chinese characters. *Journal of Experimental Psychology: Human Learning and Memory*, *3*, 621-630.

Lexical Access in Chinese: Evidence from Automatic Activation of Phonological Information

Chao-Ming Cheng
National Taiwan University

Three lexical-decision experiments were conducted to assess phonological processes in Chinese lexical access. Results of Experiment 1 show that the lexical decision to a target character was faster when preceded by a homophonic character cue than when preceded by a phonological-dissimilar character cue. This homophonic priming effect was independent of the stimulus-onset asynchrony (SOA) and visual similarity between the cue and the target. A similar pattern of results was also obtained in Experiments 2 and 3, which showed an effect of a faster decision for homophonic character pairs than for phonological-dissimilar pairs, independent of SOA and of the visual similarity between the pairs. The present experiments also obtained a finding that a brief stimulus-exposure duration which is not optimal for recognition of characters is still suitable for generating phonological information about the characters. These results are taken to support the notion that reading Chinese requires phonological mediation.

Access to an internal lexicon (i.e., a store of word representations) is a major component act of reading. A controversial issue about this act of reading has been the phonological processes in lexical access. To be precise, the issue is about whether a printed word should be converted into a speech format in order to gain its lexical access. Basically, orthographies are designed and evolved to represent speech sounds, to which objects and events are then referred. Thus the shape of a visual word itself does not carry information about the meanings that the word communicates. For this reason, visual word recognition should be based on phonology. This indirect access to lexicon through phonological mediation is especially true at the early stages of learning to read. The indirect access may equally apply to skilled reading. In skilled reading, the mapping of visual words onto phonology is expected to be executed automatically through extensive practice. However, it is also possible that a skilled reader may adopt a direct-access mode such that words are recognized on a visual basis, without reference to speech sound.

Unfortunately, research on this issue has generated contradictory findings. For example, at about the same time Forster and Chambers (1973) made strong arguments in favor of the mode of direct access, Meyer, Schvaneveldt, and Ruddy (1974) showed evidence supporting the contrary mode. Since then, contrasting observations have led to the development of dual-access models (see McCusker, Hillinger, & Bias, 1981). The idea of dual access is that a skilled reader has an option of using either the visual or the phonological route from print to meaning. These two routes are thought to operate in parallel, with a race between these two routes that determines the occurrence of phonological mediation. According to this view, phonological information is neither necessary nor obligatory for lexical access. A similar view was also proposed by Seidenberg (1985a; 1985b) in a time-course model, but the model emphasizes an activation process which begins with the extraction of visual information from the input, followed by the activation of phonological information. Whether lexical access is direct or indirect depends completely upon the time course of recognition. If sufficient visual information is extracted to permit recognition prior to the access of phonology, direct access results. On the contrary, if a word cannot be recognized prior to the activation of phonological information, indirect access results. In this model, prelexical phonological information is neither obligatory nor optional.

The theory advancement mentioned above is largely based on experimental findings using either naming or lexical-decision tasks. The naming paradigm was introduced by Baron and Strawson (1976) to measure the pronunciations of regular and exception words. Much research using this paradigm has shown a faster pronunciation for regular words than for exceptions (Baron & Strawson, 1976; Glushko, 1979; Stanovich & Bauer, 1978; Underwood & Bargh, 1982). Baron and Strawson argued that this regularity effect was based on a prelexical phonological recoding for words to be named. According to Coltheart (1978), such recoding can be accomplished only through grapheme-phoneme conversions. When such recoding is applied to regular words, whose letter sequences conform to grapheme-phoneme correspondence (GPC) rules, it results in a fast recoding and naming. On the other hand, those exceptions to GPC rules result in an incorrect or a slow naming when such recoding is used. However, it is possible that phonological information used for naming is postlexical rather than prelexical in nature. The regularity effect may simply result from a faster direct access to lexicon for regular words than for exceptions.

Seidenberg (1985) and his associates (e.g., Seidenberg, Waters, Barnes, & Tanenhaus, 1984; Waters & Seidenberg, 1985) have recently examined regularity effects for high- and low-frequency words. They found that the regularity effect was specific to low-frequency words only, but not to high-frequency words. These results were taken to support their time-course model. However, several other explanations seem plausible. First, prelexical phonological information, as it is claimed to be used to recognize low-frequency words in the time-course model, may be also used for recognizing high-frequency words. The insignificant difference in naming latency between regular and exception words of high frequency may result from a insignificant difference in generating prelexical phonological information between these two classes of words, as a result of their frequent use. As a second possibility, naming may be based on postlexical phonological information. The regularity effect specific to low-frequency words thus results from different difficulties in pronouncing words of different regularities that are seldom used. It is therefore concluded in this analysis that this pattern of regularity effects is inconclusive with respect to the issue of direct/indirect access.

The lexical-decision paradigm in various arrangements necessarily involves lexical access and does not involve more than lexical access, so that a phonological effect identified with this paradigm should be prelexical in principle. However, this effect is relevant to the issue only when it is produced by a process demand rather than by a task demand. Unfortunately, the latter tends to be the case for many findings. As an original application, a lexical-decision task was used by Rubenstein, Lewis, and Rubenstein (1971) to ask subjects to judge whether or not a string of visual letters was a legal word. Meyer et al. (1974) adopted a modified version, presenting on each trial two letter strings to subjects. The subjects were required to respond "yes" if both were legal words or to respond "no" if either of the two was illegal. In this task, words were discriminated from pronounceable nonwords. They found that word pairs that were both visually and phonologically similar (e.g., BRIBE-TRIBE) were judged faster than control pairs sharing no similarity of either dimension (e.g., BRIBE-HENCE). However, when the pairs were visually similar only (e.g., FREAK-BREAK), the decisions were longer than that for the controls (e.g., FREAK-TOUCH). These results revealed an encoding bias: subjects encode the first word phonologically by using GPC rules and are biased toward using the same rules to recode the second word if it is visually similar to the first. Consequently, if the two graphemic codes of the paired words map onto similar phonemic codes, then lexical decision is facilitated. On the other hand, if the two graphemic codes should map onto different phonemic codes, then the bias will lead to an incorrect phonemic representation of the second word, and the subject would have to make a second attempt at the word, resulting in a long decision. Clearly, this notion favors indirect access.

However, subsequent research has raised doubts about the findings by Meyer et al. (1974). For example, Hanson and Fowler (1987) and Shulman, Hornak, and Sanders (1978) have shown that both the positive rhyming and the inhibitory visual-similarity effects disappeared when the same task was used to discriminate words from consonant or random letter strings rather than from pronounceable nonwords. Shulman et al. concluded that prelexical phonological recoding, if any, is not universal and is probably an option rather than a requirement for lexical access. However, their discrimination task may have led subjects to develop a certain strategy, by which words can be distinguished effectively from consonant or random strings, without necessarily entering into lexical analysis. When this strategy is carried over to word-word pairs, they will be judged as words without priming with each other, thus no rhyming effect is to be expected.

The findings by Meyer et al. (1974) have been replicated in the studies by Hillinger (1980) and by Hsieh (1982). However, these two authors also reported a facilitative rhyming effect free from visual similarity of paired words to be judged. In the Hillinger study, a facilitative rhyming effect was produced both when the first paired word was presented auditorily and when rhyming word pairs were visually dissimilar (e.g., EIGHT-MATE). Hsieh, using Chinese characters as stimuli and native

Chinese speakers as subjects, showed that visual-dissimilar homophonic character pairs resulted in a faster decision than did their nonhomophonic counterparts (see Table 1). According to the encoding-bias notion, no facilitation should be expected in visual-dissimilar rhyming or homophonic pairs. It should be noted, however, that these positive rhyming and homophonic effects, which may require an explanation other than encoding bias, appear to confirm rather than disconfirm the mode of indirect access. Hillinger attributed this rhyming facilitation to a process analogous to semantic spreading activation (Collins & Loftus, 1975), but based on a phonological spreading in a phonological file.

Table 1
Lexical Decision Times as a Function of Pairing Condition (Data adapted from Hsieh, 1982).

Pairing condition	Decision time (msec)
Visual-similar & phonological-identical (VS-PI)	968.6
Control for VS-PI	993.2
Visual dissimilar & phonological-identical (VD-PI)	926.3
Control for VD-PI	955.8
Visual-similar & phonological-dissimilar (VS-PD)	1002.4
Control for VS-PD	960.9

In the present study, experiments were conducted to assess the role of phonological information in Chinese lexicality judgment. A general question addressed for this study was whether a study of a different orthography like Chinese may throw some light on the issue of direct/indirect access. A specific question was whether phonological processes are necessary for the visual recognition of Chinese characters which are logographic rather than alphabetic or syllabic.

Ancient Chinese characters were designed to directly represent objects and events rather than to represent speech sounds. This is evidenced by the fact that the two Chinese orthographic categories of "pictograph of objects" '象形' and "denotation of events" '指事' were developed first, followed by the development of the other four categories of "ideograph" '會意', "phonetic-logographic compound" '形聲', "phonetic loan" '假借' and "figurative extension of meaning" '轉注'. However, this orthographic development also suggests that Chinese characters are evolved to represent speech sounds, while simultaneously continuing to represent objects and events. Thus it is estimated that about 80% of modern Chinese characters are phonetic-logographic compounds, each of which consists at least of two main radicals; one is believed to carry the sound of the character and the other is to carry the meanings of the character (Li, 1977).

Given this orthographic structure, no GPC rule exists in Chinese. Further, as it is shown in Figure 1, the spelling-sound correspondences in Chinese are not rigid; visual-similar characters can be either phonologically identical or phonologically different, and so can visual-dissimilar characters. It is therefore believed that the replication of the Meyer et al. (1974) and Hillinger (1980) findings in Chinese by Hsieh (1982) cannot be accounted for by the notion of encoding bias based on either GPC or radical-sound conversions. A possible explanation considers a principle of skilled reading that applies to all writing systems: the mapping of visual words onto phonology is executed automatically as a result of extensive practice. In this light, an encounter with a first paired character in the Hsieh experiments automatically arouses the sound of the character, which alone is then used to prime or to expect the second paired character. This would result in a fast phonological recoding and recognition for the second character if it is homophonic with the first. This accounts for the positive homophonic effect free from visual similarity. The inhibitory visual-similarity effect in visual-similar phonological-dissimilar pairs is probably produced by a delay of correct phonological information about the second character. This delay is caused by a rather persistent, yet incorrect, rhyming attempt at the

Pairing condition	Chinese character pairs	
	Visual	Auditory
Visual-similar phonological-identical	培 — 陪	pei — pei
Visual-similar phonological-dissimilar	讀 — 續	du — xu
Visual-dissimilar phonological-identical	那 — 納	na — na
Visual-dissimilar phonological-dissimilar	補 — 譯	bu — yi

Figure 1. Examples of Four Different Character-Character Pairs Differing in Visual and Phonological Similarity Used in Experiment 1.

second character, induced by common visual cues shared by the paired characters.

The interpretation given above is by no means exhaustive. For example, upon receiving a pair of two characters to be lexically judged, the subject may recode the prime character phonologically after, rather than before, it is recognized; the generated phonological information is then used to prime the second character. This view also successfully accounts for the findings by Hsieh (1982), as well as those by Meyer et al. (1974).

Therefore, the priming effects observed in these two studies are not sufficient evidence that phonological recoding for the prime character (or word) is prelexical. Besides, these priming effects may have been produced in response to the task demand of judging two targets contiguously presented, rather than produced by priming a compulsory phonological recoding for the second target prior to recognition. For example, if the inhibitory visual-similarity effect is induced by common visual cues shared by two paired words simultaneously presented, then this effect should not be expected in a sequential presentation of the stimuli. In fact, the results of Meyer et al. showed this to be the case.

It is clear then that the critical evidence for indirect access, to be derived from the lexical decision to pairing words, should be evidence of a *prelexical* phonological recoding for prime words. To obtain such evidence, the approach taken in the present research is to study visual Chinese recognition by using paradigms that are likely to tap automatic activation of phonological information about prime words in lexical decision. The logic underlying this approach is that, if phonological recoding for prime words is shown to be automatically aroused, then such recoding is obligatory and compulsory and will have a chance to occur prior to, during, or as a part of recognition.

Experiment 1

In Experiment 1, phonological processes in reading Chinese were investigated in a lexical-decision task similar to that used by Posner and Snyder (1975) for investigating automatic and controlled processing. The task required subjects to judge on each trial whether or not a visual target, preceded by a visual cue, was a legal Chinese character. The variables in the experiment were: (1) visual and phonological similarities between the cue and the target, and (2) the asynchrony between the onset of the cue and that of the target (stimulus onset asynchrony, SOA).

The question asked in the experiment was whether a character simply serving as a cue in the task will result in an automatic activation of its phonological code. If it does, then the presentation of the cue character preceding a target character will produce a beneficial effect on the lexical judgment of the target, if it is homophonic with the cue as compared with that in a neutral-cue condition. Further, this beneficial effect should occur at short SOAs, as well as at long SOAs. Martin and Jensen (1988) have conducted a similar study in English. They found that a presentation of a cue word preceding a target word did not result in a positive rhyming effect on the lexical decision to the target at either short or long SOAs. This result, of course, refutes an automatic activation of phonological information in lexical decision. However, most of the stimulus pairs used in their study were rhyming pairs, which may have discouraged subjects to use phonological information for lexical decision.

Method

Subjects. Subjects were 24 undergraduates of the National Taiwan University, who were native speakers of Chinese. They participated in the experiment as a requirement for taking an introductory psychology course.

Stimulus materials. Stimuli consisted of 224 legal Chinese characters, 96 pseudocharacters, and 64 #-signs. The legal characters were selected from Cheng's frequency corpus (1982), with frequency being 2 or more in one-million occurrences of characters (but they were well known to the undergraduate subjects). The characters were of 9 to 16 strokes. Each character was composed of two radicals.

Each pseudocharacter was generated by replacing one constituent radical of a legal character by another radical, such that the resulting form was illegal, meaningless, and unpronounceable (arguably). The substituting radical matched the replaced one in number of strokes and in position on which they are conventionally arranged to compose legal characters, according to Chinese orthography. For example, Pseudocharacter 1 of Figure 2 was generated by replacing the radical *a* of Character 1 by the radical *c*. In this case, both radicals *a* and *c* are of three strokes and are upper-hand radicals of Chinese characters.

The stimuli were used to form 64 character-character, 32 #-character, 32 #-pseudocharacter, and 64 character-pseudocharacter pairs, with the first item of each pair serving as a cue and the second as a target for pair presentation. Among the 64 character-character pairs, there were 16 pairs for each of the visual-similar phonological-identical (VS-PI), visual-similar phonological-dissimilar (VS-PD), visual-dissimilar phonological-identical (VD-PI), and visual-dissimilar phonological-dissimilar (VD-PD) conditions. The #-sign served as the neutral cue in the experiment. Among the 64 character-pseudocharacter pairs, there were 32 visual-similar and 32 visual-dissimilar pairs. In addition, 20 cue-target pairs were also

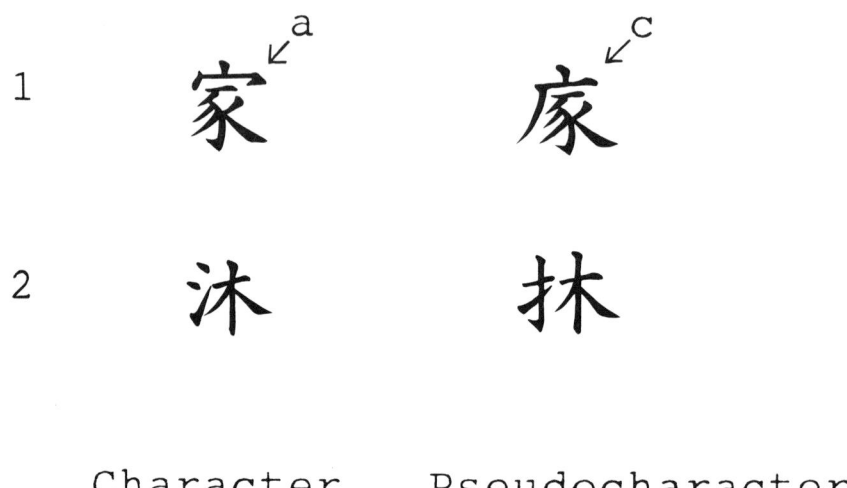

Figure 2. Examples of Chinese Characters and Pseudocharacters used in Experiments 1, 2, and 3.

prepared for practice. Each paired item was printed in black color on a slide. Examples of the four different character-character pairs are shown in Figure 1.

Apparatus. Two Kodak slide projectors (Kodak Ektagraphic AF-2) were used to present the cue and target slides, respectively. The circuit was arranged on each trial to present first a cue for a certain amount of time and then to present a target. The exposure durations of the cue and of the target and SOA were controlled by Lafayette shutters and Hunter interval timers. The cue and target appeared successively on the same position centred by a fixation point on the visual display. Two response keys were prepared and assigned for "yes" and "no" responses, respectively. A digital clock was used to measure response latencies.

Design and procedure. The experiment was carried out in a completely within-subjects design. Variables were (1) lexicality of target (character and pseudocharacter), (2) visual similarity between cue and target (similar and dissimilar), phonological similarity between cue and target (this variable is not applicable to the pseudocharacter-target condition) (identical and dissimilar), and SOA (50 and 500 msec). In total, there were eight cueing conditions. The stimuli for each cueing condition were split into two halves to be presented in two blocks. Each block thus consisted of 48 character-target and 48 pseudocharacter-target trials. The stimulus pairs in each block were randomly permuted to determine their orders of presentation, which were then fixed for all subjects. For each subject, one block was presented with 50-msec SOA and the other presented with 500-msec SOA. To insure that results could not be attributable to different stimuli used in different SOAs, the block presented with one SOA for half of the subjects was presented with the other SOA for the other half. Sequential effects associated with block presentation were completely balanced across the subjects.

The subjects were tested individually. The subject was first given the instruction for the task. For each trial, the subject was required to focus attention on the fixation point immediately upon receiving an auditory warning signal. The fixation point was exposed for two seconds and then was replaced by a cue followed by a target. The target appeared at the time the cue was terminated. This arrangement thus set the exposure duration of the cue for a trial to be equal to the SOA required by that trial. The target was always exposed for 1000 msec. Upon receiving the target, the subject was to judge as quickly as possible whether or not the target was a legal character by pressing an appropriate response key. The subject was timed from the onset of the target to the response onset. Each subject was given 10 practice trials before each block of presentation. The two blocks were separated with five minutes of rest.

Results and discussion

Results are shown in Table 2 which presents decision latencies and error percentages for all conditions. Each decision latency was the mean of correct decision latencies across all subjects in a condition. The maximum errors were 24 (subjects) x 8 (trials) = 192 for each character-cue character-target condition, and were 24 x 16 = 384 for each of the others. The error percentages were relatively low and were not different from one another by a chi-square test. Table 2 shows a tendency that the pseudocharacter targets resulted in a longer decision latency than did the character targets. This result may be attributed to a same-different (or yes-

Table 2
Mean Lexical Decision Times (in msec) and Error Percentages (in parentheses) as a Function of Cueing Condition and SOA in Experiment 1.

Cueing condition	Stimulus onset asynchrony (SOA)	
	50 msec	500 msec
Character target		
Visual-similar & phonological-identical	570.0 (3.6)	525.8 (4.2)
Visual-similar & phonological-dissimilar	613.3 (6.8)	573.3 (5.2)
Visual-dissimilar & phonological-identical	562.1 (4.2)	522.3 (5.7)
Visual-dissimilar & phonological-dissimilar	605.4 (5.7)	586.4 (7.8)
Neutral	585.4 (4.7)	547.3 (5.5)
Pseudocharacter target		
Visual-similar	694.6 (6.0)	645.7 (6.5)
Visual-dissimilar	661.3 (2.7)	619.1 (2.7)
Neutral	697.4 (5.2)	656.9 (4.8)

no) response disparity in favor of the character targets generating "yes" responses. However, as Figure 2 shows, the pseudocharacters conform to Chinese spelling rules, so that they look similar to legal characters. Thus it is also possible that, before the pseudocharacters could be rejected as legal, they may have taken a longer search in lexicon, resulting in a longer decision time, as compared with that for the character targets. This pseudocharacter effect, however, was not the main concern of the experiment. The purpose of the experiment was to examine if decision times for the target characters are influenced by the visual and phonological similarities between the cue and the target.

An analysis of variance of the latency scores for the character targets showed a significant effect of phonological similarity, $F(1,23) = 111.0$, $MSe = 1061.1$, $p < 0.001$, and of SOA, $F(1,23) = 14.3$, $MSe = 4280.7$, $p < 0.01$. The effect of visual similarity was not significant. None of the interactions resulted in a significant effect.

The effect of showing a longer decision latency at 50-msec than at 500-msec SOA may have resulted from the arrangement of a target preceded by a cue that introduces different degrees of preparedness at different SOAs. When the duration from the onset of a trial to the onset of the target for this trial is compared, the duration is shorter at 50-msec than at 500-msec SOA. This implies that the subjects may have been better prepared to respond to the targets, thereby resulting in a faster decision response, in the latter than in the former. Because the effect of SOA also appeared in the neutral-cue condition, the degree of preparedness is thought to be insensitive to the introduction and variation of the cueing situation.

The effect of phonological similarity resulted from a faster decision time for the target characters when preceded by a homophonic cue character than when preceded by a nonhomophonic cue character. This effect was independent of visual similarity and of SOA. When the four character-cueing conditions at each SOA were each compared with their appropriate neutral-cueing condition, it was found that there was no significant cost-benefit effect of visual similarity at either level of SOA. On the contrary, there was a significant cost-benefit effect of phonological similarity at each SOA. When the scores were averaged across the two levels of visual similarity at 50-msec SOA, it was found that the homophonic cueing condition resulted in a faster decision than did the neutral cueing condition (566.1 msec for the former as compared with 585.4 msec for the latter), $F(1, 23) = 5.4$, $MSe = 834.0$, $p < 0.05$, and that the nonhomophonic cueing condition resulted in a longer latency than did the neutral control

(609.4 msec for the former compared with 585.4 msec), $F(1,23) = 8.1$, $MSe = 842.1$, $p < 0.01$. A similar cost-benefit effect was also found at 500-msec SOA; the homophonic cueing condition resulted in a beneficial effect (524.1 msec for this condition compared with 547.3 msec for its neutral control), $F(1,23) = 12.1$, $MSe = 534.4$, $p < 0.005$, and the nonhomophonic cueing condition resulted in a cost effect (579.9 msec for this condition compared with 547.3 msec), $F(1,23) = 14.4$, $MSe = 886.8$, $p < 0.005$.

The present results suggest that, despite the fact that the subjects were instructed to ignore the leading cue character which was irrelevant to the task, the character was obviously recoded phonologically and acted as a prime to affect the lexical decision to a subsequent target character. This argument is supported by the present finding of a significant homophonic priming effect of cue characters on the lexical judgment of target characters. This effect was found to be independent of visual similarity, suggesting that phonological information about a cue character is generated and then is used alone to prime its subsequent target character. Further, this effect appeared at 50-msec SOA, as well as at 500-msec SOA. This finding is congruent with the findings by Neely (1977) and by others that the lexical decision to a target word benefited from a prior presentation of a semantic-related cue at both short and long SOAs. The homophonic priming effect at 50-msec SOA implies that simply seeing a character results in an automatic activation of its phonological information.

The present results also showed an inhibitory nonhomophonic-cueing effect, which not only appeared at 500-msec SOA, but also appeared at 50-msec SOA. This result is incongruent with the finding by Neely (1977) that a semantic-unrelated cue resulted in an inhibitory effect on the lexical decision only at long SOAs, but not at short SOAs. This absence of inhibitions is interpreted to be due to an automatic processing of cue words operating alone, without simultaneously involving attention, at short SOAs. If an automatic processing of a word is accompanied by attention, then it will result in an inhibition of processing a semantic-unrelated target. However, it is unlikely that the present inhibitory nonhomophonic effect at 50-msec SOA resulted from an involvement of attention at this SOA in the processing of the cue characters. This is because attention is operated slowly, unlikely to show its effects at short SOAs. Neely has shown that attentional cost was not observed at a SOA less than 250 msec, even when subjects were required to pay attention to cue words before processing targets. On the other hand, the differential sensitivity of semantic priming to SOA has been theorized in terms of semantic spreading activation in a semantic network (Posner & Snyder, 1975). The question of whether phonological entity is organized in a similar structure and is subject to an influence of this spreading activation deserves further investigations.

The experiment failed to show any visual cueing effects on the lexical decision. A potential use of visual information for priming may have been discouraged in the present experiment, either because visual information about the cue character is transient in effect in the sequential presentation of paired items, or because the subjects were instructed to ignore the leading cues which were irrelevant to the task. These possibilities are assessed in Experiment 2.

Experiment 2

In Experiment 2, two visual targets (a target in the experiment could be either a character or a pseudocharacter) were sequentially presented on each trial, separated by a prescribed SOA. Subjects were required to judge if both the targets were legal characters. The experiment was to examine how the decision times for character-character pairs are influenced by SOA and by the visual and phonological similarities between the paired characters. Because the subjects were required in the experiment to make lexical decisions about paired items on each trial, the experiment replicated the experiments by Meyer et al. (1974), except that the paired items were separated in the present experiment by a prescribed SOA that could be either short or long. It should be noted that no suitable neutral condition could be used in the experiment to assess cost and benefit effects of visual and phonological information.

Method

Subjects. Subjects were 24 undergraduates of the National Taiwan University taking an introductory psychology course. They were native Chinese speakers.

Stimulus materials. Stimulus materials consisted of 64 character-character, 24 pseudocharacter-character, 24 character-pseudocharacter, and 16 pseudocharacter-pseudocharacter pairs. They served as test pairs for the experiment. The pairs were prepared in the same way as used to prepare the stimuli for Experiment 1. Among the 64 character-character pairs, there were 16 pairs for each of the VS-PI, VS-PD, VD-PI, and VD-PD conditions. In each of the other three categories of pairs, half of the pairs were visually similar and the other half were visually dissimilar. In addition to the test pairs, 20 pairs consisting of two pairs for each of the 10 pairing conditions were prepared for practice.

Design and procedure. The apparatus, design, and procedure were the same as used in Experiment 1, except the following:

A block of presentation consisted of 72 trials, eight for each character-character, six for each character-pseudocharacter and pseudocharacter-character, and four for each pseudocharacter-pseudocharacter pairing condition.

The subjects were required to judge as quickly as possible whether two targets presented on a trial were legal characters. The subject was to press one of the two response keys if both were legal characters, and to press the other key if either one or both of the targets were illegal. The subject was timed from the onset of the second paired item to the response onset.

Results and discussion

Table 3 presents decision latencies and error percentages for all conditions. Each decision latency is the mean of all correct latencies across all subjects in a condition. The maximum errors were 192 for each character-character, 144 for each character-pseudocharacter and pseudocharacter-character, and 96 for each pseudocharacter-pseudocharacter pairing condition. The error percentage across the four character-character pairing conditions was 22.1% at 50-msec SOA, which was much higher than that at 500-msec SOA, 7.3%, $\chi^2 (1) = 16.4, p < 0.01$, and was also higher than its counterpart in Experiment 1, 5.1%, $\chi^2 (1) = 39.8, p < 0.01$. On the other hand, the error percentage at 500-msec SOA was not different from its counterpart in Experiment 1, 5.7%, by a chi-square test. These results suggest that, in the present requirement of judging two targets for a trial, a condition with 50-msec SOA is relatively taxing for processing the first paired character. The correct recognition percentage after correction for guessing (computed by subtracting error percentage from correct percentage for two-alternative or yes-no forced choice problems) was 55.8% at 50-msec SOA and was 85.4 % at 500-msec SOA. In the present analysis

Table 3
Mean Lexical Decision Times (in msec) and Error Percentages (in parentheses) as a Function of Pairing Condition and SOA in Experiment 2.

Pairing condition	Stimulus onset asynchrony (SOA)	
	50 msec	500 msec
Character-character pairs		
Visual-similar & phonological-identical	710.8 (21.4)	532.7 (7.3)
Visual-similar & phonological-dissimilar	737.3 (26.6)	554.6 (9.9)
Visual-dissimilar & phonological-identical	752.9 (16.2)	536.9 (2.6)
Visual-dissimilar & phonological-dissimilar	766.9 (24.0)	560.0 (9.4)
Character-pseudocharacter pairs		
Visual-similar	775.9 (16.7)	691.0 (18.1)
Visual-dissimilar	740.2 (6.3)	662.6 (4.2)
Pseudocharacter-character pairs		
Visual-similar	818.3 (62.5)	465.4 (11.8)
Visual-dissimilar	828.9 (63.4)	478.3 (16.0)
Pseudocharacter-pseudocharacter pairs		
Visually-similar	705.0 (13.5)	481.2 (3.1)
Visually-dissimilar	692.1 (7.3)	471.9 (5.2)

the difference between these two percentages was caused by a difficulty in processing the prime characters with short exposure duration imposed by the 50-msec SOA arrangement.

An analysis of variance of the latency scores for the four character-character pairing conditions showed a significant effect of visual similarity, $F(1, 23) = 6.459$, $MSe = 2987.9$, $p < 0.05$, of phonological similarity, $F(1, 23) = 5.898$, $MSe = 3621.3$, $p < 0.05$, and of SOA, $F(1, 23) = 88.0$, $MSe = 20996.3$, $p < 0.01$. There was also a significant interaction effect of Visual Similarity x SOA, $F(1, 23) = 5.51$, $MSe = 2171.4$, $p < 0.05$. None of the other interactions revealed a significant effect.

The effect of showing a longer latency at 50-msec SOA than at 500-msec SOA is probably not due solely to a difference in degree of preparedness between the two SOAs in favor of the condition of 500-msec SOA. When the mean decision latency across the four character-character pairing conditions was compared in Experiment 1 with Experiment 2, it was found that the mean decision latencies in Experiments 1 and 2 were 551.9 and 546.1 msec at 500-msec SOA, respectively, which were comparable to each other. However, at 50-msec SOA, the decision latency in Experiment 2 was 742 msec, which was 154.3 msec longer than in Experiment 1, 587.7 msec. These results suggest that another factor is involved in Experiment 2 to result in the effect of SOA. A possible explanation is the difficulty in reading the prime characters within an exposure duration of 50 msec, which would cause a response hesitation.

Like Experiment 1, the present experiment showed a robust phonological effect: the homophonic pairs resulted in a faster decision time than did the phonologically-dissimilar pairs. Further, this effect was independent of visual similarity and of SOA. The result relevant to the present issue is that of showing a positive homophonic effect at 50-msec SOA. Once again, this result supports the view that phonological recoding is automatically activated in reading Chinese characters. Further, the fact that the condition of 50-msec SOA resulted in a low recognition for prime characters, as observed in this experiment, and the fact that the same condition produced a robust phonological-priming effect of the prime characters, as observed in this experiment and in Experiment 1, may be combined to suggest that a taxing condition which is not optimal for recognition of characters is still suitable for generating phonological information about the characters. This would imply that phonological information about the prime characters with short exposure duration is automatically activated prior to recognition.

The significant effect of Visual Similarity x SOA was a combined result of a positive visual-priming effect occurring at 50-msec SOA, $F(1, 23) = 7.7$, $MSe = 1931.2$, $p < 0.05$, and a insignificant visual effect at the 500-msec SOA. However, the visual- and homophonic-priming effects at the short SOA were not predictable by the notion of encoding bias, because these two effects were independent of each other. Further, while the present results showed a faster decision time for the homophonic pairs than for the VD-PD pairs, the VS-PD pairs did not result in a longer decision time than did the VD-PD pairs. On the contrary, the reverse tends to be the case.

The result of showing visual and phonological priming effects at 50-msec SOA suggests that these two types of information are activated automatically, because attention is presumably not involved in this short exposure duration. The results may be taken as evidence of two routes for lexical access in this condition: one is direct from visual input, and the other is indirect through phonological mediation. This view, however, should be regarded as tentative, because given the error rate of 22.1% at the short SOA, it is estimated that about the same percentage of erroneous recognition resulting in "yes" responses, probably based on guessing, has been counted as correct to contribute in part to the mean latencies at this SOA. Thus the validity of these latency results deserves further investigations.

Experiment 3

Experiment 3 was a replication of Experiment 2, the only exception being that SOA was varied at the two levels of 150 and 750 msec, rather than at 50 and 500 msec. This modification was motivated by an attempt to reduce errors through a moderate increase of stimulus-exposure duration so that processes of lexical decision could be evaluated more properly. Cheng and Tzeng (1988) have shown that the lexical decision to a Chinese target word benefited from a prior presentation of a semantic-related prime at both 200- and 1000-msec SOAs, and the decision suffered from a semantic-unrelated prime at the long SOA only, but not at the short SOA. These results suggest that the processing of characters with an exposure duration of 150 msec will be free from attentional effects.

Method

The stimulus materials, design, and procedure used in the experiment were completely the same as those used in Experiment 2, except that SOA was varied at 150 and 750 msec.

Subjects. Subjects were 20 undergraduates of the National Taiwan University, whose native language was Mandarin Chinese.

Results and discussion

Results for the four character-character pairing conditions are presented in Table 4. The mean error percentage across the four conditions was 4% at 150-msec and was 4.7% at 750-msec SOA. These two percentages were not significantly different from each other by a chi-square test. The same test also showed that the errors committed at 150-msec SOA in the present experiment were much reduced, as compared with those at 50-msec in Experiment 2, $\chi^2 (1) = 39.38$, $p < 0.01$. An analysis of variance of the latency scores for the four conditions showed a significant effect of phonological similarity, $F(1, 19) = 8.9$, $MSe = 9647.6$, $p < 0.01$, and of SOA, $F(1, 19) = 4.4$, $MSe = 27834.8$, $p < 0.05$. The effect of visual similarity did not reach a level of significance. None of the interactions produced a significant effect.

The significant phonological effect resulted from a faster decision latency for the homophonic pairs than for the nonhomophonic pairs. This effect was independent of visual similarity and of SOA. Thus the present results were completely the same as those shown in Experiment 2, except that the visual priming effect observed at 50-msec SOA in Experiment 2 was not observed at 150-msec SOA in the present experiment. These results may lead to the conclusion that the visual effect is not genuine but specific to the taxing condition imposed by the 50-msec SOA, which also produced a significant amount of errors in Experiment 2. As the exposure duration was increased from 50 to 150 msec, errors were significantly reduced, accompanied by the extinction of the visual effect. This pattern of results is consistent with the view set forth in Experiment 2 that the decision latencies at the short SOA in Experiment 2 contributed in part to erroneous recognitions executing "yes" responses, resulting in the apparent visual effect.

Table 4

Mean Lexical Decision Latencies (in msec) and Error Percentages (in parentheses) for Character-Character Pairs as a Function of Pairing Condition and SOA in Experiment 3.

Pairing condition	Stimulus onset asynchrony (SOA)	
	150 msec	750 msec
Visual-similar & phonological-identical	708.5 (6.5)	701.4 (5.8)
Visual-similar & phonological-dissimilar	796.9 (4.4)	702.4 (4.4)
Visual-dissimilar & phonological-identical	725.2 (1.3)	656.6 (3.8)
Visual-dissimilar & phonological-dissimilar	764.7 (3.8)	712.7 (6.9)

General Discussion

The present study began with a literature review of research on phonological processes in lexical access. Special attention was paid to the experimental findings using naming or lexical-decision paradigms, on which current prevalent theories are based. A close examination on these findings found that some findings are inconclusive with respect to the issue of direct/indirect lexical access while others favor a contribution of prelexical phonological information in lexical access. And yet, lexical access tends to be produced as a task demand rather than as a process demand. Thus the issue of phonological processes in lexical access is still elusive. The result of this review also pointed out that the lexical-decision paradigm is more suitable than the naming paradigm for tapping the phonological issue of lexical access. However, phonological effects reported in previous studies using this paradigm were not necessarily prelexical and could be task-specific. For example, the Meyer et al. (1974) findings of a positive phonological priming effect and of an inhibitory visual-similarity effect are not sufficient evidence for use of prelexical phonological information in the lexical-decision task. For one thing, these effects may have been produced in response to the situation of judging two pairing words contiguously presented, rather than as a result of priming a compulsory phonological recoding for the second paired word before recognition. For another, although phonological information about the prime word, used to prime the second paired word, has been postulated to be generated prelexically based on GPC conversions, it could also be generated after recognition, then serving as a prime, to result in the priming effects.

It seems then that critical evidence for the derivation of indirect access from the lexical decision to pairing words requires that prime words are recoded phonologically and prelexically. However, to obtain such evidence directly is difficult. One way to approach this problem is to show that reading prime words results in an automatic activation of their phonological information. Phonological information activated in this way may occur prior to, during, or as a part of, recognition. The Meyer et al. (1974) lexical-decision paradigm is not suitable for assessing this automatic nature, because without a rigid control of stimulus-exposure duration in the paradigm, phonological information about prime words could be either generated automatically or generated strategically and consciously due to a long inspection.

Following this line of thinking, three experiments on Chinese lexicality judgment were conducted in the present study to assess whether a character serving as a cue or a prime would result in an automatic activation of its phonological information. Experiment 1 showed that the lexical decision to a target character was faster when preceded by a homophonic character cue than when preceded by a phonological-dissimilar cue. This effect appeared at a short SOA, as well as at a long SOA. The effect was found to be independent of the visual similarity between the cue and the target. A similar pattern of results was also obtained in Experiments 2 and 3 which showed a positive homophonic effect in a task in which, on each trial, two target characters were sequentially presented for lexical judgment, separated by a short or a long SOA. Again, this homophonic effect was found to be independent of SOA and of visual similarity between the two targets. Thus the results of the three experiments converged to a point that phonological information about the prime character is encoded automatically, which alone is then used to prime its subsequent target. Further, it was also found in the present study that prime characters shortly exposed resulted in a low recognition rate in Experiment 2, yet resulted in a robust homophonic-priming effect across the three experiments. These findings indicate that a taxing condition that is not optimal for recognition of words is still suitable for generating phonological information about the words. This leads to the conclusion that phonological information about prime characters is activated prior to recognition.

Experiment 1 failed to show a visual priming effect of the cue character. This result was not due to the instruction to ignore the cue which was irrelevant to the task, but rather resulted from a possibility that visual information is transient and is not effective in the sequential presentation of paired items. This conclusion is supported by the fact that Experiment 3 also failed to find a visual effect, even when subjects were required to pay attention to and to make decisions about the prime character. The visual effect observed at the short SOA in Experiment 2 was regarded as an apparent effect, rather than a genuine effect. It was created by or associated with high errors produced by a brief exposure duration. As the exposure duration was increased moderately, the visual effect disappeared along with a reduction of recognition errors (Experiment 3). The present finding of lacking a visual effect in lexical decision contrasts significantly with those previous findings by Hsieh (1982), by Hillinger (1980), and by Meyer et al. (1974), which showed a visual effect contingent upon phonological similarity. This contrast suggests that the latter is not general to all reading situations.

In summary, despite the facts that no GPC rule exists in logographic Chinese characters and that the radical-sound correspondences in Chinese are highly flexible, reading Chinese characters requires phonological mediation. The mechanism underlying this phonological mediation is thought to be based on character-sound correspondences which are well developed through years of extensive practice. Such phonological transformation is free from orthography and should equally apply to all writing systems.

Acknowledgements

Request for reprints should be sent to Chao-Ming Cheng, Department of Psychology, National Taiwan University, Taipei, Taiwan, Republic of China.

References

Baron, J., & Strawson, C. (1976). Use of orthographic and word-specific knowledge in reading of words aloud. *Journal of Experimental Psychology: Human Perception and Performance, 2,* 386-393.

Cheng, C.-M. (1982). Analysis of present-day Mandarin. *Journal of Chinese Linguistics, 10,* 181-258.

Cheng, C.-M., & Tzeng, C.-H. (1988). *The nature of automatic processing: Evidence from matching experiments.* Unpublished manuscript.

Collins, A. M., & Loftus, E. F. (1975). A spreading-activation theory of semantic processing. *Psychological Review, 82,* 407-428.

Coltheart, M. (1978). Lexical access in simple reading task. In Underwood, G. (Ed.), *Strategies of information processing.* London: Academic Press.

Glushko, R. J. (1979). The organization and activation of orthographic knowledge in reading aloud. *Journal of Experimental Psychology: Human Perception and Performance, 5,* 674-691.

Forster, K. I., & Chambers, S. M. (1973). Lexical access and naming time. *Journal of Verbal Learning and Verbal Behavior, 12,* 627-635.

Hanson, V. L., & Fowler, C. A. (1987). Phonological coding in word reading: Evidence from hearing and deaf readers. *Memory & Cognition, 15,* 199-207.

Hillinger, M. L. (1980). Priming effect with phonologically similar words: The encoding-bias hypothesis reconsidered. *Memory & Cognition, 8,* 115-123.

Hsieh, N.-M. (1982). *Reading of Chinese characters and words and phonological recoding.* Unpublished M.S. thesis: National Taiwan University.

Li, H.-T. (1977). *The history of Chinese characters.* Taipei, Taiwan: Lian-Jian.

Martin, R. C., & Jensen, C. R. (1988). Phonological priming in the lexical decision task: A failure to replicate. *Memory & Cognition, 16,* 505-521.

McCusker, L. X., Hillinger, M. L., & Bias, R. G. (1981). Phonological recoding and reading. *Psychological Bulletin, 89,* 217-245.

Meyer, D. E., Schvaneveldt, R. W., & Ruddy, M. G. (1974). Functions of graphemic codes in visual word recognition. *Memory & Cognition, 2,* 309-321.

Neely, J. M. (1977). Semantic priming and retrieval from lexical memory: Roles of inhibitionless spreading activation and limited capacity attention. *Journal of Experimental Psychology: General, 106,* 226-254.

Posner, M. I., & Snyder, C. R. R. (1975). Facilitation and inhibition in the processing of signals. In P. M. A. Rabbit & S. Dornic (Eds.), *Attention and performance V.* New York: Academic Press.

Rubenstein, H., Lewis, S. S., & Rubenstein, M. A. (1971). Evidence for phonemic recoding in visual word recognition. *Journal of Verbal Learning and Verbal Behavior, 10,* 645-657.

Seidenberg, M. S. (1985a). The time course of information activation utilization in visual word recognition. In D. Besner, T. G., Waller, & G. E. Mackinnon (Eds.), *Reading research: Advances in theory and practice (Vol. 5).* New York: Academic Press.

Seidenberg, M. S. (1985b). The time course of phonological code activation in two writing systems. *Cognition, 19,* 1-30.

Seidenberg, M. S., Waters, G. S., Barnes, M., & Tanenhaus, M. K. (1984). When does irregular spelling or pronunciation influence word recognition? *Journal of Verbal Learning and Verbal Behavior, 23,* 384-404.

Shulman, H. G., Hornak, R., & Sanders, E. (1978). The effects of graphemic, phonetic, and semantic relationships on access to lexical structures. *Memory & Cognition, 6,* 115-123.

Stanovich, K. E., & Bauer, D. (1978). Experiments on the spelling-to-sound regularity effects in word recognition. *Memory & Cognition, 6,* 410-415.

Underwood, G., & Bargh, K. (1982). Word shape, orthographic regularity and contextual interactions in a reading task. *Cognition, 12,* 197-209.

Waters, G. S., & Seidenberg, M. S. (1985). Spelling-sound effects in reading: Time course and decision criteria. *Memory & Cognition, 13,* 557-572.

Recognition Processes in Character Naming

Chih-Wei Hue
National Taiwan University

Three experiments were conducted to investigate the psychological processes underlying character naming. Experiment 1 was designed to investigate the locus of frequency effects in the character-naming task. The results of Experiment 1 showed that high-frequency characters were named faster than low-frequency characters, which indicated that the locus of frequency effects is in the lexical access phase of character naming. Experiments 2 and 3 investigated regularity and consistency effects and how these effects interacted with frequency. The results showed that regular-inconsistent characters and irregular characters were named much more slowly than regular-consistent characters; however, the effects were found only for low-frequency characters. Two models of visual word recognition and naming were evaluated on the basis of these results.

Despite the fact that writing systems have evolved to represent spoken languages (Hung & Tzeng, 1981), writing systems differ in the extent to which they represent phonology (Frost, Katz, & Bentin, 1987). In a shallow orthography, the correspondence between orthography and phonology is regular, whereas in a deep orthography, the correspondence is arbitrary. Frost et al. compare the orthographies of Serbo-Croatian, English, and Hebrew to exemplify this distinction. In a language such as

Serbo-Croatian, the orthography is said to be shallow in the sense that the orthographic code is isomorphic with the phonological code. Hebrew is said to have a deep orthography because the written language provides only consonants, and vowels and pronunciation must be obtained from context. English is somewhere between these two languages, with both regular words where the relationship between spelling and sound is "normal", and irregular words where it is not.

A psychological question of interest concerns how the extent of different writing systems, in the manner that they represent phonology, affects word recognition. In Frost et al.'s (1987) study, they examined naming and lexical decision latencies in the above three languages, and reported some very interesting data. First, effects of linguistic frequency on lexical decision time were rather consistent in the three languages, with high-frequency words recognized as words faster than low-frequency words, and non-words recognized even more slowly. But effects of frequency on naming latency differed across languages. In all the languages high-frequency words were named faster than low-frequency words, and low-frequency words were named faster than pronounceable non-words. Effects of frequency on naming speed were quite small in Serbo-Croatian, larger in English, and substantial in Hebrew. Second, for Serbo-Croatian, the mean naming latency was about 150 msec faster than the mean lexical decision latency. For English, the difference was in the same direction, but was smaller, about 90 msec. In Hebrew, the difference was essentially absent; subjects could decide if a stimulus was a word as fast as they could pronounce it. In fact, for high-frequency words, lexical decision latency was slightly faster than naming latency.

To explain these data, Frost et al. (1987) have argued that in shallow orthographies, phonology is generated directly from print, whereas in deep orthographies, phonology is derived from the internal lexicon. In terms of dual-route models of word recognition (Meyer, Schvaneveldt, & Ruddy, 1974), results from Frost et al.'s study imply that both visual and phonological routes are available in reading shallow orthographies, whereas only the visual route is available in reading deep orthographies. However, a number of recent studies about Chinese character naming have reported results inconsistent with this prediction (e.g., Fang, Horng, & Tzeng, 1986; Seidenberg, 1985). The results of these studies indicate that like naming English words, naming Chinese characters is an activation-synthesis process (cf. Glushko, 1979). Before discussing these studies and their results, it may be useful to review briefly a few characteristics of the written Chinese language.

Although there are more than 47,000 different characters listed in the Kang Hsi Tzu Tien (a 42-volume dictionary compiled during the reign of Kang Hsi in the Ching Dynasty), most literate Chinese know only a portion of these. Based on a huge collection of articles randomly selected from popular novels, newspapers, magazines, and textbooks, Cheng (1982) has figured out that 4,583 different characters are actually used to compose these articles. Based on this calculation, it is reasonable to estimate that a literate Chinese knows about 4,500 characters. Most characters are phonograms composed of two components: the radical (or signific) which often provides a clue to the meaning of the character, and the stem (or phonetic) which usually provides a clue to the pronunciation. According to an estimation, 82% of the characters contained in Shuowen Jiezi (121. A.D.), the oldest character dictionary, are phonograms, and this percentage is even higher today (Wang, 1981). A common strategy used by Chinese readers to pronounce a novel character is to read the stem. However, this strategy does not work all the time (Zhou, 1978). Although there is a group of "regular" characters whose pronunciations can be correctly guessed by the pronunciation strategy, there is also a group of "irregular" characters which cannot.

In a recent study, Fang et al. (1986) investigated how subjects named regular and irregular characters. According to the activation-synthesis model of word recognition proposed by Glushko (1979), presentation of a word results in the activation of lexical entries of visually similar words, and the pronunciation of the word is synthesized from the pronunciations associated with the activated entries. Two predictions of the model were tested in Fang et al.'s study. First, the relative difficulty in pronouncing a word depends on the consistency of the activated pronunciations. Using English words as examples, irregular words (e.g., HAVE) and regular-inconsistent words (e.g., WAVE) should be named more slowly than regular-consistent words (e.g., WADE). WAVE is an inconsistent word because the word body -AVE is pronounced differently in HAVE. WADE is an entirely consistent word because all its neighbors ending in -ADE rhyme. Second, lexical access does not need to be the only route to naming Chinese characters.

Fang et al. (1986) used regular and irregular characters as stimuli in a naming task. They subdivided regular characters into two types, consistent and inconsistent. The pronunciation of a regular-inconsistent character such as '油' can be correctly determined by the pronunciation strategy; however, the pronunciation of the irregular character '抽' with the same stem '由' can not be derived from the same strategy. On the other hand, the characters '距', '拒', '矩', '炬', and '苣' all with the same stem '巨' are regular-consistent characters, because their pronunciations are the same as the stem. Although Fang et al. did not find the regularity effect which was observed in experiments using English materials (e.g., Seidenberg, Waters, Barnes, & Tanenhaus, 1984), they did find that inconsistent characters were named much more slowly than consistent characters.

In the same study, Fang et al. (1986) estimated the consistency value of a group of character stems. The consistency value of a stem was defined as the percentage of the characters which contain the stem and are pronounced the same as the stem. In one experiment, they selected characters with high and low consistency stems, and in another experiment, they created pseudo-characters each containing a stem with high or low consistency value, and presented these stimuli for subjects to name. The results showed that characters and pseudo-characters with high-consistency stems were named faster than those with low-consistency stems, and subjects made more "errors" (i.e., subjects did not follow the pronunciation strategy) in naming low-consistency pseudo-characters than in naming high-consistency ones. These results are inconsistent with the orthographic depth model, because the model does not predict the consistency effect and cannot explain how pseudo-characters are pronounced.

Although Fang et al. (1986) have generated useful data to support the activation-synthesis model, their study is inconclusive and tainted by methodological inadequacies. For example, their study fails to obtain the regularity effect and does not manipulate frequency as a variable. In the studies of English word naming, word frequency has been found to have consistent effects on naming latencies (e.g., Forster & Chambers, 1973) and to interact with word regularity (e.g., Seidenberg, 1985; Seidenberg et al., 1984; Waters, Seidenberg, & Bruck, 1984). These findings are important in the development of the activation-synthesis model. In Seidenberg and McClelland's (1989) version of the model, frequency is assumed to have an effect on the processes of generating (activating and synthesizing) pronunciations. No regularity and consistency effects are expected for high-frequency words, because the pronunciation of the target word is activated or synthesized before the pronunciations of the neighboring words are activated. However, such effects are expected for low-frequency words, because the slow recognition course of these words allows the pronunciations of their neighboring words to be activated and included in the pronunciation synthesis, and thus produces regularity or consistency effects.

The results of a study conducted by Seidenberg (1985) indicate that frequency also affects character naming processes. Seidenberg examined naming latencies for regular and unique characters varying in linguistic frequencies. (Unique characters do not contain phonetics and are not phonetics in other characters. Most pictograms are of this type.) He found that regular characters were named faster than unique characters, but the effects were found only for low-frequency ones.

In the present study, three experiments were conducted to investigate the psychological processes underlying character naming. Experiment 1 investigated the locus of frequency effects in the character naming task. Experiments 2 and 3 investigated regularity and consistency effects, and how these effects interact with frequency in character naming.

Experiment 1

It is generally agreed that, one, the naming process has three phases: lexical access, pronunciation assembly, and initiation of the overt response (e.g., McRae, Jared, & Seidenberg, 1990), and two, that frequency influences primarily the processes leading to lexical access (see Henderson, 1982, for review). However, the issue is complicated by the results reported in a number of studies which investigate the locus of frequency effects in naming English words. The results of these studies show that frequency not only influences the processes leading to lexical access, but also the processes after lexical access (e.g., Balota & Chumbley, 1985; Theios & Muise, 1977); that is, it is easier to generate the articulatory codes for high-frequency words than for low-frequency words. Norris and Brown (1985) have argued that this will place the locus of the regularity effect in the production phase of word naming.

McRae et al. (1990) recently used a delay pronunciation condition, and found no low-frequency regularity effect. Furthermore, they used high- and low-frequency regular words, matched them with rhyming irregular words as stimuli, and found a word frequency by regularity interaction. Although the evidence suggests that regularity effects do not merely reflect differences in the production phase, the pronounceability of stimulus materials is an important variable to be controlled in any naming study.

Experiment 1 was to investigate the locus of frequency effect in character naming, and to examine whether special control of pronounceability is needed in character naming studies. A number of experimental paradigms have been used to investigate this issue (see McRae et al., 1990, for review). This experiment used high- and low-frequency homophones as stimuli to control pronounceability. Since homophones have the same pronunciations, an effect of frequency can not be attributed to the differences in pronounceability of the stimuli.

In this experiment, character triplets consisting of homophone pairs and control characters were used as stimuli. Each homophone pair contained a high-frequency character and a low-frequency one. The control characters were randomly selected from those with the following characteristics: first, being the most frequently used characters of their pronunciations, and second, having frequencies that match with the low-frequency homophones. The locus of frequency effect can be inferred by examining the naming latencies of the three types of characters. If the locus of the effect is in the production phase, then the naming latencies for the high- and the low-frequency homophones should be about equal, and both types of characters should be named faster than the control characters. On the other hand, if the locus is in the lexical access stage, then the naming latencies for the low-frequency homophones and the control characters should be about equal, and both types of characters should be named slower than the high-frequency homophones.

Method

Subjects. Thirty-one students from the introductory psychology classes at the National Taiwan University participated to fulfill a course requirement. All subjects were native speakers of Chinese.

Stimuli. The stimuli were characters selected from the classes described above. Examples are given in the Appendix. There were 38 characters in each class. All characters were chosen from norms prepared by the National Institute for Compilation and Translation (1967). These norms rank about 4,500 characters by frequency. High-frequency characters were chosen from the 1,000 most frequent characters in the norm, and low-frequency characters were chosen from characters occupying ranks above 3,000. The mean frequency ranks were 478 ($SD = 230$), 3525 ($SD = 380$), and 3481 ($SD = 407$) for high-, low-frequency homophones, and control characters, respectively. In addition, 20 characters were randomly chosen from the National Institute (1967) norms for practice.

Procedure. Stimuli presentation and timing of response were controlled by a Gerbrands G1176 control unit equipped with four Hunter 111c decade interval timers. Stimuli were presented singly onto a screen in the subject's room. A trial began with a fixation point (plus sign) in the middle of the screen for 300 msec. There was a 300 msec delay between the offset of the fixation and the onset of the stimulus character. The subject's task was to read the character aloud as quickly and accurately as possible. Timing was initiated with the opening of the shutter and was halted either when the subject read the character into a microphone connected to a voice key (Lafayette Model 6602A), or when a maximum allowance time (3 sec) passed. The experimenter recorded the latency and the error data.

Each subject was presented 20 practice trials and 114 experimental trials. The experimental trials were divided into two blocks. There was a two-minute break between the blocks.

Results and discussion

In this experiment, as well as the other experiments reported here, median correct response latencies for each condition were calculated for each subject and were submitted to further analyses. The mean naming latencies and error rates (in parentheses) were 536 (.00), 683 (.00) and 676 (.01) msec for high-frequency homophones, low-frequency homophones, and controls, respectively. A matched t-test indicated that the naming latencies were the same for the low-frequency homophones and the control characters. A test between the high- and low-frequency homophones showed significant differences [$t(30) = 8.54, p < .01$]; high-frequency homophones were named faster than low-frequency homophones. Because the number of errors was small, the error distribution did not permit any statistical analysis. The results of this experiment were clear and easily interpreted; the linguistic frequency of a character affects the lexical access, not the articulation of the characters in naming task.

Experiment 2

Experiment 2 was to extend Seidenberg's experiment to examine naming latencies for regular, irregular, and unique characters varying in frequencies. High-frequency characters were selected from ranks 1 to 1000

, and low-frequency characters were selected from ranks 3500 or above in the National Institute (1967) norms. All low-frequency regular and irregular characters had stems that were individually more frequent than the characters that contained them.

Method

Subjects. The subjects were 10 Chinese graduate students studying at the University of Texas at Arlington. These students have received at least 16 years of education and their Bachelor's degrees in Taiwan, where schooling is in Chinese.

Stimuli. Six sets of characters were selected by crossing frequency (high and low) and character type (regular, irregular, and unique character). Each set contained 10 characters, and examples of the characters used can be found in appendix. The average frequency ranks were 673 (SD = 395) for the high-frequency characters, and 4047 (SD = 1434) for the low-frequency characters. In addition, 20 common characters were selected for practice.

Procedure. Stimuli were created as dot patterns on a storage oscilloscope, and appeared on the screen as normal written characters. On any given trial, a fixation point appeared for 500 msec, followed by a character, which remained on the screen until a response was made. Two seconds later the next trial started. Subjects were asked to read each character aloud as rapidly as possible. A voice key was used to provide naming latencies, and the experimenter recorded the pronunciation error manually. A PDP 11/23 computer was used to control the experiment, and to collect response latencies.

Results and discussion

The results are shown in Table 1. A repeated measures analysis of variance (ANOVA) with character type (regular, irregular, and unique) and frequency (high and low) as fixed variables was performed for the data. The results indicated that there was a large frequency effect on naming latency, with high-frequency characters being named about 300 msec faster than low-frequency ones [$F(1,9) = 32.41$, $MSe = 45,833.95$], and that the effect of character type was significant [$F(2,18) = 3.70$, $MSe = 18,496.97$].

More important, the interaction between the two variables was significant [$F(2,18) = 7.73$, $MSe = 5,479.66$]. A Scheffe test indicated that effects of character type appeared only for low-frequency characters.

Table 1

Mean naming latencies (msec), Experiment 2, as a function of character type and frequency. Error rates are shown in parentheses.

Frequency	Regular	Irregular	Unique
High	684 (.01)	707 (.00)	666 (.00)
Low	901 (.05)	1095 (.27)	993 (.18)

Just like the Seidenberg (1985) study, Experiment 2 found that low-frequency regular characters were named faster than low-frequency unique characters. This result is not in agreement with the orthographic depth model which postulates that deep orthographies are recognized on a visual basis. However, the regularity effect obtained in this experiment indicates that phonological information contained in characters are used in character naming.

Low-frequency irregular characters were named much more slowly than both low-frequency regular and unique characters, which is consistent with the data from English regular and irregular words. Although this phenomenon can be explained as resulting from the activation of inconsistent neighbors, it might also be due to the competition between the pronunciations of the irregular characters and the stems contained in these characters. Since most stems are characters themselves, the pronunciations of the stems might be activated during the slow recognition processes for the low-frequency characters. The pronunciations of the stems contained in irregular characters are different from the characters themselves, which will result in the competition between the pronunciations. This interpretation is supported by the error data. In the low-frequency irregular condition, subjects often mistakenly named the stems contained in the characters rather than the characters themselves.

Experiment 3

One method to investigate the possible confounding effect in Experiment 2 is to divide regular characters into regular-consistency and regular-inconsistency characters. Since the stems in both types of characters are pronounced the same as the characters themselves, no competition is expected between the pronunciations. If inconsistent characters are named slower than consistent ones, the effect can not be attributed to the stem-character competition.

Method

Subjects. Thirty-two students from the introductory psychology classes at the National Taiwan University participated in this experiment.

Stimuli and procedure. Eight sets of characters were selected by crossing frequency (high and low) and character type (consistent, inconsistent, irregular, and unique character). Each set contained 10 characters, and examples of the characters used can be found in appendix. The average frequency rank was 551 ($SD = 305$) for the high-frequency characters, and the average frequency ranks were 4162 ($SD = 451$), 3968 ($SD = 344$), 4125 ($SD = 308$), and 3856 ($SD = 513$), for the low-frequency consistent, inconsistent, irregular, and unique characters, respectively. In addition, 20 characters were selected for practice. The procedure and equipment of this experiment were the same as Experiment 1.

Results and discussion.

The results are shown in Table 2. High-frequency characters were named faster than low-frequency ones [$F(1, 31) = 173.84$, $MSe = 78,636$]. The means were 727 and 1189 msec for the high- and low-frequency characters, respectively. The main effect of character type was significant [$F(3, 93) = 13.02$, $MSe = 30,042$], with consistent characters named faster than unique characters which in turn were named faster than irregular and inconsistent characters. In addition, the interaction between frequency and character type was significant [$F(3, 93) = 5.73$, $MSe = 23,969$], and the pattern of the interaction was as expected. A Scheffe test showed that there were no differences across character types for high-frequency characters. However, for low-frequency characters, consistent characters were named faster than the other three types of characters, unique characters were named faster than inconsistent characters, and no significant differences were found between irregular and inconsistent characters.

Table 2

Mean naming latencies (msec), Experiment 3, as a function of character type and frequency. Error rates are shown in parentheses.

Frequency	Consistent	Inconsistent	Irregular	Unique
High	682 (.00)	704 (.00)	715 (.00)	670 (.00)
Low	871 (.04)	1151 (.21)	1060 (.27)	988 (.16)

Analysis of the errors showed that subjects made more errors on low-frequency inconsistent characters than matched consistent characters, and such difference was not observed for the high-frequency characters. In the low-frequency inconsistent condition, 59% of the errors were resulted from target-and-neighbor competition. For example, the inconsistent character ' 蕪 ' (pronounced as wu) was mistakenly named as ' 撫 ' (pronounced as fuu). On the other hand, in the irregular condition, 30% of the errors resulted from target-and-neighbor competition and 37% of the errors resulted from target-and-stem competition.

The results of this experiment indicate that during the recognition process, not only the neighboring characters but also the stem of the target are activated. The pronunciations of these activated characters are used to synthesize the pronunciation of the target character. As a result, in the inconsistent and irregular conditions, subjects were more likely to make mistakes, and they took longer to name these characters.

General Discussion

The experiments of this research provides some basic information concerning the recognition processes of naming Chinese characters. In contradiction of the orthographic depth model, the results of these experiments indicate that phonological information represented in scripts are used in processing the scripts, no matter whether the scripts are shallow or deep in orthography. The similarity, rather than the difference, between the processing of Chinese (a deep orthography) and that of English (a somewhat shallower orthography) supports this conclusion; this can be shown by comparing the results of the present research and those obtained in the studies of English words naming. First, Seidenberg and his colleagues (1985; Seidenberg et al., 1984) found that low-frequency regular English words are named faster than matched irregular words. Similarly, Experiment 2 showed that low-frequency unique characters are named more slowly than matched regular characters, but more quickly than irregular ones. Secondly, Experiment 3 of the present research showed that inconsistent characters are named more slowly than consistent characters, and this effect interacts with frequency. These results are again parallel to those obtained in the studies of English word naming (e.g., Glushko, 1979; Jared et al., 1990).

The consistency and regularity effects obtained in Experiments 2 and 3 replicate Fang et al. (1986) and Seidenberg's (1985) studies. Furthermore, the interactions between these effects and character frequency confirm the activation-synthesis model. The model postulates that during character recognition, the target character activates not only its neighboring characters, but also its component characters. Since the spread of activation takes time, the pronunciations of high-frequency characters may be obtained before the neighboring characters and/or the component characters are activated. That is, high-frequency characters are rapidly recognized on a visual basis, with little interference from the pronunciations of the neighbors or from their component characters. As a result, no regularity and consistency effects were observed for these characters in this study. However, for low-frequency characters, the pronunciations of the neighbors and/or the component characters are of a greater probability to be activated before the characters are fully processed. In addition, regularity and consistency effects are expected for low-frequency characters and were obtained in this study.

Although the results of this study clearly indicate that visually similar neighbors are activated during the recognition process of the target, it is not clear the extent to which the neighbors are activated. In Glushko's original proposal, it implicitly suggests that "all" neighbors in the lexicon are activated. To support this assumption, Fang et al. (1986) manipulated character consistency value, and found that high-consistency characters were named more quickly than low-consistency characters.

However, the results of recent studies (e.g., Brown, 1987; Jared et al., 1990) indicate that in recognition of English words, only high-frequency neighbors are activated. Since the information provided by this study is not sufficient to answer this question, further investigation on the issue is needed.

Another question is how characters are recognized in context. Hue (1989) reported that multiple-character terms rather than individual characters are the processing units in reading text. It is interesting to investigate how characters are recognized in the context of a multiple-character term. Meanwhile, Seidenberg et al. (1984) have argued that the phonological information generated during word recognition process is useful in "parsing" multi-syllabic words. "The phonological code could be used to preserve information concerning the parts of words as they are processed" (Seidenberg et al., 1984, p. 397). It is equally interesting to investigate the function of the phonological information of individual characters in processing multiple-character terms.

Author Notes

Experiment 1 was presented at the 1990 meeting of the Chinese Psychological Association, Chung-li, Taiwan. I wish to thank Chia-huei Chang for her help in data collection. Correspondence concerning this article should be addressed to Chih-Wei Hue, Department of Psychology, National Taiwan University, Taipei, Taiwan 10764, Republic of China.

References

Balota, D.A., & Chumbley, J.I. (1985). The locus of word frequency effects in the pronunciation task: Lexical access and/or production? *Journal of Memory and Language, 24,* 89-106.

Brown, G.D.A. (1987). Resolving inconsistency: A computational model of word naming. *Journal of Memory and Language, 26,* 1-23.

Cheng, C.M. (1982). Analysis of present-day Mandarin. *Journal of Chinese*

Linguistics, 10, 282-357.
Fang, S.P., Horng, R.Y., & Tzeng, O.J.L (1986). Consistency effects in the Chinese character and pseudo-character naming tasks. In H.S.R. Kao & R. Hoosain (Eds.), *Linguistics, psychology, and the Chinese language* (pp. 11-21). Hong Kong: University of Hong Kong.
Forster, K.I., & Chambers, S.M. (1973). Lexical access and naming time. *Journal of Verbal Learning and Verbal Behavior, 12*, 627-635.
Frost, R., Katz, L., & Bentin, S. (1987). Strategies for visual word recognition and orthographical depth: A multilingual comparison. *Journal of Experimental Psychology: Human Perception and Performance, 13*, 104-115.
Glushko, R.J. (1979). The organization and activation of orthographic knowledge in reading aloud. *Journal of Experimental Psychology: Human Perception and Performance, 5*, 674-691.
Henderson, L. (1982). *Orthography and word recognition in reading*. London: Academic Press.
Hue, C.W. (1989). Word superiority and inferiority effect: A study of Chinese word recognition. *Chinese Journal of Psychology, 31*, 33-39.
Hung, D.L., & Tzeng, O.J.L. (1981). Orthographic variations and visual information processing. *Psychological Bulletin, 90*, 377-414.
Jared, D., McRae, K., & Seidenberg, M.S. (1990). The basis of consistency effects in word naming. *Journal of Memory and Language, 29*, 687-715.
McRae, K., Jared, D., & Seidenberg, M.S. (1990). On the roles of frequency and lexical access in word naming. *Journal of Memory and Language, 29*, 43-65.
Meyer, D., Schvaneveldt, R., & Ruddy, M. (1974). Functions of graphemic and phonemic codes in visual word recognition. *Memory and Cognition, 2*, 309-321.
National Institute for Compilation and Translation. (1967). *A Study on the high frequency words used in Chinese elementary school reading materials*. Taipei, Taiwan: Chung Hwa.
Norris, D., & Brown, G. (1985). Race models and analogy theories: A dead heat? Reply to Seidenberg. *Cognition, 20*, 155-168.
Seidenberg, M.S. (1985). The time course of phonological code activation in two writing systems. *Cognition, 19*, 1-30.
Seidenberg, M.S., & McClelland, J.L. (1989). A distributed, developmental model of word recognition and naming. *Psychological Review, 96*, 523-568.
Seidenberg, M.S., Waters, G.S., Barnes, M., & Tanenhaus, M.K. (1984). When does irregular spelling or pronunciation influence word recognition? *Journal of Verbal Learning and Verbal Behavior, 23*, 383-404.
Theios. J., & Muise, J.G. (1977). The word identification process in reading. In N.J. Castellan, Jr., D.B. Pisoni, & G.R. Potts (Eds.), *Cognitive theory* (Vol. 2). Hillsdale, NJ: Erlbaum.
Wang, W.S.-Y. (1981). Language structure and optimal orthography. In O.J.L. Tzeng, & H. Singer (Eds.), *Perception of print*. Hillsdale, NJ: Erlbaum.
Waters, G.S., Seidenberg, M.S., Bruck. M. (1984). Children's and adults' use of spelling-sound information in three reading tasks. *Memory and Cognition, 12*, 293-305.

Zhou, Y.G. (1978). To what degree are the "phonetics" of present day Chinese characters still phonetic? *Zhongguo Yuwen, 146,* 172-177.

Appendix

Examples of Characters Used in This Research

Character Type	Frequency	Character Pronunciation	Stem Pronunciation	English Translation
Experiment 1				
Homophone	High	Baw 報		Report
Homophone	Low	Baw 豹		Panther
Control	Low	Pye 瞥		Glance
Experiment 2				
Regular	High	Bau 胞	Bau 包	Countryman
Regular	Low	Meei 鎂	Meei 美	Magnesium
Irregular	High	Ann 暗	In 音	Dark
Irregular	Low	Iong 邕	I 邑	Harmony
Unique	High	Mau 毛		Hair
Unique	Low	Linn 吝		Stingy
Experiment 3[a]				
Consistent	High	Ji 機	Ji 幾	Machine
Consistent	Low	Keen 啃	Keen 肯	Bite
Inconsistent	High	Faan 返	Faan 反	Return
Inconsistent	Low	Guei 珪	Guei 圭	Jade

[a] Irregular and unique characters are similar to those used in Experiment 2, and are not illustrated in the Table.

Part II

LEXICAL STRUCTURE AND WORD PROCESSING

Psychological Reality of the Word in Chinese

Rumjahn Hoosain
University of Hong Kong

While the notion of the word is relatively clear to ordinary English speakers, it is not so to the Chinese. Word boundaries, as distinct from morpheme boundaries, are not marked in Chinese text. A lot of disagreement as to word boundaries in quite simple sentences is found amongst Chinese students. Psychological correlates of this fuzziness in the concept of the word and salience of the character in multi-character words are reviewed, including perceptual, eye-movement, and memory phenomena. The nature of the lexicon in Chinese is discussed.

The question of psychological reality of the word amounts to whether a linguistic distinction has any psychological correlates. In the modern history of psycholinguistics, perhaps the best known investigation of psychological reality is that of transformational grammar (e.g., Miller, 1962). In that case, the linguistic notions (such as passive transformation) are clear although the locus of psychological effects (whether it is the required transformation, frequency of usage, or only surface sentence length that requires more processing time) may be open to question. As we shall see, in the case of the Chinese word, not only do we have to consider possible psychological implications of the linguistic distinction, but the concept of the linguistic unit itself, to many people, is unclear in the first place.

The Word

For English, it can be said that "Everybody of course knows what a word is" (Chao, 1968a, p. 53). Most people would simply identify it in terms of space at either end of a letter string in a text. But, actually, other considerations such as whether a letter string is free or bound, whether its occurrence is restricted, its phonology, etc. are relevant (Chao, 1968a). In the case of Chinese, two different words, 字 (zi) and 詞 (ci) can have usages corresponding to the English word, depending on the context. When a teacher wants an essay of so many words, it is zi that is the unit. (We shall soon see why ci is not the unit.) Chao (1968b) called zi "the sociological word" meaning that it is the unit "the general, nonlinguistic public is conscious of, talks about, has an everyday term for, and is practically concerned with in various ways" (p. 136). Zi actually means a morpheme-syllable which is written as one Chinese character -- the written character is almost always a morpheme and monosyllabic (cf., Hoosain, 1991). Chinese is invariably written or printed with individual characters each occupying more or less a uniform space, with no additional spatial demarcation for syntactic word boundaries. Thus, even a person who cannot speak or read Chinese should find it possible to delineate characters in a text.

Ci, on the other hand, is the syntactic word and can be made up of one or more characters. As we will see, identification of such word boundaries is not a straightforward matter. To the ordinary Chinese, zi is by far the more familiar unit of language. The frequency counts for ci and zi are 36 and 359 respectively per about a million words, according to Liu, Chuang, and Wang (1975). The usage of ci to refer to the syntactic word is only a few decades old, and one of its older usages refers to diction or wording (Chao, 1968b). It also refers to a literary form popular in the *Song dynasty*, as well as words set to music (and all these usages together amounted to the frequency count of 36 noted above). In the rest of this paper, ci is the topic of discussion when I refer to "word". "Character" will be used for zi.

Before we proceed, it would be helpful to look at how the word is defined. Although there is a view that the word has to be defined separately for each language (cf., Greenberg, 1957), Bloomfield's definition (not for Chinese particularly) as "a minimum free form" is generally one of the best known. In fact, many introductory linguistics texts for Chinese define *ci* as the smallest unit capable of free or independent usage. Chao found Bloomfield's definition of the word too drastic, and, in his classic study of Chinese grammar (1968b), added other criteria such as pause and versatility. As a rule of thumb, I find the criterion that words should be able to accept insertions at their boundaries but not within them (Greenberg, 1957) applicable to Chinese as well as English, although not languages with infixes. According to this, single characters which stand alone as unbound morphemes (e.g., 人 meaning 'person') are words, just as two- or multi-character words like 超人 ('superman') or 太空人 ('astronaut'). Insertions at their boundaries 女超人 ('superwoman') or 女太空人 ('female astronaut') retain their meanings, but insertions within their boundaries (超女人 or 太空女人) mess up their original meanings. This criterion for the syntactic word will be used in this paper.

Let us look at some ways in which Chinese multimorphemic words are formed, bearing in mind that the majority of modern Chinese words are bimorphemic (according to Lin, 1971, 80% of words in Chinese speech is bisyllabic): (1) There are some morphemes which combine with other more substantive morphemes as prefixes or suffixes to form words, corresponding to what Chao(1968b) referred to as morphemes that are start-free but end-bound in the case of prefixes (e.g., 可 as in 可愛 'lovely' and 可靠 'reliable') and end-free but start-bound in the case of suffixes (e.g., 們, the plural suffix). (2) Two synonymous or antonymous morphemes can also be combined to form new words, in the former case resulting in a richer if somewhat redundant unit (such as 富貴 'wealthy-exalted'), and in the latter case resulting in a word referring to the underlying dimension of the antonym pair (such as 大小 , 'big-small' meaning 'size'). (3) Most morphemes form words in a manner which Chao called start-free or end-free, but not both (in the same word). These morphemes can be joined with other morphemes in front or following them (see Figure 1). The words thus formed can have many different structures such as adjective + noun, verb + object, verb + adjective complement, etc. (cf., Chao, 1968b).

Of course, affixation and compounding are frequently used means for word formation in English too, and it is important to bring out the difference between the languages. One aspect is that in Chinese, the bound morphemes in multimorphemic words all have visual salience in the form

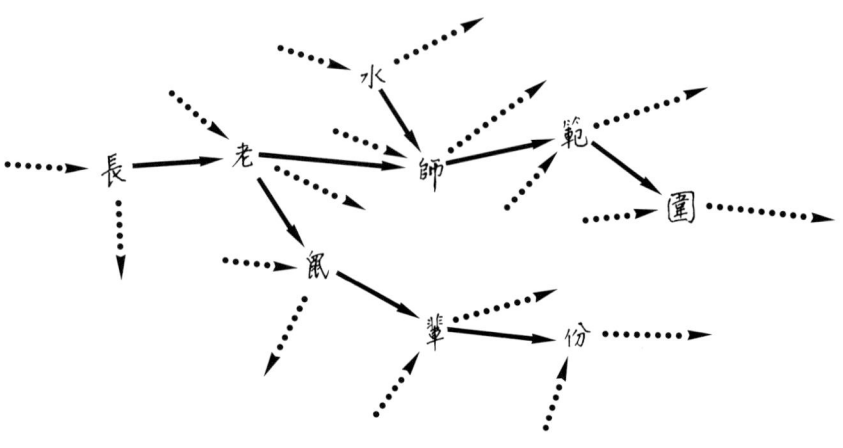

Figure 1. Network of bimorphemic words. A solid arrow indicates an actual combination of characters forming a two-character word. A dotted arrow indicates that an indeterminate number of other combinations are possible. The words thus formed are: 長老 "elder", 老師 "teacher", 水師 "navy", 師範 "teacher-training", 範圍 "area", 老鼠 "rat", 鼠輩 "thief", 輩份 "generation".

of separate characters. But even this can be found in English sometimes. English nominal compounds (cf., Lees, 1968), particularly those that combine single morphemes that are otherwise unbound, like *tear gas*, have many of the characteristics of Chinese bimorphemic words. They function like single words and insertions within their boundaries alter their meanings (*strong tear gas* is fine but *tear strong gas* changes the meaning). In this regard, they are not ordinary noun phrases like *copper block*, in which case we can have *copper and zinc block*. However, the English nominal compound is usually a noun equivalent, and the constituents do not compound productively anything like Chinese, as indicated in Figure 1. Most compound words in English do not have spacing between the constituent words (e.g., *courtyard, foodstuff, wasteland*), clearing up their word status. It is useful to bear in mind the relatively few English nominal compounds like *tear gas* when we discuss Chinese morphology and its psycholinguistic implications, since they are the closest kind of English linguistic item to Chinese bimorphemic words.

Meanings of the constituents of multimorphemic Chinese words are more manifest than often is the case with constituents of multimorphemic English words. In English, we can have groups of syllables within words that are individually meaningless or with meanings that are obscure (e.g., *helicopter* versus 直升機 , 'vertical', 'rising', 'machine'). Chinese almost always avoids having constituent characters of words that are meaningless on their own. Thus, Chinese text is a continuous parade of meaningful individual characters (morphemes). One purpose of this paper is to see how the word comes in.

Individual Differences in Segmentation

A first question we wish to ask regarding psychological reality of the word is whether ordinary Chinese speakers have any clear conception of what a word is. This can be answered by asking people directly what they think, or indirectly by asking them to segment sentences into constituent words. The following study indicates that they have somewhat varying ideas about the word.

Two sets of materials were used. The first consisted of nine of the seven-character long sentences used in the study by Liu, Yeh, Wang, and Chuang (1974). The purpose of the study was to see if demarcating word boundaries, with additional spacing placed between words over and above spacing between characters, might facilitate perception of Chinese sentences. Figure 2 shows the nine sentences printed with additional spacing marking the boundaries between the six words of each sentence. Although the criterion for deciding on word boundaries was not stated in Liu et al. (1974), it appears that the actual demarcations coincided with the criterion adopted in this paper. In the present study, the nine sentences were printed on a sheet of paper, but without any additional spacing between word boundaries. All the seven constituent characters of each sentence were evenly spaced.

Fourteen undergraduates at the University of Hong Kong were tested. They were all native Cantonese speakers, and used Chinese as the medium

1. 她 到 公園 去 找 你。(5)
2. 她 不 曉得 你 是 誰。(9)
3. 你們 坐 幾 號 車 呢？(8)
4. 他 給 你 不 少 資料。(13)
5. 你 在 家 裏 做 什麼？(10)
6. 她 有 許多 話 要 說。
7. 你 知道 你 有 錯 嗎？(6)
8. 她 要 拿 那 條 繩子。(6),(6)
9. 你 是 否 要 去 學校？(13),(6)

有 許多 科學， 從前 學者 不 把(4) 它們 當作 自然 科學(4) 看 的； 現在 因為 研究 方法(2) 的 變異， 已 進(2) 了(2) 自然 科學(4) 的 領域 了。 如 心理學 和 地理學 就 是(6) 這樣 的 科學。

Figure 2. Chinese sentences to be segmented.

of instruction in grade school. They studied Chinese language and literature as a subject in high school, although their medium of instruction for other school subjects was English. Subjects were simply asked to segment each of the nine sentences into their constituent words by drawing slashes at word boundaries. Afterwards, they were asked to write down, in an open format, what they considered to be the criteria for deciding on what was a word.

Figure 2 shows that, with the exception of sentence 6, there were substantial disagreements as to what were word boundaries in the sentences. In fact, none of the subjects agreed with the original authors in all the demarcations. Only demarcations indicated by at least five of the 14 subjects, differing from those of Liu et al. (1974), are shown in the figure. In each case, the subjects' demarcation is shown by the extent of the underline for a word, and the number of subjects doing so is indicated. Two points might be noted in connection with these results. The sentences involved are by no means difficult or complex. Also, while sentences in the study have a large proportion of single-character words, in all disagreements with the original authors, word boundaries had been extended by the subjects to include morphemes beyond the word in each case.

Figure 2 also shows a second set of materials, consisting of a few consecutive clauses taken from a grade 10 Chinese language text for Hong Kong schools. Seven high school students who had studied this text at school within the previous year were asked to segment it into constituent words. For illustration, the text is shown in Figure 2 with additional spacing between word boundaries determined according to the criterion adopted in this study. Disagreements with the experimenter's expectations indicated by at least two of the seven subjects are shown in Figure 2. As with the nine sentences above, all disagreements involved extensions of word boundaries. Also, only one of the seven subjects agreed with the experimenter in all the demarcations.

To illustrate aspects of the subjects' conceptions of the word, a few of the discrepancies indicated in Figure 2 will be reviewed. Some of these involve phrases that could be mistaken for what Chao (1968b) called compounds (two or more words bound together to form a single word). For example, 就是 ('namely is') resembles adverb-verb compounds but is actually a phrase, since the adverb is separable from the verb it modifies (see Chao, 1968b, p. 405). For example, we can have 就一定是 ('namely definitely is'). Three of the discrepancies involved the adverb 不 ('not'). One of the criteria used by Chao to decide if these 'not'-X combinations are actually compounds rather than phrases is whether X occurs free (Chao, 1968b, p. 413). Accordingly,不曉得, for example, is a phrase since 曉得 occurs free (the sentence where this phrase occurs is just as grammatical if we delete the 不).

Perhaps the most interesting discrepancies shown by the subjects, for the purpose of this discussion, are 自然科學 and 研究方法 ('natural science' and 'research method'), with each of the four-character phrases made up of two two-character words. It should be noted that subjects were asked to demarcate words (詞) and not terms (名詞). In both cases, some of the high school subjects considered the two-word phrases as single words. It is illuminating to look at the reports of what subjects themselves thought a word was. In some cases subjects resorted to knowledge of form class and used this to identify words. But most of the subjects decided according to what they thought were "independent meanings" or what amounted to "one thing", as demarcating word boundaries. In this regard, natural science and research method were each one thing to some subjects, and therefore the respective phrases were each considered a word. We might note that, in this vein, it is easy to come to see many modifier-modified constructions as "one thing" each. Actually, "that which expresses an idea" is also a common definition of a word, but, as pointed out by Chao (1968b), the difficulty then becomes how to decide what is one idea.

We have seen that similar people (classmates in school or university) have different ideas about what are actual word boundaries in the case of quite ordinary sentences. This is so even though the subjects thought they knew what was a word when they saw one. What could be the reasons for this state of affairs?

Morpheme and Word Boundaries

There are a number of factors that could lead to individual differences in distinction between morphemes and words. These factors could also result in a somewhat more fluid distinction of the two in the minds of Chinese speakers. While classical Chinese had predominantly fmonosyllabic words (that is, individual morphemes were usually free), words in modern Chinese tend to be bisyllabic, although what amount to function words are usually monosyllabic. As an example, the character 師 meaning 'teacher' is a word in classical Chinese (e.g., 吾師 means 'my teacher'), but does not have independent occurrence in modern Chinese (however, it has another meaning, referring to an army division, in which case it is a word in modern usage). It is now combined with 老 ('old') to mean 'teacher' ('my teacher' becomes 我的老師). All educated Chinese are aware of a certain amount of classical literature and usage, and classical Chinese is still used in some formal written domains. Although 師 is a bound morpheme and not a word in modern usage, its classical usage could be in the back of the mind of some people. Thus, historically, many single-character words have become (bound) morphemized and both variations are familiar to many people. We should also note that the morphemization of single character words is ongoing, since this is the main method of coining new words in Chinese (rather than creating genuinely new characters). For example, the Chinese for AIDS is 愛滋病 , 'love', 'propagated', 'disease' (and 愛滋 together are even pronounced like AIDS!).

The fluidity of the morpheme/word distinction is also reinforced by dialect differences. For example, according to Chao (1968b), while 梨 ('pear') is a free form 桃 ('peach') is bound in Mandarin. However, 桃 is free in my Cantonese dialect, as indicated in 我買桃 ('I buy peaches'). Chao also noted dialect differences in morpheme differentiation or blending. As in the case of classical Chinese, many educated Chinese speak more than one dialect, and the result would again be some degree of fluidity of morpheme/word distinctions.

Morpheme/word distinction can also vary according to context, even with identical characters and to the same person. An example given by Chao (1968b) was 第九 . In most contexts they are a two-word phrase meaning 'number nine'(we can make insertions resulting in 第八和九 ('numbers eight and nine'). But in specific contexts they constitute a single word and is an epithet for an unwanted person, according to Chao, but also meaning inferior generally in my Cantonese usage, as in 這意見 眞第九 'This idea is really inferior.') with no insertion acceptable within the boundaries of the word.

Finally, the morphology of Chinese words also means that bound morphemes have a versatility beyond those in the English language. In the latter case, each morpheme has its characteristic location in words they constitute and meanings are more or less stable. For example, *pre-* occurs at beginnings of words and means something like 'before'. However, in the case of Chinese, most characters can occur at the beginning of some multi-character words and the end of others (Chao's "start free or end free, but not both") as bound morphemes of large numbers of multimorphemic words, in a multitude of morphological and semantic relations, although some typically occur only at the beginning or end in any combination. Figure 1 illustrates how a few such characters combine in a network of bimorphemic words. The same character can occur in other parts of the extended network, as part of other words. This interspersing of characters (bound morphemes) in a diversity of multimorphemic words indicates how monosyllabic morphemes weave an intricate fabric of semantic interrelations in Chinese vocabulary. This situation is also reinforced by the possibility of names of places, institutions, etc., taking on one or the reversed order in two-character combinations. For example, 珠海 and 海珠 are the names of a town and a bridge respectively, both near Hong Kong. For some time, I was not sure if the name of my mechanic's shop was 精藝 or 藝精, just by looking at the sign-board, since Chinese characters can be printed left-to-right or right-to-left, although predominantly the former. It turned out to be the latter, which is actually in the noun-adjective order and not the usual prenominal order for adjective-noun combinations. But then there are a florist and a curtain shop withthe reversed name. If characters do not occupy habitually front or end locations when they combine to form larger units, the result is some degree of perceived fluidity of word boundaries.

We have seen how a number of factors, including diachronic change involving morphemization of single-character words, dialect and context variations, and Chinese morphology all result in fluidity of word boundaries. All these, plus possible individual differences in the notion of what is a thing or an idea, mean that the word is not the hard and fast entity that it appears to be in English. We should be curious about what implications this might have on psycholinguistic processes, including the nature of lexical representation or the lexicon.

Psychological Correlates of the Fluid Word

There are a number of cognitive phenomena suggesting that in the case of Chinese words made up of two or more characters, the constituents have a life of their own that is not found in multimorphemic English words. This liveliness is related to the fluidity of the notion of the word due to the factors reviewed above.

It has been demonstrated that in the case of English, a letter is perceived better when presented as part of a word, compared with being part of a non-word or standing alone (Reicher, 1969). This word superiority effect can be taken to mean that the word as a whole is a perceptual unit and the context it provides facilitatesperception of letters within the word (cf., Osgood & Hoosain, 1974). Cheng (1981) found a similar word superiority effect generally for two-character Chinese words. Characters were perceived better in tachistoscopic presentation when they were part of two-character words, compared with two-character non-words. This would imply that generally, two-character words have perceptual salience and are not perceived as two separate units side by side. However, there was one exception: high frequency characters with low stroke numbers and occurring in the second position of words were actually perceived slightly better (although not significantly so) when presented as a part of a non-word rather than a word.

In the case of English studies, the letter D, for example, was presented in the context of *WORD* and subjects were asked to decide whether *K* or *D* was presented, in a forced-choice situation. This amounted to precisely a combination of high familiarity, low stroke number, and end position of the presented word, and showed the word superiority effect. However, the same effect was not found in the corresponding Chinese situation. It would seem that constituent characters of two-character Chinese words can have individual salience, admittedly only when all the perceptual factors are favorable -- high familiarity and low stroke number amounting to low spatial frequency in a state-limiting situation (cf., Sergent, 1983).

In a task comparing how quickly subjects pronounced characters (Liu, 1988), we again have some indication of the salience of individual characters. Subjects were asked to pronounce characters either in isolation or occurring in two- or three-character words or nonwords. Characters in two-character words were not pronounced faster than the same characters in isolation, although both were pronounced faster than characters in nonwords. In the case of three-character words, there was no significant difference between characters occupying the first position and the same characters presented in isolation (and both were pronounced faster than characters in nonwords). Characters occupying the second and third positions of words as well as nonwords were actually pronounced slower than the same characters in isolation. Given that nonword combinations are unnatural, we should pay more attention to the comparisons between characters in isolation and characters as constituents of words. The absence of facilitation in pronunciation times for constituents of words would mean that, at least as far as pronunciation is concerned, they stand on their own.

On the other hand, Liu's Chinese-English bilingual subjects showed a facilitation effect for English words embedded in compounds (like *base-ball*) -- constituent words were pronounced faster than when presented in isolation or embedded in nonwords. While this brings out the contrast between Chinese and English, it should be noted that the subjects were not native English speakers and that the hyphen linking the words in each English compound is not natural.

Apart from the above evidence from the perception and pronunciation of individual characters and words, there are studies using sentences. As noted earlier, Liu et al. (1974) presented seven-character sentences to subjects, with word boundaries accentuated by additional spacing. They were compared with the same sentences having all constituent characters evenly spaced irrespective of word boundaries, as in the case of ordinary written or printed texts. The threshold exposure times required for seeing the sentences were compared. There was no facilitation effect found for marking word boundaries with additional spacing, and in some cases it resulted in higher perceptual thresholds for the sentences. One obvious answer for this result is that subjects were not accustomed to the novel experimental format for printed sentences. But, given the findings shown in Figure 2 that different individuals could have different ideas about word boundaries (using the same sentences designed by Liu et al.), it should not be surprising that the predetermined word boundaries could actually be disruptive in some cases.

A main finding with Chinese eye-movement studies is that saccadic lengths are shorter than the case with reading English. Printed Chinese text is actually more dense than English. Translation equivalents, as found in bilingual publications for example, usually have the English text something like 50% longer in terms of physical printed length. If saccadic lengths, in terms of physical distance, are comparable for Chinese and English texts it would mean that Chinese passages are read faster than English. However, independent studies have found that saccadic lengths are shorter for Chinese (Peng, Orchard, & Stern, 1983; Sun, Morita, & Stark, 1985; Sun & Stark, 1986). Fixation times, on other hand, tend to be about the same for the two languages. When saccadic lengths are measured in terms of number of words covered in each eye movement, instead of physical distance, the two languages become comparable. Each saccade covers about one and three quarters of a word in either language. Sun and Stark (1986) took this to mean that limitation in processing capabilities of the brain apply similarly to both languages. This comparability of saccadic length in terms of words does not have to mean that reading processes for Chinese and English are similar (cf., Hoosain, 1991). This assumption has to be questioned particularly with the finding that the notion of what is a word is fuzzy for Chinese.

For English, the facilitation of reading by gross word shapes in peripheral vision has been demonstrated (Haber, Haber, & Furlin, 1983). In Chinese, particularly with the uniformity of gross character shapes in most cases in peripheral vision, there is little peripheral visual information available. This means that, in terms of data-driven processes, eye movement in reading Chinese has to be more restrained and depend largely on focal vision. This dependency is also dictated by the generally higher spatial frequency of Chinese text, and high spatial frequency information is less useful in peripheral vision. Together with the emphasis on individual script-sound associations rather than grapheme-phoneme conversion regularities, the focus of reading could be the character rather than the syntactic word (cf., Hoosain, 1991). Thus, a combination of data-driven processes (including salience of the character, lack of word shape variation, and high spatial frequency), and conceptually driven processes (including fluidity of the concept of the word) influences factors related to the pattern of eye movements in reading Chinese.

The fluidity of words and salience of constituents of words are also reflected in memory phenomena. Short-term memory span studies (Yu, Jing, & Sima, 1984; Zhang & Simon, 1985) indicate that two-character words are not memorized as "compact chunks". On the other hand, they do not behave like individual and separate characters either, but as "loosely packed" units. In simultaneous presentation, memory spans varied from a mean of 3.15 for low frequency single-character words to 8.30 for high frequency single-character words. For two-character words, the mean varied only from 3.45 for low frequency words to 3.73 for high frequency items (Yu, et al., 1984). The means for low and high frequency four-character idioms were both 2.65. (Frequency of component characters in words and idioms was not controlled.)

In terms of chunks, each item of single-character word, two-character word, and idiom constitutes one chunk, provided of course that subjects know them equally well. The fact that memory span in terms of such chunks is not stable across the three types of items suggests the possibility that two-character words, for example, do not function as single chunks in short-term memory. Of course, item length and particularly the sound length of the respective items should also be a factor (cf., Baddeley,

Thomson, & Buchanan, 1975). But, it is particularly interesting that the span for low and high frequency two-character words did not vary much. Constituent characters of either low or high frequency two-character words can themselves occur with low or high frequency (either as components of other words or in some cases as words on their own), and there is no necessary connection between frequency of any particular two-character word and that of its component characters. If memorization of two-character words is strictly a matter of the item as a whole, we would expect memory span to be influenced by frequency of each word as a whole, which was not the case. If component characters of such words have individual salience, we would expect frequency of two-character words not to matter as much as frequency of their constituent characters. On the other hand, if constituent characters of multi-character words function as independent units, memory span should be simply a function of number of characters in the items. This was not the case either. Thus multi-character words behaved more like "loosely packed" units, and Zhang and Simon (1985) suggested that short-term memory capacity is in terms of a weighted sum of chunks and syllables.

Memory association data also indicate some individual salience of components of multi-character words. Huang (1979) independently monitored the frequency of usage of two-character words as wholes and the frequency of their component characters. Four types of items were then obtained: HHH, with each of the component characters as well as the resulting two-character word as a whole being high frequency; LHH, with each of the component characters being high frequency but the word as a whole being low frequency; LHL and LLH, with either one of the component characters being high frequency but the other being low frequency, and the word as a whole being low frequency; and LLL, with both of the component characters as well as the word as a whole being low frequency. Number of association words produced by subjects, when there was no time limit, showed that there was no significant difference between the HHH and LHH conditions (in fact, the respective mean associations were 7.80 and 7.86 respectively). When the HHH condition was compared with the average of all the other conditions (LHH, LHL, LLH, and LLL), there was a significantly greater number of associations produced for HHH items. Thus, it appears that frequency of two-character words as a whole was not the crucial factor in number of association words produced, although this would be the impression if frequency of component characters was not controlled. This contrasts with the situation for English, where word frequency and number of associations produced is correlated. Huang also showed that subjects tended to produced associates first by responding to the whole two-character word and its first constituent character, and later to the second constituent character.

Miron and Wolfe (1964) studied word associations produced by Chinese subjects compared with subjects speaking most of the major languages. They asked subjects to produce an associate word to complete a sentence frame like *The (noun) is* _____. The total number of associate words (tokens) produced by the Chinese subjects was similar to those of the others, given the constraint imposed by the presented sentence frames. However the variety (types) of associate words produced was far greater for the Chinese subjects compared with those of all the other eleven groups. There is no obvious explanation for this distinct situation with Chinese, except that constituents of multi-character words have their own individuality within the words, and subjects could be responding to the words as a whole or to their component morphemes. With the morphology of Chinese words illustrated in Figure 1, the constituents in turn become associated with a multitude of other words. The result of such an intricate web could well result in the rich fabric of associate words reported for Chinese.

A study by Tzeng, Hoosain, and Osgood (1987) provided some insight into Chinese word meanings. Affective meanings of emotion terms (such as *fear, devotion*, and *laughter*) in 23 languages, obtained from the respective subjects, were compared with denotative codings for the same terms. While denotative meanings are more specific, affective meanings are subject to each individual's feelings about the words and whatever they might arouse at the time of testing. The correlations between denotative meanings and affective meanings for the same respective concepts provide a kind of goodness-of-fit indication. Chinese subjects produced one of the lowest goodness-of-fit amongst the 23 groups. A likely explanation, in line with that for the data of Miron and Wolfe (1964), would be that a greater variety of other things come to the mind of the Chinese subjects when they thought about each item, enhanced by the salience of constituent characters of Chinese words. Given the primacy of affective response (Zajonc, 1980) we have the resulting greater variation of Chinese affective meanings relative to denotative meanings.

Mental Lexicon

Given the various indications of greater individuality of constituent characters in multi-character words and the vagueness of the notion of the word to ordinary people, what can we say about the nature of the lexicon or representation of word meanings for Chinese? Models of the lexicon proposed for English usually assume that the word is psychologically real, and discussion is centered on the subsequent question of whether each word is entered separately in lexical representation (the full listing hypothesis, cf., Butterworth, 1983). An alternative is described vividly by Aitchison (1987) as that the lexicon contained only bits of words. What is stored then are only common headings of related forms (based morphemes), together with rules of their formation. For example, *work, working, worker*, etc. would be stored under the same heading. This serves to minimize the number of listings required.

A distinction is usually made between inflection and derivation in discussion of the mental lexicon. *Working* is an example of inflection and *trans-late* an example of derivation. Proposals about lexical representation tend to suggest that inflectional suffixes are added on as needed in the course of the language act, but words obtained by derivation are listed individually in the lexicon (e.g., Aitchison, 1987). Inflection is not used in Chinese. But, we have noted that some Chinese words are formed by adding morphemes either as prefixes or suffixes. Some of these (e.g., 可靠 and 可愛 with the morphological structure of 'worth ...-ing') would be the likeliest candidates for being "added on as needed" rather than being already assembled in the lexicon.

What about other Chinese words? In his review, Butterworth (1983) concluded that a model of lexical representation that lists only base forms of words (morphemic units) is not well supported by the evidence, and was inclined towards a model that included both base forms and multimorphemic words, including compounds. Given the fluidity of the notion of words in Chinese, it would be likely that a greater proportion of multimorphemic words in Chinese (compared with English) is not necessarily listed in the lexicon but instead have meanings arrived at in the course of language use. What we have then is a lexicon comprised of a large number of individual morphemes, functioning together with what Aitchison (1987) calls the "lexical tool-kit" which allows us to create and understand multimorphemic words. This is possible only with our knowledge of the world (cf., Murphy, 1990) which allows us, for example, to realize that apple pie is made of apple but apple basket is not, or to understand what is corporate clothing the first time we come across the phrase. Imagine how morphemic knowledge and knowledge of the world permit the "lexical tool-kit" to work on multimorphemic words like 大學 ('big' and 'learning' meaning 'university'), and 天堂 ('sky' and 'hall' meaning 'heaven'). In fact, this is how the Chinese speaker needs to know only a relatively small number of characters in order to be able to use at least a few times that number of multimorphemic words. Of course, with familiarity of usage, these multimorphemic words can come to be represented as wholistic entries in the lexicon (just as *tear gas* would, in English). And there could be parallel activation of both the entry for the word as a whole and those of its component morphemes separately. The emphasis of one or the other route could depend on the context and demand of the task at hand (such as in word association). Given the many ways in which Chinese multimorphemic words come to be (cf., Chao, 1968b), the understanding and representation of their meanings must rely heavily on functioning of the "lexical tool-kit" and knowledge of the world. In the case of English, it has been suggested that a back-up information store, secondary and attached to the lexicon proper, holds information regarding bits of words as extra information (Aitchison, 1987). I would suggest that, in the case of Chinese, the store for information concerning such bits of words plays a more prominent role.

    A serious problem with the full listing hypothesis for Chinese is the fuzziness of the notion of the word itself. The full list of lexical entries for some of the subjects in the word demarcation task indicated in Figure 2 would have to include 'research method', in addition to 'research' and 'method', while only the latter two entries are needed for other subjects. We would have to say that the lexicon of the two groups of subjects are organized differently. But, on the other hand, it is not expected that any other meaningful behavioral measure would differentiate the two groups of subjects, along the line of the difference in the notion of the lexical status of 'research method'. Alternatively, we would have to say that the lexicon is built up, with a growing list of lexical entries, independent of a person's awareness of the identity of words. This amounts to a functional independence hypothesis.

    What this means, in effect, is that both groups of subjects have the same understanding and usage of what is 'research method', etc., and that they have similarly organized lexicon. It is only the separate and perhaps artificial act of demarcation of word boundaries based on a vague notion which differs, and this may not be an essential aspect of language competence in the first place. There is a view that the concept of the word may be inapplicable to some languages (Greenberg, 1957). On the other hand, many proposed grammars of language adopt words as their building blocks.

Recall that all the discrepancies shown by the subjects in their demarcation of words involved extensions of word boundaries. Given that the purpose of reading a text is to arrive at meanings of larger and larger units of language, up to and beyond the sentence, the boundary of what a subject considers to be one thing or one idea could vary according to whichever chunk of information the subject is focused on at the time, from that of a morpheme anywhere upwards. With regard to 'natural science' and 'research method' respectively (see Figure 2) the numbers of subjects who thought that one or the other was a word were not the same. This suggests that subjects were not using common morphological or other linguistic criteria to judge these two items, in which case we would expect the same classification for both items across subjects. Instead, it appears that subjects were appealing to their intuitions of what constituted one thing or idea within the respective contexts.

To conclude, my guess is that even if the Chinese lexicon individually lists all multimorphemic words in the language, the store for morphemes, "bits of words", or the "back-up store" plays a greater role than is the case of English. This accounts for the various psycholinguistic phenomena reviewed above, including the absence of the word superiority effect in some situations, the smaller saccadic span for Chinese despite the greater density of the text, loosely packed characters in word memory span, and the greater variety in word associations.

References

Aitchison, J. (1987). *Words in the mind*. Oxford: Basil Blackwell.
Baddeley, A.D., Thomson, N., & Buchanan, M. (1975). Word length and the structure of short-term memory. *Journal of Verbal Learning and Verbal Behavior*, 14, 575-589.
Butterworth, B. (1983). Lexical Representation. In B. Butterworth (Ed.), *Language production*, vol. 2. New York: Academic Press.

Chao, Y.R. (1968a). *Language and symbolic systems.* Cambridge: Cambridge University Press.
Chao, Y.R. (1968b). *A grammar of spoken Chinese.* Berkeley: University of California Press.
Cheng, C.M. (1981). Perception of Chinese characters. *Acta Psychologica Taiwanica,* 23, 137-153.
Greenberg, J.H. (1957). *Essays in linguistics.* Chicago: University of Chicago Press.
Haber, L.R., Haber, R.N., & Furlin, K.R. (1983). Word length and word shape as sources of information in reading. *Reading Research Quarterly,* 18, 165-189.
Hoosain, R. (1991). *Psycholinguistic implications for linguistic relativity: A case study of Chinese.* Hillsdale, NJ: Erlbaum.
Huang, J.T. (1979). Time-dependent separability hypothesis of Chinese words association. *Acta Psychologica Taiwanica,* 22, 41-48.
Lees, R.B. (1968). *The grammar of English nominalizations.* Bloomington: Indiana University.
Lin, Y.T. (1971). *Chinese-English dictionary of modern usage.* Hong Kong: Chinese University of Hong Kong.
Liu, I.M. (1988). Context effects on word/character naming: Alphabetic versus logographic languages. In I.M. Liu, H.C. Chen, & M.J. Chen (Eds.), *Cognitive aspects of the Chinese language* (pp. 81-92). Hong Kong: Asian Research Service.
Liu, I.M., Chuang, C.J., & Wang, S.C. (1975). *Frequency count of 40,000 Chinese words.* Taipei: Lucky Books.
Liu, I.M., Yeh, J.S., Wang, L.H., & Chang, Y.K. (1974). Effects of arranging Chinese words as units on reading efficiency. *Acta Psychologica Taiwanica,* 16, 25-32.
Miller, G.A. (1962). Some psychological studies of grammar. *American Psychologist,* 17, 748-762.
Miron, M.S., & Wolfe, S. (1964). A cross-linguistic analysis of the response distributions of restricted word associations. *Journal of Verbal Learning and Verbal Behavior,* 3, 376-384.
Murphy, G.L. (1990). Noun phrase interpretation and conceptual combination. *Journal of Memory and Language,* 29, 259-288.
Osgood, C.E., & Hoosain, R. (1974). Salience of the word as a unit in the perception of language. *Perception and Psychophysics,* 15, 168-192.
Peng, D.L., Orchard, L.N., Stern, J.A. (1983). Evaluation of eye movement variables of Chinese and American readers. *Pavlovian Journal of Biological Sciences,* 18, 94-102.
Reicher, G. (1969). Perceptual recognition as a function of meaningfulness of stimulus material. *Journal of Experimental Psychology,* 81, 275-280.
Sergent, J. (1983). Role of input in visual hemispheric asymmetries. *Psychological Bulletin,* 93, 481-512.
Sun, F.C., Morita, M., & Stark, L.W. (1985). Comparative patterns of reading eye movement in Chinese and English. *Perception and Psychophysics,* 37, 502-506.

Sun, F.C., & Stark, L.W. (1986, April). *The analysis of reading eye movements in Chinese and English -- an approach to study information processing in the central nervous system.* Paper presented at the Shanghai Symposium on Neuroscience, Shanghai.

Tzeng, O.C.S., Hoosain, R., & Osgood, C.E. (1987). Cross-cultural componential analysis on affect attribution of emotion terms. *Journal of Psycholinguistic Research*, 16, 443-465.

Yu, B., Jing, Q., & Sima, H.A. (1984). STM capacity for Chinese words and phrases under simultaneous presentation. In H.W. Stevenson & Q. Jing (Eds.), *Issues in cognition* (pp. 317-329). Washington, DC: National Academy of Sciences and American Psychological Association.

Zajonc, R.B. (1980). Feeling and thinking: Preferences need no inferences. *American Psychologist*, 35, 151-175.

Zhang, G., & Simon, H.A. (1985). STM capacity for Chinese words and idioms: Chunking and acoustical loop hypotheses. *Memory and Cognition*, 13, 193-201.

Decomposed Storage in the Chinese Lexicon

Biyin Zhang and Danling Peng
Beijing Normal University

This study investigated the hypothesis that representations of Chinese words are stored in morphologically decomposed form. Three lexical decision experiments are reported in which the character frequency, word frequency and morphological structure of word stimuli were varied. Results show that when word frequency is controlled, the frequency of the two characters of coordinative words determines the latencies of the stimuli, but for modifier words, only the second character's frequency affects the response to stimulus words. When character frequency is controlled, word frequency determines the latencies of two-character words. It is proposed that Chinese words are accessed via the character, and that the morphological structure has a role in the representation of characters in the lexicon.

Recently, various works have focused on the issues of mental representation of morphology (e.g. Henderson 1989; Hankamer 1989). Of the many issues concerning the representation of morphology which have been addressed by psychologists, there are three of particular interest here.

The first is whether or not words are represented in the lexicon in morphologically decomposed form. The Word Access (WA) model assumes that word representations are the only units of access in the lexicon (Rubin, Becker & Freeman, 1979; Manelis & Tharp, 1977). But the Morpheme Access (MA) model assumes that only morphemes (roots, or stems, and affixes) are stored in the orthographic input lexicon (Taft & Forster, 1975; Taft 1979; Taft 1981; Taft 1985; Taft 1987). The Augmented Addressed Morphology (AAM) model assumes that access to lexical representation may take place through a whole-word access procedure for known words, or through a morpheme address procedure for novel words (Caramazza, Miceli, Silveri & Laudanna, 1985; Caramazza, Laudanna & Romani, 1988).

The second issue is whether or not there is an affix "stripped off" procedure for word recognition. Both the WA and the AAM model predict there is no affix "stripped off" procedure before lexical access. The MA model predicts that for visually-presented prefixed words the recognition of the word involves the stripping off of the prefix and the subsequent location of the lexical entry in terms of the stem (Taft & Forster, 1975).

The third issue concerns the effects of morphological structure in lexical decisions for word versus non-word stimuli. The MA model predicts morphological structure effects in lexical decision tasks for both words and non-words. The WA Model predicts no effects of morphological structure for either type of stimulus, whereas the AAM model predicts effects of morphological structure only for non-words.

Since Chinese uses a logographic system, there are some recognition differences between Chinese and alphabetic words. But the recognition of Chinese words also has some similarities with alphabetic words. When we study the orthographic input lexicon of Chinese, we have to face all three issues.

The Chinese writing system is a logographic orthography in which most characters correspond to morphemes: units that have some meaning. For example, the Chinese logograph for tricycle is made from three characters meaning "three-wheel vehicle". From the point of view of cognitive economy, the character is the most convenient unit for storage. Beijing Language College (1986) have counted 1,310,000 words in various Chinese books. But only 4,574 characters were found in these materials. This means that if one can recognize 4,574 characters, one can be considered a mature reader. Just, Carpenter, and Wu (1983) have found that the correlation between gaze duration on a Chinese word and the logarithm of the word's frequency was 0.71, and that the correlation between gaze duration and the logarithm of the sum of the frequencies of the characters of the word was 0.50. These results suggest that at least some characters are treated as units of access in the lexicon.

The affix "stripped off" procedure cannot be applied to all other alphabetic systems. For example, Hankamer (1989) has pointed out that the morphological parsing for agglutinative languages involves a root-first strategy rather than an affix "stripped off" procedure. For Chinese the affix "stripped off" procedure will be more difficult to apply than in an agglutinative language.

In Chinese there are only four prefixes: 初阿第老 These four prefixes can make 133 prefixed words. Chinese has several suffixes: 子兒頭巴者然 . They can make up 998 suffixed words. According to Beijing Language College (1986), the 1,131 affixed words constitute only 3.63% of all Chinese words. Thus, that the affix "stripped off" procedure may not be applicable to Chinese word recognition.

In Chinese word recognition, one also needs information about morphological structure. The Chinese morphological structure is different from the morphological structure of Italian. In the Caramazza et al.'s (1988) study, the morphological structure suggests a possible organizing principle for verb stems and verbal infections. But in Chinese the morphological structure for a two-character word involves the relationship between the two characters. In Chinese there are two kinds of relationships for two stems (characters). First, the two stems may be equally important: for example, coordinative words. Second, the two stems may not be equally important: for example, modifier words. In modifier words the second character (morpheme) is more important than the first. The first one is the modifier of the second character.

Just et al. (1983) found that both characters and words demonstrate frequency effects. In order to explain this phenomenon we propose that if lexical representations are morphologically decomposed, then we can expect to find an effect of character frequency in lexical decision tasks. Meanwhile, the lexicon's order is ranged in the word order, so we should also expect to find word frequency effects in our experiments.

Experiment 1

The purpose of Experiment 1 was to examine whether or not coordinative words are morphologically decomposed. The logic of this experiment was the same as that used by Taft (1979), Bradley (1979) and Cole et al. (1989). Items were selected in pairs. All of the items had the same word frequency (surface frequency). However, the character frequency (cumulative root frequency) of the two matched words differed markedly. If character frequency has a significant effect on decision speed and accuracy, this result would be taken as evidence for morphological decomposition. An absence of significant differences in response speed and accuracy would suggest that there is no morphological decomposition in coordinative words and that morphological structure does not influence the word recognition process.

In this experiment an attempt was made to make the character frequency differences as large as possible both for the first and, later, the second character. Thus we have two parts of the experiment. In the first part we controlled the second character frequency and made the first character frequency differences as large as possible, and vice versa in the second part of the experiment.

Method

Subjects. Forty subjects from Beijing Normal University took part in the experiment.

Stimuli and design. The stimuli were coordinative words that conformed to a factorial manipulation of character frequency (high or low). The word frequency for all items was 2. The pairs were matched to the number of words that came from the same root. Matching this variable was necessary in order to equate the two conditions for the number of possible interfering entries in each case. The number of strokes in the matched words was also controlled. Frequencies were estimated using the Beijing Language College's frequency dictionary (1986). The frequency counts reported here are per million.

In the first part of the experiment, there were 20 items in two groups of 10. The second character frequency was 128 for one group and 125 for the other. The first character frequency for one group was high, with a mean frequency of 125, and for the other group was low, with a mean frequency of 57. In the high frequency group, the number of mean interfering entries for the first character was 18.5, and for the second character was 17.4. In the low frequency group, the number for the first character was 17.3, and for the second character was 17.3. The mean number of strokes were 18.6 and 16.3, respectively, for the two groups.

In the second part of the experiment the first character frequency was closely matched for the two groups with a mean frequency of 187 and 188. The mean frequency of the second character for one group was high, 359, and for the other was low, 71. In the high frequency group the mean number of interfering entries for the first character was 24, and for the second character was 25.4. In the low frequency group the mean number of interfering entries for the first character was 22.8, and for the second character was 20.1. The two groups had mean numbers of strokes of 16.9 and 20.7 respectively.

In addition to these experimental words, there were 20 filler words and 40 non-words. The 20 fillers included 10 coordinative words and 10 modifier words. The 40 non-words were constructed by replacing one character at random in coordinative and modifier words.

Each subject saw 80 stimuli composed of 20 test words, 20 filler words, and 40 non-words. These 80 stimuli were presented in a random order.

Procedure and apparatus. Subjects were run individually in a 15-minute session. They were told to decide, as quickly and as accurately as possible, whether or not the two characters were or were not a word. The subject's task was to press the "yes" button if the presented was a word, and the "no" button if it was not a word. All subjects were right-handed. A fixation point was presented for 1000 ms. After a 1000 ms blank internal, the item was presented on the screen for 250 ms. Twenty practice trials were run before the first and second parts of the experiment.

Stimuli were presented on an IBM-PC computer screen. The screen was situated about 70 cm in front of the subject. Stimulus presentation time and response collection were controlled by the computer.

Table 1

Mean Reaction Times and Percentages of Errors in Experiment 1, Part I.

First Character Frequency	RT(ms)	Error(%)
High	518.3	9
Low	563.8	24

Results and discussion

Table 1 presents the means from the first part of the experiment for the two experimental conditions. A comparison of the two conditions reveals a significant difference of mean lexical decision time in both the subject, $F(1,19) = 6.848$, $p < 0.025$, and the item analyses $F(1,18) = 7.80$, $p < 0.025$. The items where the first character frequency was high were more quickly recognized than the items where the first character frequency was low. A significant difference of error rate was also obtained in subject analyses, $F(1.19) = 17.44$, $p < 0.005$, and in item analyses $F(1,18) = 10.22$, $p < 0.005$. There was a positive relationship, therefore, between error rate and reaction time.

Table 2

Mean Reaction Times and Percentages of Errors in Experiment 1, Part II.

Second Character Frequency	RT(ms)	Error(%)
High	495.8	15.5
Low	535.1	10

Table 2 presents the item means from the second part of the experiment. In this experimental condition, the second character's frequency was either high or low. A comparison of these two conditions revealed a significant difference of mean lexical decision time in both the subject, $F(1.19) = 18.5$, $p < 0.005$, and the item analyses, $F(1,18) = 6.57$, $p < 0.025$. Although there was a negative correlation between lexical decision time and error rate, there was no evidence to suggest that this was a result of a speed-accuracy trade off, since the error difference was by no means significant in both the subject, $F(1,19) = 3.32$, $p > 0.05$, and the item analyses, $F(1,18) = 2.26$, $p > 0.05$.

The result we obtained for coordinative words gave strong support to the hypothesis that such words are morphologically decomposed and are accessed by their stems. According to Taft (1979), the difference between high-frequency characters and low-frequency characters will occur at the stage when the lexical entry for the stem is located. Since high-frequency characters can be located more quickly than low ones, the high-frequency group will be recognized more quickly than the low-frequency group.

The results of Experiment 1 can also explain how the lexical decision performance for words is affected by the morphological structure of the stimuli. Our results are consistent with the AAM model (Caramazza et al., 1988); the lexicon includes morphological structure in the representation of lexical items and in the procedures for lexical access. Taft and Forster (1976) have demonstrated that for the compound non-words, the first constituent is particularly important for accessing a compound word in the lexicon and the second morpheme has at least some importance. In our experiment the first and second character are similar in importance, probably because in coordinative words the two items are of equal importance. This will not be the case for modifier words.

Experiment 2

In Experiment 2 the stimulus items were modifier words, where the second character was the main morpheme and the first character was a modifier morpheme. We predicted that the second character would be a unit of access in the lexicon, but the first character might not be.

Method

Subjects. Forty subjects from Beijing Normal University took part in the experiment.

Stimuli and design. The design was the same as in Experiment 1. The word frequency for all items was 2. In the first part of the experiment there were 20 items in two groups of 10. The second character frequency was closely matched in both groups with a mean frequency of 272. The first character frequency in one group (10 items) was high, 669.8, and in one group (10 items) was low, 152.6. In the high frequency group, the mean number of the mean interfering entries for the first character was 34.6, and for the second character was 32. In the low frequency group the mean number for the first character was 33.2, and for the second character was 33.3. The two groups' mean strokes were 16.4 and 17.2 respectively.

In the second part of the experiment there were also 20 items. The first character frequency was closely matched, one group (10 items) having a value of 140, and the other group (10 items) having a value of 139. The second character frequency for the high group was 377, and for the low group was 84.9. In the high group the mean number of interfering entries for the first character was 24.9, and for the second character was 25.8. In the low group, the mean number of interfering entries for the first character was 24, and for the second character was 23.6. The two groups had mean numbers of strokes of 18 and 19.6 respectively.

The filler words, non-words, and design were the same as in Experiment 1.

Procedure and apparatus. The same as in Experiment 1.

Table 3
Mean Reaction Times and Percentages of Errors in Experiment 2, Part I.

First Character Frequency	RT(ms)	Error(%)
High	526.9	15.5
Low	552.5	15

Results and discussion

Table 3 presents the mean reaction times, i.e., lexical decision time and error rates for the first part of Experiment 2. It can be seen from the table that neither the decision time nor the error rate differences were significant in both the subject [RT: $F(1,19)=3.483$, $p>0.05$; error rate: $F(1,19)=2.044$, $p>0.05$] and the item analyses [RT: $F(1,18)=0.212$, $p>0.05$; error rate: $F(1,18)=0.01$, $p>0.05$].

The mean reaction times and error rates for each condition in the second part of Experiment 2 are presented in Table 4. A comparison of the high frequency and low frequency groups revealed no significant difference for the reaction times in both the subject ($F<1$) and the item analyses ($F<1$). But there appeared to be a speed-accuracy trade off, since the error difference was highly significant in both the subject, $F(1.19)=55.6$, $p<0.0005$, and the item analyses, $F(1,18)=6.76$, $p<0.025$.

Table 4
Mean Reaction Times and Percentages of Errors in Experiment 2, Part II.

Second Character Frequency	RT(ms)	Error(%)
High	554.1	3
Low	587.9	2

These results appear to support the decomposition hypothesis only for the second characters in the modifier word. In the coordinative word the two stems are equally important, but in the modifier word the second character is the main morpheme, and the first character is only a modifier. It does not provide clues to word meaning. The morphological structure may inhibit the activation of the first character. Under this condition morphological decomposition does not appear to function.

Experiment 3

This experiment followed the same logic as that of Experiments 1 and 2. But this time character frequency was held constant while word frequency was varied. The purpose of this experiment was to determine the separate role of character and word in the organization of the lexicon.

Method

Subjects. Twenty subjects from Beijing Normal University took part in the experiment.

Stimuli and design. The stimuli were twenty two-character words, including both coordinatives and modifiers, in two groups of 10. In one group the mean word frequency was high, 38. In the other group the mean word frequency was low, 4.5. In the high frequency word group, the mean first character frequency was 188, the second was 199. In the low frequency word group, the mean first character frequency was 194, the second was 173. In the high frequency word group, the mean number of interfering entries for the first character was 28.3, and for the second character was 27.5. In the low frequency word group, the mean number of interfering entries for the first character was 28.2, and for the second character was 30.1. The mean number of strokes for the two groups were 19.4 and 18.5.

The design, filler words and non-words were the same as in Experiments 1 and 2.

Procedure and apparatus. These were the same as in Experiments 1 and 2.

Table 5
Mean Reaction Times and Percentages of Errors in Experiment 3.

Word Frequency	RT(ms)	Error(%)
High	764	12
Low	833.5	19

Results and discussion

Table 5 presents the item means for the high and low word frequency conditions. It can be seen from the table that high frequency words were recognized faster than low frequency words. The reaction time differences were significant, $F(1,19) = 8.571$, $p < 0.01$. The error rates did not discriminate, $F(1,19) = 4.0$, $p > 0.05$.

The results of Experiments 1, 2 and 3 are similar to those of Taft (1979). Taft found that both base frequency and surface frequency have effects. How can one resolve this paradox? Taft suggests that the lexical accessing system is conceptually divisible into two distinct stages. First, there is the "master file" or lexicon proper. This is where all information about every word is stored. In addition, there is a set of peripheral access files: orthographic, phonological, and semantic. The orthographic file is used for visually presented language. Both Taft's study and our experiment only involved visual word recognition. We thus only consider the role of the orthographic file in our discussion. Taft (1979, 1985) has proposed that the representations stored in the orthographic file are the stems, or BOSSs of words. Taft (1987) defines the BOSS as the first part of the stem morpheme of a word, up to and including all consonants following the first vowel, but without creating an illegal consonant cluster in its final positions. Each of these entries (either entire stem or BOSS) in the peripheral file provides an address to an entry or entries in the master file. Taft's proposal is consistent with Forster's (1979) model of word recognition. Forster postulated that in the lexicon there are two independent access files that permit rapid access to the lexicon from either a visual or an acoustic stimulus. The search and matching process takes place in the access files, not the lexicon.

In order to explain the effect of base frequency and surface frequency, Taft (1979) suggested that words are stored in their base forms in the peripheral file but in their surface forms in the master file. Taft assumes that frequency plays a role in two places: the peripheral and the master file.

Taft's hypothesis cannot be applied to the organization of Chinese lexicon. Chinese is a logographic written language where each character represents a syllable. In our experiments one character also is a stem morpheme. We cannot separate a character and differentiate its vowel and consonant cluster in Chinese orthography. If we have to define the BOSS in Chinese, our proposal is that the BOSS is a character or a stem.

In fact, most Chinese dictionaries have two files. The peripheral file contains the character's orthographic and phonological information. Based on this information one can then find the character or word in the master file which contains all the information concerning the character and word. With this organization of the dictionary one character will be represented many times in the lexicon. For example, the character " 不 " (No) can be used to construct 500 words. It will then appear 500 times in the master file.

Cole et al. (1989) made another assumption about the mental lexicon. They suggested that affixed words (prefixed and suffixed) are stored in the lexicon in a whole word form, while their morphological structure is reflected by the organization of the family. The members of the family are related by the affix frame which encodes the morphological, syntactic, and phonological properties of the affixes, while the root constitutes the "head" of the morphological family (Cutler et al., 1985). In order to explain the cumulative root frequency effects and the surface effects, they suggested that both the members of the root and morphological families are examined in a frequency-ordered search.

Cole et al. found that while the processing times of suffixed words varied significantly according to their cumulative root frequency, this was not the case for prefixed words. For prefixed words, access to the root did not precede whole word access. Thus, the recognition process for these words should operate on the basis of the whole word form.

In Experiment 2, we demonstrated that for modifier words the second character is the main morpheme. It can work as the head of the morphological family, although the modifier frequency did not influence word decision time. The recognition of the modifier word should not operate on the basis of the whole word form, because the main morpheme frequency can influence reaction time.

In order to explain our finding, we suggest a new model, one in which the characters are stored in the lexicon as a network, rather than as two separate files or in a whole word form.

General Discussion

Both our and Caramazza et al.'s (1988) studies demonstrated that words are morphologically decomposed in the lexicon. But Caramazza's stimuli were all non-words, whereas in our experiment the stimuli evaluated in the three experiments were words. Henderson (1986) has noted that non-word stimuli may be used to draw inferences about the processing of unfamiliar words, but that it will be inappropriate to draw inferences about familiar words from such results. In our study, we did not use data from non-words. The conclusions to be drawn from our study thus more precisely reflect the organization of the orthographic lexicon.

In Experiments 1 and 2, we found the morphologically decomposed form for both coordinative and modifier words. These findings allow us to assume that lexical representations are stored in the orthographic input lexicon in a morphologically decomposed form. Our results are incompatible with the whole-word access models as well as the affix-stripping model. To some extent they are compatible with the augmented addressed morphology model. But we do not agree with the AAM model's assumption that morphological representations for known (previously experienced) words are not accessed through an active, pre-lexical decomposition process (or parsing) of the orthographic input string. Experiments 1 and 2 indicate that even frequently experienced words have to be accessed through the words' stems.

There is, however, an exception. In Experiment 2, there were no significant differences on either decision time or the error rate for the first character variable. This means that for modifiers, activation of the node representing the first morpheme does not feed activation to the whole word node. Why do we conclude, then, that in our experiments all words are stored in the morphologically decomposed form?

We suspect that the modifier word is stored in the morphological form. However, since it is a modifier word, the morphological structure gives the modifier the inhibitory information. Modifier compounds are accessed only through their second stem. Otherwise we can not explain why for the same character, for example " 母 " (mother) in Experiment 2, (first part) the character frequency did not affect the reaction time, but in the second part the same character worked as the main morpheme in the modifier word. Here it was clearly demonstrated that this character frequency did affect the error rate.

In the AAM model (Caramazza et al., 1985; Laudanna & Burani, 1985; Caramazza et al., 1988) morphological structure has important roles in the representation of lexical items and in the procedures for lexical access.

In the AAM model, Caramazza assumes that the morphological structure contains lexical/linguistic information, which is represented at the level of the orthographic input lexicon. It is at this level that information about the combinability of characters or letters is specified. The information needed to determine the legal combinability of morphemes is quite complex and abstract. It thus appears that quite distinct sorts of information - "prelinguistic" and linguistic - are needed for the efficient and accurate determination for the lexicality of a string of letters. The results that Caramazza et al. obtained for morphologically legal and illegal non-words are consistent with their hypothesis: morphologically illegal non-words may be rejected at the "prelinguistic" level of processing, whereas morphologically legal non-words engage linguistic-level processing mechanisms and are rejected on the basis of information activated by these mechanisms.

In the AAM model the morphological structure mainly refers to the organizing principle for verb stems and verbal inflections: the stem of regular verbs and the "major" stem of (predictably) irregular verbs are only linked to the relevant set of irregular suffixes. In addition to these positive links between stem and suffix sets, inhibitory links are assumed to exist between the "major" stems of irregular verbs and the specific suffixes for verbal forms that are irregular for a particular verb. Thus in the AAM model the orthographic input lexicon consists of facilitatory and inhibitory activations, whose sum determines whether or not a particular stem/suffix pair will be accepted as a word.

In Chinese, this kind of relationship between stem and suffix (as in the verbs in Italian) does not exist. As we have described in this article, in Chinese there are very few affixed words. Most words are two-character words. Of these kinds of words there are five types: coordinative, modifier, supplement, subject and predicate, and verb and object words. This kind of relationship is also found for three and four-character words, as well as phrase words. We have divided two-character words into two types. One type involves two stems of equal importance. For the second type the two stems are not equally important: one character is the main morpheme, the other is the modifier or supplementary morphemes.

The morphological structure information for Chinese word recognition also involves two levels: prelinguistic and linguistic. Non-words may be rejected at the prelinguistic level. If the character is legal, the linguistic level information has to be engaged to determine whether it is a word or not.

Since there are two types of two-character words, one can infer both positive and inhibitory links between the two characters. The positive links will facilitate the activation of characters, whereas the inhibitory links will inhibit the activation of characters.

For example, in the coordinative word when the character classes are the same, the two characters can be noun morphemes, adjective morphemes, adverb morphemes and so on. The same class link is the positive link and will activate the two characters.

In the modifier word the situation is different. The word class and the main morpheme class have to be consistent. If there is some inconsistency, the relationship will be checked by the morphological structure and will inhibit the illegal one.

In modifier and supplement words, the two characters are not of equal importance. In the modifier word the second character is the main morpheme and vice versa for the supplement word. If the first character of the modifier word is the main morpheme, the word will be a supplementary word. If the first character is of equal importance as the second character, it will be a coordinative word. In this case it will have to be inhibited. Thus the same character in different positions (first or second) in the modifier words will have different effects on speed of recognition.

For example, in the first part of Experiment 2 " 母 " (mother) was a modifier of frequency 422, and the matched character was " 灰 " (gary) of frequency 157. We obtained no significant difference for the modifier character in the two groups. In the second part of the experiment " 母 " was the main morpheme, and the matched character was " 珠 " (pearl), and the frequency was 115. In this situation we obtained a significant difference for the main characters. How can we explain this effect? We think it is due to the morphological structure. The sum of the facilitatory and inhibitory activations determine the situations in which a character can express its role and why in other places it cannot. From this point of view, although we did not obtain a significant difference in Experiment 2 (first part), our conclusion is that coordinative and modifier word representations in the orthographic lexicon are stored in morphologically decomposed form.

Since two-character words are stored in morphologically decomposed form, we do not agree with Taft's (1979) model that there is a peripheral file and a master file in the lexicon. We also do not agree with the Cole et al.'s (1989) model which holds that affixed words are stored in the lexicon as whole word form. Our model suggests that all two-character words are stored in decomposed form, the morphological structure determining their relationship. The morphological structure information includes the word type, the grammatical class of the characters, the distance and the strength between the two characters in the lexicon, etc. Meanwhile, both the word and the character's frequency also have effects for the storage of Chinese words.

Zhang et al. (1990) have found that in the lexicon, some characters have stronger associations than others. For example, the characters which share the same radical have stronger associations in the lexicon than the characters which share the same phoneme. According to this study, we can assume that in the two-character word, there are different associations between the characters, and some of them are stronger than others.

In Experiments 1 and 2 we found that, in the coordinative word, the two characters are accessed during word recognition. In the modifier word only the main character is accessed. In the orthographic lexicon these three stems can constitute the "head" of the character's network. In the coordinative word the head can associate with the equally important stems, and the stems must belong to the same class. If this is not the case, the morphological structure information will inhibit the association. In the positive association there are different strengths between the two characters.

Their different strength reflects the word frequency for the coordinative word. The word frequency effect routinely employs published word counts to define word frequency operationally. The higher frequency two-character word will establish stronger associations than the low one. In the coordinative word, the two characters are equally important: either the first character or the second character can work as the head. In the modifier words the relationship is different. The two characters are not of equal importance; the second character is the main morpheme. The morphological structure information will facilitate the second character activation and inhibit the first character activation. Thus, only the second character can work as the head in the lexicon, and only the first character can be associated with the second character. The associate has different strength just as in the coordinative words.

In the process of word recognition we first have to locate the head character. If the frequency of this character is high, it will be more quickly located. This is where the character frequency had its effects in our experiment.

The strength between the two characters reflects the different frequency of the word. Once the head is located, then the strength of the two characters' association will be checked. The stronger association will be checked early, or the stronger association will be activated to reach its threshold earlier. Thus, the word frequency also has its effect in our experiment.

The character and word frequency interactively influence word recognition. In Experiments 1 and 2 the word frequency was the same, but the character frequency influenced reaction time. In Experiment 3 the character frequency was the same, and word frequency was found to influence reaction time. These results suggest that in the orthographic lexicon there are both facilitatory and inhibitory effects operating for both character and word frequency. The character frequency can inhibit the word frequency effects as in Experiments 1 and 2. The word frequency can inhibit the character frequency as in Experiment 3. These effects emanate from the orthographic lexicon: the character network.

References

Beijing Language College (1986). *Modern Chinese frequency dictionary.* Beijing Language College Press.

Bradley, D. (1979). Lexical representation of derivational relation. In M. Aronoff & M.L.Kan (Eds), *Juncture.* Cambridge, MA: MIT Press.

Caramazza, A., Miceli, G., Silveri, M.C., & Laudanna, A. (1985). Reading mechanisms and the organization of the lexicon: Evidence from acquired dyslexia. *Cognitive Neuropsychology, 2*, 81-114.

Caramazza, A., Laudanna,A., & Romani, (1988). Lexical access and inflectional morphology. *Cognition, 28*, 297-332.

Cole, P., Beauvillain, C., and Segui, J. (1989). In the representation and processing of prefixed and suffixed derived words: a differential frequency effect. *Journal of Memory and Language, 28*, 1-13.

Cutler, A., Hawkins, J.A., & Gilligan, G. (1985). The suffixing preferences: A processing explanation. *Linguistics, 23*, 723-758.

Forster, K.I. (1979). Levels of processing and the structure of the language processor. In W.E. Coope & E.C.T. Walks (Eds.), *Sentence Processing: Psycholinguistic studies presented to Mirril Carrott.* Cambridge, MA: MIT Press.

Hankamer, J. (1989). Morphological parsing and the lexicon. In W. Marslen-Wilson (Ed.), *Lexical representation and process.* Cambridge, MA: MIT Press.

Henderson, L. (1986). From morph to morpheme: The psychologist gaily trips where the linguist has trodden. In G. August (Ed.), *New trends in graphemics & orthography*, 197-217. Berlin/New York: Walter de Gruyter.

Henderson, L. (1989). In mental representation of morphology and its diagnosis by measures of visual access speed. In W. Marslen-Wilson (Ed.), *Lexical Representation and Process.* Cambridge, MA: MIT Press.

Just, M.A., Carpenter, P.A., & Wu, R. (1983). Eye fixations in the reading of Chinese technical text (Technical Report). Pittsburgh: Carnegie-Mellon University.

Laudanna, A., & Burani, C. (1985). Address mechanisms to decomposed lexical entries. *Linguistics, 23*, 775-792.

Manelis, L., & Tharp, D. (1977). The processing of affixed words. *Memory & Cognition, 5*, 690-695.

Rubin, G.S., Becker, G.A., & Freeman, R.H. (1979). Morphological structure and its effects on visual word recognition. *Journal of Verbal Learning and Verbal Behavior, 18*, 757-767.

Taft, M., & Forster, K.I. (1975). Lexical storage and retrieval of prefixed words. *Journal of Verbal Learning and Verbal Behavior, 14*, 638-647.

Taft, M., & Forster, K.I. (1976). Lexical storage and retrieval of polymorphemic and polysyllabic words. *Journal of Verbal Learning and Verbal Behavior, 15*, 607-620.

Taft, M. (1979). Recognition of affixed words and the word frequency effect. *Memory and Cognition, 7*, 263--272.

Taft, M. (1981). Prefix stripping revisited. *Journal of Verbal Learning and Verbal*

Behavior, 20, 289--297.
Taft, M. (1985). The decoding of words in lexical access: A review of the morphographic approach. In D. Besner, T. Waller, & G. Mackinnon (Eds.) *Reading research: Advances in theory and practice (Vol. 5).* New York: Academic Press.
Taft, M. (1987). Morphographic processing: The BOSS re-emerges. In M. Coltheart (Ed.), *Attention and Performance XII: The psychology of reading.* Lawrence Erlbaum Associates, 265--279.
Zhang, B.Y., Guo, D.J., & He, L. (1990). *The mental dictionary of complex Chinese characters.* Paper presented at the Fifth International Symposium on Cognitive Aspects of the Chinese Language.

Appendix: Experimental Stimuli

Experiment 1

Part I (First character frequency)		Part II (Second character frequency)	
High	Low	High	Low
丟棄	揣摩	殘缺	廢棄
浮躁	斑駁	考究	儉樸
富麗	良善	傲慢	獎賞
更改	假設	批鬥	刻薄
父兄	淺薄	寬厚	辯駁
艱辛	廉潔	測驗	湖沼
遲延	並攏	悲壯	奔赴
迷茫	赤誠	監察	疑滯
吹捧	俊秀	傳佈	低落
奔波	刊載	封存	簡捷

Appendix: Experimental Stimuli (continued)

Experiment 2

Part I (First character frequency)		Part II (Second character frequency)	
High	Low	High	Low
涼棚	糞坑	怒罵	殘疾
唱盤	怒潮	零錢	茶爐
極目	畫片	鬧鐘	猛虎
黨務	龍船	附件	橫貫
奇景	逼供	荒野	牧童
民團	金質	宮城	崗亭
飯桶	餐廳	繼母	棉珠
彈殼	翠竹	慣例	蜂蜜
技藝	燈節	絕技	歌詞
母校	灰沙	貨船	巨靈

Experiment 3

Word frequency: High	Word frequency: Low
麻煩	鼓掌
功課	春季
炮彈	環抱
透鏡	寶珠
園林	江輪
田野	擺弄
優良	奇景
激烈	富足
禁止	假案
檢察	巨浪

Judging Homophony in Chinese: The Influence of Tones

Marcus Taft
University of New South Wales

Hsuan-Chih Chen
The Chinese University of Hong Kong

When making judgements about whether one character is homophonic with another, both Mandarin and Cantonese speakers encounter difficulties in saying "no" when the characters have the same phonemes but different tones, regardless of whether the task is performed silently or aloud. These difficulties were demonstrated using two different experimental paradigms. Mandarin speakers were poorer than Cantonese speakers at deciding whether two presented characters were homophonic, and compared to previous data collected with English materials, were extremely poor at deciding that a presented character was not homophonic with any other character. Theoretical consideration was therefore given to the difficulty observed when tones differed, and to the difference in performance between Mandarin and Cantonese speakers, as well as to the general difficulty observed in the homophone-generation task.

The impetus for the research to be described in this chapter came from an experience that the first author had when lecturing in China. I (the first author) presented a seminar on the topic of lexical processing in Chinese during which I described an experiment that I had carried out many years ago using Chinese (Mandarin) speakers and materials. Subjects were required to discriminate real characters from non-characters by pressing a "yes" or "no" button to individually presented stimuli. The real characters were of two types: Those which were pronounced identically to another character (i.e., homophones, like ' 企 ') and those which had a unique pronunciation (i.e., non-homophones, like ' 晃 '). Even though I am not at all proficient in the Chinese language, I was able to construct what I thought was a well-designed set of materials using a Chinese dictionary and the assistance of a Chinese-speaking friend. It came as a bit of a shock, therefore, that when I presented examples of my non-homophones during the seminar, many members of the audience immediately called out that these were actually homophones. For example, they said that ' 晃 ', which I had classified as being a non-homophone, was actually pronounced in the same way as ' 黃 '.

While I stood there disconcerted, however, the audience began to waver on their claim. They qualified what they had said by acknowledging that such characters were only homophonic if one were to ignore the tone. Now, this seemed to me to be a very odd thing to say, given what I understood about Chinese. Why would one ignore the tone when deciding how a character is pronounced? One of my constant problems when attempting to speak the occasional Chinese phrase has been that I fail to produce the correct tone and therefore the listener does not understand what I am saying. From this I had assumed that the tone was as crucial to the identity of the syllable as were the individual segments (i.e., phonemes). But now I was finding that the tonal structure appeared to be relatively unimportant in identifying the pronunciation of the character. Why should this be?

This experience in China was not the first occasion where I had observed difficulty in judging that two utterances were homophonic. Some years ago, I reported an experiment using English stimuli whereby subjects were presented with a series of words and asked to say whether there existed another word which was pronounced identically to each (Taft, 1984). For half of the items for which a "yes" response was correct, the homophonic word had a different morphological structure to the presented word, and for half it did not. For example, the word GOLD is a single morpheme while the homophonic word GOALED comprises two morphemes (GOAL and ED); whereas both the word HEAL and its homophone HEEL are single morphemes. What I found was that, when the task was performed silently, there were a considerable number of errors in responding to the morphologically different homophones (i.e., subjects said "no") as compared to the morphologically congruent homophones. On the other hand, when the subjects could read the words aloud before making their decision, the morphologically different homophones were handled just as well as the morphologically congruent homophones.

The way I interpreted these results was to suggest that the silent task was tapping into a more abstract representation of the word's pronunciation than was the vocalized task. The abstract representation of a polymorphemic word is structured differently to that of a monomorphemic word (e.g., GOALED is represented as something like [gol + past tense], while GOLD is represented as something like [gold]), and therefore, at this abstract level, the two morphologically different homophones do not correspond while the two morphemically congruent homophones do (e.g., both HEAL and HEEL would be represented as something like [hil]).

To draw a parallel to the situation with Chinese tones, one could suggest that in the abstract representation of the Chinese syllable, the tone is treated separately from the segmental information (i.e., the phonemic information), and is only integrated with the segmental information when the syllable is converted into a form that is overtly vocalized. If this were so, the tone would play an important role when attempting to identify a spoken character, but might be ignored when making a judgement about the pronunciation of an unvocalized character. Such a view accords with linguistic theories of the abstract representation of Chinese syllables, whereby segmental information is kept quite distinct from tonal information (e.g., Cheng, 1966; Wang, 1967). In Cheng's account of Mandarin, for example, the underlying representation of a syllable is separable into segments and tone with independent rules being applied to each in order to generate the surface form. In fact, the tone that is actually produced is seen as being generated from an underlying tone. In particular, Cheng claims that the 2nd (rising) tone is the same as the 1st (level) tone in the underlying representation, but the addition of a "dynamic" feature causes it to emerge as a different tone in the surface pronunciation. Similarly, the 3rd (dipping) tone is supposedly generated from the 4th (falling) tone by the addition of this dynamic feature.

The aim of the experiments to be reported in this chapter was to empirically demonstrate what I had anecdotally observed, namely, that when asked to make judgements about homophony in Chinese, subjects would be quite insensitive to tonal differences. Further, it was expected that if this insensitivity arose at the abstract phonological level, it would be manifested more strongly when the syllables which were to be judged were spoken silently than when spoken aloud.

Experiment 1

In the first experiment, the homophone judgement was made on two characters presented sequentially. There were 90 such pairs. Half of the time the two characters were pronounced identically in Mandarin (e.g., '保' and '飽', both pronounced $bǎo^1$) and half of the time they were not. The non-homophonic pairs were the items of interest and fell into three conditions. Either the two members of the pair had the same segments, but different tone (e.g., '曲' and '去', i.e., $qǔ$ and $qù$ respectively), the same tone, but a different vowel (e.g., '氣' and '去', i.e., $qì$ and $qù$), or different segments and tone (e.g., '年' and '去', i.e., $nián$ and $qù$). There were three lists of items constructed such that no list repeated the same character, while each list contained 15 non-homophonic pairs in each condition. So, for example, List 1 contained ' 曲去 ', List 2 ' 氣去 ', and List 3 ' 年去 '. Characters were presented in their simplified form as used in the People's Republic of China, and the characters in the three different conditions were approximately matched on their complexity in terms of number of strokes and their frequency of occurrence as determined from a compilation of Chinese word frequency norms (National Institute for Compilation and Translation, 1967). Ten practice item pairs were given to subjects at the beginning of the experiment.

Subjects were divided into 6 groups. Three groups performed the task silently while the other three were instructed to read the characters aloud before making their response. There were three groups for each task condition in order that each of the three lists could be presented to the same number of subjects. There were 6 subjects in each of the three "silent" groups, and 5 subjects in each of the three "aloud" groups. All subjects were students from the People's Republic of China aged in their 20's and studying at the University of Arizona.

The characters were presented via computer on a T.V. monitor. The first member of a pair appeared for 1 sec on its own, and remained on the screen when the second member of the pair appeared next to it. After a further 1 sec the two characters were removed. By pressing a foot pedal, subjects were able to bring up the next pair of characters. Subjects were asked to decide whether or not the pairs of characters were pronounced identically in Mandarin, by pressing a "yes" or "no" button as quickly but as accurately as possible. Response latencies were measured from the onset of the second member of the pair. The reaction times for correct responses were analyzed, as well as the error rates.

It was predicted that when the task was performed silently, the subjects' ability to say "no" to the non-homophones would be poorer when the characters differed in tone than when they differed in segmental structure, but that this difference would be reduced when the characters were spoken aloud.

Table 1
Reaction times for correct responses (RT in msec) and percentage error rates (%E) for the pairs of characters in Experiment 1 (Mandarin).

Condition	Example		Silent RT	%E	Aloud RT	%E
Different Tone	曲去	qǔ qù	1115	27.8	1057	43.1
Different Vowel	氣去	qì qù	947	5.2	967	9.3
Control	年去	nián qù	896	4.0	922	7.1
Homophones	保飽	bǎo bǎo	917	16.9	899	15.8

The mean reaction times and error rates are presented in Table 1. It can be seen that the tone different items did cause problems, but this difficulty was not systematically greater in the silent task compared to the aloud task. While there was a tendency toward such a reduction in difficulty on reaction times, the reverse was true for errors.

The difference between the Different Tone condition and the Different Vowel condition was significant on both reaction times and errors for both the silent and the aloud task, with all F's significant at $p < .02$, as was the difference between the Different Tone and Control conditions. The difference between the Different Vowel condition and the Control was not quite so reliable: While the reaction time difference was highly significant in the silent task, $p<.001$ for both the subject and item analyses, it was significant by subjects but not by items in the aloud task, $F_s(1,12)=7.23$, $p<.02$; $F_i(1,42) = 3.34$, $p>.05$. In addition, the error difference was far from significant in both the silent and the aloud tasks, all F's at $p>.1$. There were no significant interactions between conditions and task, $p>.1$ in every case.

It seems then that tones do tend to be ignored when judgements are made about the pronunciation of characters. The fact that this is the case even when the character is spoken aloud, might suggest that the explanation has nothing to do with abstract phonological representations. Even if it does (see later discussion for further consideration of this question), there is no support for the particular account of abstract phonological representations given by Cheng (1966). According to Cheng, the underlying forms of the 1st and 2nd tones are identical apart from one feature, as are the 3rd and 4th tones. Yet there was no sign in the present experiment of greater confusion between these tones and any others. There was a reaction time difference of 144 msec and an error difference of 22.1% between the Different Tone and Different Vowel conditions in the silent task for the 9 cases where the tone difference was between the 1st and 2nd tone or the 3rd and 4th tone. These differences were of the same (or if anything, smaller) magnitude as the remaining 36 cases, where the differences were 174 msec and 22.7%.

In attempting to explain why tonal information is frequently ignored in making homophone judgements, certain artifactual accounts must be addressed. First, it is likely that two syllables which differ only in tone are acoustically (or phonetically) more similar than two syllables which differ by a single segment. If so, it could be argued that there is no special difficulty with tones per se, but rather, that the more acoustically similar two sounds are, the more readily they will be confused. The argument against this, however, is that the members of the Different Vowel pairs were much more acoustically similar to each other than those of the Control pairs, yet the confusion between them was not dramatically greater, and not even significantly so when looking at errors. Thus, it would be hard to sustain the argument that the much greater difficulty observed in the Different Tone condition than the Different Vowel condition, particularly in terms of errors, was purely a result of greater acoustic similarity.

A second argument that could be mounted against the present experiment is that the subjects came from a variety of regions in China. As a result, a number of the subjects did not speak Mandarin as their primary dialect, and may have spoken it with a non-standard accent. Perhaps this fact could explain the difficulties observed with the Different Tone items, since some of the pairs used in this condition may actually be pronounced the same in some dialects. It is unlikely, however, that this could provide a complete explanation for the results. Differences in pronunciation would be logically more likely to affect responses to homophones than to non-homophones. It seems more likely that two syllables that are normally pronounced the same might differ in another dialect, rather than the other way around. If two syllables which are pronounced differently in standard Mandarin turn out to be pronounced the same in a particular dialect, this would be pure coincidence and certainly infrequent, unless that dialect systematically collapsed together two different sounds (e.g., 1st and 2nd tone). However, the difficulty with tone differences observed in the present experiment generalized statistically across both subjects and items, and this suggests that the majority of subjects and items showed the same pattern (despite the fact that a variety of tone contrasts were used).

Nevertheless, the fact that subjects spoke in a variety of accents makes one somewhat wary of drawing strong conclusions from this experiment. For this reason, and also to explore the generalizability of the results beyond Mandarin, we decided to repeat the experiment in Cantonese, where all of the subjects spoke with the same accent.

Experiment 2

The experiment run with Cantonese materials and native speakers was basically of the same design as the experiment run with Mandarin materials. There was, however, an additional non-homophone condition. Rather than just having a Different Vowel condition to compare to the Different Tone condition, a Different Consonant condition was included. In this condition, the two characters of a pair were pronounced with the same tone and vowel, but differed on their initial consonant. The only other change to the design of the materials was, of course, that homophony was determined on the basis of Cantonese pronunciation.

Stimuli were 36 homophonic pairs and 36 non-homophonic pairs. There were four types of non-homophonic pairs: Different Tone pairs (e.g., ' 告 ' and ' 高 ', i.e., /go$_3$/ and /go$_1$/), Different Vowel pairs (e.g., ' 家 ' and ' 高 ', i.e., /ga$_1$/ and /go$_1$/), Different Consonant pairs (e.g., ' 租 ' and ' 高 ', i.e., /jo$_1$/ and /go$_1$/), and Control pairs (e.g., ' 魚 ' and ' 高 ', i.e.,

/yue₄/ and /go₁/). All stimuli were presented in their traditional form as used in Hong Kong, and the four different types of pairs were matched as closely as possible on their complexity and their frequency of occurrence according to a Hong Kong Chinese word frequency count (Educational Research Establishment, 1986).

Forty-eight native Cantonese speakers (with a mean age of about 20) drawn from the introductory psychology subject pool at the Chinese University of Hong Kong participated in the experiment. Half of them performed the silent task and the other half the aloud task. Each subject was presented with the 36 homophonic pairs and nine of each of the four types of non-homophonic pairs.

The stimuli were presented on the screen of an IBM PC/AT compatible computer. At the beginning of the experiment, instructions and four practice trials were given. Each trial began with the presentation of a star signal for 500 msec in the centre of the computer screen followed immediately in the same position by the display of the first character of a pair. After another 500 msec the second character of the pair appeared next to the first character for 2 sec. Then the two characters were covered by a masking field. The subjects were instructed to press the space bar on the keyboard to start a trial and to respond by pressing a "yes" or "no" key.

The results can be found in Table 2. In terms of reaction time, the conclusions that can be drawn from these data are the same as those arising from Experiment 1. The Different Tone condition took longer to respond to than the other non-homophone conditions in both the silent task, $F_s(1,22) = 14.06$, $p < .01$, $F_i(1,35) = 24.36$, $p < .001$, and the aloud task, $F_s(1,22) = 8.82$, $p < .01$, $F_i(1,35) = 5.08$, $p < .05$. While there was a tendency for the size of this effect to be reduced in the aloud task compared to the silent task, the interaction between task and conditions failed to reach significance, all F's at $p > .1$. Unlike the Mandarin experiment, the Different Vowel condition did not statistically differ from the Control condition, and neither did the Different Consonant condition, all F's at $p > .1$. This lack of difficulty with the pairs which differed by one segment, accentuates the point that the primary difficulty in judging homophony comes from judging tone differences. It seems, therefore, that in Cantonese as well as in Mandarin, information about tones is not of primary importance when determining the pronunciation of a character.

Interestingly, the error data are very different to those of Experiment 1. The difficulty in judging tone differences does not manifest itself in the error rates, though there is a non-significant tendency for the effect to be

Table 2
Reaction times for correct responses (RT in msec) and percentage error rates (%E) for the pairs of characters in Experiment 2 (Cantonese).

Condition	Example			Silent RT	%E	Aloud RT	%E
Different Tone	告高	/go$_3$/	/go$_1$/	910	2.3	1103	4.6
Different Vowel	家高	/ga$_1$/	/go$_1$/	816	2.8	1023	2.3
Different Consonant	租高	/jo$_1$/	/go$_1$/	808	1.4	1050	2.3
Control	魚高	/yue$_4$/	/go$_1$/	794	1.9	1022	2.3
Homophones	色昔	/sik$_1$/	/sik$_1$/	870	6.0	1021	3.8

greater in the aloud task than the silent task (a trend also observed in the Mandarin experiment), all F's at $p > .1$. Not only do the Different Tone pairs present little difficulty for the Cantonese readers as far as accuracy goes, but the error rates overall are much lower than for the Mandarin readers. One can only speculate about why this might be the case.

Firstly, it might have something to do with the structure of Cantonese compared to the structure of Mandarin. The fact that there are nine tones in Cantonese as opposed to four in Mandarin means that homophony is less frequent in Cantonese. As a result, homophones may be specifically noted in lexical memory in some way, just as English speakers may have noted the homophony between THEIR and THERE, for example. However, this would not explain why the problem with the Different Tone condition was reflected in reaction times and not in errors. In fact, one might have predicted that Cantonese would be even harder than Mandarin since there are more tones to get confused between.

A second possible explanation lies in the way in which reading is taught in Hong Kong compared to China. In China, an alphabetic system of writing (pinyin) is typically used at the early stages of learning to read, while in Hong Kong the children are only taught character-to-pronunciation mappings, without the mediation of an alphabetic system. Whether this fact could have led to the pattern of differences in accuracy observed between the two groups is something that may be worth pursuing (perhaps by testing Cantonese speakers from China). Since the pinyin system distinguishes the segments from the tones, it is possible that readers from China are more likely to distinguish segments and tones in their lexical representations than readers from Hong Kong. However, this would not explain why there was a tone effect in the Cantonese experiment on reaction times, even though not on errors, and neither would it explain the overall lower error rate compared to the Mandarin experiment. Moreover, adult readers from China have had little or no need for pinyin after childhood, and most would claim that it plays no role in their thinking about characters. Nevertheless, it would be interesting to ascertain whether there actually is an unconscious influence of these childhood practices on adult lexical representations.

When it comes to comparing homophone decision performance in Chinese with that in English, there is little that can be concluded in relation to Experiments 1 and 2. There are not to our knowledge any studies reporting a homophone decision task on pairs of English words (like SAIL and SALE). Previous experiments using the homophone decision task have typically used single nonwords as the stimuli, like BRANE and RIST (e.g., Taft, 1982; McCann, Besner, & Davelaar, 1988). However, as mentioned earlier, Taft (1984) did report a study using single English words as items. For example, subjects were asked whether there is another word that is pronounced identically to SAIL. On finding a different pattern of results when the words were spoken silently compared to when they were spoken aloud (depending on the morphological structure of the words), Taft concluded that the silent task was tapping a more abstract level of lexical representation than the aloud task. In the Mandarin and Cantonese experiments reported here, however, there was no difference in the pattern of responses observed between the silent and the aloud task. There are several interpretations that can be given to this result.

First, it may be the case that tones are represented in the same way in both the abstract and the surface representation of a syllable in Chinese. Alternatively, it may be the case that there are no such things as abstract representations in Chinese, or that if there are, they are not tapped into when reading silently. Note that these explanations have difficulty explaining why tone differences are problematical, since they suggest that homophone judgements are being made on the basis of a representation that is equivalent to the surface phonetic representation of the syllable, and tones should be an integral part of this phonetic representation. Another explanation that can be offered is that, even in the aloud task, responses are made at an abstract level where tonal information is imperfectly represented. If so, this would mean that the abstract level of phonological representation has more impact for Chinese readers than English readers since the aloud task seems to be performed by the latter at the surface level.

Another possible explanation for the difficulty that Chinese subjects encountered in both the aloud and silent tasks with the Different Tone condition, is that the subjects simply mispronounced some of the characters, and that this happened to be particularly so for the Different Tone items. The possibility that mispronunciations had an influence on the results was examined in the Cantonese study, where the pronunciations given by subjects were monitored by asking them to read out the full list of characters after they had performed the homophone decision task. It turned out that errors of pronunciation were reasonably common (12.2% of responses), but that the least number of errors were made with the Different Tone condition items (5.6%). There were 319% errors of pronunciation amongst the Different Consonant, Control, and Homophone items, and 8.3% errors amongst the Different Vowel items. It seems, therefore, that there was no special difficulty in pronouncing the Different Tone pairs, and in fact, the relative lack of difficulty with these items compared to the other non-homophonic pairs could possibly have counteracted the tone effect on error rates. In point of fact, an explanation in terms of inappropriate pronunciations is really only relevant to the examination of error rates, and not to the differences observed in reaction times. If a character is not pronounced correctly, it could lead to an error in the judgement of homophony (depending upon the mispronunciation), but should have no impact on the time taken to make a correct response.

Perhaps the difference in experimental paradigms accounts for the contrast between the aloud/silent difference in English and the lack of an aloud/silent difference in Chinese. In Experiments 1 and 2, subjects were asked to compare the pronunciations of two presented characters. In the English study (Taft, 1984), subjects were presented only one word and asked if it was possible to generate another word with the same pronunciation. Since it is conceivable that these two paradigms tap into somewhat different processes, we decided to try out the latter paradigm with Mandarin readers to see if problems with tone differences still emerged, and also if the pattern was still the same regardless of whether the syllables were read silently or aloud. Furthermore, since the conclusions drawn from the English study were based on incorrect responses given to homophones rather than to non-homophones, Experiment 3 included a manipulation of homophones in addition to the manipulation of non-homophones.

Experiment 3

In Experiment 3, native Mandarin speakers were presented with single characters and asked to respond by button press whether or not there existed in their vocabulary another character pronounced identically to the presented character. Half of the items were homophones for which a "yes" response was correct, and the other half were non-homophones for which a "no" response was correct. There were two types of non-homophones: A Competing Tone condition, where there existed at least one other character pronounced with the same segments as the presented character, but with a different tone (e.g., ' 肉 ' which is the only character pronounced *ròu*, though ' 柔 ' is pronounced *róu*), and a No Competing Tone condition, where there were no other characters pronounced with the same segments as the presented character (e.g., ' 丢 ' being the only character pronounced *diū*, while no characters are pronounced *diú*, *diǔ*, or *diù*). The two conditions were approximately matched overall on number of strokes and frequency of occurrence according to the "Modern Chinese Frequency Dictionary".

Similarly there were two types of homophones: A Competing Tone condition, where there was more than one character pronounced with the same segments as the presented character, both with the same tone and different tones (e.g., ' 洪 ' pronounced *hóng*, while ' 紅 ' is also pronounced *hóng*, but ' 轟 ' is pronounced *hōng*), and a No Competing Tone condition where there was more than one character pronounced with the same segments as the presented character, but only with the same tone (e.g., ' 若 ' is pronounced *ruò*, as is ' 弱 ', but there are no characters pronounced *ruō*, *ruó* or *ruǒ*). The two conditions were approximately matched overall on number of strokes and frequency of occurrence according to the "Modern Chinese Frequency Dictionary".

Items were presented on a video display unit under computer control. Each item was displayed for 2 sec, and because the results from a pilot subject suggested that the task was very difficult, an inter-stimulus interval of 8 sec was used. Subjects were instructed to decide whether or not the presented character was pronounced identically in Mandarin to any other character. Response was to be made by button press. The same subjects were used in the silent and the aloud task, with the former always being conducted before the latter. That is, in the first phase the subjects were told not to read the character out aloud, while in the second, they were told that now they should do so and that they should listen to themselves in order to make their decision. By using the same subjects, it was anticipated that performance in the aloud task would be better than performance in the silent task, but the question of interest was whether this would be equally true across all four conditions.

Fifteen subjects participated in the study. All were graduate students from the People's Republic of China studying at the University of New South Wales. Only 5 of the subjects were not from the north part of China.

The results are presented in Table 3. Turning first to the non-homophones, there appears to be a delay in response times when there exists a character with the same segments as the presented character, but with different tone. However, the main effect of tone competition was only significant on the subject analysis, $F_s(1,14)=6.34$, $p<.05$, $F_i(1,48)=0.17$, $p>.1$. On the other hand, the analysis of errors did prove to be significant, $F_s(1,14)=19.42$, $p<.001$, $F_i(1,48)=6.78$, $p<.02$. There was no significant interaction between tone competition and task, for either response times or error scores.

It can be seen then that the task of thinking of other characters with the same pronunciation as the presented character produces similar results to the task of comparing the pronunciation of two presented characters, particularly in terms of the errors made. Tonal information appears to be less important than segmental information in making judgements about pronunciation, and it does not make any difference whether the judgement is made on a silently read character or on a spoken character. That is, in making a decision about the homophony of a character, tonal differences are sometimes ignored.

The results for the homophonic items may at first seem paradoxical. It appears that the presence of characters with competing tones actually facilitates both response latencies and accuracy: While the difference between the Competing Tone and No Competing Tone conditions was nonsignificant on response times, neither for subjects nor for items, $F_s(1,14)=1.32$, $p>.1$, $F_i(1,48)=0.57$, $p>.1$, the error data produced a significant difference, $F_s(1,14)=21.66$, $p<.001$, $F_i(1,48)=4.59$, $p<.05$. Again, there was no interaction between tone competition and task on either measure.

The explanation for this result would actually appear to be quite simple. If tonal information is ignored, then the pool of characters which are considered to be homophonic with the presented word will be increased when there exist characters pronounced with the same segments and different tone. In other words, on a number of occasions with the Competing

Table 3
Reaction times for correct responses (RT in msec) and percentage error rates (%E) for the pairs of characters in Experiment 3.

Condition	Example		Silent RT	%E	Aloud RT	%E
Non-homophones						
Competing Tone	肉	ròu	3214	63.6	2967	59.5
No Competing Tone	丢	diū	3134	48.2	2730	44.6
Homophones						
Competing Tone	洪	hóng	2104	12.8	1957	13.3
No Competing Tone	若	ruò	2209	26.7	1996	27.2

Tone items, subjects will make their "yes" response on the basis of the wrong character. Since this will unavoidably register as a correct response, performance in this condition will appear to be better than in the No Competing Tone condition where such errors do not occur. So, it seems that the homophonic items are reflecting the same phenomenon as the non-homophonic items, namely, that tones are not an important part of the phonological representation of a Chinese syllable.

In addition to the tone effect, however, what is particularly striking about the results of this experiment is the fact that the task was extraordinarily difficult for subjects to carry out. Reaction times of around 3 secs would seem to be extremely long, though one cannot draw a comparison with studies in English since there are no equivalent English data. However, error rates on this task using English materials are available from Taft (1984). On comparing the data from the English and Chinese studies, it can be seen that performance in the homophone decision task is very different in the two languages. The error rate for correct "no" responses in English (e.g., for words like ACHE) was very low (1.9% in the silent task and 0.3% in the aloud task), while in Mandarin, performance was not much better than chance for the equivalent items (i.e., the No Competing Tone condition). The error rate for correct "yes" responses was not so dramatically different, though accuracy was still greater for English than for Mandarin. For the silent task in English there were 17% errors for homophones with the same morphological structure, and for the aloud task it was 14%. This compares to error rates of around 27% in the No Competing Tone condition for both tasks in Mandarin.

An attempt will now be made to explain the difficulty experienced by Chinese subjects in making homophone judgements in Experiment 3. After this, we will try to home in on the source of the tone effect found in all three experiments.

The first idea that comes to mind in attempting to account for the poor performance observed in the homophone decision task is that the link between orthography and phonology is not as strong in Chinese as it is in English, owing to the greater arbitrariness of the relationship for the former compared to the latter. It has been shown, for example, that phonological recognition is slower and less accurate than graphemic recognition for Chinese characters, while the reverse is true for English words (Chen & Juola, 1982). In the homophone decision task, a weak link between orthography and phonology could manifest itself at two loci; when the pronunciation of the presented character is generated, and when an alternative orthographic representation for that pronunciation is sought. Given that characters can typically be given their correct pronunciation, it is more likely that difficulties arise in the homophone decision task at the latter stage, when alternative orthographic forms are being sought.

The problem with this account, however, is that the link between phonology and orthography may be weak, but it must be strong enough to account for the fact that Chinese language users are nevertheless able to generate a correct graphemic representation for a spoken syllable, even out of context. One could envisage that it takes longer to think of the graphemic representation of a monosyllabic word in Chinese than in English, but it is difficult to see why there would be such a dramatic difference in error rates.

Instead of using such vague concepts as strong or weak links between orthography and phonology, we should look more precisely at how homophone judgements might be made. Consider the single item task used in Experiment 3 and by Taft in 1984. Intuitively, it has been assumed that one is able to make one's decision by determining the pronunciation of the item and then ascertaining whether that pronunciation can be graphemically represented in any other way. This involves access on a visual basis to the lexical entry for the presented item, extraction of the pronunciation associated with that entry,[2] and then an attempt to access the lexicon using this pronunciation in order to discover a lexical entry which is associated with a different orthographic representation to the one that has been presented.

While this may seem to be an intuitively obvious way to perform the homophone decision task, the fact is that in English (or any alphabetic language) there is actually another way in which the task could be successfully carried out. Having determined the pronunciation of the letter string, (for example, after establishing that PLAIN is pronounced /plein/), one could then generate other ways of spelling that pronunciation, (e.g., PLANE, PLEIN, PLEIGN, PLAYNE) and attempt to access these on a visual basis. If a lexical entry is so accessed, as it would be in the case of PLANE, a "yes" response could be made. If not, a "no" response could be made. Evidence for the use of this approach would be if a word like HEED were sometimes mistakenly thought to be homophonic with HEAD, since the pronunciation of HEED (namely, /hi:d/) can be spelled HEAD. Treiman, Baron, and Freyd (1983) provide some indication that such errors do occur, though they did not directly address this issue, while Taft (1982) found that such errors occurred using letter strings which were nonwords (like THREED being thought to be homophonic with THREAD).

Now, this second way of determining homophony is impossible in Chinese. One cannot reliably generate potential orthographic representations of specific pronunciations since the relationship between pronunciation and orthography is quite arbitrary. Instead, one can only use the first method. But what if this method were extremely inefficient (at least in Chinese and perhaps in English also)? If it were, we would witness a great deal of difficulty in performing homophone decisions on single characters in Chinese compared to English, since there would be no alternative approach to fall back on.

So, why might the attempt to access other characters on the basis of the pronunciation of the presented character be inefficient? One explanation could rest on the fact that a character in Chinese frequently combines with a second character to form a word. Therefore, when determining whether different characters may be used to represent a spoken syllable, all of these two character words must be considered. For example, when presented with '肉', one establishes that it is pronounced *ròu*, but then must think of all words that include that syllable in order to determine whether any of these use a different character to '肉'. Given that subjects can never be sure that they have thought of all possible words containing a particular syllable, they can never be sure that there is no other way of orthographically representing that syllable if they cannot actually think of one. This problem is compounded by the fact that there are no constraints on what that alternative orthographic representation might be, given the arbitrary mapping of pronunciation and orthography.[3] In such circumstances, they might take a guess and perform at around chance level. This would result in around 50% errors for non-homophones, but a rather better performance for homophones, since subjects would occasionally actually think of the alternative orthographic representation of the syllable. In this way, the general difficulty with the task used in Experiment 3 can be explained. The relative ease of performing the task used in Experiments 1 and 2 is also explained. A phonological-orthographic association is not necessary in these experiments at all, since the homophony judgement is based on two given characters. All that is required in this task is for the pronunciation of the two characters to be generated and then for these two pronunciations to be compared.

This leads us then to an attempt at explaining the source of the tone effect. Since Experiments 1 and 2 did not require the generation of orthographic representations from phonological ones, the observed tone effect must have arisen at some locus other than this, a locus which was common to the pronunciation-matching task of the first two experiments and the homophone-generation task of the third experiment.

One might consider the stage at which pronunciation of the characters is determined and suggest that the confusion between different tones results from an inaccuracy in pronouncing tones. However, the confusion between syllables with different tones was just as great when the task was performed silently as when it was performed aloud, and Chinese readers have not been observed to make a large number of tonal errors in reading aloud, at least not with characters of the frequency of occurrence that were used in the present experiments. As mentioned earlier, in the Cantonese study, reading errors were monitored and if anything, there were fewer errors with the Different Tone items. Similarly, the pronunciations given in the aloud task of Experiment 3 were monitored and inappropriate tones were found to be rarely given. So it seems that an alternative explanation is required.

Another possibility might reside in the fact that both tasks require working memory. In the pronunciation-matching task, subjects must hold the pronunciation of the first character in memory while they determine the pronunciation of the second and compare it to the first. In the homophone-generation task, the pronunciation of the presented character must be held in working memory while alternative orthographic representations are being sought. It has been amply shown that working memory involves an articulatory component (see Baddeley, 1990). To illustrate, the immediate recall of a list of digits (digit-span) is correlated with the speed with which the digits can be uttered, such that the shorter the names of the digits, the greater the digit-span. For example, digit-span in Cantonese is greater than in English (Hoosain & Salili, 1988), presumably because of the fact that the mean articulation rate of Cantonese digits is considerably faster than that of English.

Now, in order to explain the tone confusions observed in the homophone decision tasks, what can be suggested is that pitch characteristics are hard to represent in the articulatory coding of the syllable in working memory. It would not be surprising if such concretely defined articulatory features as the position of the tongue and lips (which contribute to a description of the vowels and consonants) are easier to represent in a memory code than the frequency of laryngeal vibration (which describes the tone). If so, we can say that the difficulty in deciding that two syllables with different tones are pronounced differently arises from the traces laid down in working memory.

There are several points that can be raised as being potential problems for this claim, however. First, it has recently been demonstrated (Xu, 1991) that immediate memory for the ordering of a visually presented list of characters whose pronunciations rhyme (e.g., *bān, gān, ān, tān*) is poorer than that for a list of characters whose pronunciations rhyme except for having different tones (e.g., *bàn, gǎn, ān, tán*). This implies that tones are able to be represented in short-term memory, since different tones seem to be used as cues for discriminating between stored syllables. In response to this point though, the claim being challenged is not that tones cannot be represented, but rather that the representation is imperfect. Thus, it would presumably be the case that the list of rhyming characters with different tones would not be as well remembered as a list of characters which did not rhyme but which had the same tone (e.g., *bān, gōng, āng, tā*), and this would be equivalent to the tone effect observed in Experiment 1.

A second possible argument against the suggestion that the source of the tone effect is working memory, is that one might have expected that the effect would disappear when the characters were pronounced aloud. In other words, one might expect that the implicit pronunciation of the character in the silent task, where the tone is imperfectly represented, would be replaced by an explicit pronunciation where the tone is correctly produced. If so, it might be supposed that the echoic trace of the explicit pronunciation would take the place of working memory, and that therefore, different tones would not be confused. However, this assumption does not necessarily follow. It may be the case that a simple echoic trace is inadequate when a decision is required about the relationship of that trace to a second trace (Experiments 1 and 2) or to other pronunciations stored in lexical memory (Experiment 3). Under such circumstances, an articulatory-based working memory may still be required.

Conclusions

The only thing that can be definitely concluded from the research reported here is that tonal information is difficult to use when making a homophone decision. Several loci for this difficulty with tones were considered:

First, tones are possibly poorly represented in the underlying phonological representation of a syllable. If this were the case, though, one might have expected a reduction in difficulty when the characters were overtly pronounced, but this did not happen.

Second, subjects possibly mispronounced the characters, either because of dialect variations or because of ignorance. Yet no systematic mispronunciations were detected when subjects' overt responses were monitored. In addition, since the difficulty observed in the pronunciation-matching task of Experiments 1 and 2 arose from the non-homophones, the mispronunciation would have had to have fortuitously coincided with the pronunciation of the other character.

Third, tonal information may be hard to represent in working memory. In the pronunciation-matching task, the match would be attempted on traces of the pronunciation of the two syllables held in working memory. In the homophone-generation task, a representation of the pronunciation of the presented character must be held in working memory while a syllable that is homophonic with it is sought within lexical memory. While this is the favoured explanation (through lack of alternatives), one must make the assumption that such a working memory is used even when a self- generated overt phonetic representation is available.

Two other issues emerged from the research. The first was that it is very difficult to generate a homophone in Mandarin compared to English, and more particularly, to decide that a singly presented character is not homophonic with any other character. The explanation for this was thought to reside in the fact that one must often generate a character in conjunction with another character since they form a single word, and one cannot be sure that one has thought of all the words that contain a character which is homophonic with but different to the presented character. Furthermore, unlike in English, there is no orthographic basis for generating homophones if the phonological mechanism is difficult to implement.

The other issue concerned the difference between the performance of Cantonese and Mandarin readers in the pronunciation-matching task. While both groups were relatively slow in discriminating two characters which had different tones as opposed to different segments, only the Mandarin speakers made more errors when so doing. In fact, Mandarin speakers made more errors overall than Cantonese speakers. Two possible causes for this were considered, though neither seemed greatly appealing: The structure of the two dialects and the nature of childhood instruction. It would be interesting to ascertain whether Cantonese speakers have a similar difficulty with homophone-generation as Mandarin speakers do, though this would be unlikely to provide further clues about the source of the difference. An examination of Cantonese speakers from Canton rather than Hong Kong might prove illuminating.

Acknowledgments

The first experiment was conducted at the University of Arizona while the first author was on study leave. The authors wish to thank Ken Forster for the use of his facilities, and Xing Kongliang for generously giving up his time to conduct the experiment and perform the analyses. The authors also acknowledge the help provided by Nancy Chen in designing the items.

The second experiment was supported by a UPGC Direct Grant for Research from the Social Science and Education Panel of the Chinese University of Hong Kong. The authors wish to thank Fong Kong for constructing the stimuli, conducting the experiment, and analyzing the data. We are also grateful to Ng Ching Man for assistance in computer programming.

The third experiment was carried out at the University of New South Wales with support from a grant provided by the Australian Research Council. The authors wish to thank Nancy Chen and Xu Ming Yang for constructing the items, Huang Jishan for conducting the experiment, and Bruce Russell for analyzing the data.

Notes

1. The alphabetic Pinyin script will be used to indicate pronunciation.

2. In English, but not in Chinese, it would also be possible to determine the pronunciation of the item on the basis of subcomponents of the item. For example, the pronunciation of PLAIN could be determined from the combined pronunciations of P, L, AI and N. The pronunciation of a nonword, like PRAIN, would need to be determined in this way, since there is no lexical entry for a nonword.

3. In an alphabetic language there are considerable constraints. For example, the pronunciation of the word PLAIN could never be alternatively spelt GRONK.

References

Baddeley, A. (1990). *Human memory: Theory and practice.* Hove, East Sussex: Lawrence Erlbaum Associates.
Chen, H.-C., & Juola, J.F. (1982). Dimensions of lexical coding in Chinese and English. *Memory & Cognition, 10,* 216-224.
Cheng, R.L. (1966). Mandarin phonological structure. *Journal of Linguistics, 2,* 135-262.
Educational Research Establishment (1986). *A study on Chinese lexical units for Hong Kong junior secondary students.* Hong Kong: Hong Kong Education Department.
Hoosain, R., & Salili, F. (1988). Language differences, working memory and mathematical ability. In M.M. Gruneberg, P.E. Morris, & R.N. Sykes (Eds.), *Practical aspects of memory: Current research and issues, Vol. 2.* Chichester: John Wiley & Sons.
McCann, R.S., Besner, D., & Davelaar, E. (1988). Word recognition and identification: Do word-frequency effects reflect lexical access? *Journal of Experimental Psychology: Human, Perception and Performance, 14,* 693-706.
Modern Chinese frequency dictionary (Xianda Huayu pinlu zidian). (1985). Beijing: Beijing Language Institute Press.

National Institute for Compilation and Translation (1967). *A study on the high frequency words used in Chinese elementary school reading materials*. Taipei: Chung Hwa.

Taft, M. (1982). An alternative to grapheme-phoneme conversion rules? *Memory & Cognition, 10*, 465-474.

Taft, M. (1984). Evidence for an abstract lexical representation of word structure. *Memory & Cognition, 12*, 264-269.

Treiman, R., Freyd, J.J., & Baron, J. (1983). Phonological recoding and use of spelling-sound rules in reading sentences. *Journal of Verbal Learning and Verbal Behavior, 22*, 682-700.

Wang, W.S-Y. (1967). Phonological features of tone. *International Journal of American Linguistics, 33*, 93-105.

Xu, Y. (1991). Depth of phonological coding in short-term memory. *Memory & Cognition, 19*, 263-273.

Part III

SENTENCE AND TEXT COMPREHENSION

Reading Comprehension in Chinese: Implications from Character Reading Times

Hsuan-Chih Chen
The Chinese University of Hong Kong

In this chapter major features of the Chinese language are described and compared with those of Indo-European languages with alphabetic systems, particularly with those of English. Language-specific differences are shown to be related to differences in processing strategies in reading Chinese and English texts. It is argued that Chinese readers rely less on information carried by individual characters or words and more on context, whereas readers of English pay considerable attention to specific syntactic and semantic information embedded in the individual words. This was demonstrated in two experiments using a specially designed moving-window method to collect character and/or word reading times. In the paradigm, a reader moves an optical mouse to see each successive Chinese character or English word in a text presented in a spatially appropriate location. In the first experiment, character reading times were analyzed in multiple-regression analyses to identify regression effects at various textual levels. In the second experiment, lexical, syntactic, and semantic information were separately violated at certain points in short Chinese and English passages. The results from the two experiments are qualitatively compared to those obtained in English studies with similar methods. Character reading times in Chinese were not generally affected by properties of characters or words, but longer pauses were often found at either syntactic or physical boundaries. In contrast, both word-level and sentence-level effects were quite robust in English. These results suggest that Chinese and English languages activate different processing strategies for reading comprehension such that Chinese text induces a diffused strategy and English text a more focused strategy.

Reading involves very complex mental activities, and the ability to read well is critical for academic and job success in our society. Considerable attention has thus been devoted to the study of reading and related processes ever since Huey (1908/1968). However, most research in reading has been conducted in major Indo-European languages with alphabetic systems, and only a small amount in Chinese, despite the fact that Chinese has a number of unique and important features and is probably the most widely used language in the world. This bias presents a problem in developing a general theory of reading, because it does not account for the processing roles played by linguistic and orthographic features not found in the alphabetic languages.

In this chapter I will attempt to focus on how people read and comprehend written Chinese. I will begin by briefly reviewing major, distinguishing features of the Chinese language related to reading and comprehension. I will then survey major on-line paradigms reading researchers have used to understand how written words are comprehended. A new paradigm (i.e., a specially designed, moving-window technique) will be introduced. Two studies that have been carried out using this new technique will be reported. These experiments were designed to identify factors that are important to the process of reading comprehension in Chinese. I will relate the results of these experiments with those of others in the literature and will try to address whether or not language-specific features would affect the reading process in Chinese.

The Chinese Language and Some of Its Major Features

In this section I will describe major orthographic and linguistic features of the Chinese language that are especially revealing of the structure of written Chinese as compared with those of Indo-European languages with alphabetic systems. I will mention these features here and then discuss them in more detail below. (1) Characters represent lexical morphemes, and they vary in construction complexity. (2) Character boundaries, but not word boundaries, are indicated by spaces. (3) Chinese words can be formed by one or more characters. (4) Chinese words generally have no inherently marked lexical categories nor inflectional markings. (5) Context plays a crucial role in reading and comprehension in Chinese. In most cases, comparison and discussion will be done with English, because English is the most extensively studied and widely used alphabetic language. I will also try to discuss psychological implications of these features in relation to reading and comprehension.

Written Chinese is formed by strings of lexical morphemes called characters. Each character occupies a constant, square-shaped area and is separated from other characters by a space in texts (although a Chinese word can include more than one single character, word boundaries in Chinese are not marked by extra spacing). Different characters vary in number of strokes (e.g., ' 囚 ' vs. ' 國 ') and in manner of construction (e.g., ' 此 ' is constructed by combining two components horizontally, whereas ' 尖 ' is formed by two components along the vertical dimension) but not in their overall character size. In general, there is a relatively large number of visual details (a character can include up to about 29 strokes) packed in a constant, square-shaped area for each Chinese character. The complex and fine details of each character are particularly important in differentiating and identifing a character among others, resulting in an emphasis on visual encoding and holistic processing strategies (see, e.g., Chen & Juola, 1982; Chen & Tsoi, 1990, for relevant results and discussions). From a data-driven point of view, an apparent consequence of characters with relatively high construction complexity is that recognizing characters may only be done in the center of vision (i.e., the foveal area), because visual acuity drops off rapidly from the fixation point. Taylor (1965), for example, reported that visual acuity is about 75% within one degree of visual angle around fixation (i.e., in the foveal area), and it quickly drops off to about 45% when the visual area subtends about two degrees of visual angle.

It is interesting to note that the physical features of written Chinese reviewed above can be related in meaningful ways to results of Chinese eye-movement studies. Although there are very few eye-movement studies with Chinese materials, a characteristic finding is that Chinese readers generally make smaller saccades, measured in visual angle and/or in number of saccades per line of Chinese text than do English readers (Peng, Orchard, & Stern, 1983; Shen, 1927; Stern, 1978; Sun, Morita, & Stark, 1985). Another relevant finding is that eye movements are less variable and more regular for Chinese reading than for English reading (Shen, 1927; Stern, 1978). There is evidence in the literature to indicate that the movement of the eyes (e.g., fixation position and saccade length) appears to be influenced by parafoveal information such as spacing and word length to the right of fixation (see, e.g., O'Regan, 1979; Pollatsek & Rayner, 1982; Rayner & Pollatsek, 1981; for a comprehensive review, see Rayner

& Pollatsek, 1989). Note that texts in alphabetic languages consist of word strings with spaces between individual words. Various words, such as those in English, differ in length (e.g., *so* vs. *some*), in height (e.g., *do* vs. *no* vs. *go*), and in form (e.g., *WE* vs. *we*). In other words, a great deal of parafoveal information (e.g., form, height, and length) is available to guide saccades and to provide partial preview for the words not being fixated. In contrast, in written Chinese, characters with high construction complexity are equally spaced with similar box-liked shapes. Consequently, very little parafoveal information is available in reading, and character recognition may only be done in the foveal area. It is, then, no surprise to find that English readers tend to make larger and more variable saccades than do Chinese readers.

Although morphemes and words are different linguistic units, only character boundaries, but not word boundaries, are marked in written Chinese. An obvious consequence of written Chinese with clearly marked character boundaries is that characters become basic perceptual units in Chinese reading in a way similar to words in alphabetic reading. This is supported by empirical evidence. For example, Healy and Drewnowski (1983), asked subjects to read an English passage and to detect every instance of a target letter. They discovered that subjects made many more errors on correct words than on misspelled words. Parallel to this word inferiority effect found in English, Chen (1984, 1986) demonstrated a character inferiority effect in reading Chinese texts using a component detection task (Chinese characters are formed by strokes and components). The results showed that more detection errors were found when a target component was embedded in correct characters than in misconstructed characters. In a follow-up study, Chen (1987) used a character detection task, rather than the component detection task, and demonstrated a word superiority effect that character detection was facilitated by familiar word contexts. This word superiority effect in Chinese stands in strong contrast to both the character inferiority effect in Chinese and the word inferiority effect in English. Taken together, these results indicate that Chinese characters, rather than words, become important perceptual units in reading which may function as coding units similar to those of alphabetic words.

It is also important to note that the meaning of a Chinese character can be highly context-dependent for two main reasons: (1) many individual characters have several meanings and can be independently used as words in text; and (2) single characters can also be used with other characters to form multi-character words with distinctively different meanings. For example, '生' has several meanings itself (e.g., "give birth to", "living", "premature", "uncooked", or "student"); it can also join other characters to form very different words such as ' 生長 ' meaning "grow", '生意' meaning "business", ' 生命 ' meaning "life", ' 花生 ' meaning "peanut", ' 衛生 ' meaning "health", and ' 接線生 ' meaning "operator". Thus, context is particularly important in helping to disambiguate the meaning of a character. This actually is another important feature of the Chinese language.

There is evidence to suggest that Chinese relies more heavily on context to disambiguate the meaning of its perceptual units than do alphabetic languages like English (for further discussion, see Aaronson & Ferres, 1986). For example, by comparing Chinese and English word frequency corpora (i.e., Liu, Chuang, & Wang, 1975; Kucera & Francis, 1967) Cheng (1982) reported only 2460 characters or 15708 words are needed to account for 99% of the 1177984-character (982119-word) Chinese corpus, whereas 40000 English words are needed to account for the same proportion of the one million-word English corpus. Because the two corpora are assumed to contain the same amount of information, and also because that total information is communicated in Chinese with fewer units (using either characters or words as units of measurement) than English, Aaronson and Ferres (1986) therefore argued that the meanings of Chinese characters and even those of Chinese words are less precise and more variable than those of English words.

Although the meaning of a Chinese word is generally better defined and less ambiguous than a character, as we shall see, the concept of the word is very fuzzy in Chinese (see Hoosain, this volume, for relevant discussion). Identifying words and segmenting word boundaries in written Chinese are not simple and straightforward matters even for skilled readers for at least two reasons. First, the size of a Chinese word is not constant and word boundaries are not marked by extra spacing. As mentioned above, Chinese words can be formed by one or more characters. The proportions of single-, two-, and three-or-more-character words in Chinese are about 55%, 40%, and 5%, respectively (Sun et al., 1985). Second, many characters can be independently used as words in text, but they can also join other characters to form different words. In this context, Hoosain (this volume) provided evidence that skilled Chinese readers have vague and different ideas about how to segment words in sentences.

Another point to note regarding Chinese words is that they generally have very little morphological complexity: Chinese words generally have no inherently marked lexical categories and have no inflectional markings to indicate the number, gender, and case for nouns or the tense and aspect for verbs (Li & Thompson, 1981; Wang, 1973). Furthermore, intrasentence concordance rules, such as subject-verb agreement, are also absent in Chinese. In fact, various forms of semantic and syntactic information are not carried by individual words. Rather, these syntactic information are usually carried by the context as a whole. In contrast, words in alphabetic languages generally have inflectional markings to indicate various grammatical attributes, though different alphabetic languages vary to some extent in terms of their morphological complexity. Thus, Chinese words generally carry less meaning and structural information in sentential context than do alphabetic words.

As for sentence structure in Chinese, because Chinese words generally do not have inflections, it seems reasonable to expect that word order plays a crucial role in sentence processing in Chinese (see, e.g., Chang, this volume; Taylor & Taylor, 1990). This kind of reasoning is in line with observations that in some alphabetic languages, which are heavily inflected (e.g., Latin, Polish, and Russian), word order can be quite flexible, whereas in languages which are less inflected (e.g., English) word order is pivotal (see, e.g., Danks & Kurcz, 1984; Ellis & Beattie, 1986; MacWhinney, Bates, & Kliegl, 1984). As contemporary researchers are actively discussing and debating the basic word order in Chinese (see, e.g., Huang, 1978; Li & Thompson, 1981; Tang, 1988), there are empirical data indicating that word order is not the dominant linguistic cue to sentence comprehension in Chinese (see, e.g., Li, Bates, Liu, & MacWhinney, this volume; Miao, 1981). Li et al., for example, asked Chinese subjects to state which noun was the actor for simple transitive sentences involving one verb and two nouns. The choice data revealed that the Chinese subjects relied most heavily on an "animacy" strategy, selecting the animate, rather than the inanimate noun, as the actor, although other linguistic cues such as word order also played certain roles. These results, in conjunction with the following facts: (1) Chinese has a relatively small scope of syntactic information compared with other languages, and (2) devices indicating syntactic information, such as functional characters (e.g., '的', '被', '們', and '把'), are not always present in sentences, nor do they always provide constant and reliable syntactic information (for further discussion, see, e.g., Chao, 1968; Li & Thompson, 1981; Tang, 1988), suggest that syntactic factors may not be very critical for comprehension in Chinese. Rather, semantic and pragmatic factors seem to play more crucial roles.

The preceding review indicates that a Chinese reader needs to rely more heavily on sentential context than does a reader of an alphabetic language for four major reasons: (1) the meanings of basic perceptual units in Chinese (i.e., characters) are generally not very precise and highly variable; (2) Chinese words are not very well defined, partly because they don't have clearly marked boundaries; (3) Chinese words do not usually contain explicitly marked syntactic information; and (4) sentence structure and other syntactic devices are not reliable sources to obtain precise and constant syntactic information. Thus, it seems reasonable to predict that Chinese readers would have a more diffused strategy (i.e., they may pay very little attention to individual sentence units, characters or words), whereas readers of alphabetic languages would have a more focused strategy (i.e., they may pay considerable attention to process the specific syntactic and semantic content of each word). However, this specific prediction regarding the general processing strategy of Chinese readers has not been verified yet.

Up to this point, we have reviewed several major features of the Chinese language relevant to the task of reading. Although we have seen that some of the features (i.e., construction of characters and words and their arrangement in text) can be related to patterns of eye movements and to basic perceptual units used in Chinese reading, possible effects of other language-specific features, such as the context dependency of Chinese characters and words, on on-line reading processing strategies in Chinese have not been systematically investigated. In the following sections I will report some preliminary experiments carried out to tackle this issue using a moving-window method.

On-Line Methods of Studying Reading

One major method of studying reading is to monitor and record a reader's eye movements as the reader progresses through a text. The idea is to capture the momentary changes in processing load and to isolate the factors contributing to it. Researchers using the eye-monitoring procedure have found that the eye-movement data are sensitive to various textual variables and are capable of revealing major aspects of the moment-to-moment cognitive processes that occur while the subject is reading a text (see, e.g., Just & Carpenter, 1987; Rayner & Pollatsek, 1989, for recent reviews). However, a precise record of eye movements is both expensive and difficult to obtain, because it requires a very costly and highly accurate recording system and a fair amount of expertise in setting up, using the system, and interpreting the record. In addition, in using the monitoring procedure, frequent calibration tests are needed throughout the recording period to ensure that there is a correct alignment between the subject and the system. These features thus limit the use of eye-monitoring procedures in reading research.

Recently, as the low-cost microcomputer technology has evolved, other subject-paced methods of studying silent reading "on-line" have been developed. These methods include various single-word display procedures (e.g., Aaronson & Ferres, 1984; Aaronson & Scarborough, 1976; Just, Carpenter, & Woolley, 1982) and multiple-word display paradigms (e.g., Graesser & Riha, 1984; Mitchell & Green, 1978). These procedures are more cost effective and easier to implement than the eye-monitoring procedure. In addition, there is substantial evidence to indicate that the subject-paced tasks, particularly for those single-word procedures, are sensitive to different situational and linguistic variables and can produce reliable data to reflect the momentary cognitive processing load (see, e.g., Aaronson & Ferres, 1984; Haberlandt & Graesser, 1985; Just et al., 1982; Mitchell, 1984). Thus, the subject-paced, on-line tasks have been widely used to study reading and related processes (e.g., Aaronson & Scarborough, 1976; Chan & Chen, 1991; Graesser & Riha, 1984; Haberlandt, 1984; Haberlandt, Graesser, & Schneider, 1989; Just et al., 1982; Mitchell, 1984). Among various subject-paced tasks, the single-word procedures are preferred to the multiple-word paradigms because data collected under the multiple-word methods (i.e., reading durations for entire clauses, idea units, or sentences) do not allow for the fine grain data analyses possible with the data from the single-word methods (reading durations for individual words).

The moving-window method

One commonly used single-word method is the moving-window method (Just et al., 1982). In the moving-window method, each word of text appears one at a time in their spatially appropriate locations on a display screen. The display is initially filled with strings of dashes corresponding to the words and spaces in the conventional layout of the passage to be presented. A subject progresses through the passage by pressing a key, thus simultaneously making a new word appear as the previous word disappears. The reading time of a word is then measured as the interval between two successive key presses.

Note that, in contrast to the eye-monitoring and other multiple-word procedures, in the moving-window method an accurate record of word reading times can be obtained rather easily and economically, and the relationship between what is being read and how long that information is processed is fairly clear and straightforward. In addition, the moving window method closely resembles a conventional reading situation in two major aspects: (1) important parafoveal and peripheral information such as spacing, punctuation, and the length and location of the words in the text are available; and (2) normal left-to-right scanning within a line and return sweeps from the end of a line to the next, similar to those involved in the conventional reading, are preserved. More crucially, it has been demonstrated that the reading data collected using the moving-window method are comparable in important ways to those obtained from the eye-monitoring procedure, indicating it is a valid research tool that can be used to study a wide range of issues in reading comprehension (see, e.g., Haberlandt & Graesser, 1985; Just & Carpenter, 1984; Just et al., 1982).

The modified moving-window method

The moving-window method has been chosen to investigate the moment-to-moment cognitive processes in reading Chinese texts in our laboratory for the following reasons: (1) Compared with the eye-monitoring procedure, the moving-window method not only is much more economical to set up, but it also is a reliable method that enables the study of ongoing reading processes without at the same time greatly interfering with conventional reading behavior. (2) Compared with other methods of studying reading "on-line" as reviewed above, this method closely resembles the conventional reading situation.

It is important to note, however, that the original moving-window method differs in a number of ways from the conventional text display format. First, in the conventional condition, readers execute eye movements to process textual information, whereas in the moving-window condition they exercise key-pressing activities. The use of key-pressing to read is obviously less efficient than moving the eye. In fact, Just et al. (1982) reported that, compared with the conventional reading condition, the reading time in the moving-window condition was almost twice as long per word (i.e., 239 and 441 msec, respectively). Thus, a major problem with the moving-window method is that its key-pressing feature does not allow readers to read as fast as they can, and it actually slows down their reading speed to a great extent (see, e.g., Danks, 1986; Rayner & Pollatsek, 1989). Second, subjects cannot reread in the moving-window condition, whereas they can in the conventional reading situation. It has been suggested that regressive eye movements can help resolve syntactic ambiguity (e.g., Frazier & Rayner, 1982). Kenney and Murray (1984) have actually reported that the availability of prior text on reading could affect subjects' sensitivity to syntactic ambiguity when reading syntactically ambiguous sentences. However, other researchers (e.g., Chen, 1986; Chen, Healy, & Bourne, 1985; Juola, Ward, & McNamara, 1982; Just et al., 1982), using technical and prose passages as materials, have demonstrated that whether or not prior text is available makes no difference to subjects' reading and comprehension performance. Finally, in the moving-window condition, readers have no option of skipping over words, whereas in the conventional condition, they have such an option. Previous investigators (e.g., Chen, 1986; Chen et al., 1985; Juola et al., 1982) have compared results obtained under these two conditions and found that this factor is not critical for comprehension.

To overcome some of the problems mentioned above, the original moving-window method has been modified to make it more closely resemble a conventional reading condition. In the modified paradigm, an optical mouse is linked to the display computer to control the stimulus presentation on the screen. Under this paradigm, subjects view Chinese texts displayed on the computer screen one character at a time by moving a mouse horizontally on a mouse pad in front of the screen. The position of the mouse is represented on the screen as a pointer under a certain line of the text. Whenever the pointer moves into the area under one certain line segment, a character corresponding to that position is displayed right above that line segment. The display time of a character is then recorded in milliseconds as the reading time of that character. Thus, by moving the mouse from left-to-right, characters within a line appear successively on the screen. At the end of a line or at the end of a page, a right-to-left return sweep is required to move the mouse to the horizontal beginning position. Subjects can then read characters in the next line or page. This modified paradigm, also allows subjects to read preceding characters by moving the mouse backward (i.e., from right-to-left within a line), though this feature was not used in the following experiments.

In the modified moving-window paradigm, subjects can read or scan very rapidly to the extent that can not possibly be done under the original moving-window method. In fact, when 20 control subjects were asked to search for a target character using either the original key-pressing procedure or the modified mouse-moving procedure, the average character display times under the two procedures were about 280 and 130 msec, respectively. Furthermore, when 10 additional control subjects were asked to use either the key or the mouse to advance the displays but did not read the characters, the average character display times were about 270 and 15 msec, respectively. These results clearly indicate that the modified procedure has resolved quite successively the rate-limiting problem of the original procedure.

Experiments on Reading Strategies in Chinese

This section describes results from two experiments using the modified moving-window method. The first experiment investigated and compared reading strategies for the recall and comprehension tasks in Chinese. The second explored and compared comprehension processes in reading Chinese and English texts by introducing lexical, syntactic, and semantic violations at specific points in the texts.

Component processes in reading Chinese

Many recent reading researchers have considered reading an interactive process in which the reader utilizes information from different levels of text structure to form a cognitive representation that consists of major ideas and relations expressed by the text (see, e.g., Danks & Glucksberg, 1980; van Dijk & Kintsch, 1983; Just & Carpenter, 1987; Perfetti, 1985; Rayner & Pollatsek, 1989). It is generally assumed that different levels of text (e.g., word, sentence, and text level) are associated with specific processes, and that various processes impose a cognitive load during reading. Similarly, it is assumed that in reading Chinese text, different levels of processing contribute concurrently to the overall reading task. Different levels of text structure in Chinese include character, word, sentence, and text levels. Character-level processes presumably consist of encoding, identification, and lexical access. Word-level processes include segmentation and lexical access. Sentence-level processes include intrasentence interpretation and integration. Text-level processes consist of intersentence integration, macrostructure construction, and topic identification.

The main purpose of the experiment reported here is to investigate and to estimate the cognitive load associated with some of the processes mentioned above, as it is reflected in character-reading times. This was done by using multiple regression analysis to relate the character-reading times (i.e., the dependent variable) to the properties of the characters (i.e., the predictor variables). Similar multiple regression techniques have been fruitfully used by reading researchers to analyze reading times for various linguistic units in English (e.g., Just & Carpenter, 1980; Kieras & Just, 1984; Haberlandt & Graesser, 1985). In the present experiment, the properties of characters were coded along five major classes of predictor variables, including character-level, word-level, sentence- level, text-level, and layout variables. The classification of levels and the choice of predictor variables were made according to the structure of written Chinese reviewed above and results from relevant experiments with English materials (e.g., Just & Carpenter, 1980; Just et al., 1982; Graesser & Haberlandt, 1986; Haberlandt & Graesser, 1985; Haberlandt, Graesser, & Schneider, 1989; Haberlandt, Graesser, Schneider, & Kiely, 1986).

The character-level variables included the complexity of the character expressed in number of strokes, the logarithm of its occurrence frequency (Hong Kong Education Department, 1986), and the complexity and logarithm of the frequency of the previous character. The word-level variables basically included the same four variables as those in the character category, except that the complexity variable was replaced by word length as expressed in number of characters. The word-level variables contained one additional variable: new argument noun (i.e., whether it was a new argument noun to the reader, see Haberlandt et al., 1986). The sentence-level variables included two clause-boundary factors (beginning of clause and end of clause) and the amount of new information expressed in number of new argument nouns in the sentence. There was one text-level variable: the serial position of the sentence in the passage. Finally, four physical layout variables were used: beginning of line, end of line, beginning of screen, and end of screen.

When using multiple regression techniques, it is important that the predictor variables approach independence (see, e.g., Kerlinger & Pedhazur, 1973). The degree of independence of the predictor variables was examined by inspecting bivariate correlations between the predictors. According to Graesser and Riha (1984), a bivariate correlation with an absolute value of 0.80 or higher is a sign of collinearity problems. Among 136 possible bivariate correlations for the 17 predictor variables, there were 128 with absolute values of 0.30 or less, five in the range 0.31 to 0.52, and three with relatively high values of 0.72 (i.e., a negative correlation between number of new argument nouns in a sentence and serial position of a sentence), 0.73 (i.e., a negative correlation between length and frequency of the previous word), and 0.74 (i.e., a negative correlation between length and frequency of a word). Because most variables were not highly collinear, potential collinearity problems were considered to be minimal.

Twenty-four native Chinese-speaking undergraduate students at the Chinese University of Hong Kong participated in the experiment. They read two scientific passages with 182 and 169 characters using the modified moving-window method. These passages were Chinese translations of English texts originally selected from *Newsweek* and *Times* by Just and Carpenter (1980). The subjects were randomly and equally divided into two groups (i.e., comprehension and recall groups). All subjects were instructed to read each passage carefully and were tested individually. After reading a passage, subjects in the comprehension group were asked to answer five four-alternative forced-choice comprehension questions, whereas subjects in the recall group were instructed to recall the passage just read.

Stimulus presentation and data collection were controlled by a SIGMA 386DX computer. All stimuli were presented on a MITSUBISHI multiscan color monitor using the modified moving-window method. In the present and the following experiments, characters were successively presented from left to right along the horizontal dimension, not only because this has become a common way to print Chinese, but also because it has been shown that Hong Kong Chinese undergraduates comprehend Chinese texts presented on computer displays better from left to right horizontally than from right to left vertically (Chen & Chen, 1988; see also Chan & Chen, 1991; Chen & Ho, 1986). From the subjects' viewing distance of about 50 cm, a Chinese character subtended about 0.5 degrees of visual angle both in width and in height. To reduce glare on the computer screen the experiment was conducted in a semidarkened room.

The mean reading times per character were 397 msec ($SD = 324$ msec) in the comprehension condition, as opposed to 859 msec ($SD = 608$ msec) in the recall condition. Furthermore, the mean percentage of correct responses in the comprehension condition was 89%, and the mean percentage of idea units correctly recalled in the recall condition was 85%. The mean reading times in each condition were analyzed using multiple regression with 17 predictor variables. All predictors were entered simultaneously into the regression equation. Table 1 shows standardized regression coefficients (i.e., beta weights) derived from the regression analyses. The standardized regression coefficients reflect the relative contribution of a specific predictor variable after all variables were transformed in standard score form. A positive standardized regression coefficient indicates that mean reading times per character increases with increasing values on the corresponding predictor variable, whereas a negative sign indicates the opposite relationship.

The regression analysis applied to the data in the recall condition and that in the comprehension condition revealed different patterns of results. In the recall condition, the set of predictor variables accounted for a significant 55% of variance in the mean character reading times ($p < .05$). Character reading times significantly increased at the ends of clauses, when characters formed new concepts, at the ends of lines, with an increase in the number of new concepts in the sentence, and at the beginnings of lines. Character reading times significantly decreased with an increase in the length and frequency of the previous word, with an increase in the frequency of the character, and at the ends of pages. In the comprehension condition, however, the set of predictors significantly accounted for 16% of variance in the dependent variable ($p < .05$). Three predictor variables had a significant and positive impact on character-reading times: the number of new argument nouns in the sentence, new argument noun, and end of line.

The results indicate that in the comprehension condition, subjects tended to use a semantic or meaning-oriented strategy. Thus, the reading time patterns for the comprehension subjects mainly reflect the semantic content of the passage (e.g., new argument noun and number of new argument nouns in the sentence). There is evidence to indicate that the comprehension subjects performed text integration at line boundaries (i.e., the reading times increased at the ends of lines) rather than at syntactic boundaries such as at the end of clauses. For recall subjects, however, they relied heavily on a syntactic or structure-oriented buffering strategy as reflected by the following results: (1) among the 17 predictor variables, the end-of-clause variable had the highest bivariate correlation with mean reading time (i.e., 0.61); and (2) there was a lag effect showing that the processing of the current word was influenced by features (i.e., length and frequency) of the previous word. The results for the recall subjects thus suggest that when reading for memory, sentence units are buffered and grouped into chunks according to linguistic structure at syntactic boundaries.

Table 1
Standardized Regression Coefficients from Multiple Regression Analysis on Mean Character Reading Times.

	Condition	
Factor	Recall	Comprehension
Character level		
Complexity	-.01 (.67)	-.09 (.67)
Frequency	-.14 * (.58)	.03 (.50)
Previous complexity	.04 (.67)	.07 (.58)
Previous frequency	-.06 (.67)	.04 (.50)
Word level		
Length	-.04 (.42)	.04 (.50)
Frequency	.08 (.67)	.12 (.58)
Previous length	-.18 * (.83)	.08 (.58)
Previous frequency	-.22 * (.75)	.05 (.58)
New argument noun (NAN)	.24 * (.83)	.17 * (.75)
Sentence level		
Beginning of clause	.05 (.58)	.06 (.42)
End of clause	.61 * (.75)	-.03 (.42)
Number of NAN	.16 * (.92)	.21 * (.75)
Text level		
Serial position of sentence	-.09 (.58)	.00 (.50)
Layout		
Beginning of line	.12 * (.67)	-.04 (.50)
End of line	.22 * (.58)	.20 * (.42)
Beginning of screen	-.03 (.58)	-.06 (.50)
End of screen	-.14 * (.83)	-.13 (.50)
Multiple R square	.55	.16

Note. The agreement between average and individual subject's data is in parentheses. The agreement measure expresses the proportion of subjects whose standardized regression coefficient for each factor had the same direction as the average values.

* $t = p < 0.05$.

Note that the recall and comprehension subjects not only differed in task demand, they also varied in terms of the amount of time they spent in reading. Thus, it is not clear whether these two factors (i.e., task and total reading time) could have independently or jointly contributed to the different reading time patterns in the two conditions. To address this issue, in each condition two reading-speed groups of six subjects each were formed using a median-split format according to the total reading time on the passages. The mean reading times per character were 520 and 1203 msec for the fast and slow subjects in the recall condition (their average recall scores were 83% and 87%, respectively), as opposed to 269 and 526 msec for the fast and slow subjects in the comprehension condition (their average comprehension scores were 90% and 87%, respectively). Separate multiple regression analyses were performed on these data and the results are summarized in Table 2. Because the fast recall subjects and the slow comprehension subjects had highly comparable reading times, their patterns of results were compared. As can be seen in Table 2, the slow comprehension subjects tended to pause longer at physical boundaries rather than at syntactic boundaries, indicating that they paid little attention to process structure, whereas the fast recall subjects paid attention to both physical and syntactic structure and showed a lag effect. These results are generally consistent with the earlier results from the average subjects in the recall and comprehension conditions, indicating that it was task demand, not total reading time, that affected the patterns of results.

The present results thus suggest that recall and comprehension tasks place different sorts of demands on the reader and affect the reader's processing strategy. This suggestion and the results discussed up to this point are generally consistent with findings from other experiments with English materials (e.g., Aaronson & Ferres, 1983; Haberlandt et al., 1989). However, other results of the present study stand in interesting contrast to findings of prior research in English. English investigators (e.g., Haberlandt & Graesser, 1985; Just et al., 1982) using similar procedures (i.e., moving window method and multiple regression techniques) have typically reported that word-level predictor variables such as word length and word frequency have very reliable and robust effects on word reading times, regardless of which type of task is used (e.g., recall or comprehension). The present experiment, however, demonstrated that in general, properties of characters (i.e., basic perceptual units in Chinese) such as complexity and frequency and those of words (e.g., word length and frequency) had no reliable, immediate impact on character reading times in

Table 2
Standardized Regression Coefficients from Multiple Regression Analysis on Mean Character Reading Times for Fast and Slow Readers.

Factor	Recall		Comprehension	
	Fast	Slow	Fast	Slow
Character level				
Complexity	-.01 (.67)	-.01 (.67)	.03 (.33)	-.10 (.67)
Frequency	-.15 (.33)	-.12 (.83)	.02 (.50)	.02 (.50)
Previous complexity	.07 (.67)	.02 (.67)	.08 (.33)	.06 (.83)
Previous frequency	-.13 (.67)	-.05 (.67)	-.14 (.67)	.07 (.67)
Word level				
Length	.12 (.67)	-.07 (.50)	.00 (.50)	.03 (.50)
Frequency	.11 (.67)	.09 (.67)	.12 (.67)	.08 (.50)
Previous length	-.21*(.83)	-.13 (.83)	.03 (.50)	.08 (.67)
Previous frequency	-.24*(.67)	-.19*(.83)	-.04 (.50)	.10 (.67)
New argument noun (NAN)	.10 (.67)	.24*(1.0)	.19*(.67)	.10 (.67)
Sentence level				
Beginning of clause	.17*(.67)	.00 (.50)	-.12 (.67)	.13 (.50)
End of clause	.16*(.50)	.63*(1.0)	-.10 (.67)	.06 (.50)
Number of NAN	.10 (1.0)	.15*(.83)	.32*(1.0)	.12 (.50)
Text level				
Serial position of sentence	.02 (.67)	-.12 (.83)	.04 (.67)	-.02 (.67)
Layout				
Beginning of line	-.02 (.50)	.14*(.83)	-.07 (.67)	-.05 (.33)
End of line	.34*(.50)	.16*(.67)	.23*(.67)	.27*(.50)
Beginning of screen	.02 (.67)	-.04 (.50)	.05 (.50)	-.07 (.67)
End of screen	-.18*(1.0)	-.11 (.67)	.04 (.50)	-.16 (.83)
Multiple R square	.22	.56	.24	.15

Note. The agreement between average and individual subject's data is in parentheses. The agreement measure expresses the proportion of subjects whose standardized regression coefficient for each factor had the same direction as the average values.

* $t = p < 0.05$.

both the comprehension and recall conditions. This, however, doesn't mean that our subjects did not immediately process the meanings of characters or words at all: one word-level predictor variable, new argument nouns (i.e., nouns that introduce a person, object, location, or concept in the passage for the first time), had a reliable and unique impact on character-reading times in both reading conditions. Furthermore, the predictor variables that specify either syntactic or physical boundaries had an important impact on character-reading times. These results, in conjunction with results of previous studies with English materials (e.g., Just et al., 1982; Haberlandt & Graesser, 1985), thus suggest that, compared to readers of alphabetic languages, Chinese readers tend to pay relatively less attention to individual sentence units, either characters or words, and relatively more attention to the ends of syntactic or physical boundaries.

Comprehension processes in Chinese reading

In the experiment reported in the previous section, different predictor variables were not systematically varied within the text. Multiple regression analyses were thus adopted to assess the effect of each predictor variable of interest after the effects of other variables, including those of extraneous variables, had been statistically partialled out. Consequently, one can't be certain that a relation between the variation in a predictor variable and the dependent variable is causal. In the experiment reported in this section, however, different types of linguistic information were experimentally manipulated to investigate comprehension processes in Chinese reading. Specifically, lexical, syntactic, and semantic information were separately violated at certain points in short Chinese and English passages. Patterns of disruptions caused by various violations were compared and discussed in relation to the processing strategies involved in reading text written in different languages. This paradigm was used originally by Danks and his colleagues in studying comprehension processes, using oral reading performance as an on-line indicator of the processes (Danks, Bohn, & Fears, 1983; Danks & Kurcz, 1984; Polkowska, Kurcz, & Danks, 1986). Since the primarily focus of the present experiment was on silent reading, character and word viewing times rather than oral reading performance were measured using the modified moving-window method.

If, as argued in the previous sections, Chinese tends to be more context dependent and less word dependent than alphabetic languages like English, then Chinese readers would use a more diffused processing strategy, whereas readers of English or other alphabetic languages would use a more focused strategy of attending to both the semantic content of each word and the syntactic information (e.g., various inflectional markings) embedded in the word. Consequently, in the present experiment one would expect to find a larger disruption of reading performance, resulting from the various types of violations of information, in English than in Chinese. In addition, different patterns of violation effects would also be expected in the two languages.

In the English version of the task, lexical, syntactic, and semantic violations should all produce significant disruptions in word reading times, because the English language presumably activates a relatively focused processing strategy. In the Chinese version of the task, however, violating lexical information would produce substantial disruptions because lexical information is crucial in lexical access, the fundamental processing component in reading comprehension. Violating syntactic information by modifying a critical word, however, should not produce a reliable disruption because syntactic information in Chinese is usually generated from the sentential context. Similarly, introducing a semantic violation by replacing the critical word with an anomaly would probably not yield a significant disruption, because Chinese readers would attempt to use contextual information to resolve the violation. These predictions were verified in the experiment reported here.

In many cross-language studies, the major factor of interest (i.e., difference in language structure) has often been confounded with extraneous subject factors such as educational history and family and cultural backgrounds (for relevant discussion and possible solutions, see Au, this volume; Chen & Tsoi, 1990). To minimize possible influences of subject factors, the subjects in the present experiment included 40 proficient Chinese-English bilingual undergraduates. They participated for research credit in an introductory psychology class at the Chinese University of Hong Kong. All subjects had learned Chinese as their first language and had studied English, their second language, for more than 12 years at different stages of school. These subjects were randomly divided into two groups (i.e., Chinese and English groups), with 20 subjects in each group. The two groups of subjects thus had similar individual and social characteristics. Subjects in each group were given instruction and stimuli in the corresponding language only.

Forty narrative passages were excerpted from issues of the Chinese edition of *Reader's Digest* published before 1975 to minimize the chance

每月總有兩三次,全校學生列隊在圖書館集合,總有一個或兩個壞孩子,會給推進隔壁房間,鞭打(學裕,鞭打著,量度)得皮破血流,其餘的人坐在那裡,哆嗦著聽他們呼號尖叫。我恨透了這個學校,那兩年多提心吊膽的日子,真不知道是怎麼過的。

Two or three times a month the whole school was marshaled in the library, and one or more delinquents were haled off to adjoining apartment and there flogged (seprool, flogging, measured) until they bled freely, while the rest sat quaking, listening to their screams. How I hated this school and what a life of anxiety I lived there for more than two years.

Figure 1. An example of a Chinese passage and its English version. The critical word is underlined. The lexical, syntactic, and semantic violations introduced are indicated in parentheses.

that the subjects might have encountered the passages before. All the passages were selected from the bilingual sections of those issues in which each Chinese passage was published with its English version. The average passage length was 83 characters in the Chinese version of the passages and 57 words in the English version. Figure 1 presents one Chinese passage and its original version in English. In each passage, one critical word was selected for manipulation, being either a verb or an adjective and usually located at the central portion of the passage. The Chinese and English versions of a passage always had the same critical word. Three types of violations (i.e., lexical, syntactic, and semantic) were introduced in the critical word of each passage as described in the following paragraphs.

A lexical violation was introduced by replacing the critical word with a pseudoword. The critical words in English were replaced by pronounceable nonwords. Because all critical words in Chinese were two- or three-character words, they were replaced by meaningless words (i.e., words containing randomly selected individual characters) of the same length. Semantic information was violated in Chinese and English by replacing the critical words with words that were semantically anomalous but syntactically appropriate.

To violate syntactic information in English, the inflectional ending of the critical word was altered to make it clearly inappropriate within the context of the sentence. This could be done by making tense or category changes (e.g., *break* to *broke* and *clear* to *clearly*). Note that syntactic manipulations are relatively easy to construct in alphabetic languages like English, because they generally have a wide variety of inflectional markings to indicate various grammatical attributes; similar manipulations in Chinese are extremely difficult, because Chinese words generally have no inflectional markings. However, Chinese has some functional characters that can be used, mostly as suffixes, with other characters to indicate grammatical attributes. And yet these functors often play multiple syntactic roles, and their presence in sentences is optional rather than obligatory (see, e.g., Chao, 1968; Li & Thompson, 1981). Thus, the syntactic violation in Chinese was introduced by either inserting after the critical word a functional character (e.g., ' 的 ' or ' 著 ') or replacing the suffix of the critical word with another one to make similar tense or category changes as those in the English passages.

In both the Chinese and English versions of the experiment there were four violation conditions (lexical, syntactic, semantic, and control). Every subject in each group (Chinese or English) read 10 passages in each of these conditions. Across subjects in each group, each passage occurred five times in each violation condition. The order of passage presentations was randomized for each subject. The apparatus and viewing conditions and the procedure for each trial were basically the same as those used in the experiment reported in the previous section, except that in the present experiment only one multiple-choice comprehension question was given after the display of each passage.

Because various violations were manipulated in terms of words in both the Chinese and English versions of the experiment, the display duration of individual words was used as the unit of analysis. This was easily accomplished in English, because the functional stimulus units were individual words. In Chinese, however, each character of a passage was treated as the functional stimulus unit. In addition, the syntactic violation in Chinese was often introduced by inserting a functional character after the critical word. Thus, the number of characters involved in a critical word varied across different conditions in Chinese. To overcome this problem, the dependent measure in the Chinese version was calculated by averaging, rather than adding, character reading times across the number of characters involved in each word unit.

The average comprehension scores for the Chinese and English groups were 91% and 90% correct, respectively. The reading time data for subjects in each group were submitted to two separate analyses of variance with two within-subjects factors (i.e., type of violation and word position). Post hoc comparisons were conducted using the protected t-test procedure (Fisher's least significant difference). The differences between the average viewing times of the experimental and control conditions for the Chinese and English groups are shown in Figure 2. The average character reading time per word in the control condition for the Chinese group was 365 msec, whereas the average word reading time in the control condition for the English group was 435 msec. Note that although the subjects, stimuli, violation manipulations, general procedures, and units of analyses in the Chinese and English versions of the experiment were matched as colosely as possible, there were enough unavoidable differences to prevent direct comparison between the Chinese and English groups. Consequently, only the patterns of results of the two groups will be compared.

As Figure 2 shows, the disruption profile for the Chinese group is generally very flat with two minor peaks in the lexical violation conditions. Specifically, the analysis for the Chinese group revealed a significant main effect for word position, $F(10, 190) = 3.42$, $p < .01$, indicating that

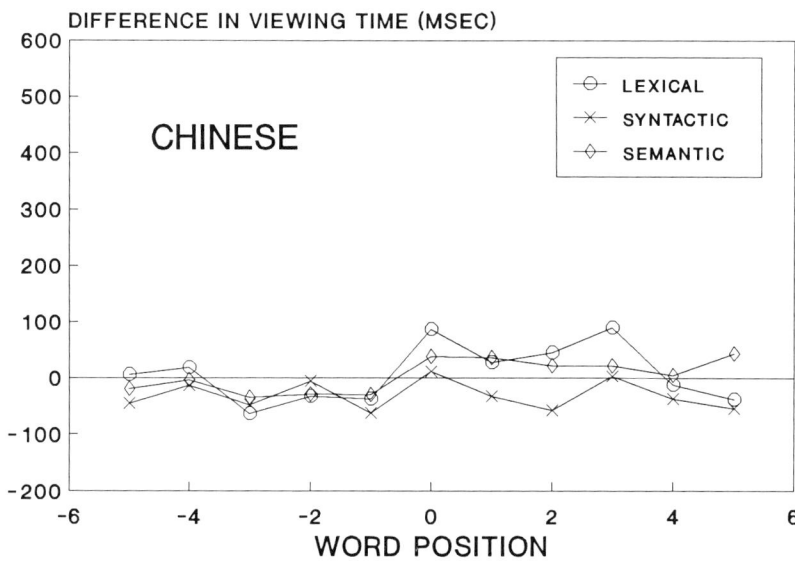

Figure 2. Differences in mean reading times between the lexical, syntactic, and semantic violations and their controls for Chinese stimuli.

subjects' average reading time was affected by word position. The main effect of violation type, however, was not significant, $F(3, 57) = 1.23$. Most critically, the interaction between violation type and word position was significant, $F(30, 570) = 1.71, p < .05$. Post hoc comparisons revealed that the lexical violation produced significant disruptions at the critical word and at the word +2 position. In contrast, the syntactic violation did not produce a significant disruption at any word position. As for the semantic violation, although it seemed to produce some disruptions, especially at the word +5 position (see the top panel of Figure 2), no significant result was found.

As shown in Figure 3, all violations were distinctively different from their controls for the group of English readers. In fact, all main effects and the two-way interaction were significant at $p < .001$: type of violation, $F(3, 57) = 23.42$; word position, $F(10, 190) = 210.13$; and violation x word, $F(30, 570) = 22.94$. Among various types of violations,

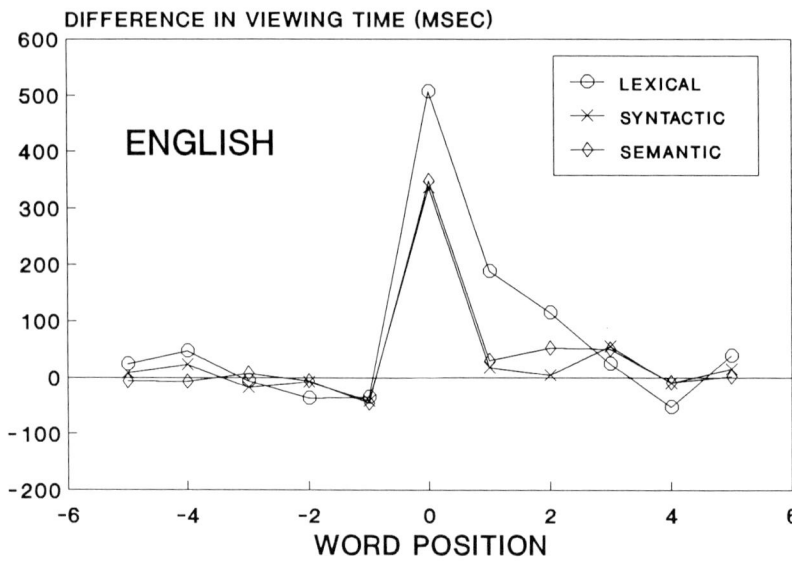

Figure 3. Differences in mean reading times between the lexical, syntactic, and semantic violations and their controls for English stimuli.

the lexical violation produced the largest disruption, beginning at the critical word and continuing through the word +2 position with a peak at the critical word position. The syntactic and semantic violations both produced a significant disruption, but only at the critical word.

In the Chinese group, only the lexical violation produced significant disruptions at the critical word, providing support for the notion that Chinese readers do not heavily rely on the word-dependent processing strategy. Furthermore, there is evidence to indicate that Chinese readers attempted to use contextual information to resolve the syntactic and semantic violations: both types of the violations, but not the lexical violations, produced significant disruptions at the end of the clause, $F(3, 57) = 2.85$, $p < .05$. In contrast, all violations created dramatic interference at the critical word in English. Thus, English readers appear to use a more focused, word-dependent processing strategy than do Chinese readers, probably because various aspects of information carried by individual words in English are rather informative.

An interesting point to note here is that Danks et al. (1983) have previously demonstrated that lexical, syntactic, and semantic violations in English all produced significant disruptions in oral reading performance of American readers; the syntactic and semantic violations both created similar disruption effects, but the lexical violations produced a larger effect. The study of Danks et al. differs from the present one in three important respects (i.e., type of the subject, dependent variable, and method of data collection). In the present experiment proficient Chinese-English bilinguals were used, and their word viewing times were collected via the modified moving-window method; in the previous study, native English speakers were asked to perform oral reading tasks and their oral production times were scored. Despite these differences between the two studies, the overall pattern of results is highly consistent and is distinctively different from that for the Chinese group in the present experiment. These results therefore indicate that the effects created by manipulating various linguistic violations are very robust and reflect language-specific processing strategies.

There is another point to note regarding the issue of language processing in bilingual speakers. The present finding that proficient Chinese-English bilinguals' patterns of results in English are generally comparable to those from English monolinguals is in line with results from many previous studies with similar subjects (see, e.g., Chen & Ho, 1986; Chen & Tsoi, 1988; Chen & Tsoi, 1990). These findings are consistent with the concept-mediation hypothesis that the first and second languages of proficient bilinguals can be operated rather independently, so that information in the two languages are not directly or strongly associated but are connected through an amodal conceptual system (see, e.g., Chen, 1992; Chen, 1990; Chen & Leung, 1989; Chen & Ng, 1989, for relevant results and discussion about this hypothesis and related issues).

Taken together, the present violation results in Chinese and English illustrate that different processing strategies are activated in reading text written in logographic Chinese and that in alphabetic English. That the same type of Chinese-English bilingual subjects showed different patterns of violation effects in Chinese and English clearly suggests that readers are sensitive to the differences in the cognitive demands imposed by different linguistic structures in reading comprehension and that they adapt their processing strategies to meet the cognitive demands of the situation.

Conclusions

The issue that I have tried to address in this chapter is: can language-specific features affect reading strategies in Chinese? If so, how? The unique features of Chinese that I briefly reviewed in the beginning of the chapter suggest that both orthographic and linguistic features of Chinese can be related in meaningful ways to specific results obtained in reading research conducted to observe patterns of eye movements and basic perceptual units. Furthermore, I presented some preliminary experimental evidence in support of the notion that unique features of the Chinese language can affect processing strategies used in reading Chinese text. The results from the correlational and experimental studies reported here converge nicely, suggesting that the Chinese language activates a reading strategy relying more on context and less on individual characters or words than an alphabetic language such as English.

Furthermore, there is evidence in the literature to support the hypothesis that reading words written in different systems activates different processing mechanisms (see, e.g., Chen & Juola, 1982; Chen & Tsoi, 1990; Hoosain, 1991; Hung & Tzeng, 1981). However, such evidence is mainly obtained from studies using various lexical tasks (e.g., Stroop-like tasks or character/word recognition in visual-half-field experiments). This has lead to the suggestion that the locus of processing difference due to variation in writing systems may be located at an encoding and perceptual level for simple lexical-processing tasks, but not at higher levels of information processing, such as parsing and integration for more complex tasks such as reading for comprehension (see, e.g., Chen & Juola, 1982; Hung & Tzeng, 1981). However, the studies reviewed and reported here, in conjunction with other studies using different tasks (e.g., Danks & Kurcz, 1984; Li et al., this volume; MacWhinney & Bates, 1989; MacWhinney et al., 1984), illustrate that processing differences due to orthographic and/or language variation exist at higher levels of processing in complex tasks such as sentence interpretation and text comprehension.

Another issue that emerged from the research reported here is that readers appear to have very flexible processing strategies and mechanisms that are sensitive to a great variety of variables, including, for example, task demand (recall vs. comprehension), type of text or text difficulty (technical vs. prose passage or difficult vs. easy), and language structure (Chinese vs. English). It was demonstrated in the first experiment reported here that task demand could affect patterns of character reading times. In the second experiment, it was shown that differences in language structure affected the pattern of violation results. When comparing the results of the two experiments, there is also some evidence to show that the type of the text could affect the pattern of reading performance: the average character reading time in the comprehension condition of the first experiment where technical passages were used as stimuli was longer than that in the second experiment in which prose passages were used.

The final issue concerned the modified moving-window method. This method has been shown to be a quality research tool that is sensitive to important situational and linguistic variables and applicable for testing hypotheses about text processing. This method is rather easy to set up and less expensive than other on-line procedures that obtain a comparable amount and validity of reading data. These features make the modified moving-window method a useful complement to eye monitoring and other on-line self-paced methods used in the study of reading.

Acknowledgements

The preparation of this chapter was supported by a research grant from the Hong Kong University and Polytechnic Grants Committee. The research reported in this chapter was supported by the same grant. I would like to thank Tze-Chau Chiu, Chun-Kit Lo, Ruth Fan, and William Lam for the valuable contributions they made to the work described here.

References

Aaronson, D., & Ferres, S. (1983). Lexical categories and reading tasks. *Journal of Experimental Psychology: Human Perception and Performance, 9*, 675-599.
Aaronson, D., & Ferres, S. (1986). Sentence processing in Chinese-American bilinguals. *Journal of Memory and Language, 25*, 136-162.
Aaronson, D., & Ferres, S. (1984). The word-by-word reading paradigm. In D.E. Kieras & M.A. Just (Eds.), *New methods in reading comprehension research* (pp. 31-68). Hillsdale, NJ: Erlbaum.

Aaronson, D., & Scarborough, H.S. (1976). Performance theories for sentence coding: Some quantitative evidence. *Journal of Experimental Psychology: Human Perception and Performance, 2*, 56-70.

Au, T.K. (this volume). Cross-linguistic research on language and cognition: Methodological challenges.

Chan, K.-T., & Chen, H.-C. (1991). Reading sequentially-presented Chinese text: Effects of display format. *Ergonomics, 34*, 1083-1094.

Chang, H.W. (this volume). The acquisition of Chinese syntax.

Chao, Y.R. (1968). *A grammar of spoken Chinese*. Berkeley, CA: University of California Press.

Chen, H.-C. (1987). Character detection in reading Chinese: Effects of context and display format. *Chinese Journal of Psychology, 29*, 45-50.

Chen, H.-C., (1986). Component detection in reading Chinese characters. In H.S.R. Kao and R. Hoosain (Eds.), *Linguistics, Psychology, and the Chinese Language* (pp. 1-10). Hong Kong: Hong Kong University Press.

Chen, H.-C. (1984). Detecting radical components of Chinese characters in visual reading. *Chinese Journal of Psychology, 26*, 29-34.

Chen, H.-C. (1986). Effects of reading span and textual coherence on rapid-sequential reading. *Memory & Cognition, 14*, 202-208.

Chen, H.-C. (1990). Lexical processing in a non-native language: Effects of language proficiency and learning strategy. *Memory & Cognition, 18*, 279-288.

Chen, H.-C. (1992). Lexical processing in bilingual and multilingual speakers. In R.J. Harris (Ed.), *Cognitive processing in bilinguals* (pp. 253-264). Amsterdam: Elsevier.

Chen, H.-C., & Chen, M.J. (1988). Directional scanning in Chinese reading. In I.M. Liu, H.-C. Chen, and M.J. Chen (Eds.), *Cognitive Aspects of the Chinese Language* (Vol. 1, pp. 15-26). Hong Kong: Asian Research Service.

Chen, H.-C., Healy, A.F., & Bourne, L.E., Jr. (1985). Effects of presentation complexity on rapid-sequential reading. *Perception & Psychophysics, 38*, 461-470.

Chen, H.-C., & Ho, C. (1986). Development of Stroop interference in Chinese-English bilinguals. *Journal of Experimental Psychology: Learning, Memory, & Cognition, 12*, 397-401.

Chen, H.-C., & Juola, J.F. (1982). Dimensions of lexical coding in Chinese and English. *Memory & Cognition, 10*, 216-224.

Chen, H.-C., & Leung, Y.-S. (1989). Patterns of lexical coding in a non-native language. *Journal of Experimental Psychology: Learning, Memory, and Cognition, 15*, 315-326.

Chen, H.-C., & Ng, M.-L. (1989). Semantic facilitation and translation priming effects in Chinese-English bilinguals. *Memory & Cognition, 17*, 454-462.

Chen, H.-C., & Tsoi, K.-C. (1988). Factors affecting the readability of moving text on a computer display. *Human Factors, 30*, 25-33.

Chen, H.-C., & Tsoi, K.-C. (1990). Symbol-word interference in Chinese and English. *Acta Psychologica, 75*, 123-138.

Cheng, C.M. (1982). Analysis of present day Mandarin. *Journal of Chinese*

Linguistics, *10*, 282-358.
Danks, J.H. (1986). Identifying component processes in text comprehension: Comment on Haberlandt and Graesser. *Journal of Experimental Psychology: General, 115*, 193-197.
Danks, J.H., Bohn, L., & Fears, R. (1983). Comprehension processes in oral reading. In G.B. Flores d'Arcais & R.J. Jarvella (Eds.), *The process of language understanding* (pp. 193-223). Chichester, Sussex: Wiley.
Danks, J.H., & Glucksberg, S. (1980). Experimental psycholinguistics. *Annual Review of Psychology, 31*, 391-417.
Danks, J.H., & Kurcz, I. (1984). A comparison of reading comprehension processes in Polish and English. *International Journal of Psychology, 19*, 245-269.
Ellis, A., & Beattie, G. (1986). *The psychology of language and communication.* London: Weidenfeld & Nicolson.
Graesser, A.C., & Haberlandt, K.F. (1986). Research on component processes in reading: Reply to Danks. *Journal of Experimental Psychology: General, 115*, 198-200.
Graesser, A.C., & Riha, J.R. (1984). An application of multiple regression techniques to sentence reading times. In D.E. Kieras & M.A. Just (Eds.), *New methods in reading comprehension research* (pp. 183-219). Hillsdale, NJ: Erlbaum.
Haberlandt, K.F. (1984). Components of sentence and word reading times. In D.E. Kieras & M.A. Just (Eds.), *New methods in reading comprehension research* (pp. 219-251). Hillsdale, NJ: Erlbaum.
Haberlandt, K.F., & Graesser, A.C. (1985). Component processes in text comprehension and some of their interactions. *Journal of Experimental Psychology: General, 114*, 357-374.
Haberlandt, K.F., Graesser, A.C., & Schneider, N.J. (1989). Reading strategies of fast and slow readers. *Journal of Experimental Psychology: Learning, Memory, & Cognition, 15*, 815-823.
Haberlandt, K.F., Graesser, A., Schneider, N.J., & Kiely, J. (1986). Effects of task and new arguments on word reading times. *Journal of Memory and Language, 25*, 314-322.
Healy, A.F., & Drewnowski, A. (1983). Investigating the boundaries of reading units. *Journal of Experimental Psychology: Human Perception and Performance, 2*, 413-426.
Hong Kong Education Department. (1986). *Frequency count of Chinese words used in Hong Kong secondary school reading materials.* Hong Kong: Hong Kong Government Press.
Hoosain, R. (1991). *Psycholinguistic implications for linguistic relativity: A case study of Chinese.* Hillsdale, NJ: Erlbaum.
Hoosain, R. (this volume). Psychological reality of the word in Chinese.
Huang, S.F. (1978). Historical change of prepositions and emergence of SOV order. *Journal of Chinese Linguistics, 6*, 212-242.
Huey, E.B. (1968). *The psychology and pedagogy of reading.* Cambridge, MA: MIT Press. (Originally published, 1908.)
Hung, D.L., & Tzeng, O.J.L. (1981). Orthographic variations and visual information

processing. *Psychological Bulletin*, *90*, 377-414.
Juola, J.F., Ward, N., & McNamara, T. (1982). Visual search and reading of rapid, serial presentations of letter strings, words, and text. *Journal of Experimental Psychology: General*, *111*, 208-227.
Just, M.A., & Carpenter, P.A. (1980). A theory of reading: From eye fixation to comprehension. *Psychological Review*, *87*, 329-354.
Just, M.A., & Carpenter, P.A. (1987). *The psychology of reading and language comprehension*. Newton, MA: Allyn & Bacon.
Just, M.A., & Carpenter, P.A. (1984). Using eye fixations to study reading comprehension. In D.E. Kieras & M.A. Just (Eds.), *New methods in reading comprehension research* (pp. 152-182). Hillsdale, NJ: Erlbaum.
Just, M.A., Carpenter, P.A., & Woolley, J.D. (1982). Paradigms and processes in reading comprehension. *Journal of Experimental Psychology: General*, *111*, 228-238.
Kerlinger, F.N., & Pedhazur, E.J. (1973). *Multiple regression in behavioral research*. New York: Holt, Rinehart & Winston.
Kieras, D.E., & Just, M.A. (Eds.). (1984). *New methods in reading comprehension research*. Hillsdale, NJ: Erlbaum.
Kucera, H., & Francis, W.N. (1967). *Computational analysis of present-day American English*. Providence, RI: Brown University Press.
Li, C., & Thompson, S. (1981). *Mandarin Chinese: A functional reference grammar*. Berkeley, CA: University of California Press.
Li, P., Bates, E., Liu, H., & MacWhinney, B. (this volume). Cues as functional constraints on sentence processing in Chinese.
Liu, I.M., Chuang, C.J., & Wang, S.C. (1975). *Frequency count of 40,000 Chinese words*. Taipei, Taiwan: Lucky Books.
MacWhinney, B., & Bates, E. (Eds.). (1989). *The crosslinguistic study of sentence processing*. Cambridge: Cambridge University Press.
MacWhinney, B., Bates, E., & Kliegl, R. (1984). Cues validity and sentence interpretation in English, German and Italian. *Journal of Verbal Learning and Verbal Behavior*, *8*, 295-301.
Miao, X.C. (1981). Word order and semantic strategies in Chinese sentence comprehension. *International Journal of Psycholinguistics*, *8*, 109-122.
Mitchell, D.C. (1984). An evaluation of subject-paced reading tasks and other methods for investigating immediate processes in reading. In D.E. Kieras & M.A. Just (Eds.), *New methods in reading comprehension research* (pp. 69-89). Hillsdale, NJ: Erlbaum.
Mitchell, D.C., & Green, D.W. (1978). The effects of context and content on immediate processing in reading. *Quarterly Journal of Experimental Psychology*, *30*, 609-636.
O'Regan, J.K. (1979). Eye guidance in reading: Evidence for the linguistic control hypothesis. *Perception & Psychophysics*, *25*, 501-509.
Peng, D.L., Orchard, L.N., & Stern, J.A. (1983). Evaluation of eye movement variables of Chinese and American readers. *Pavlovian Journal of Biological Sciences*, *18*, 94-102.
Perfetti, C.A. (1985). *Reading ability*. New York: Oxford University Press.

Polkowska, A., Kurcz, I., & Danks, J.H. (1986). Verification of an interactive model of text comprehension. In I. Kurcz, G.W. Shugar, & J.H. Danks (Eds.), *Knowledge and language* (pp. 237-258). Amsterdam: Elsevier.

Pollatsek, A., & Rayner, K. (1982). Eye movement control in reading: The role of word boundaries. *Journal of Experimental Psychology: Human Perception and Performance, 8*, 817-833.

Rayner, K., & Pollatsek, A. (1981). Eye movement control in reading: Evidence for direct control. *Quarterly Journal of Experimental Psychology, 33A*, 351-373.

Rayner, K., & Pollatsek, A. (1989). *The psychology of reading*. Englewood Cliffs, NJ: Prentice Hall.

Shen, E. (1927). An analysis of eye movements in the reading of Chinese. *Journal of Experimental Psychology, 10*, 158-183.

Stern, J.A. (1978). Eye movements, reading, and cognition. In J.W. Senders, D.F. Fisher, & R.A. Monty (Eds.), *Eye movements and the higher psychological functions* (pp. 145-155). Hillsdale, NJ: Erlbaum.

Sun, F., Morita, M., & Stark, L.W. (1985). Comparative patterns of reading eye movement in Chinese and English. *Perception & Psychophysics, 37*, 502-506.

Tang, T.C. (1988). *Studies on Chinese morphology and syntax*. Taipei, Taiwan: Student Book Co.

Taylor, S.E. (1965). Eye movements in reading: Facts and fallacies. *American Educational Research Journal, 2*, 187-202.

Taylor, I., & Taylor, M.M. (1990). *Psycholinguistics*. Englewood Cliffs, NJ: Prentice Hall.

Van Dijk, T.A., & Kintsch, W. (1983). *Strategies of discourse comprehension*. Orlando, FL: Academic Press.

Wang, W.S.Y. (1973). The Chinese language. *Scientific American, 228*, 50-60.

Cues as Functional Constraints on Sentence Processing in Chinese

Ping Li, Elizabeth Bates, Hua Liu
University of California, San Diego

Brian MacWhinney
Carnegie Mellon University

The language-specific properties of Chinese provide a unique testground for theories in sentence processing. This chapter examines the psycholinguistic mechanisms underlying Chinese sentence comprehension processes with results from two experiments. First, an off-line experiment was designed to investigate how Chinese speakers use word order and animacy cues in processing simple sentences. The results are largely compatible with previous studies in that Chinese speakers rely more on animacy than on word order. Second, an on-line experiment was designed to tap into the role of word order, animacy, the object marker BA, and the passive marker BEI in real-time processing of Chinese sentences. Consistent with the results from the off-line experiment, this experiment shows that different cues play different roles in the interpretation process, but they interact with each other as a function of competition and convergence that correspond to the patterns of cue use in the language. These studies also provide clues to the dynamic properties of sentence processing in general.

Crosslinguistic methods have in recent years become very important in the field of language acquisition and language processing. Because of the diversity of the world's languages with respect to their specific linguistic properties, comparison across languages allows researchers to disentangle variables that are likely to be confounded in a single language. Crosslinguistic comparison also allows investigators to identify the role of specific variables that may not be transparent in a single language. However, most of the languages that have been well examined so far are the Indo-European languages, all of which have, to different degrees, some kinds of grammatical devices that mark number, gender, or case relations between nouns, or nouns and verbs. Chinese, in contrast to these languages, makes virtually no use of such morphological devices. There are no case markings, no agreement markings, and no tense suffixes. The impoverished system of grammatical morphology in Chinese thus provides a good opportunity for the study of language processing from a crosslinguistic perspective.

A large body of recent crosslinguistic studies have been carried out within a research paradigm called the Competition Model (Bates & MacWhinney, 1982, 1989; Bates, McNew, MacWhinney, Devescovi, & Smith, 1982; MacWhinney, 1987). This model is an interactive activation model of language comprehension and language use, in which the cue validity or the information value of linguistic forms in a given language plays a probabilistic role in the process of mapping between surface forms and underlying functions. The surface forms that can be used to assign meaning include grammatical devices and semantic cues. The underlying functions that can be extracted from these surface cues include categories like agent and topic. The strength of the connection between forms and functions vary from language to language. A cue, in this context, is a particular piece of information for the speaker or listener to identify the functions of linguistic forms.

The major predictive construct in the Competition Model is cue validity, which is evaluated as the product of a cue's availability (how often the cue is available) and its reliability (when the cue is available, how often it leads to the right answer) in a given language. Cue validity serves as the primary determinant of cue strength, i.e., the weights that speakers assign to different cues in real-time sentence processing. For example, word order has a higher cue validity in English than animacy or morphology, while the reverse is true in Italian. Thus English speakers rely more on word order while Italian speakers rely more on animacy and morphology in sentence interpretation.

Different cues cooperate and compete with each other in the comprehension process. If two or more cues point to the same interpretation, their strengths are combined, leading to a greater activation of that interpretation than the activation produced by a single cue acting alone. If the cues disagree, the interpretation with the highest activation is chosen.

In contrast to most nativist models of language processing, the Competition Model emphasizes linguistic variation rather than linguistic universals in explaining language behaviors. Because this model was formulated from the beginning as a crosslinguistic model, it has been applied in studies of a wide range of languages, including Dutch, English, French, German, Hebrew, Hindi, Hungarian, Italian, Japanese, Serbo-Croatian, Turkish, and Warlpiri (see MacWhinney & Bates, 1989 for representative works). However, it has not been applied systematically to the study of Chinese, a major Sino-Tibetan language spoken by a fifth of the world's population. The goal of this study is to examine the basic principles of the Competition Model in Chinese. We are interested in the question of how Chinese speakers, in the absence of grammatical morphology, make use of other types of cues, and how these cues interact in determining Chinese speakers' performance in real-time sentence processing.

Most previous studies within this framework have adopted a sentence comprehension task in which native speakers of different languages are presented with simple sentences that contain two nouns and one transitive verb, and are asked to identify the agent of the sentence, i.e., the performer of the action described in the sentence. In these studies, competing and converging combination of surface cues are often incorporated into sentence stimuli. For example, in the English sentence *The cow is hitting the ball*, there are three cues: (1) the pre-verbal position of the first noun (which is usually the agent in English); (2) agreement between the first noun and the main verb in person and number; (3) a contrast in animacy between the first and the second noun (first noun animate, second noun inanimate). All three cues converge to indicate *the cow* as the agent of the sentence. In contrast, in the sentence *The pencils is kissing the elephant*, the word order cue which promotes *the pencils* as the agent competes with the agreement and the animacy cues which promote *the elephant* as the agent. Performance on these sentences with converging and competing cues would provide us with information on the processing strategies that native speakers adopt in sentence interpretation.

There are only a few studies that have adopted this paradigm to investigate some aspects of Chinese sentence processing. Miao (1981) and

Miao, Chen, and Ying (1986) studied the role of word order and animacy in interpreting simple Chinese sentences. In the first study, Miao found that native Chinese speakers relied more on noun animacy than on word order in determining the agent of a sentence. In fact, the main effect of word order did not even reach statistical significance. There was only a slight tendency for subjects to choose the first noun as the agent in NVN (Noun-Verb-Noun) sentences, i.e., to interpret NVN as SVO. This was a surprising finding, since in traditional grammars word order was considered to be almost the only syntactic device in Chinese (cf. Chao, 1968). In the second study, using the same procedure as in the first one, Miao et al. still found that animacy was a stronger cue than word order. However, this time the main effect of word order was significant. For NVN sentences, adult subjects (the study also involved children) chose the first noun as agent 77.5% of the time, as compared with 51.4% for NNV (Noun-Noun--Verb) and 40% for VNN (Verb-Noun-Noun) sentences. They also found that there was an interaction between word order and noun animacy. When these two cues agree with each other, e.g., in AVI sentences (first noun animate, second noun inanimate), interpretation was uniform across subjects (100% first noun choice), and when these two cues conflict, e.g., in IVA sentences (first noun inanimate, second noun animate), subjects depended more on animacy (35.8% first noun choice). These authors claimed that results from the second study should be regarded as more reliable since there were 20 subjects in the second study and only 8 in the first.

In a study of sentence interpretation in Chinese aphasia, Chen, Tzeng, and Bates (1990) looked at both aphasic patients and normal controls. They found that both normal controls and aphasic patients were sensitive to animacy and word order cues in processing simple NNV, NVN, and VNN sentences. Consistent with Miao's studies, their results indicate that the effect of animacy was much stronger than that of word order. There was also a significant interaction between animacy and word order. However, the aphasic patients were not significantly different from the normal controls in their performance on these sentences. The only difference was a small overall tendency for a few aphasic patients to choose the first noun as agent. Their results thus demonstrate that aphasic patients, in spite of focal brain injury, preserve the basic processing strategies of their native language.

So far, these studies have concentrated on two types of cues, word order and animacy, and their conclusions were drawn from results of off-line experiments. Our study reported in this chapter will, in addition to word order and animacy cues, examine a number of other cues. Moreover, we will use both off-line and on-line techniques to tap into issues of real-time sentence processing. We shall see that the on-line method will, on the one hand, complement what has been found in off-line experiments, and on the other, reveal some new dynamic aspects of cues as functional constraints on sentence processing.

Before reporting our experimental results in detail, let us look at some facts about the Chinese language. In particular, we want to examine some of the syntactic and semantic properties of the major cues to Chinese sentence processing.

An Analysis of Four Cues in Chinese

In the absence of inflectional morphology, Chinese makes use of a number of devices in indicating sentence roles between different constituents. These devices include word order, animacy, free-standing morphemes such as the object marker *ba*, the passive marker *bei*, the locative preposition *zai*, the dative marker *gei*, and the aspect marker *-le* (For detailed discussions of some aspects of these morphemes, see Li & Thompson, 1981; Li, 1990). In the following, we will briefly discuss four cues in Chinese that will be examined in our experiments: word order, the object marker *ba*, the passive marker *bei*, and animacy.

According to traditional grammars, word order is the primary syntactic device in Chinese. This is not only true on sentential level, but also true on phrasal level (see Chao, 1968; Tai, 1985; Li, 1989 for discussions of head modifier relations and the ordering of temporal and locative prepositional phrases). The basic word order in Chinese is SVO (Sun & Givón, 1985).[1] However, there are some word order variations. Three other word orders, OSV, SOV, and OVS are available in the spoken language, although they are marked in a number of ways. The basic SVO sentences are neutral in meaning with respect to the status of both the subject and the object. In contrast, OSV and SOV sentences place special emphasis on the object. In OSV, the object is the topic of the sentence. It is assumed to involve information that is given to both the speaker and the hearer. In SOV, the object is definite and is usually preceded by the object marker *ba*. SOV sentences with *ba* are semantically associated with highly transitive, resultative events (Li, 1990); those without *ba* are pragmatically restricted to situations in which the speaker provides information counter to the expectation of the hearer (Li & Thompson, 1981). This second type of SOV is particularly marked: given a simple NNV string with no *ba* marking, it is more likely to be OSV than SOV in Chinese. Finally, VOS sentences are only possible if S is an afterthought, as in *kan -le nabu dianying, tamen* (see -LE that movie, they) (see Lu, 1980 for a detailed discussion).

To illustrate the word order variations discussed above, let us look at the following examples:

(1) *Zhangsan mai -le yi ben shu.* (SVO)
 Zhangsan sold a book.

(2) *Shu Zhangsan mai -le.* (OSV)
 Book Zhangsan sold.

(3) *Zhangsan (ba) shu mai -le.* (SOV)
 Zhangsan (BA) book sold.

(4) *Mai -le shu, Zhangsan.* (VOS)
 Sold book, Zhangsan.

The existence of SOV sentences indicates that the pre-verbal position is not particularly associated with a fixed function in Chinese. It contrasts with the post-verbal position in which only the object of the sentence can occur. Thus, the way in which word order cues are configured in Chinese is almost the opposite of the way they are configured in English. In English, it is pre-verbal positioning which is the single most reliable cue to sentence interpretation (MacWhinney & Bates, 1989). Postverbal positioning is a useful cue to the identification of the object, but not nearly as strong as the pre-verbal cue to the identification of the subject. Furthermore, the subject can often be omitted in Chinese when the context is clear, frequently resulting in simple VO and (less often) OV sequences. Subject omission also reduces the reliability of the pre-verbal position as a cue to the subject in Chinese. Omission is common in Chinese. Not only the subject, but also other constituents of the sentence can frequently be omitted, as long as the context provides clues as to who does what to whom. In general, omission reduces the reliability of word order cues.

As mentioned above, the object marker *ba* is associated with SOV sentences. It cannot be used in the basic SVO sequence. Although the original meaning of *ba* as a verb ('take hold of', 'grasp') is very weak or nonexistent in modern Chinese, its trace can still be seen in that *ba* requires an object that is highly affected by the activity denoted by the verb. Traditional grammars have termed the *ba* construction "the disposal construction" (Wang, 1957), due to this property of the form. Two other features of *ba* have also been widely noted (Chao, 1968). First, the object noun phrase must be definite or specific; that is, indefinite noun phrases cannot normally occur following *ba*. Second, the verb phrase in these constructions must be structurally complex (Ding, 1961; Li, 1990). In particular, causative and resultative verbs (e.g., verb-complement structures like *da-po* ('hit-break')) are required in the *ba* construction. Developmental evidence indicates that children are sensitive to the properties of this morpheme and acquire its use at an early stage (Li, 1990, 1991; Chang, 1986).

The passive marker *bei* is another important device like *ba* in Chinese grammar. Although *bei* does not occur frequently in spoken language, it is extremely reliable as a cue to role assignment in that the noun phrase after it always indicates the agent of the sentence. On the surface, the *bei* construction is structurally similar to the *ba* construction (i.e., both appear in front of the second noun in an NNV string), but their functions in indicating sentence roles are different: *bei* marks an OSV structure while *ba* marks an SOV structure. However, they also share some features in common. For example, the *bei* as well as the *ba* construction requires the verb phrase to be highly transitive or to indicate a causative meaning, and structurally the verb phrase has to be complex, i.e., single monosyllabic verbs cannot occur alone in sentences with *bei* or *ba*.

There are at least two reasons why *bei* does not occur very often. First, Chinese often uses the topicalized object construction (OSV) to express the same meaning for which other languages would use a passive construction, e.g., *douzi xiaohai reng -le* (beans child throw -LE = the beans were thrown away by the child). Second, the *bei* construction in Chinese is traditionally associated with an adverse meaning. It is used when the speaker wants to indicate that something unfortunate or undesired has happened.[2]

Sentence roles are not determined solely by grammatical devices. It can also be influenced by the semantic properties of the noun phrase itself, such as animacy, i.e., whether a noun phrase indicates an animate (including human and animals) or an inanimate object.[3] Comrie (1981) discusses in detail the interrelations of animacy with other syntactic and semantic factors, e.g., number, gender, and case marking, showing that animacy is relevant and important to grammatical distinctions. As Corrigan (1988) has shown, many verbs expect to have an animate agent and an inanimate patient. If there is an animate-inanimate contrast involved in an action, it is usually the case that an animate agent is acting on an inanimate patient. These semantic biases for particular verbs hold across many languages (Gass, 1987) and should be available to Chinese speakers just as they are to speakers of other languages.

We have thus far discussed the importance of word order, animacy, *ba*, and *bei* in Chinese as a function of their validity in natural speech. In order to evaluate these different cues and their interaction patterns in Chinese sentence processing, we have carried out two experiments in which different cues were crossed over in different sentences, so that subjects had to rely on one or more competing or converging cues to identify the agent role. The first experiment was an attempt to replicate previous studies, in particular, Miao (1981) and Miao et al. (1986), using an off-line method (Liu, Bates, & Li, 1991). The second experiment was an attempt to tap into issues of dynamic processes of sentence interpretation, using an on-line technique (Li, MacWhinney, & Bates, 1991). In the second experiment, sentences and pictures were digitized for computer presentation and the subject's task was to press a button when he decided which of the two pictures indicates the agent of the sentence. On the basis of results from these experiments, we hope to be able to disentangle the role of individual cues and their interactions in the processing of Chinese sentences. In the following, we will report the major results from both experiments, first the off-line study, then the on-line study. For technical details of these studies, see Liu, Bates, & Li (1991) and Li, MacWhinney, & Bates (1991).

Experiment One: Off-line Sentence Interpretation

Method

Subjects. Eight native Mandarin Chinese speakers participated in this experiment (6 females and 2 males, age range 28 - 44). Six of these subjects were family dependents of Chinese graduate students who were studying at the University of California, San Diego; the other two were visiting scholars. All of them had been exposed to the English speaking environment for no more than half a year by the time of the beginning of the experiment, and had received little or no formal training in English when they were in mainland China. At the time of testing, all of them reported using Chinese almost all of the time while they were staying in the United States.

Materials. The two variables manipulated in this study were word order sequences (NVN, NNV, and VNN) and noun animacy (AA: both nouns animate; AI: first noun animate and second noun inanimate; IA: first noun inanimate and second noun animate). The crossing of the three levels of word order with the three levels of animacy yielded nine types of sentences: AAV, AIV, IAV, AVA, AVI, IVA, VAA, VAI, VIA. Each test sentence was generated by a random selection of two nouns and a verb from a pool of nouns and verbs (see Appendix 1 for a complete list of the nouns and verbs used in this experiment), appropriate to that particular sentence type. The nouns and verbs used in this and the following experiment are all familiar items to the subjects. There were six individual tokens for each of the nine types, resulting in a total of 54 test sentences. There were three versions of the test sentences. Each subject was randomly assigned one of the three versions for testing. Below are some examples of the test sentences:

AVA: *Xiaoma ti xiaoniu.*
Horse kick cow.

IAV: *Luobo daishu xi.*
Carrot kangaroo wash.

VAI: *Qiao nuhai chuanghu.*
Knock girl window

Procedure. Each subject was tested individually in a quite room. All the instructions and the test sentences were recorded by a native Chinese speaker before the test and then played back on a tape-recorder one sentence after another. There was a pause for subjects to give verbal responses after each sentence had been played. Subjects received the stimuli via an earphone.

The instructions were as follows (translated from Chinese), "In this experiment you will hear a series of short sentences in Chinese. Each sentence describes an action and there will be two objects involved in the action. One of the objects will be the actor of the action. Your task is to determine who is the actor, depending upon your understanding of the sentence. There are no right or wrong answers here, but we need you to listen carefully to each sentence."

Data analysis. In this kind of sentence interpretation experiment, the notion 'percent correct' is not meaningful. Thus we followed the scoring procedure adopted in other studies (see MacWhinney & Bates, 1989), to derive the dependent variable 'percent choice of the first noun as agent'. For each test sentence, subjects were given a score of 1 for choosing the first noun as the agent, a 0 for choosing the second noun. The values were summed for the six individual sentences belonging to the same sentence type and were then entered as the raw data for subsequent statistic analysis. In all text and figures reported below, these results have been converted to percentages. Hence a score close to 100% means that the first noun was reliably chosen as the agent, a score close to 0% means that the second

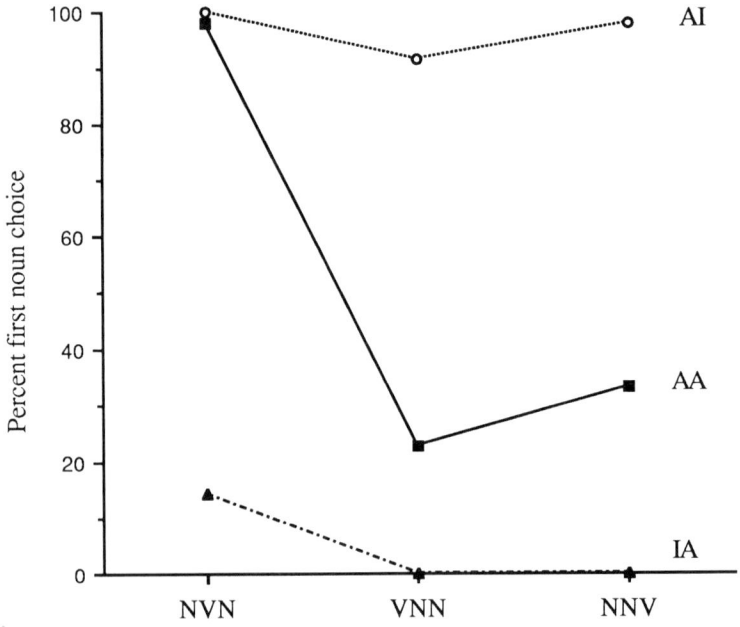

Figure 1. Choice responses in Experiment 1.

noun was reliably chosen as the agent, and scores in the 50% range indicate random performance.

Results

The results from this experiment are summarized in Figure 1. A 3 X 3 within-subject analysis of variance (i.e., with three levels of word order and three levels of animacy) indicates that there were both main effects of word order, $F(2,14) = 91.21$, $p < 0.001$, and animacy, $F(2,14) = 15.68$, $p < 0.001$, and there was also a significant interaction between the two, $F(4,28) = 18.27$, $p < 0.001$.

It should be clear from Figure 1 that these native speakers of Chinese relied primarily on the animacy cue to interpret simple sentences. On the AI and IA items, where there was an animacy contrast, subjects chose almost exclusively in favor of the animate noun (96.5% first noun choice on AI, and 4.9% on IA), irrespective of the order differences. On the AA items, where there was no animacy contrast, subjects showed a strong tendency to choose the first noun in NVN (97.9%, an SVO strategy), and somewhat weaker tendency to choose the second noun in VNN (22.9%, a VOS strategy) and NNV (33.3%, an OSV strategy). These word order strategies are stronger than the ones reported by Miao (1981, 1986) and Chen et al. (1990). In particular, the second noun strategy in the non-canonical word orders NNV and VNN was absent in Miao's and Chen's studies. However, they are consistent with results from our on-line sentence interpretation study (cf. Li et al., 1991). We will return to these similarities and differences later in the discussion.

A direct comparison of the strength of word order vs. animacy can be obtained by looking at the critical "competition cells", i.e. items in which word order and animacy lead to opposite conclusions. For example, in the cell IVA (where animacy must compete with canonical SVO word order), subjects chose the second noun 85% of the time. The same is true for the competition cells VAI and AIV, where animacy competes with the default VOS and OSV word order strategies. Here too, subjects chose in favor of animacy close to 100% of the time. It shows that animacy plays a predominant role as a cue to Chinese speakers' identification of sentence constituents.

Experiment Two: On-line Sentence Interpretation

The experiment discussed above used the traditional configurations of materials and procedures, and subjects' responses were measured in an off-line fashion after initial processing has been completed. The experiment only considered word order and animacy and did not take other important cues into account. To overcome the limit of the off-line experiment, we moved to on-line techniques in the second experiment, in which we could measure not only how often subjects choose a particular noun, but also how fast they do so as a function of cue use. In the following, we will discuss two kinds of results from the on-line experiment, choice responses and reaction times. As will be seen, these results are highly consistent with each other, and with results from the off-line experiment.

Method

Subjects. Twenty native adult Chinese speakers participated in this experiment (11 males and 9 females, age range 22 - 44). These subjects were either college students, visiting scholars, or their family dependents, and had been in the United States for no more than a year by the time of the testing. None of these subjects took part in Experiment One. Two subjects were dropped from the final analysis because their responses contained more than 10% missing values.

Materials. The experimental materials contained three sets of stimulus sentences: simple sentences, *ba* sentences, and *bei* sentences.[4] The simple sentences were structurally identical to the sentences used in the off-line experiment. The *ba* and *bei* sentences had the object marker *ba* and the passive marker *bei* in front of the second noun, respectively. Word order and animacy were also systematically varied in these sentences. Thus, the contribution of *ba* and *bei* as markers of sentence roles can be evaluated by comparing results from *ba* and *bei* sentences with those from simple sentences.

To match the number of sentences tested in the off-line experiment, we used 54 sentences for each of the three types of sentences, which resulted in a total of 162 sentences. Within each type, there were nine sub-types identical to those in the off-line experiment. Each sub-type represents an individual cell in which one level of word order is crossed with one level of animacy. There were six test sentences in each of these sub-types. All sentences were generated randomly by combining two nouns and a verb from a pool of lexical items (for a complete list of these items, see Appendix 2). A sample of the test sentences are presented below:

(1) Simple sentences

    AVI: *Xiaomao ti chuanghu.*
           Cat kick window.

    AIV: *Daishu putao zhai.*
           Kangaroo grapes pick.

    VIA: *Xi damen nanhai.*
           Wash door boy.

(2) *Ba* sentences

    A*ba*IV: *Xiaoya ba dashu reng-diao.*
            Duckling BA tree throw-away.

    AV*ba*I: *Houzi chi-diao ba xiangjiao.*
            Monkey eat-up BA banana.

    VI*ba*A: *Fang-zou fengzheng ba mianyang.*
            let-go kite BA sheep.

(3) *Bei* sentences

    I*bei*AV: *Qiqiu bei nuhai reng-diao.*
            Balloon BEI girl throw-away.

    AV*bei*I: *Xiaozhu yao-lan bei dashu.*
            Pig bite-mash BEI tree.

    VA*bei*I: *Da-po xiaogou bei pingguo.*
            Hit-break dog BEI apple.

The test sentences were first recorded on a high bias audio tape by a native Mandarin speaker and then digitized into the computer. All sentences were read in a smooth and flat intonation. Each sentence was matched with two pictures that represented the objects described in the sentence. Pictures were selected from Abbate and LaChappelle (1978, 1984). The pictures were digitized with an AST Turbo scanner and displayed on a high resolution RGB monitor.

Procedure. During the testing, subjects heard a sentence played back on a speaker, and simultaneously saw a pair of pictures corresponding to the two objects of the sentence on the computer screen. They were instructed to listen to the sentence and look at the pictures at the same time. The task was to determine which of the two objects did the action in each sentence. The subjects were asked to express their choices by pushing one of the two buttons on a button box as soon as possible.

The experiment was conducted in a dimly-lit room so that the subject could concentrate on the computer screen where the pictures were displayed. Each subject was tested individually. The experiment was run on a Macintosh IIsi model. The experimental program was configured so that the onset time of the pictures being displayed on the screen was the same as the onset time of the sentence being played on the speaker. The onset of each sentence started the button box timer for subjects' response times to that sentence. Each time after the subject pressed a button, the current pictures disappeared. There was then a two second silence with a blank screen before the next pair of pictures appeared and the next sentence began to play. Subjects were given a maximum of three seconds to respond after the sentence had been played. This amount of time was sufficient to allow full responses for most subjects under most of the conditions, while still putting some pressure on the response speed. Within each of the four types of sentence, the order of presentation was randomized for each subject. Subjects' responses, i.e., choice responses and reaction times, were recorded automatically by the program for later analyses.

At the beginning of the testing, each subject had a warm-up session in which he or she practised with ten sentences similar to the test sentences. Simple sentences were tested first, and then *ba* sentences, and then *bei* sentences. This was to ensure that performance on sentences with markers would not influence performance on simple sentences without any markers. Subjects were given a five minute break after the testing of each type of sentences.

Results

Simple sentences. Figure 2 presents the choice responses for the simple sentences, averaged across 18 subjects. Analysis of variance on the raw data showed a significant main effect of animacy, $F(2,34) = 75.54$, $p < 0.001$. Collapsed over word order types, subjects chose the animate noun as the agent 85% of the time on AI items and 88% of the time on IA items. This animacy effect accounts for 72% of the experimental variance. There was also a significant main effect of word order, $F(2, 34) = 21.61$, $p < 0.001$. When there was no animacy contrast, i.e., on the AA items, subjects chose the first noun in NVN 87% of the time, 34% in NNV, and 25% in VNN. This reflects a first noun strategy in the canonical order NVN, and a second noun strategy in the non-canonical orders NNV and VNN. However, as compared with the main effect of animacy, the word order effect is smaller, accounting for only 23% of the experimental variance. Finally, the word order by animacy interaction was also strongly significant, $F(4,68) = 11.46, p < 0.001$.

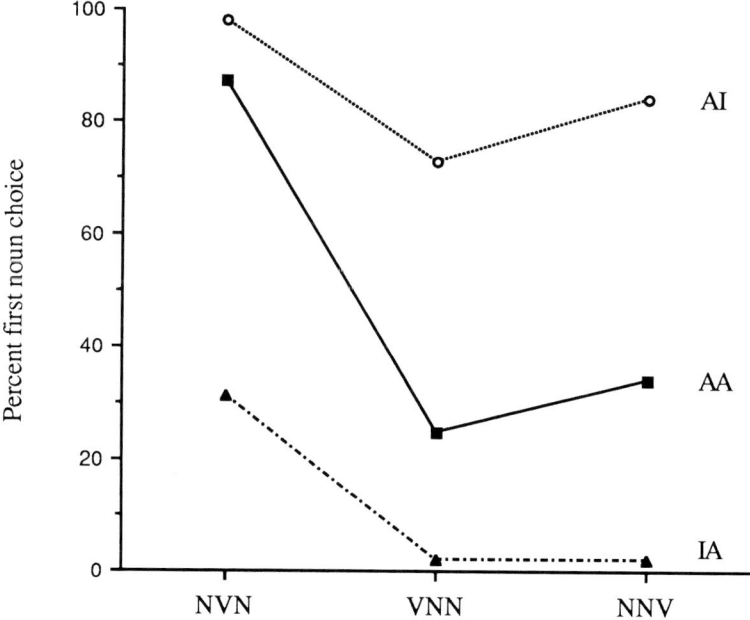

Figure 2. Choice responses for the simple sentences in Experiment 2.

These results are highly compatible with those from the off-line experiment. In both cases, animacy was the dominant cue, and word order interacted with animacy. Comparing Figures 1 and 2, we can see that there was only a slightly stronger word order effect in the on-line experiment. For example, subjects chose the first noun in VAI sentences 91% of the time in Experiment One, but only 73% of the time in this experiment.

The reaction time data, averaged across 18 subjects, are summarized in Figure 3. RTs in this and the remaining graphs represent the response times in milliseconds from the beginning of the sentence to the point where the subject pressed the button for his choice decision.

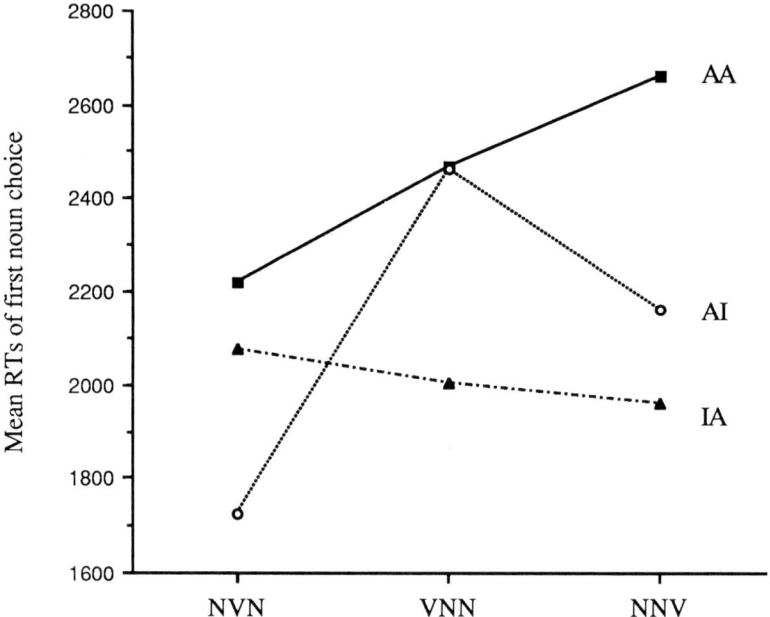

Figure 3. Reaction times for the simple sentences in Experiment 2.

Consistent with the choice response data, the main effects of animacy and word order and the interaction effect between the two all reached significant level ($p < 0.001$). In general, subjects were faster when the animacy cue was present (AI and IA items) than when there was no animacy contrast (AA items). When the animacy cue and the word order cue agree with each other, sentence processing was facilitated and subjects' response speed was faster. For example, the mean reaction time for AVI (mean = 1724 ms) was faster than that for any other type of sentences, because both cues agree with the SVO configuration, thus promoting a first noun choice. In contrast, when the two cues conflict with each other, sentence processing was inhibited and subjects' response speed was slower. The IVA sentences, in which word order promotes first noun while animacy promotes the second noun as agent, produced significant slower reaction times (mean = 2077 ms) as compared with AVI. In the non-canonical order VNN, VIA elicited much faster RTs (mean = 2002 ms) than VAI sentences (mean = 2462 ms). This may reflect the fact that VOS is a possible string in Chinese, while VSO is not: only the object can occur at the post-verbal position. In NNV, subjects were slower with AIV (mean = 2162 ms) than with IAV (mean = 1958 ms), which probably reflects the fact that in adult Chinese OSV is more common than SOV for simple NNV strings.

BA sentences. Turning to the results with the *ba* sentences, we found that in general, the presence of the *ba* marker did not change the underlying pattern that was seen in the simple sentences. In a combined analysis incorporating data from both the simple sentences and the *ba*

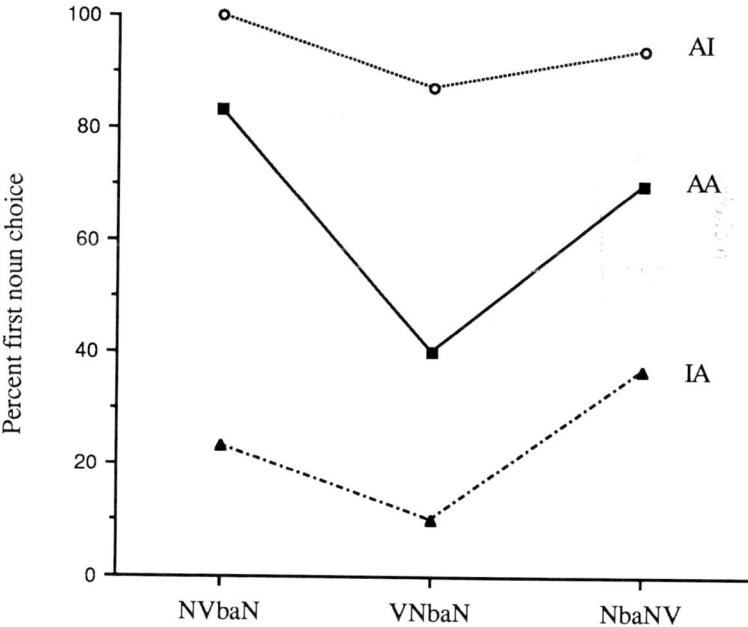

Figure 4. Choice responses for the BA sentences in Experiment 2.

sentences, animacy is still the dominant cue and the shape of its significant main effect ($F(2,34) = 115.75, p < 0.001$) is similar across sentences with and without *ba*. The significant interaction between word order and animacy ($F(4,68) = 15.80, p < 0.001$) also has the same shape as in the results of the simple sentences without *ba*. Figure 4 illustrates the results from subjects' choice responses to the *ba* sentences.

The contribution of *ba* marking was mainly shown in the non-canonical orders, but not in the canonical order NVN. The presence of *ba* had its effect most clearly on the NNV word order, since this is the only order in which *ba* occurs naturally in the language. In the combined analysis, there was a significant main effect of *ba* marking in that the presence of *ba* tended to lead to a higher level of first noun choice. This effect can be clearly seen by comparing A*ba*AV with AAV sentences. In AAV, subjects chose the first noun only 34% of the time, whereas in A*ba*AV, they chose the first noun 70% of time. This difference accounts for much of the effect of *ba* marking. However, counter to expectation, the presence of *ba* did not elevate the first noun choice to an even higher level. According to traditional grammars, the *ba* construction is exclusively associated with the SOV structure.

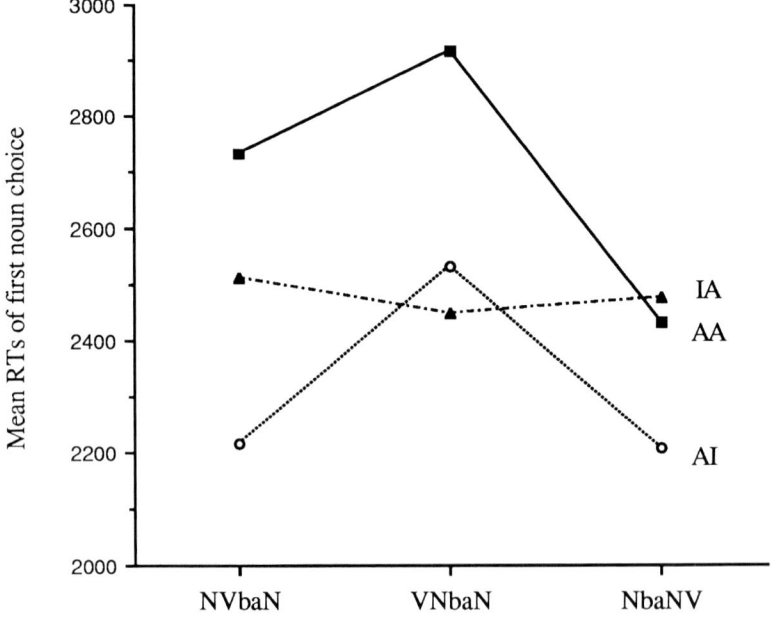

Figure 5. Reaction times for the BA sentences in Experiment 2.

An inspection of the reaction time data for the *ba* sentences shows that subjects' response speed was highly consistent with their choice responses. In addition, these RTs revealed facts about on-line competition and convergence that were not apparent in the choice data. Figure 5 presents the RT results from subjects' performance on the *ba* sentences.

As can be seen from Figure 5, A*ba*IV and AV*ba*I elicited fastest response times of all sentence types (mean = 2209 ms, and mean = 2217 ms, respectively) because both animacy and *ba* marking point to the first noun as agent in these sentences.

A comparison with the results from simple sentences indicates that for NVN sentences, the basic pattern of response speed is the same whether *ba* was present or absent. This similarity is entirely consistent with the choice response data in which the presence or absence of *ba* did not make a difference to subjects' performance on NVN sequences. However, in the non-canonical VNN sentences, the presence of *ba* produced a facilitation of response speed from VA*ba*A (mean = 2915 ms) to VA*ba*I (mean = 2531 ms); the convergence of animacy and *ba* marking was enough to overwhelm the word order cue in VA*ba*I. In contrast, when the *ba* marker was absent (cf. Figure 3), there was no facilitation from VAA (mean = 2470 ms) to

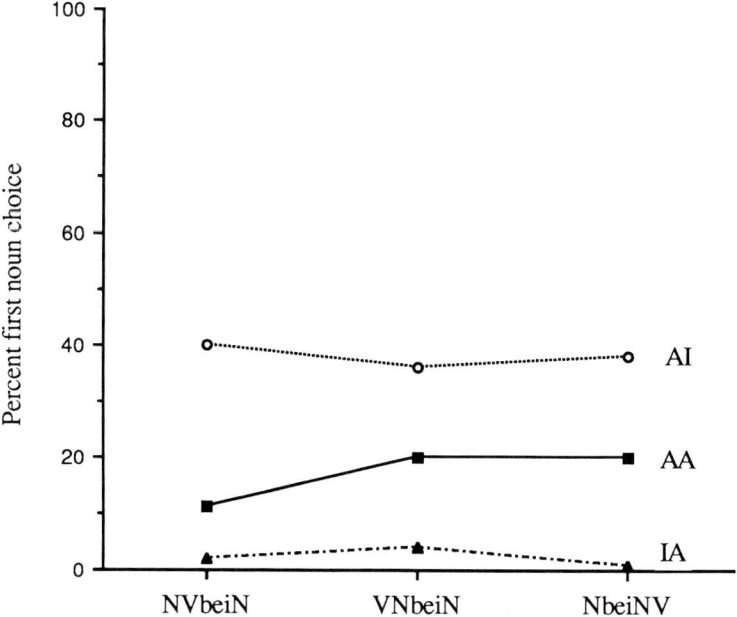

Figure 6. Choice responses for the BEI sentences in Experiment 2.

VAI (mean = 2462 ms), indicating that both kinds of simple VNN strings were equally difficult for subjects to process, given that the animate noun occurs at the post-verbal position.

BEI sentences. The results with the *bei* sentences are summarized in Figure 6. As can be seen, unlike the object marker *ba*, the passive marker *bei* was clearly dominant over all other cues in sentence interpretation. Subjects chose the second noun predominantly for all different conditions of word order and animacy, although animacy still has a strong effect, $F(2,34) = 12.80$, $p < 0.001$. There was no main effect of word order, $F(2,34) = 1.51$, $p > 0.05$. The interaction between word order and animacy was barely significant, $F(4,68) = 2.89$, $p < 0.05$.

These results indicate that native Chinese speakers rely on the passive marker almost exclusively and ignore other cues whenever *bei* is present. In other words, *bei* wins over word order and animacy when these cues are set into competition. However, we can still see a small effect of animacy in these data. On the AI items, first noun choice was pushed to about 40% for different orders.

In the RT data (Figure 7), although there are main effects of both word order, $F(2,34) = 5.87$, $p < 0.01$, and animacy, $F(2,34) = 7.99$,

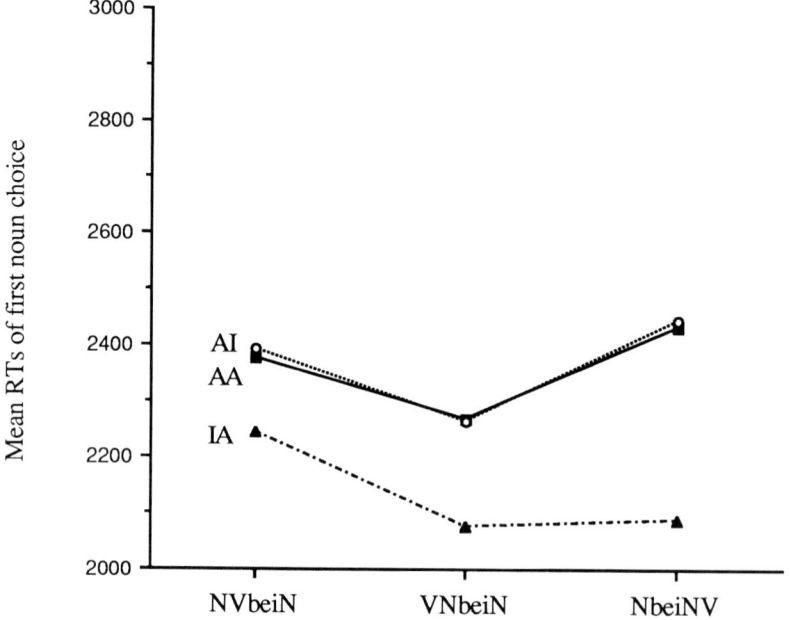

Figure 7. Reaction times for the BEI sentences in Experiment 2.

$p < 0.01$, the differences between different word orders are small (in a given animacy condition, all differences were within 200 milliseconds), and of less interest. The effect of animacy is shown by comparing IA with AA or AI conditions. In the IA condition, response times were faster by about 150 milliseconds for NV*bei*N, 200 ms for VN*bei*N, and 250 ms for N*bei*NV sentences. These facilitations are compatible with the fact that in Chinese *bei* is followed by the agent and preceded by the patient. IA sentences produced the fastest responses among the different animacy conditions because animacy converges with *bei* marking in promoting the second noun as agent in these sentences.

Discussion

The main results from our off-line and on-line experiments on simple sentences are highly consistent with each other. We found a strong main effect of animacy, a reliable word order effect, and an interaction effect between animacy and word order. In both studies, animacy was shown to win over word order when the two were set into competition. These results are also compatible with Miao (1981), Miao et al. (1986), and Chen et al. (1990). Furthermore, it was shown that the passive marker *bei* plays a dominant role in Chinese sentence processing whenever it occurs. The object marker *ba* is less as important as *bei* to the assignment of sentence roles, but its presence also strongly promotes the first noun as agent in sentences with non-canonical word orders, in particular, the NNV sentences. Overall the hierarchy of cue strength we found in these experiments was: passive marker > animacy > word order > object marker. Because the passive marker *bei* is rare in informal speech, overall, it is noun animacy that is the most valid cue in Chinese sentence processing.

As previous crosslinguistic studies of sentence processing have shown, the types and functions of cues vary across different languages and accordingly determine the processing strategies by speakers of different languages. Results from our two experiments further confirm these predictions. Studies in English (Bates & MacWhinney, 1982; Bates et al., 1982) have indicated that word order is the most important cue to English speakers in the assignment of sentence roles. Although our results have also shown that Chinese speakers rely on word order in addition to other cues, the word order pattern is not the same in these two languages. English speakers exclusively depend on word order cues whenever there is a competition between word order and animacy. In contrast, Chinese speakers rely more heavily on animacy than on word order when conflict between the two occurs. Moreover, English speakers tend to rely on the pre-verbal position as a cue to the subject of the sentence (an SV strategy) while Chinese speakers rely on the post-verbal position as a cue to the object of the sentence (a VO strategy), since the post-verbal position in Chinese is a better predictor of the object than the pre-verbal position as a predictor of the subject (see earlier discussion on Chinese).

Although our results are largely compatible with Miao (1981), Miao et al. (1986), and Chen et al. (1990), there are some discrepancies. In particular, subjects in our study showed a second noun strategy in the non-canonical VNN and NNV orders, while this processing strategy was absent in Miao's studies. The reason for this difference is so far unclear. However, we would like to argue that this second noun strategy fits in well with the fact of word order patterns in adult Chinese. The strong post-verbal cue as an indicator of the object clearly promotes a VOS interpretation for VNN strings, while the more frequent use of OSV over the marked SOV in simple sentences (see earlier discussion) tend to lead the subject to interpret the second noun in NNV as the agent.

The role of the *ba* and *bei* markers as functional cues in adult sentence interpretation has not been well examined in previous studies. Although our main results are clear in showing that these cues are important to sentence processing in Chinese, our on-line experiment has revealed a surprising finding which was not expected: contrary to expectation, the object marker *ba* did not serve as a strong cue to the identification of patient, in contrast to the passive marker *bei* which played a predominant role in marking the agent role. The first noun choice in A*ba*AV sentences reached only 70% of the time. However, a detailed analysis of the adult language suggests that this discrepancy may have well stemmed from the differences between *ba* and *bei* with respect to their functions. First, *ba* functions to mark the pre-verbal object in an SOV sentence. Unlike morphological markings of the accusative in inflectional languages, it does not mark the object in post-verbal positions. Second, grammatical analysis has identified the *ba* construction as conveying a highly transitive or causative meaning, due to the original meaning of the verb *ba* (cf. Sun, 1991). Third, *ba* marks a definite rather than an indefinite object. These syntactic, semantic, and pragmatic constraints on *ba* would probably reduce the validity of *ba* as a pure object marker, and accordingly, *ba* is less prominent to speakers as an indicator of sentence roles.

Bei, unlike *ba*, is not particularly associated with definiteness, and thus carries a more uniform function. Furthermore, the fact that simple NNV strings without any marker are more strongly associated with an OSV than with an SOV interpretation could have influenced our results since both *ba* and *bei* appear in NNV strings. *Ba* indicates an SOV structure while *bei* indicates an OSV structure. The higher probability of NNV as OSV rather than SOV shows that there is a conspiracy between the more frequent OSV and the passive marker *bei*, whereas there is a competition between the OSV and the object marker *ba*. Given that word order is an important cue and that the NNV order is more compatible with *bei* than with *ba*, it comes as no surprise that subjects more uniformly chose the second noun in *bei* sentences than they chose the first noun in *ba* sentences.

Conclusion

The experimental results summarized in this chapter have systematically investigated four cues in Mandarin Chinese with respect to their functional roles in sentence processing: word order, animacy, the object marker *ba*, and the passive marker *bei*. Using both on-line and off-line methods, we have attempted to address the question of how sentence processing in Chinese, the language in which there is no explicit inflectional marking, is determined as a function of cue use. Our results are, in general, highly consistent with previous crosslinguistic work that has examined the predictions of the Competition Model. The results clearly argue for an interactive point of view in which cues differentially affect speakers' performance by means of competition and convergence. The results indicate that Chinese speakers, in the absence of inflectional morphology, make use of almost all possible cues and integrate them interactively in identifying the functional roles of different linguistic constituents. In a language like Chinese, speakers cannot rely only on one type of information, either because single pieces of information would not give unique answers to the processing task, or because some of them, such as the passive marker *bei*, although highly reliable, are not always available (*bei* is optional even for a sentence for which other languages would use a passive construction, see earlier discussion on Chinese).

In the discussion above we have pointed out that animacy is overall the most important cue to Chinese sentence processing. This result is consistent with the fact that Chinese is a context-oriented language in which speakers use "supra-syntactic" information, i.e., semantic and pragmatic information to determine who does what to whom. In contrast to many other languages, syntactic information has only a very limited range in Chinese (cf. Chao, 1968) and cannot possibly be the major functional determinant in Chinese sentence processing.

Although we have taken a crosslinguistic perspective in our study, we did not try to directly compare our results with results from other languages. Such comparisons would be most relevant in the context of bilingualism, where it is important to see how different patterns from different languages influence bilingual speakers' performance. In future studies, we plan to use both on-line and off-line techniques to study sentence interpretation and grammaticality judgment in Chinese-English bilingual speakers. Some pilot work is currently underway in our laboratory (Liu, Bates, & Li, 1991).

Acknowledgements

The research reported here was supported by the Human Frontier Science Program Organization. The construction of the experimental system was supported by a grant from NICHHD, and some of the expenses of data collection were provided by a grant from NIDCD. The authors wish to thank the granting organizations and the following institutions for their support: Center for Research in Language and Department of Cognitive Science, University of California, San Diego and the Department of Psychology, Carnegie Mellon University. We are grateful to Darius Clynes, Larry Juarez, Edward Yang, and Shuhong Zhu for their assistance to our experiments.

Notes

1. In a simple sentence like *the dog chases the cat*, the noun *dog* can be categorized as a subject, an agent, an initiator and so on, in contrast with the noun *cat* which can be viewed as an object, a patient, a theme, etc. As the distinctions between these categories are highly disputable in linguistics, we do not make a particular commitment here and would like to treat the difference between *dog* and *cat* as a contrast along any of these dimensions.

2. Both Wang (1957) and Chao (1968) have noted that in modern Chinese the adverse meaning is becoming weak because of the influence from massive translation works of Western science and literature in which passive constructions in Western languages were simply translated with the *bei* construction.
3. This cut-off is somewhat idealized since noun animacy may be a continuum on the human-animal-inanimate scale rather than a discrete phenomenon. As Comrie (1981) points out, some languages use finer distinctions while others use less fine distinctions.
4. In the original design we had included another set of sentences with the indefinite marker *yi*. Since these sentences constitute a completely separate piece of the design and the effect of the indefinite marker was not clear from the experiment, we will not report the results here. See Li, MacWhinney, and Bates (1991) for discussion of these results.

References

Abbate, M. & LaChappelle, N. (1978). *Pictures, please: a language supplement.* Communication Skill Builders, Inc.

Abbate, M. & LaChappelle, N. (1984). *Pictures, please: an articulation supplement.* Communication Skill Builders, Inc.

Bates, E., & MacWhinney, B. (1989). Functionalism and the competition model. In B. MacWhinney & E. Bates (eds.), *The crosslinguistic study of sentence processing.* Cambridge University Press.

Bates, E., & MacWhinney, B. (1982). Functionalist approaches to grammar. In Wanner, E., & Gleitman, L. (eds.), *Language acquisition: the state of art.* New York: Cambridge University Press.

Bates, E., McNew, S., MacWhinney, B., Devescovi, A., & Smith., S. (1982). Functional constrains on sentence processing: A cross-linguistic study. *Cognition, 11,* 245-299.

Chang, H-W. (1986). Young children's comprehension of the Chinese passives. In H. Gao & R. Hoosain (eds.), *Linguistics, psychology, and the Chinese language.* Center of Asian Studies, University of Hong Kong.

Chao, Y-R. (1968). *A grammar of spoken Chinese.* Berkeley: University of California Press.

Chen, S., Tzeng, O., & Bates, E. (1990). Sentence interpretation in Chinese aphasia. In *Proceedings of the tenth meeting of the second language research forum,* Department of Linguistics, University of Oregon, Eugene, Oregon.

Comrie, B. (1981). *Language universals and linguistic typology: syntax and morphology.* Oxford: Basil Blackwell.

Corrigan, R. (1988) Who dun it? The influence of actor-patient animacy and type of verb in the making of casual attributions. *Journal of Memory and Language, 27,* 447-463.

Ding, S-S. (1961). *Xiandai Hanyu yufa jianghua* (Lectures on Modern Chinese

Grammar). *Yuwen Huibian* (Collections in Linguistics), *17*, Beijing.
Gass, S. (1987). The resolution of conflicts among competing systems: A bidirectional perspective. *Applied Psycholinguistics, 8,* 329-350.
Li, C., & Thompson, S. (1981). *Mandarin Chinese: A functional reference grammar.* Berkeley: University of California Press.
Li, P. (1991). "Zai" and "ba" constructions in child Mandarin. CRL Newsletter, Vol.5, No.5, University of California, San Diego.
Li, P. (1990). *Aspect and aktionsart in child Mandarin.* Ph.D. dissertation, Leiden University, the Netherlands.
Li, P. (1989). *What cues can Chinese speakers use in sentence processing?* Paper presented at the Workshop on Crosslinguistic Study of Sentence Processing, Dept. of Psychology, Carnegie Mellon University, Pittsburgh, July.
Li, P., MacWhinney, B., Bates, E. (1991). *Processing a language without inflections: An on-line study of sentence processing in Chinese.* CRL Technical Report, 9102. Center for Research in Language, University of California, San Diego.
Liu, H., Bates, E., & Li, P. (1991). *Sentence interpretation strategies and grammaticality judgments in bilingual Chinese-English speakers.* Manuscript, University of California, San Diego.
Lu, J-M. (1980). Hanyu kouyu jufa-li -de yiwei xianxiang (On reversed sentence patterns in spoken Chinese), *Zhongguo Yuwen* (The Chinese Language), *1,* 28-41.
MacWhinney, B. (1987). The Competition Model. In B. MacWhinney (ed.), *Mechanisms of language acquisition.* Hillsdale, NJ: Erlbaum.
MacWhinney, B., & Bates, E. (eds.). (1989). *The crosslinguistic study of sentence processing.* Cambridge University Press.
Miao, X-C. (1981). Word order and semantic strategies in Chinese sentence comprehension. *International Journal of Psycholinguistics, 8,* 109-122.
Miao, X-C., Chen, G., & Ying, H. (1986). Sentence comprehension in Chinese. In M. Zhu (ed.), *Studies in child language development.* Shanghai: East China Normal University Press.
Sun, C-F. (1991). *Transitivity and the "ba" construction.* Paper presented at the 3rd North American Conference on Chinese Linguistics, Cornell University, Ithaca, May.
Sun, C-F., & Givón, T. (1985). On the so-called SOV word order in Mandarin Chinese: a quantified text study and its implications. *Language, 61,* 329-351.
Tai, J. (1985). Temporal sequence and Chinese word order. In J. Haiman (ed.), *Iconicity in syntax, typological studies in language.* Vol.6. Amsterdam: J. Benjamins.
Wang, L. (1957). *Zhongguo xiandai yufa* (Modern Chinese grammar). Shanghai: Zhonghua Book Co.

Appendix 1

Nouns and Verbs Used in Experiment One.

A. Nouns

1. Animate nouns:

   daxiang (elephant), *daishu* (kangaroo), *gongji* (cock), *gouxiong* (bear), *houzi* (monkey), *mama* (mother), *mianyang* (sheep), *nanhai* (boy), *xiaohai* (child), *nuhai* (girl), *xiaogou* (dog), *xiaoma* (horse), *xiaomao* (cat), *xiaoniu* (cow), *xiaotu* (rabbit), *xiaozhu* (pig);

2. Inanimate nouns:

   chuanghu (window), *fengzhen* (kite), *luobo* (radish), *pingguo* (apple), *qiqiu* (balloon), *xiangjiao* (banana), *yifu* (clothes), *yizi* (chair).

B. Verbs

   chi (eat), *da* (hit), *fang* (let go), *kan* (look), *qiao* (knock), *ti* (kick), *wan* (play), *xi* (wash), *zhai* (pluck), *zhui* (chase).

Appendix 2

Nouns and Verbs Used in Experiment Two.

A. Nouns

1. Animate nouns:

   chongzi (insect), *daxiang* (elephant), *daishu* (kangaroo), *gongji* (cock), *gouxiong* (bear), *houzi* (monkey), *hudie* (butterfly), *laoshu* (mouse), *mama* (mother), *mianyang* (sheep), *nanhai* (boy), *nuhai* (girl), *xiaogou* (dog), *xiaoma* (horse), *xiaomao* (cat), *xiaoniao* (bird), *xiaoniu* (cow), *xiaotu* (rabbit), *xiaoya* (duckling), *xiaozhu* (pig);

2. Inanimate nouns:

   beizi (cup), *chuanghu* (window), *damen* (door), *dashu* (tree), *fengzhen* (kite), *luobo* (radish), *pingguo* (apple), *putao* (grapes), *qiqiu* (balloon), *qingcai* (vegetable), *shitou* (stone), *xiangjiao* (banana), *yifu* (clothes), *yizi* (chair).

B. Verbs

1. Monosyllabic single verbs:

   chi (eat), *da* (hit), *fang* (let go), *gan* (drive), *kan* (look), *qiao* (knock), *ti* (kick), *wan* (play), *xi* (wash), *yao* (bite), *za* (smash), *zhai* (pluck), *zhua* (seize), *zhuang* (bump), *zhui* (chase);

2. Disyllabic complex verbs:

   chi-diao (eat-up), *da-bai* (hit-defeat), *da-lan* (hit-mash), *da-po* (hit-break), *fang-zou* (let-go), *gan-pao* (drive-go), *kan-jian* (look-see), *reng-diao* (throw-away), *ti-dao* (kick-down), *tui-kai* (push-open), *yao-lan* (bite-mash), *za-po* (smash-break), *zhua-zhu* (seize-stop).

Part IV

LANGUAGE ACQUISITION

Language Development in Chinese Children

Xiaochun Miao and Manshu Zhu
East China Normal University

This paper reviews the studies conducted by psychologists in mainland China on children's language development in the past decade. It consists mainly of four parts: children's phonological development, lexical development, syntactic development, and theories of language acquisition. Comparisons are made between the results of some of these studies and those of comparable studies conducted in other countries and districts. Finally, some brief comments are made on these studies.

Children's language development, having an important bearing on the development of cognition and socialization, is an essential aspect of psychological development. Since children's language acquisition is a major issue in psycholinguistics, knowledge of this process is conducive to the solution of some basic problems in psycholinguistics. Therefore, the process and mechanisms of children's language development are a common concern of many disciplines, including developmental psychology and general linguistics, as well as psycholinguistics. In the past three decades or so, a great deal of research has been done by scholars all over the world, especially in the United States, which has resulted in an abundance of findings and theoretical hypotheses.

Chinese is a very peculiar language. There are important differences between Chinese and other languages such as English, French, German, and

Russian. Besides, it is the most widely spoken language in the world. Therefore, the study of the language development (or language acquisition) of Chinese-speaking children is of special significance. A comparative study of our discoveries regarding the language development of Chinese-speaking children and the findings of scholars in other countries might reveal whether there are any similarities or dissimilarities between the acquisition of Chinese and that of other languages, and whether or not dissimilarities, if any, result from the differences in linguistic structures. In our view, a comprehensive and profound understanding of the laws of Chinese- speaking children's language development will be a great contribution to the understanding of the universality of language and language acquisition. It is for this reason that psychologists in mainland China[1] have conducted studies on some of the problems regarding children's language development since the end of the 1970s.[2] In what follows we give a brief survey of the studies conducted in the past decade.

Speech Sounds in Children

Wu and Xu (1979), Zhang and Zhu (1987), and Li (1991) observed and recorded pronunciations of several Chinese infants. Wu and Xu used Hanyu Pinyin in their analysis, and the others used the international phonetic symbols. Their observations of the Chinese infants' sounds were basically in agreement with each other.

According to these observations, the sounds pronounced by Chinese infants during their first four months are mostly monosyllables, with vowels, including monophthongs and diphthongs. These emerge first, followed by consonants when they are about three to four months old. These consonants, however, are normally pronounced in combination with vowels. Towards the end of this period, the infants' pronunciations seem to be similar to their mother-tongue syllables and intonation pattern. However, they do not seem to have grasped the skills of pronouncing any particular sound. Therefore, they are still unable to imitate adults' pronunciation, and the sounds which they pronounce are still devoid of meaning.

Starting from four months old, the infants enter the initial stage of babbling which lasts until they are about one year old. During this period they demonstrate a strong desire to communicate when they are babbling away at toys or the reflections of themselves in the mirror. Meanwhile, this period witnesses an enormous increase in the number of sounds which they are capable of pronouncing, including not only combinations of consonants and vowels but also single consonants and vowels. Besides monosyllables, they are also able to pronounce many dissyllables and multisyllables. According to Wu and Xu (1979), the first few dissyllables which infants utter are all repetitions of monosyllables, such as "mama" and "baba". It takes some time before they can pronounce combinations of different monosyllables, such as "ouma" and "bawa", etc. According to the research of Zhang and Zhu (1987), however, infants learn to pronounce both types of dissyllables at the same time. In any case, such sounds are very similar to some words in adults' speech and are the basis of children's first words.

In addition, infants at this stage begin to imitate the pronunciation of adults. In Zhang and Zhu's (1987) research, for example, seven and a half month old babies were able to pronounce "ma" in imitation of adults; one of Wu and Xu's (1979) eleven month old subjects could imitate the pronunciation of "ba ba". According to Wu and Xu's research, when the subjects are about one year old their near speech sounds increase sharply, and they can imitate the pronunciation of some adult speech sounds quite correctly, e.g."jie jie" (older sister), "mei mei" (younger sister), "mao mao" (cap), etc. Even their tones are very similar to those of adults, including the high and level tone in the first syllable and the neutral tone in the second. Such imitated sounds can be recalled after a lapse of several days. Also, children begin to associate certain syllables with particular things.

According to Li's research (1991), children's acquisition of vowels seems to follow this pattern: non-rounded vowels precede rounded vowels, blade vowels precede apical vowels, non-retroflex vowels precede retroflex vowels, and low vowels precede high vowels. This finding coincides with Zhang and Zhu's (1987) results. These researchers suggest that the order of vowel acquisition depends on two factors: (a) the openness and closeness of the oral cavity and (b) the shape of the lips. The sounds which are pronounced when both the oral cavity and the lips are in natural or near natural states are acquired earlier than others. As regards the order of consonant acquisition, there seems to be a back-front-middle tendency in terms of the position of articulation. The first consonants which the infants acquire are those pronounced with back parts of the articulator, such as the pharynx, larynx and uvula, e.g. /h/ and /k'/, etc. Next, bilabial consonants, such as /m/ and /p/, appear which will develop into labiodental consonants such as /v/ and apical consonants such as /l/, /t/, /n/. In terms of the methods of pronunciation, nasals, fricatives and unaspirated stops are generally acquired earlier than laterals, affricates, and aspirated stops.

The above mentioned observations regarding the order of Chinese children's phonetic development are on the whole in accordance with the results of research conducted in other countries. This may be due to the fact that children's phonetic development is mainly determined by their biological development, and the maturation of the organs of speech does not seem to vary with children of different nationalities.

In Jakobson's opinion (1968), although children learn to pronounce many sounds in the initial stage of their language learning, there is no regular pattern in the order of their emergence; children's babbling sounds are not subject to any restrictions and therefore have no relevance to their acquisition of adult speech sounds in later stages. This is obviously at variance with the results of our research. As mentioned above we found that there are certain regularities in the initial stage of children's speech sounds, and that there is a certain connection between the babbling sounds of babies and their first words. Before they learn such words as "ma ma", "pa pa", and "tia tia", for instance, similar sounds must have already emerged in the babbling stage.

Children's Lexical Development

Words are the building blocks of language. We normally use words as the basic units of semantic and syntactic analyses. Children's acquisition of words can be divided into the understanding of word meanings and the use of them. Some studies in China involve both of these aspects, while others only touch upon one of them.

Brief survey of the early stage of lexical development

Around age one, children begin to use their first words, which are mainly those denoting people, objects, and some actions (e.g. "mummy", "milk", "sock", and "bye bye") that are most easily accessible to them. In other words, the first words which children learn to use are nouns and verbs. Other parts of speech begin to find their way into children's language after they are one and a half years old. These include adjectives (e.g. big, small, red, bad), adverbs (e.g. also, all), pronouns (e.g. you, me), and more abstract numerals and conjunctions which are rarely used by children less than two years old.

According to the investigations of the Cooperation Study Group of Oral Speech of Preschool Children (1981), Wu and Zhu (1980), and Wu and Xu (1979), the speech of two year olds already encompasses most parts of speech, including nouns, verbs, adjectives, pronouns, numerals, adverbs, auxiliaries, prepositions, conjunctions, and interjections. According to Wu and Zhu's data, nouns and verbs constitute the majority (about 70%) of the words in the speech of two to four year old children. Similar results were found in the investigations conducted in Zhejiang Province. However, Wu and Xu's study indicates that these two parts of speech account for 70% of the words used by children one and a half years to two years old; the percentage decreases to 60.1% when they are two to two and a half years old and further drops to 51.8% with children two and a half to three years old. This seems to suggest that the growth of children is accompanied by a continuous increase in the proportional usage of other parts of speech. The differences in the results of different investigations may be attributed to error variances due to different samples used and districts where the investigations were conducted. They may also be due to different methods of data calculation (some investigators calculated the occurrences of words while others calculated the number of different words which appeared in children's speech).

As regards the ratio between content words and function words in the speech of two to six year old children, the former constitute the main part whereas the latter account for only about 10 - 20%. Interjections account for about half of the function words used by children two to two and a half years of age whereas conjunctions and prepositions are rather rare in their speech. It should be noted, however, that the proportion of interjections seems to decrease gradually with the growth of children, while that of conjunctions, prepositions, and adverbs increases slowly but steadily (The Cooperation Study Group of Oral Speech of Preschool Children, 1981). Due to the lack of statistics on the ratio between content words and function words, and on the proportions of nouns and verbs in adults' speech, the above mentioned results are hardly sufficient for a reliable appraisal of the distributional features of different parts of speech in Chinese children's speech.

The authors of these studies basically use adult criteria to analyze the word classes in children's utterances, though they occasionally consider the situation in which the children use the words. However a child's production of a word is not necessarily in accordance with its class specified in the dictionary. For example, a word that is a noun according to adult criteria, while children use it as a verb. Consequently, the results of the above mentioned studies may not describe the real picture of children's word classes.

Children's comprehension of temporal words

Zhu, Wu, Ying, Zhu and Zhuang (1982) conducted a special study on this problem. Their subjects were between two to eight years old. The children were asked to act with toys according to the experimenter's instructions. The instructions comprised three classes of temporal words: (1) those denoting sequence of time, such as "xian" (before), "hou" (after), "yiqian" (earlier), "yihou" (later), "tongshi" (at the same time), etc.; (2) those denoting different periods of time, such as "jintian" (today), "shangwu" (morning), "qunian" (last year), etc.; and (3) those denoting the tenses of actions, such as "zhenzai" (right now), "yijing" (already), "jiuyao" (will soon, be going to), etc. The following are examples of the instructions used in the study:

(a) Xiao wawa zai da wawa yiqian/yihou shangche.
(The little baby gets on the bus before/after the big baby.)
(b) Xiaoming cong jiali chulai, jiuyao dao xiaoqiao le.
(Xiaoming leaves home. He'll soon reach the small bridge.)

The results of this research indicate that, in general, children three to four years old can understand the meanings of "xian" (before), "hou" (after), and "tongshi" (at the same time), but most children are not able to understand "yiqian" (earlier) and "yihou" (later) until they are five years old. Children four to five years old can understand the meanings of "zuotian" (yesterday), "jintian" (today), and "mingtian" (tomorrow), but it is another year before they can understand words denoting parts of a day, such as "zaochen" (early morning) and "shangwu" (morning), and "xiawu" (afternoon). Words denoting longer periods of time, such as "jinnian" (this year), "qunian" (last year), and "mingnian" (next year) are not comprehensible to children until they are six years old. In other words, children's comprehension of temporal words starts from "jintian" (today), "zuotian" (yesterday), and "mingtian" (tomorrow), and then spreads to those denoting shorter and longer periods of time. As for words denoting tenses of actions, children learn "zhenzai" (right now) first at three to four years old, "yijing" (already) next at five years old, and finally "jiuyao" (will soon, be going to) at six years old. This shows that children's comprehension starts from the present point of time and then spreads to the past and the future. All this agrees with the results of studies conducted abroad (Beilin, 1975). In the mode of expression, Chinese is different from English and some other languages in that it uses a separate word or words in front of the verb to indicate the time of event described by the sentence, because Chinese verbs have no morphological inflexion. This seems to suggest that the above mentioned developmental sequence probably depends mainly on children's cognitive development. Since actions which are taking place are directly observable, "zhenzai" (right now) is therefore easily comprehensible. Past actions have been experienced and are thus still traceable; whereas future actions are rather elusive as they require prediction, therefore, "jiuyao" (will soon, be going to) is more difficult to comprehend than"yijing" (already).

Children's acquisition of spatial words

In Chinese there are altogether sixteen spatial words. Zhang (1985) and the Cooperation Study Group of Language Development (1986b) tested two to six year old children with the ten spatial words which are most commonly used, namely: "qian" (front), "hou" (back, rear, behind), "zuo" (left), "you" (right), "shang" (above, upper), "xia" (under, below, lower), "li" (in, inside), "wai" (out, outside), "zhongjian" (middle, center), and "pang" (side). First, the researchers tested the children's comprehension of these words by asking them to carry out instructions containing these words, such as:

(a) Ba wawa fangzai qiche li.
   (Put the doll in the car.)
(b) Ba xiaoshizi fangzai wawa de qianmian.
   (Put the little stone in front of the doll.)

Next, the experimenters placed objects at certain spatial locations or showed the children some objects at certain spatial locations, and then asked them to describe in spoken language these actions and the spatial locations of the objects. In this way they tested the children's ability to use these words. The results indicate that the order of the children's comprehension of these spatial words is: "li" (in, inside), "shang" (above, upper), "xia" (under, below, lower), "wai" (out, outside), "hou" (back, rear, behind), "zhongjian" (middle, center), "qian" (front), "pang" (side), "zuo" (left), "you" (right); the order of their production of these words is: "xia" (under, below, lower), "li" (in, inside), "shang" (above, upper), "hou" (back, rear, behind), "qian" (front),"wai" (out, outside), "zhong" (middle, center), "zuo" (left), "you" (right). These investigations show that in the comprehension and production of spatial words, children make the most obvious progress when they are three to four years old, and there is no noticeable difference between five year old children and six year old children. On the basis of these observations, the researchers divided children's acquisition of spatial words into two stages. The first stage is when they are two and three years old; the second stage is when they are four to six years old. As regards the relationship between comprehension and production, comprehension always precedes production. The younger the children are, the greater the time gap between comprehension and production, and the discrepancy between them decreases gradually as the children grow older.

The results of the above mentioned studies seem to agree with comparable studies abroad (Kuczaj and Maratsos 1975; Washington and Naremore 1978) in respect to the order and ages of children's acquisition of spatial words. For instance, both Chinese and non-Chinese children acquire "li" (in, inside) and "shang" (above, upper) first, and they begin to understand most spatial words at about the same age. However, there are also some disparities. H.Clark and E.Clark (1977) hypothesized that where there was a pair of words denoting two opposites, the positive word was acquired earlier than the negative word because the use of the negative word involves an additional negation rule. Contrary to this, the results of Zhang's (1985) research, like those of many others abroad, suggest that this may not be so in comprehension or production. The acquisition of "qian" (front), for example, may not precede that of "hou" (back, rear, behind). Therefore, H.Clark's hypothesis does not enjoy the full support of experimentation as it cannot interpret all the results of this research. In comparison, this problem seems to be better explained by E. Clark's hypothesis (1973b, 1980) that the order of lexical acquisition is jointly determined by the semantic complexity of words and non-linguistic strategies of children.

Children's acquisition of pronouns

Pronouns such as "zhe" (this), "na" (that), "wo" (I, me), and "ni" (second person singular 'you') do not have clear, denotive meanings in the sense that their referents change when the situation and the roles of the speaker and listener change. Thus, one and the same person is sometimes referred to as "wo" (I, me), sometimes referred to as "ni" (second person singular you) or "ta" (he/she). Similarly, one and the same object can be referred to either "zhege" (this) or "nage" (that), depending on the situation. The comprehension and production of these words require adjusting and shifting the reference by means of complicated intellectual operations.

Zhu, Cao, and Zhang (1986) studied how children three to seven years old comprehended the four demonstrative pronouns "zhe" (this), "na" (that), "zhebian" (this side, here), and "nabian" (that side, there). They designed three different situations. In the first situation, the children sat near the experimenter facing the model of a zoo. The experimenter then asked the children to carry out her instructions which contained demonstrative pronouns, such as: "ba tuzi fangdao dongwuyuan de nabian" (Put the rabbit on that side of the zoo). In the second situation, experimenters A and B sat face to face with the model of the zoo between them. The subject sat at a point that was equidistant from A and B. A gave B some instructions which B asked the subject to perform. In the third situation, the experimenter and subject sat face to face with each other, and the experimenter gave instructions for the subject to perform. They found that the children's performances were different in the three different situations. They performed most satisfactorily in the first situation and quite poorly in the third. This means that the situation of linguistic activities influences children's comprehension of demonstrative pronouns. The researchers suggested that in the first situation, because the children sat beside the experimenter, their reference point was identical with that of the experimenter's. Therefore, they did not need to shift the reference point while trying to comprehend the demonstrative pronouns. In the third case, the children sat face to face with the experimenter, so they had to shift the reference point in order to understand the demonstrative pronouns. They had to interpret "zhebian" (this side, here) as "nabian" (that side, there) which added to the difficulty of comprehension, because children of this age have a strong egocentric tendency. In the second case, the children could not rely entirely on their own reference point, nor did they have to change it completely. The difficulty of comprehension, therefore, lay between the first and the third cases. In the third case, the rate of correct comprehension responses was very low. Even seven year olds scored only about 40%, which is lower than the success rate (about 50%) of five and a half year olds reported by Tai (1986) in Taiwan. As regards children's comprehension of "zhe" (this) and "na" (that), Zhu et al.'s (1986) research did not find any substantial difference. This is at variance with the research results of Tai, whose subjects found "zhe" (this) easier than "na" (that). All this may be due to different standards of analysis.

Another type of pronoun is the personal pronoun. Zhu, Cheng, and Zhang (1986) studied children's comprehension of first, second, and third person pronouns. The subjects were a group of three and a half year olds, four and a half year olds, and five and a half year olds. The first part of the research allowed the children to watch a video recording of three party conversations. Next, the children participated in real conversations as the listener and the third party. In both parts the children were asked to identify the referents of the personal pronouns which they heard. Statistics showed that four and a half year olds performed better than three and a half year olds, but there was no significant difference between the performances of five and a half year olds and four and a half year olds. All the age groups found "wo" (I, me) the easiest, "ni" (second person singular 'you') more difficult, and "ta" (he/she) the most difficult to comprehend. It was noted that when the children were acting as the third party in a conversation, they seldom realized that "ta" (he/she) referred to themselves, and they normally took "ni" (second person 'you') for themselves. In such situations, less than 20% of the five and a half year olds' responses were correct, whereas in other situations, more than two-thirds of them could correctly comprehend the three personal pronouns "wo" (I, me), "ni" (second person singular 'you'), and "ta" (he/she). This may also be due to the fact that different situations call for different degrees of adjustment of the reference.

Xu and Min (1988) studied children's production of personal pronouns. They made a longitudinal study of how a group of children learned personal pronouns from six months old to three and a half years old and how three to four year old children used personal pronouns with the experiment method. According to their findings, Chinese speaking children's acquired order of personal pronouns is: "wo" (I, me) precedes "ni" (second person singular 'you') which in turn precedes "ta" (he/she). Children begin to use "wo" (I, me) in subjective and possessive cases correctly when they are about twenty months old; the use of "wo" (me) and "ni" (second person singular 'you') as objects emerges soon afterwards. However, children often substitute "wo" (I, me) for "ni" (second person singular 'you') or vice versa until they are about two years old. The emergence of the third person singular "ta" (he/she) occurs when the children are about two and a half to three years old, but the reference point is not very clear until after they are thirty-nine months old. During the age of three to four, children's use of "wo" (I, me) is still much better than that of "ni" (second person singular 'you') and "ta" (he/she), but there is no noticeable gap between their acquisition of "ni" (second person singular 'you') and "ta" (he/she). These researchers also found that four year olds are much more proficient than three and three and a half year olds in the use of personal pronouns. By the age of four, the three personal pronouns are used equally well, which seems to suggest that Chinese children's acquisition of personal pronouns is in a period of rapid development around that age. This tendency of development agrees with Zhu et al.'s findings regarding children's development of comprehension of personal pronouns.

Tai's (1986) and Chang's (1988) studies in Taiwan, and Deutsch & Pechmann's (1978) and Charney's (1980) studies all came to the conclusion that the order of children's acquisition of personal pronouns is: first person singular precedes second person singular which in turn precedes third person singular. It thus seems that this order of acquisition is universal.

Children's use of adjectives

In children's oral speech adjectives emerge later and are used less frequently than nouns and verbs. The Cooperation Study Group of Language development (1986a) conducted an investigation on the use of adjectives involving 942 children from six districts in China, ranging in age from one and a half to six years old. The researchers elicited children's use of adjectives by showing materials and pictures, asking children to describe those materials and pictures, and talking with children about the events and stories familiar to the children. A 50% correct answer rate was the criterion for deciding whether children of a particular age group could use a particular adjective correctly. The results of the investigation show that one and a half year olds can not yet use adjectives, because not a single adjective was used correctly by 50% of this age group. After age one and a half, children's proficiency in the use of adjectives undergoes a gradual improvement. The adjectives which they acquire emerge in the following sequence: first, those describing the characteristics of objects and substances, such as "big" "red", "hot"; second, those describing physical feelings, such as "hungry", "full", "painful"; third, those describing actions and people's physical shapes, such as "quick", "slow", "light", "fat", "thin"; fourth, those describing emotions, personalities and characteristics, such as "happy", "clever", "brave", and finally, those describing events and situations, such as "dangerous", "quiet", "difficult". On the whole, the tendency of development seems to be from the concrete to the abstract and from the external world to the internal world.

As regards children's acquisition of adjectives describing spatial dimensions, studies abroad have revealed certain orders. Studies in China have found that the order of children's acquisition of this type of adjective is roughly: "da" (big), "xiao" (small); "chang" (long), "duan" (short), "gao" (high), "ai" (low), "cu" (thick, wide in diameter), "xi" (thin, slender); "hou" (thick), "bao" (thin), "kuan" (wide), "zhai" (narrow). This finding coincides with the results of Chang and Yang's investigation (as summarized in Chang, 1988) in Taiwan and those of some others worldwide. According to Clark and Clark (1977), these pairs of adjectives are not acquired at the same time, but this hypothesis has been challenged by some. The Chinese research in question revealed that children began to use the majority of these pairs of adjectives at the same time. However in each age group there were some children who failed to do so. These children normally used the positive poles of the dichotomies first. For instance, they would use "gao" (high, tall) before "di" (low), and "kuan" (wide) before "zhai" (narrow). This seems to lend partial support to Clark and Clark's hypothesis.

Children's use of classifiers

One characteristic of Chinese language is its extensive repertoire of frequently used classifiers. In Chinese, when numerals precede nouns, the nouns must be modified by classifiers, which are placed between numerals and the nouns, forming a "numeral + classifier + noun" construction. In modern Chinese, there are a great number of classifiers. Their collocation with nouns is normally accepted through common practice, but there is a certain flexibility which has so far frustrated all those who have attempted to generalize all-inclusive rules about their usage. Naturally, this characteristic of the Chinese language presents tremendous difficulty for children in their acquisition of classifiers.

Ying, Chen, Song, Shao, and Guo (1983) investigated a group of four to seven year old children's use of 40 individual classifiers (e.g. "ge" '個', "zhi" '隻', "kuai" '塊', "ben" '本', etc.), 8 makeshift classifiers: the name of a container as the classifier (e.g. "wan" ['碗' bowl] in "yi wan fan" [a bowl of rice], and "tong" ['桶' bucket] in "yi tong shui" [a bucket of water]), and 8 collective classifiers (e.g. "shuang" ['雙' pair] in "yi shuang kuaizi" [a pair of chopsticks], and "chuan" ['串' bunch] in "yi chuan putao" [a bunch of grapes]). They used the picture elicitation method on the subjects and found that the four year olds could only use two individual classifiers: "ge" and "zhi"; the five year olds had acquired "ge", "zhi", "tiao" '條' and "ban", and the six year olds and seven year olds could use ten and thirteen classifiers respectively. The children under five could scarcely use makeshift classifiers, but the rate of success went up quickly when they were six. With respect to collective classifiers the success rate was very low: even the seven year olds had acquired only one of the tested items, viz. "shuang". These results suggest that children have to go a long way before they can possibly acquire the Chinese classifiers.

This study also reveals that the acquisition of Chinese classifiers depends not only on rote memorization, but also to a large extent on children's cognitive development. To use classifiers correctly, one has to abide by the formula "numeral + classifier + noun" and the collocation of the classifier and the noun. Four year olds can apply this rule to a certain degree, but their employment of classifiers is limited to the two most commonly used ones, "zhi" and "ge", which have been generalized to such an extent that whichever noun they use, they always put either "zhi" or "ge" in front of it, e.g. "yi zhi yifu" (a coat), "yi ge beizi" (a quilt), etc. This shows that they have not yet developed any rule about the collocation of nouns and classifiers. Some six year olds are able to choose relevant classifiers for different classes of nouns. For instance, they will use "liang" '輛' incorrectly to modify "feiji" (plane) and "lunchuan" (ship) since they are all means of transportation. Meanwhile, they are beginning to realize that makeshift classifiers are actually nouns used as classifiers. That explains why the success rate of classifiers in their utterances rises quickly. By the time they are seven, they have already grasped the basic rule about the use of makeshift classifiers: that is, they are actually nouns denoting containers. Thus makeshift classifiers no longer present much difficulty for them.

Fang (1985) conducted a study on four to six year old children's acquisition of classifiers which yielded very similar results to those of Ying et al.'s investigation. According to this research, four year olds' competence in the use of classifiers is still very insufficient, but it soon enters a period of rapid development. The first classifier which children acquire is the extremely commonly used general classifier "ge". The next ones which they acquire are much less commonly used classifiers such as "ben" and "shuang". The most difficult classifiers are the typical classifiers which denote the spatial perceptions of objects, such as "zhang" '張' and "kuai" '塊'. In order to test the validity of the hypothesis about the close relationship between the acquisition of classifiers and the development of cognition, Fang used some quaint objects with artificial names in his research which, according to their physical shapes, should be modified by "zhang", "li" '粒', "tiao" and "kuai" respectively. The results show that four year olds' ability for generalization regarding these classifiers is very poor and, consequently, they commit errors in the use of classifiers. In contrast, most six year olds have already developed the necessary ability. For example, they say "Zhe shi yi zhang ... " (This is a piece/sheet of ...) because it is "thin and flat, like a piece of paper"; similarly, they will say "Zhe shi yi li"... (This is a ...) when referring to something "small and round". This further proves that in addition to rote memorization, children's acquisition of classifiers involves thinking activities such as abstract generalization.

Summary

The following conclusions can be drawn about children's comprehension and production of words from the above discussions:

The order of development and its dependence on the situation.
There is a basic order in children's comprehension and production of words, but there is no absolute cutoff line between children of different ages. One and the same word may get different responses from one and the same child in different situations. It often happens that children can understand or produce certain words in certain situations but fail to do so in other situations. This is because different situations have different psychological requirements for the comprehension and production of a particular word. Therefore, in describing the process of children's lexical development, we must specify the situations and the ages of children in question. Needless to say, when children reach a higher level of language and cognitive development, they will be able to comprehend and produce these words in any situation.

Non-uniformity and the stages of development. There are different stages of development in children's comprehension and production of words. They develop at different speeds at different ages, sometimes very quickly, sometimes very slowly, and sometimes at a standstill. However, this non-uniform motion and the different stages of development are not consistent in the acquisition of different classes of words, which reflects the disequilibrium of development. For instance between age three and four children make very rapid progress in the acquisition of spatial words but there is no noticeable gap between these two ages group in the comprehension of demonstrative pronouns. Obvious progress is made when they are between four to five and six to seven years of age. Thus far no uniform turning points and stages have been found in the acquisition of different parts of speech.

The gradual development of the accuracy and generalization of word meanings. In the early stages of children's lexical acquisition, there are two seemingly opposite phenomena, namely, the widening and narrowing of the scopes of the applications of words. On the one hand, many words, such as "qian" (front), "hou" (back, rear), "zuo" (left) and "you" (right), are often confused; on the other hand, a particular word is often related to one thing only, for example, for some children "jiaohua" (cunning) can modify "huli" (fox) only. However, they at least know that "qian", "hou", "zuo" and "you" denote the spatial position, while "cunning" refers to the feature of the animates and cannot be used to describe other objects. This indicates that although children have not yet grasped all the meanings of the words, they have acquired part of the words' semantic features. Later, they will learn to distinguish words like "qian", "hou", "zuo" and "you" and realize that they refer to two different spatial dimensions. In due time, they will be able to distinguish two words referring to two different points on the same dimension, thus reaching the accuracy level of acquisition. In addition, they will be able to classify all the referents of the words which they are learning according to the sum total of their semantic implications and, thus, free themselves from the predicament of one track associations between modifiers and nouns. All this is, in nature, the process of the gradual acquisition of several semantic features of one and the same word; the process of achieving semantic accuracy and generalization. Such phenomena, to a certain extent, also lend support to E.Clark's hypothesis on semantic features (Clark, 1973a).

Children's Sentence Development

The development of sentences mainly depends on syntactic development. It also involves comprehension and production. The question of how children transform their syntactically non-adult utterances into adult utterances in a few years has attracted a great deal of research endeavors, but this has still remained a controversial issue in psycholinguistics. The theoretical dispute about children's language acquisition is, in fact, focused on their syntactic acquisition.

It is universally acknowledged that each language has its own syntactic rules. The syntactic rules of Chinese are very different from those of Indo-European languages such as English. Morphologically, Chinese words have many fewer changes than those of Indo-European languages. Chinese is more flexible in the use of words than English. Many Chinese verbs and adjectives, for example, can be used as subjects or objects without being nominalized. Besides, Chinese nouns can be more freely used as modifiers of other nouns than English nouns can. Therefore, Chinese speaking children do not have to spend such a long time wrestling with morphological difficulties as do English speaking children in the process of their language development. Syntactically, unlike the grammatical systems of Indo-European languages which are based upon sentences and clauses, the grammatical system of Chinese is based upon phrases. Simple sentences with complex structures are, without exception, made up of two more phrases, e.g.

  (a) Da jia zai yi qi wan jiu hao le.
     (We all played together would be good.)
  (b) Xiao peng you kan jian ta ku jiu qu gao su lao shi.
     (Little friends saw him cry so went to tell the teacher.)

which in English would have to be expressed by complex sentences. These characteristics of Chinese might account for the differences between the syntactic acquisition of Chinese-speaking children and that of English-speaking children, especially in the later stage of children's language development.

Children's production of sentences

The length of children's sentences. The mean length of utterances

(MLU) has been widely used as one of the indexes in the measurement of children's language development. Considering the morphemic structures of their language, American and European researchers normally take morphemes as the basic units of calculation. In light of the fact that Chinese characters lack morphological changes, and the boundaries of morphemes in Chinese are not so clear as in English, the Chinese researchers Zhu, Wu and Miao (1979) used words as the unit of calculation in their analysis of a group of two to six year old children's sentences. Wu and Xu (1979) on the other hand, used Chinese characters as the unit of calculation in their investigation of the sentences produced by children of several age groups. Zhu et al.'s research found that the MLU of two year olds was 2.91, that of two and a half year olds was 3.76, and that of three year olds increased to 4.61.

Although MLU is commonly used in the measurement of children's language development, it only indicates quantitative changes, not qualitative changes, and is therefore not capable of demonstrating the nature and complexity of sentence structures. After children have overcome the incompleteness of most simple sentences, sentences of the same length might have entirely different structures. The development of syntactic structures, therefore, is a more important index in the measurement of language development.

Syntactic development

Wu and Xu (1979), Zhu et al. (1979), and Wu, Zhu, and Miao (1987), the Cooperation Study Group of Oral Speech of Preschool children (1981), and Peng (1984) conducted several studies on children's syntactic development with the methods of both longitudinal and cross sectional studies and reached basically unanimous conclusions, which are summarized below.

Most of the sentences uttered by one and a half year old children are incomplete, including one word, two word and multi-word utterances. In one word utterances the words are generally nouns, but there is also a small number of verbs. However, as children at this age can only produce one word at a time, the words are not functionally distinguishable. The word "pa wu", for example, can be understood either as a noun, meaning a car or bus, or as a verb, meaning driving a car or a bus. Two word and multi-word sentences are also called "telegraph sentences". According to the observation of Guo (1988), a fourteen month old girl's two word utterances included three structures, namely, verb + noun, adjective + noun, and noun + noun, the majority being the verb + noun construction.

From one and a half to about two years of age, while continuing to use telegraph sentences, children begin to produce syntactically complete, though modifier free, simple sentences which include SV, VO and SVO sentence patterns. The available data show that more than 50% of the two year olds' utterances are complete sentences, and by the time they are three to three and a half, their utterances are mostly complete sentences. In the complete sentences produced by children, there is no substantial difference between the percentages of SVO, SV, and VO sentences produced by one and a half to two year old children; after they are two years of age, SVO sentences account for the highest percentage, SV sentences are second in number, and VO sentences are the lowest in numbers. After they are four years of age, the percentage of SVO sentences rises substantially, while the other two types of sentences drop quickly.

An important issue in the study of syntactic development is whether children's utterances are in accordance with the rules of word order of the language they are learning. The studies indicate that Chinese-speaking children's two word utterances normally follow the rules of Chinese word order. For instance, agents come before actions, and possessors are placed in front of their possessions. Although omissions of certain elements occasionally occur, such as prepositions, the possessive marker "de", and even verbs and subjects, their utterances are on the whole correct in word order. In the early stages of their language acquisition, some of the children's utterances seem to violate the standard word order of Chinese. An obvious phenomenon is the "fronting" of the object, which converts VO and SVO sentences into OV and OSV structures. e.g.

(a) Mianbaoche, mianbaoche wo zuo guo de.
   (The minibus, the minibus I have travelled in.)
(b) Zhege huaidan xiao pengyou kanjian le.
   (This bad egg the little boy saw.)

Another interesting structure is the postponing of prepositional object after the verb with the preposition omitted. Thus the noun looks like the object of the verb, e.g.

(c) Ni chi kuaizi, wo chi tiaogeng.
   (You eat the chopstick, I eat the spoon.)

which actually means "You eat with the chopsticks, and I eat with the spoon." Here, sentences (a) and (b) might be due to the influence of the "ba" construction in Chinese, because this construction requires the "fronting" of objects. Some linguists have suggested that the two main sentence patterns in Chinese are SVO and SOV. When children have just learned the "ba" construction, they tend to overgeneralize the OV structure in other contexts. However, judging from the context and the semantic meanings of these utterances, the influence of the topic-comment structure in Chinese would seem to be a more probable reason. It might be worth mentioning that the prevalence of the topic-comment structure in Chinese has led some linguists to classify it as a topic prominent language. Thus it can be seen that, in fact, (a) and (b) are normal sentences in Chinese. As regards a sentence like example (c), this may be incorrect or it may be due to the flexibility of word order in Chinese. In fact, such sentences as "Wo chi kuaizi" (I eat the chopsticks) are occasionally produced by adults also. The confusion of word order in children's utterances is a reflection of this phenomenon. Therefore, Chinese-speaking children in general are, from the very outset, extremely sensitive to the word order, like the children who speak other languages. The word order of their utterances are basically in accordance with the canonical word order of Chinese sentences.

In Chinese there are some peculiar syntactic structures which are absent in other languages like English. One of them is the "ba" construction, which is very frequently used. In this construction, the object is placed in front of the verb and preceded by the preposition "ba", so as to emphasize the result of the action. Li, Zhou, and Kong (1990) conducted research on the use of this construction by two to five year old children. The results of this research indicate that two year olds are already able to produce some basic patterns of this construction, which contain the four essential semantic elements: agent, recipient, action, and result, for example, "Wo ba zhe qiu shuai diao" (I throw off the ball), "Wo ba shoupa fang dao koudai li" (I put the handkerchief into the pocket). When children are four and a half years old, their use of this construction is fairly close to that of adults, except that the two most difficult patterns are still absent in their utterances. The subject and object of this construction are often missing in their utterances. The researchers further pointed out that the "ba" construction might not be a transformation of the SVO sentence as suggested by some. In fact, this construction is most closely related to sentences with recipient or patient subjects such as "Yifu dou xi ganjing le" (The clothes have all been washed clean). As to whether children acquire the sentences with recipient or patient subjects before they acquire the "ba" construction, further studies are still needed.

In Chinese there is a type of simple sentence which contains several conjoined structures or those with one or more structures which contain one or more embedded structures. Wu et al. (1987) recognize three kinds of such simple sentences in two and a half to six year old children's speech: (a) those with several verbal expressions in series, such as "Xiao pengyou kanjian le jiu qu gaosu laoshi" (The child/children saw it and so went to tell the teacher); (b) those consisting of an SV structure plus a VO structure - also called "concurrent sentences"- such as "Laoshi jiao women zuo youxi" (The teacher teaches us how to play games); and (c) those in which a subject or object contains an SV structure, such as "Liang ge xiao pengyou zai yiqi wan jiu hao le" (Two little friends playing together would be wonderful). The experiment's subjects began to produce these sentence patterns at two and a half, but extremely few in number at first, which gradually increased as they grew older. Wu and Xu's (1979) subjects, on the other hand, started to use sentences containing more than one predicate at one and a half to two, e.g. "Mama gai jiejie xiu shubao" (Mummy repaired the schoolbag for my elder sister). This seems to indicate that children begin to produce this type of sentence very early, although they have to undergo a very long process of development later.

Compound sentences consist of two or more simple clauses, which may be either in a coordinate or in a non-coordinate relationship. In general, children begin to produce relatively simple compound sentences at two to two and a half years of age, which are very small in number at first but then gradually increase. The rate of development quickens when they are between four and five. An analysis of children's utterances shows that most of the compound sentences produced by two to six year old children are coordinate sentences, of which the majority are those with semantically coordinated clauses. Those with sequentially fixed coordinated clauses are fewer, and still fewer are those with explanatory coordinated clauses, such as "wo da dongxi, wo da giao" (I'm building something, I'm building a bridge). In the non-coordinate sentences produced by children of this age group, most are those expressing cause and effect relationships. Other types of complex sentences occur much less frequently.

The most obvious peculiarity of children's compound sentences is the absence of conjunctions. Although conjunctions are omissible in most compound sentences, they are normally obligatory in non-coordinate sentences. Researches (Wu et al., 1987; Peng, 1984) show that two year olds never use conjunctions in their non-coordinate sentences. It is not until they are three years old that they begin to use subordinating conjunctions, which increase gradually afterwards. The development of conjunctions is manifest not only in the frequency of their occurrence, but also in the richness and complexity of the conjunctions. The conjunctions most frequently used by three to four year old children are "hai" as in "haiyou" (also, besides) and "haiyao" (also, in addition), "ye" (also), and "you" (again). "Houlai" (later) and "name" (then, in that case) emerge slightly later. Conjunctions denoting causal, adversative, and conditional relations, such as "yinwei" (because), "jieguo" (as a result), "yaoburan" (otherwise), "keshi" (but), as well as such correlatives as "meiyou......zhiyou" (no...only), and "ruguo......jiu" (if... then), begin to emerge when they are five to six years of age.

The fact that simple sentences emerge in children's utterances earlier than compound sentences seems to suggest that the developmental order of their sentences in terms of syntactic complexity is from simple to compound. However, as is revealed by the above mentioned studies, compound sentences emerge when children's simple sentences are still far from perfect in structure. Therefore, compound sentences begin to develop side by side with simple sentences. According to Zhu et al.'s (1979) investigation, 40% of two year olds' simple sentences are syntactically incomplete, and 80% are without any modifiers. It is in this state of affairs that compound sentences emerge. The majority of these early compound sentences are also incomplete. They have no conjunctions and are structurally very simple and loose. Their development and perfection occur simultaneously with the development and perfection of simple sentences. Furthermore, it is observed that when most of a child's simple sentences are syntactically complete, the omissions of the main elements of the simple clauses in their compound sentences still occur fairly frequently. This may be due to the fact that children's psychological energy available at any certain moment is still very limited.

Zhu et al. (1979) summed up the following three points with respect to the tendencies of the development of declarative sentences in children's utterances.

The first is the gradual development from an originally confusing mass of utterances into clearly differentiated sentences. The differentiation of children's utterances involves these aspects: function, parts of speech, and syntax. The early utterances of children normally have three functions: expressive, desiderative, and referential. Initially, these three functions are inseparable. As time goes on, they gradually branch off, and the referential and expressive functions become increasingly distinct. Secondly, the words in the early utterances of children are not distinct parts of speech. Gradually, nouns and verbs, as well as central words and modifiers, are differentiated. Lastly, children's early utterances are only one word or two word sentences without any subject predicate distinction. Eventually, they develop into structurally stratified sentences.

The second point is the gradual development of structurally loose sentences into concise and compact sentences. The earliest two-word sentences produced by children are only a sequence or words which have no syntactic structure. The basic structural framework of Chinese sentences are not established until the emergence of complete simple SV and SVO sentences. But at first the relationships between different elements of the sentences are still unclear, as some of the main elements are often missing. After the children are three and a half, the relationships between different sentence elements become more and more strict. The same is true of the development of compound sentences. Initially, we have only two juxtaposed simple clauses. It is some time before they are linked by conjunctions.

The last point is the gradual development of structurally compressed and rigid sentences into expanded and flexible sentences. Initially, children's utterances contain only one or two phrases which have no subject and predicate, and thus lack the distinction of basic sentence elements. Due to their cognitive limitations and their limits in vocabulary, the children can only utter a very limited number of stereotyped compressed sentences with a very limited number of words to express a very limited number of ideas, such as "Mama shangban" (Mummy goes to work), "Didi chifan" (Brother eats the meal), "wawa shuijiao" (The baby sleeps). Gradually, more and more complicated modifiers emerge which greatly expand the sentences. Finally, they are able to combine different sentence elements flexibly, producing a wide range of sentences. This tendency of development is clearly demonstrated in the expression of one and the same idea by means of different sentence structures.

Children's comprehension of sentences

Children's comprehension of questions. Children begin to ask and answer questions, especially yes/no questions, at a very early stage. It is common sense in daily life, but, unfortunately, little is known about development in this regard. To the best of the authors' knowledge, only Miao (1986) in China has conducted research to explore the developmental peculiarities of children's answers to "wh" questions, and through their answers, to learn more about children's comprehension of this type of question. The researcher posed some questions containing "what", "who", "where", "when", "how", and "why" to his subjects, and asked them to answer the questions according to pictures provided or simply from memory. The results showed that the order of "wh" questions which children can answer is: first, those containing "who", "what", "where" (three years old); next, those containing "when" and "how" (four years old); and finally, those containing "why" (five years old). Comparable studies abroad (Cairns & Hsu, 1978; Tyack & Ingram, 1977) also found that questions with "who", "what", and "where" are easier for children than those with "how" and "when". The main discrepancy between these studies lies with the results regarding "why" questions. According to some studies abroad children respond correctly to "why" questions at an earlier stage than they do to "when" and "how" questions. But according to Miao's research, correct answers to "why" questions occur at a later stage of development. This difference may be due to the different contents of the questions used in the different researches, or it may be that some clues in the questions of some studies induced the children to adopt certain strategies which led to the correct answers. It may also be attributable to the different conditions of education in different countries which are responsible for the different questions that children are more likely to hear in their daily life.

Children's comprehension of negative sentences. Negation is not only an important linguistic phenomenon, but also one of the principal linguistic expressions of the reversible operations of the human cognitive system. It is also one of the problems studied in the field of psycholinguistics. Zhu and Wu (1984) and Xu (1990) studied children's comprehension of negative and double negative sentences. Xu's research indicates that four year old children can already comprehend simple negative sentences and those with universal quantifiers as in sentences (a) and (b) respectively:

(a) Panzi li meiyou pingguo.
   (There are no apples on the plate.)
(b) Suoyou de panzi li dou meiyou pingguo.
   (There are no apples on all the plates.)

However, as the youngest of his subjects were four years old, we cannot conclude that children under four cannot understand these two types of negative sentences. According to Xu (1990), five to six year olds can already understand simple double negative sentences such as "Panzi li bushi meiyou pingguo" (The plate does not have apples). According to Zhu and Wu's study, on the other hand, the percentage of five year olds' correct responses to double negative sentences is very low, with increasing improvement to over 95% when they are seven. They deduced that the age of seven may be a turning point in children's comprehension of double negative sentences. The differences in the results of these two studies may be due to the fact that Xu used the picture sentence matching method, whereas Zhu and Wu asked their subjects to act out the sentences with real objects, which, as was proved by Xu's own study, is more difficult than the picture sentence matching. If we complicate the simple double negative sentences by introducing some syntactic transformations and quantifiers, children's comprehension of such sentences will be developed even later. Since there is certain correspondence between syntactic and semantic complexity of sentences and the percentages of children's correct responses, we can predict the order of the sentences which children will comprehend according to their syntactic and semantic complexity.

Children's comprehension of passive sentences. In modern Chinese, there are mainly six types of passive sentences, the most typical being the "bei" construction. In general, children's development of the "bei" construction takes place rather late. Zhu and Wu (1984) tested children's comprehension of passive sentences by asking them to act out what they thought the sentence meant. Their five-year-old subjects' scores were still rather low, but their six-year-old subjects could already understand most passive sentences. On this basis, the researchers suggested that the age of six is probably a turning point in children's comprehension of passive sentences. This is different from the results of Chang's research (1988) in Taiwan which indicated age five as the turning point.

Tang (1984) made a careful study of nine to thirteen year old elementary and middle school students' comprehension of various types of passive sentences. He designed ten groups of active and passive sentences which embraced all the passive structures in modern Chinese, including those containing "jiao", "rang" and "gei" instead of "bei", those with "wei...suo", and pseudo-active sentences. The subjects were asked to take a multiple choice test on voice transformation, which was intended to test their comprehension of passive sentences. He found that his nine year old subjects had already acquired the ability to do such transformations, and his ten to eleven year old subjects did remarkably better. When tested on almost all types of passive sentences, the rate of correct answers for eleven year olds was as high as 95%. This means that it takes five to six years for children to perfect their comprehension of passive sentences: from five to six years of age when they have already grasped the basic idea of the passive voice to about eleven when their knowledge of this structure is comparable to that of adults.

Children's comprehension of compound sentences

In Chinese, there are two classes of compound sentences, namely, coordinate sentences and non-coordinate sentences. The relationships between the clauses in compound sentences are expressed either by clause order or by correlatives which are obligatory in most cases. As each relationship is expressed by a particular group of correlatives, readers or listeners can easily decide, according to the correlatives which they read or hear, whether a particular sentence is a compound sentence and, if so, what relationship exists between the component clauses.

Miao and Zhu (1989) tested a group of four to six year old children's comprehension of compound sentences which contained seven types of correlatives, namely, "hai"(also), "bushi...ershi" (not...but), "budan...erqie" (not only, ... but also), "huozhe ... huozhe" (either ... or), "bushi ... jiushi" (if not...then), "zhiyou...cai" (only...can). Here, "hai" and "bushi...jiushi" express coordination; "budan...erqie" expresses succession or addition, "houzhe...huozhe" and "bushi...jiushi" indicate alternation or selection; "zhiyou...cai" and "ruguo... name" indicate condition. The subjects were asked to carry out experimenter's instructions which contained above mentioned correlatives, for instance, "If I take the yellow, square block, you take the white, round block", "Not only give me the blue, round block, but also give me the green, square block". The results of the study showed that most four year olds can understand coordinate sentences; most six year olds can understand sentences denoting succession and condition, but they have not yet reached the level of basic comprehension of sentences denoting alternation or selection. This indicates that of all the compound sentences, coordinate sentences and the sentences denoting alternation or selection are the easiest and the most difficult respectively, and the difficulty in comprehension corresponds to the complexity of the relations expressed by the compound sentences. Coordinate sentences and the sentences denoting succession or addition express the conjunctive relation, the sentences with conditional clauses express the implicative relation, and the sentences containing clauses of alternation express the disjunctive relation. Obviously, since different types of compound sentences express different logical relations, the cognitive activities which are necessary for the comprehension of such sentences also have different degrees of difficulty. On the other hand, modes of expression also exert certain influence on children's comprehension. Among the sentences expressing the conjunctive relation, for example, those containing "budan...erqie" (not only...but also) seem to be more difficult than others; similarly, in sentences denoting alternation or selection, those with "bushi...jiushi" (if not...then) are more difficult than those with "huozhe...huozhe" (either ...or). The reason may be that the word "bu" (no, not) in these sentences misleads children into thinking that the first clauses of these sentences are negative in meaning.

Compound sentences denoting causal relations are another type of frequently used sentence. A recent study conducted by Zhu (in preparation) showed that the rate of first graders'(eight years old) correct responses to compound sentences denoting causal relations, such as "Zhang Wen ma Li Ming, yinwei ta zuoshi tai bu renzhen" (Zhang Wen scolded Li Ming, because he was too careless) is 67.5%, which increases with the growth of the children. It reaches 95.4% with fourth graders (eleven years old). However, not many children can correctly comprehend ambiguous sentences denoting causal relations. For instance, only 16% of the fifth grade subjects could appreciate the ambiguity of the sentence, "Li Ming ma Zhang Wen, yinwei ta xiangxin bieren de yaoyan" (Li Ming scolded Zhang Wen, because he believed other people's rumour), due to the ambiguity of the pronoun "ta" (he) whose referent could be either "Li Ming" or "Zhang Wen". This indicates that most elementary school students take ambiguous sentences as non-ambiguous sentences, and they tend to take the subject of the subordinate clause "ta" (he) as co-referential with that of the main clause. When contextual clues are provided to turn ambiguous sentences into non-ambiguous sentences, the rate of first graders' correct responses are at a chance level, which increases to 80.8% with fourth graders, and to 89.5% with fifth graders. Due to the fact that such sentences are more complicated, both syntactically and semantically, than simpler sentences like "Zhang Wen ma Li Ming, yinwei ta zuoshi tai bu renzhen" (Zhang Wen scolded Li Ming, because he was too careless), the percentages of correct responses of all these age groups are comparatively lower. This testifies to the impact of the syntactic and semantic complexity on children's comprehension of compound sentences.

Children's strategies in the comprehension of sentences

Children resort to certain strategies in the comprehension of sentences. These strategies refer to the rules generalized by the individuals from their linguistic and non-linguistic experiences in the past. Such rules sometimes facilitate their comprehension of sentences and sometimes lead to errors, which calls for further revision and enrichment of the rules. In this way, children's comprehension strategies gradually develop. Studies abroad (Strohner & Nelson 1974; Cromer 1976; Slobin & Bever 1982) have identified some of the strategies commonly adopted by children, such as word order strategy, the semantic strategy (i.e. event probability strategy), and non-linguistic strategies. Various interpretations have been proposed for these strategies.

Miao (1981) and Miao, Chen, and Ying (1984) studied the roles of word order and word meaning in the comprehension of sentences by four to eleven year old children and adults. Using three words, two nouns and one verb, which were arranged into various word orders, he asked his subjects to act out the meanings of these "sentences". He discovered that generally Chinese people's comprehension depends on both word order and meanings, and that there are very complicated relationships between these two factors. However, for adults, word meanings play a more important role than word order, whereas for five to seven year olds the role of word order seems to be more obvious in their comprehension of NVN sentences (which are normal in word order). Sentences consisting of inanimate noun + verb + animate noun, such as "Qiu tui gou" (The ball pushes the dog), which violate the normal possibilities of events and where the syntactic information contradicts the semantic information, are still comprehended by most five to seven year olds according to the word order, by taking the inanimate being as the agent and the animate being as the patient or recipient. When faced with NNV and VNN sentences, which are abnormal in word order, children in most cases have recourse to the semantic strategy and take the animate beings as the agents. In general, with the exception of the period from five to seven years of age, Chinese children rely more on the semantic strategy than on the word order strategy in the comprehension of simple sentences. This finding is basically in agreement with that of Chang and Chen's research (as summarized in Chang, 1988) in Taiwan. At first, this seems to contradict the fact that word order is basically the only syntactic information available, since Chinese words lack morphological distinctions. However, because word order in Chinese is not as strict as in many other languages, such as English, Chinese speakers have to rely heavily on semantic information in the comprehension of sentences.

Wang (1986) studied three to seven and a half year old children's strategies in the comprehension of instrumental and dative sentences which are composed of two nouns, one verb and a preposition arranged in various orders. He found that most younger children tend to adopt the meaning-based, event probability strategy. For instance, they often tend to act "Song gei piqiu xiao gou" (Give to the ball the little dog) and "Yong xiao yang da bianzi" (To beat the whip with the little sheep) as " Song gei xiao gou piqiu" (Give to the little dog the ball) and "Yong bianzi da xiao yang" (Beat the little sheep with the whip) respectively. As children grow up, however, the event probability strategy gradually gives way to the word order strategy in the comprehension of dative sentences (after age three and a half) and instrumental sentences (after age four and a half). The four and a half year old and five and a half year old subjects, for instance, still used the strategy of treating the first noun in a sentence as a moving object. The influence of this strategy continues until children are seven and a half. This trend in development agrees with the results of comparable research abroad.

One of the manifestations of the event probability strategy in the comprehension of sentences is the expectation of sentence meanings stemming from one's experiences. Where sentence meanings match with one's expectations, the sentences are easy to comprehend; otherwise, it is difficult. This was borne out by Zhu and Wu's research (1981) with Chinese children. In the research, they presented to their subjects two types of passive sentences with identical syntactic structures and of the similar length, but the contents of one type were compatible with the children's past experiences, whereas those of the other type were not. e.g.

(a) Linlin bei Xiao Zhen zhuangdao zai dishang, laoshi ba ta fu qilai.
(Linlin was knocked down by Xiao Zhen, the teacher helped her up.)
(b) Zhang laoshi bei Xiao Hua bei zhe qu jiaoshi, ta de tui dieshang le.
(The teacher, Mr Zhang, was carried to the classroom by Xiao Hua, because his leg was injured.)

The study shows that there is a great difference between seven year olds' interpretation of these two types of sentences. They often ignore the syntactic structure of the second group of sentences and misinterpret their meanings. This clearly points to the influence of the expectations stemming from their experiences. The research also shows that nine and ten year old children can overcome the interference of subjective expectations and correctly respond to such sentences. However, if the content of a sentence is entirely new, then the syntactic factor will play an important role in seven year olds' comprehension.

The comprehension strategies of Chinese-speaking children and their developmental tendencies as revealed by the above mentioned studies share certain similarities with those of non-Chinese children. This lends support to the opinion that there are certain universals with respect to comprehension strategies. On the other hand, besides being consistent with the general tendencies of children's development, the selection and application of the syntactic and semantic strategies in the comprehension of sentences seem to vary with the characteristics of the sentences involved and the relationships between the children and the contents of the sentences. When a sentence is simple in structure and its content is familiar to the children, the children tend to adopt the semantic strategy; otherwise, they interpret it according to the syntactic information. From these findings we can conclude that the process of children's syntactic acquisition and sentence comprehension is one in which children actively explore the laws of language in linguistic materials, evolve hypotheses, and constantly test and revise these hypotheses in the practice of linguistic communication. In a sense, it is also a process of the gradual integration of children's subjective initiatives with the objective laws of language.

Children's Pragmatic Competence

Besides the acquisition of basic phonological, syntactic, and semantic rules, language acquisition also involves the development of pragmatic competence: the appropriate use of language for effective communication. Since the late 1970s, pragmatic studies, including children's acquisition of pragmatic competence, have received more and more attention of researchers world-wide. In China, the study of pragmatics is still in its infancy. To the best of our knowledge, only a few reports have touched upon it.

One's pragmatic competence includes the ability to adjust the contents and forms of one's utterances according to the specific characteristics of the listener. Zhang and Lin (1989) studied this ability of six to six and a half year old children when playing games. They asked their subjects to explain the name of a new toy and the way of playing with it to their teachers, children of their own age, and younger children in specially designed situations. They found that the subjects spoke fewer sentences to the teachers than to other children. An analysis of these sentences reveals that the sentences used in introducing the name of the toy and how to play with it to three different types of listeners were basically the same in number; the main difference rested in the number of explanatory sentences. For young listeners they often used explanatory sentences to help explain how to play with the toy, which were frequently repeated in order to remind and correct mistakes. Furthermore, there were also some differences in the moods and tones of the sentences. When the listeners were the teachers, the majority of the sentences were declarative sentences, and the tones were rather tentative and gentle; when the listeners were children of their own age, more imperative, interrogative and exclamatory sentences were used, the conversations were more casual, and the tones were stronger and livelier; when the listeners were younger, the conversations were also casual but to a different degree. In the last case, the explainers tended to behave like "elders", urging and criticizing the "youngsters". All this indicates that six year old children are already capable of selecting appropriate contents and forms of utterances in accordance with the listeners' needs, knowledge and abilities.

Hua (1990) investigated five to seven year old children's ability to adjust their speech in different situations. She put a coin under a big, yellow round building block, and then asked the subjects to tell where the coin was. This big, yellow round block was successively placed beside a red round block; a yellow square block; a yellow square and a red round block; and a yellow square, a red round, and a small yellow round block. Thus, this big, yellow round block, compared with its neighbours, should be called yellow block, round block, yellow and round block, and big yellow and round block respectively. The five year olds involved in the investigation could select appropriate words only in the first two cases, whereas most of the seven year olds could successfully express these notions. When they committed errors, they could also correct their own utterances according to the experimenter's feedback. The results of this investigation indicate that five and six year old children are capable of adjusting their own utterances in simple situations, and that the age of seven might be a turning point in the regulation of utterances according to different situations.

Explorations of Language Acquisition Theories

As studies of children's language acquisition started rather late in China, and Chinese researchers, for the most part, are still in the stage of accumulating materials concerning children's acquisition of the Chinese language, it is difficult to do any thorough theoretical analysis on the basis of these materials. So far, only a few Chinese researchers have conducted some preliminary theoretical explorations of language acquisition. These explorations focused mainly on two theoretical aspects. One was the relationship between language acquisition and cognitive development; the other was the role of imitation in language acquisition.

The relationship between language acquisition and cognitive development

International scholars have different views about the relationship between language acquisition and cognitive development. Chinese researchers, in general, think that cognitive development is the basis of language acquisition, which is similar to the position of the Piagetian school. With respect to the acquisition of lexical items, for example, Chinese scholars believe that lexical development has to be based on cognitive development and the formation of related concepts. Many studies have proven that the order of lexical development is in accordance with the complexity of the intellectual operations required of the acquisition of the particular words involved. Even the acquisition of the classifiers, which seems to require only rote memory, is in fact closely related to cognitive development. The same is true of syntactic development. The more complex the required intellectual operations are of a particular syntactic structure, the older children are when they acquire it. Similarly, since the comprehension of passive sentences, negative, and double negative sentences call for reverse intellectual operations, children who have not yet achieved this intellectual level cannot possibly comprehend such sentences.

This relationship between language acquisition and cognitive development, to a certain extent, can also be illustrated by comparative studies of normal children, deaf and mute children, blind children, and mentally retarded children. Tang (1984) compared the comprehension levels of normal children, deaf and mute children (including congenitally acquired), and moderately retarded children in his study of children's comprehension of active passive transformation. He found that the level of comprehension of normal children is higher than that of deaf children, which in turn, is higher than that of mentally retarded children. Although deaf children suffer from the loss of oral speech, the level of their cognitive development is still higher than that of mentally retarded children. Therefore, they surpass mentally retarded children in the comprehension of passive sentences. Zhu and Wu's (1982) comparative studies of normal children, blind adolescents, and deaf and mute adolescents showed that their seven year old normal subjects and blind subjects were more advanced than their deaf and mute counterparts in class inclusion, and conservation, but there was no significant difference between the normal subjects and the deaf and mute subjects. These different levels of cognitive development were reflected in their comprehension of passive and double negative sentences: the seven year old normal children's comprehension was similar to that of the blind children, and both of these groups did better than the deaf and mute subjects. All these results supported the position that language acquisition is based on the development of cognition. The fact that the process and order of Chinese children's acquisition of the Chinese language are in many ways similar to the processes and order of non-Chinese children's acquisition of their mother tongues is perhaps mainly due to the dependence of language acquisition on cognitive development, which is to a certain extent universal: children of different countries undergo basically the same processes of cognitive development.

However, cognitive development is not the only, nor is it a sufficient condition for language acquisition. After all, language acquisition and cognitive development are not one and the same process. Language acquisition is also subject to the influence of the characteristics of language itself. For instance, there are a variety of different ways of expressing one and the same concept or cognitive operation, some of which are more complicated and difficult than others, and consequently, they cannot possibly be acquired at the same time. The above mentioned fact, that one and the same logical relation can be expressed by several different correlatives, and children's comprehension performances of these correlatives are different, is a convincing piece of evidence. This may also be one of the principal reasons why the process and order of Chinese children's language development are in some respects different from those of other children. This opinion agrees with Slobin's (1988) position on the relationship between cognitive development and language acquisition.

In Zhu and Wu's (1982) study, the blind subjects did better than the deaf and mute subjects both in the comprehension of active, passive, as well as double negative sentences, and in intellectual operations. This is contrary to the results of the research cited by Piaget of M.Vincent, P.Oleron, H.Furth, and Y.Hatwell (Piaget & Inhelder, 1969). Piaget cited the fact that the level of deaf and mute children's intellectual operations is higher than that of blind children. He attempted to show that blind children's sensorimotor mechanisms are impaired from the very beginning, and that their adjustments or adaptations by linguistic means are not sufficient to compensate this cognitive deficit. This means that cognitive development plays a decisive role in the development of cognition and language. Zhu and Wu, on the other hand, believe that their materials indicate that language development plays a certain role in cognitive development. In their opinion, the deaf and mute children's loss of oral speech and blind children's fairly well developed linguistic competence help explain why the blind children are cognitively better developed than deaf and mute children. Their deaf and mute subjects' thoughts, for example, were confined to their intuitions about the present circumstances and were rather rigid and difficult to change; in contrast, their blind subjects were capable of generalization with the help of language. Therefore, they were, to some extent, free from the constraints of the present conditions and could apply the relevant knowledge which they had learned in their responses to the experimenter's questions. It is thus evident that the relationship between cognitive development and language development is a two-way operation.

The role of limitation in language acquisition

The role of imitation in language acquisition has been a controversial issue. From the 1920s to the late 1950s, the dominant theoretical position was that language was acquired by virtue of imitation. After the birth of the Chomskian transformational generative grammar, the role of imitation was for a while totally negated. Since the late 1970s, some scholars have partially "rehabilitated" its "reputation" by arguing that imitation is conducive to language acquisition under certain conditions. A few Chinese scholars have also addressed this problem in their studies on the processes of language acquisition. Wu and Zhu (1982) and Guo (1988) observed many linguistic inventions of one to three year old children. They noted that their subjects occasionally uttered some words, phrases, and sentences which they had never learned or even heard before. This suggests that children's language is not simply a copy of adults' language. In other words, it is not acquired through mere imitation. On the other hand, they also observed that imitation did play a certain role in language acquisition. Gao Xiaochao found that 86.42% of the words and phrases which a girl acquired from age eleven to fourteen months were taught by adults and repeatedly imitated by her. It is clear that adults' teachings and children's imitations are important sources of children's language acquisition, as well as important influences on language acquisition, especially phonological and lexical acquisition. Wu and Zhu's observations proved that imitation also plays a certain role in syntactic acquisition. According to their observations, there are four types of linguistic imitations: (1) instant and complete imitation; (2) instant but incomplete imitation; (3) delayed imitation; and (4) selective imitation. When children are expressing new ideas in new situations according to the syntactic structures of model sentences, they are in fact both imitating and creating at once. For example, a thirty-two month old girl once heard her grandfather say "Xiao pengyou wei ge yuangquan zai zuo youxi" (The children are playing games in a ring). Later, when she saw three teachers speaking with each other in a ring, she said "San ge ren wei ge quan jianghua" (Three people are talking in a ring). In general, of the four types of imitations, the most important one is selective imitation, not instant imitation. It should be pointed out, however, imitation is not the only source of language acquisition. According to Guo (1988), for example, 13.58% of his subject's new vocabulary was not acquired through imitation. What is more important is that not all of the words and phrases taught by adults are imitated by children, and not all the words and phrases which they imitate can be acquired. What children imitate are the words and sentences which they are capable of reproducing. They cannot possibly imitate, for example, sounds which require complicated pronunciation skills which their pronunciation mechanisms are not yet mature enough to produce. Similarly, they will not imitate or completely imitate the words or sentences which are far beyond their language development level or which they cannot comprehend and memorize.

In another study, Zhu and Wu (1984) specially studied the role of imitation. They asked their five to six year old subjects, who could not yet use passive and double negative sentences, to imitate these two types of sentences produced by adults. After doing such imitation exercises, some of the children were able to produce passive and double negative sentences on other topics, which means that imitation does have some positive influence on language acquisition. However, such positive influence was observed only in subjects who had some foundation in comprehension. Only one subject learned to use, through imitation, some sentences which he did not understand at all originally. The results of this study seem to suggest that imitation serves to facilitate the transition from comprehension to production, and that what is learned by imitation are the forms of linguistic expressions, not intellectual operations, which cannot be acquired through instant imitation. That is why imitation has little or no effect with children lacking a foundation in comprehension.

In short, these researchers confirmed the role of imitation in children's language acquisition; however, they pointed out that imitation is not the only way to acquire language. It has some prerequisite conditions and is limited by the levels of children's language skills and cognitive development.

Concluding Remarks

Since the late 1970s, psychologists in mainland China have conducted studies in many areas of children's language development. These areas include phonological, syntactic, semantic, and pragmatic developments, the bilingualism of minority children, and the relationship between cognitive development and language development, as well as the role of imitation in language development. Our ongoing research has included subjects from various age groups, ranging from infants to adolescents, but mainly preschoolers. Besides normal children, we have also studied exceptional children (i.e. blind, deaf-and-mute, and mentally retarded children), and have made comparative studies of their language development with that of normal children. With respect to the methods of research, we have made some longitudinal studies, cross-sectional studies, the combination of both, observations, natural experiments, and laboratory experiments. Owing to more than a decade of efforts, we have accumulated a great deal of first-hand data and have gained a preliminary and rough understanding of various aspects of Chinese-speaking children's language development, which is a good foundation for further research work and theoretical generalizations.

Nevertheless, our studies so far are still rather insufficient in quantity, due to the short time span of our research history and the shortage of our manpower and material resources. Moreover, language development is an extremely complicated issue which involves numerous aspects and problems. Our research to date has dealt with almost all of them, but regarding each aspect, we have touched upon only a few problems. Only one or two of our studies have been conducted on each of these problems. It is, therefore, difficult to generalize reliable conclusions from these studies. Furthermore, the fact that there are some differences between the individual studies in sampling, data-collecting, methodology, and standards of measurement also adds to the difficulty of comparison and contrast. In our view, only after we have conducted a great deal of research work on all the problems and have amassed an abundance of data can we possibly understand some laws and, thereby, reach a comprehensive and thorough understanding of the language development of Chinese-speaking children.

Early childhood (from about one to three years of age) is a crucial period in children's language development. The study of children's language development in this period is of supreme significance for the revelation of the laws of children's language development. The principal research method with children of this age group should probably be longitudinal studies, which were adopted by Brown (1973), Slobin (1985), Bloom (1970), and others in their very fruitful studies. In the late 1970s, a small number of Chinese scholars also conducted some longitudinal studies, but their analyses of the materials were not thorough and exhaustive enough. Since then, due to many reasons, most studies on the language development in China have investigated a certain problem of three year olds and older children's speech and have employed the cross-sectional method, which is an unfortunate drawback. In our opinion, more longitudinal studies should be conducted from now on which focus on recording the utterances of children under three and doing comprehensive syntactic and semantic analyses of these utterances.

Although we have conducted some studies on Chinese-speaking children's language development in the past decade or so, and the materials which we have used were all Chinese words and sentences, many of the research questions were introduced from abroad. So far we have not developed enough research projects which focus the features of the Chinese language itself. In Chinese language there are some very peculiar linguistic features which are absent in other languages; besides, there are also some linguistic rules in Chinese which exhibit peculiar characteristics. Such phenomena and their influence on children's language development are now deserving our attention. Moreover, the complex nature of Chinese grammar and the theoretical dispute among the Chinese linguists have given rise to additional difficulties in our studies. Therefore, more research must be devoted to the analysis of the features of the Chinese language and studies of Chinese children's acquisition of the linguistic rules which are peculiar to Chinese. Until we do that, we cannot possibly make more contributions to the understanding of the universalities and peculiarities of language acquisition.

Notes

1. For the sake of convenience, we shall call mainland China "China" in the rest of this paper. Therefore, "China" in this paper refers to mainland China only, exclusive of other parts of China.

2. As concerns the subjects of these studies, most of them learn dialects at home and speak Putonghua (Mandarin) at nursery, kindergarten and school. Only the subjects in Fang (1985), Guo (1988), Wu and Xu (1979), Xu and Min (1988), Zhang and Zhu (1987) are exposed to Putonghua from their birth. While conducting the studies, the experimenters and children communicate with each other in Putonghua.

References

Beilin, H. (1975) *Studies in the cognitive basis of language development.* Academic Press, 84-122.
Bloom, L. (1970) *Language development: form and function in emerging grammars.* The M.I.T.Press.
Brown, R. (1973) A first language. Cambridge, MA: Harvard University Press.
Cairns, H. and Hsu, J. (1978) Who, why, when and how: a development study. *Journal of Child Language, 5,* 477-488.
Chang, H.W. (1988) *Acquisition of Mandarin Chinese: A review of recent research in Taiwan.* Paper presented at XXIV International Congress of Psychology Sydney, Australia.
Charney, R. (1980) Speech role and the development of personal pronouns. *Journal of Child Language, 7,* 509-526.
Clark, E. (1973a) What's in a word? On the child's acquisition of semantic in his first language. In Moore, T. (ed.) *Cognitive development and the acquisition of language.* Academic Press, 65-110.

Clark, E. (1973b) Nonlinguistic strategies and the acquisition of word meaning. *Cognition*, 2, 161-182.
Clark, E. (1980) Here's the top: nonlinguistic strategies in the acquisition of orientational terms. *Child Development*, 51, 329-338.
Clark, H.and Clark, E (1977) *Psychology and language: An introduction to psycholinguistics.* Harcourt Brace Jovanorich, Inc.
Cromer, R. (1976) Developmental strategies for language. In Hamilton, V. and Vernon, M.D.(eds.) *The development of cognitive process.* Academic Press. 305-308.
Deutsch, W. and Pechmann, T. (1978) On the acquisition of pronouns in German children. *Cognition*, 6, 155-168.
Fang, F.X. (1985) An experiment on the use of classifiers by 4 to 6-year olds. *Acta Psychologica Sinica*, 17, 384-391.
Guo, X.C. (1988) *Adult's language instruction, children's imitation learning and language acquisition.* Paper presented at the Conference of the Committee of Developmental Psychology of Chinese Psychological Association.
Hua, H.Q. (1990) Investigation into pragmatic skills in children of 5-7 years old. *Information on Psychological Sciences*, 2, 53-54.
Jakobson, R. (1968) *Child language, aphasia and phonological universals.* The Hague: Mouton Publishers
Kuczaj, S. and Maratsos M. (1975) On the acquisition of front, back and side. *Child Development*, 46, 202-210.
Li, X.N., Zhou, G.G., Kong, L.D. (1990) A preliminary investigation of 2 to 5-year old children's production of the sentences with "ba". *Literacy Research*, 4, 43-50.
Li, Y.M. (1991) a case study of a baby's phonological development from 1 to 120 days old. *Psychological Science*, 5, 21-25.
Miao, X.C. (1981) Word order and semantic strategies in Chinese sentence comprehension. *International Journal of Psycholinguistics*, 8, 109-122.
Miao, X.C., Chen, G.P., Ying, H.C. (1984) Reexamination of the roles of word order and lexical meaning in Chinese sentence comprehension. *Information on Psychological Sciences*, 6, 1-7.
Miao, X.C. (1986) Young children's understanding of interrogative --the developmental peculiarities of answering WH questions in young children. *Information on Psychological Sciences*, 5, 1-5.
Miao, X.C., Zhu, M.S. (1989) Preschool children's comprehension of some types of compound sentences. *Information on Psychological Sciences*, 6, 1-6.
Peng, Z.Z. (1984) *Preliminary analysis of language development in 3 to 6-year old children.* Paper presented at the Conference of Chinese Psychological Association.
Piaget, J. and Inhelder, B. (1969) *The psychology of the child.* Basic Books, Inc.
Slobin, D. (1985) *The cross-linguistic study of language acquisition.* Lawrence Erlbaum Associates.
Slobin, D. (1988) From the garden of Eden to the tower of Babel. In Kessel, F.(ed.) *The development of language and language researchers: Essays in Honor of Roger Brown.* Lawrence Erlbaum Associates.

Slobin, D. and Bever, T. (1982) Children use canonical sentence schemes: A cross-linguistic study of word order and inflections. *Cognition, 12,* 229-265.

Strohner, H. and Nelson, K. (1974) The young children's development of sentence comprehension: Influence of event probability, nonverbal context, syntactic form and strategies. *Child Development, 45,* 567-576.

Tai, C.J. (1986) *A development study of the singular pronoun in spoken Chinese.* Unpublished M.A. thesis, Fu Jen Catholic University.

Tang, J. (1984) A study on the comparison of children's ability to transform active and passive forms in Chinese sentence structure. *Acta Psychologica Sinica, 16,* 182-192.

Tyack, D. and Ingram, D. (1977) Children's production and comprehension of questions. *Journal of Child Language, 4,* 211-224.

Wang, Y.M. (1986) Children's comprehension of dative and instrumental sentences and their comprehension strategies. *Information on Psychological Sciences, 2,* 16-22.

Washington, D. and Naremore, R. (1978) Children's use of spatial prepositions in two and three dimensional tasks. *Journal of Speech and Hearing Research, 21,* 151-165.

Wu, H.Y., Zhu, J.Q. (1980) An investigation of 2 to 6-year old children's language development. *Child Psychology and Educational Psychology 3-4,* 19-25.

Wu, J.Z., Zhu, M.S. (1982) Some factors that influence language acquisition, *Information on Psychological Sciences, 5,* 23-28.

Wu, J.Z., Zhu, M.S., Miao, X.C. (1987) Analysis of the structure of compound sentences in preschool children in Zhu, M.S. (Ed.) *Researches on Child language development.* (p.9-19) East China Normal University Press.

Wu, T.M., Xu, Z.Y. (1979) A preliminary analysis of language development in children during the first three years. *Acta Psychologica Sinica, 2,* 153-165.

Xu, H.H. (1990) Chinese children's understanding of quantified negation sentence. *Information on Psychological Sciences, 4,* 13-18.

Xu, Z.Y., Min, R.F. (1988) *A study of Chinese personal pronoun acquisition.* Paper presented at the conference of the committee of the Developmental Psychology of Chinese Psychological Association.

Ying, H.C., Chen, G.P., Song, Z.G. Shao, W.M., Guo, Y. (1983) Characteristics of 4 to 7-year-old children in mastering quantitatives. *Information on Psychological Sciences, 6,* 24-32.

Zhang, J.G., Lin, J. (1989) Preliminary study of upper grade kindergartners' language ability in playing. *Information on Psychological Sciences, 3,* 42-44.

Zhang, R.J. (1985) On children's mastery of expressions denoting space. *Journal of East China Normal University (Educational Science Edition), 4,* 35-46.

Zhang, R.J., Zhu, M.S. (1987) The development of infant's sounds. *Information on Psychological Sciences, 5,* 7-11.

Zhu, M.S., Wu, J.Z., Miao, X.C. (1979) An investigation of the development of oral speech in preschool children. 1. Analysis of the structure of simple declarative sentences in preschool children. *Acta Psychologica Sinica, 3,* 281-286.

Zhu, M.S., Wu, J.Z. (1981) Factors affecting the comprehension of sentences by children. *Information on Psychological Sciences, 1,* 23-27.

Zhu, M.S., Wu, J.Z. (1982) A comparative study in normal, deaf-mute and blind children --- on relationship between the development of language and thinking. *Information on Psychological Sciences, 1,* 15-21.

Zhu, M.S., Wu, J.Z., Ying, H.C., Zhu, L.M., Zhuang, X.J. (1982) Children's comprehension of several kinds of temporal words in sentences. *Acta Psychologica Sinica, 14,* 294-301.

Zhu, M.S., Wu, J.Z. (1984) Chinese children's comprehension and production of passive voice and double negation sentences. *International Journal of Behavioral Development, 7,* 67-76.

Zhu, M.S., Cao, F., Zhang, R.J. (1986) Young children's interpretation of demonstrative pronouns. *Information on Psychological Sciences, 3,* 1-6.

Zhu, M.S., Cheng, G.P., Zhang, R.J. (1986) Young children's comprehension of personal pronouns. *Acta Psychologica Sinica, Vol.18, No.4,* 356-364.

Zhu, M.S. (in preparation) School children's comprehension of causality sentences

The Cooperation study Group of Oral speech of Preschool Children (1981) Investigation on the development of the oral speech of preschool children. *Information on Psychological Sciences, 5,* 30-37.

The cooperation study group of language development (1986a) An investigation of using adjectives in young children. *Child Development and Education, 1,* 39-43.

The Cooperation Study Group of Language Development (1986b) Young children's mastery of expressions denoting space. *Child Development and Education, 4,* 34-39.

The Acquisition of Chinese Syntax

Hsing-Wu Chang
National Taiwan University

This article is concerned with recent research data on the development of Chinese syntax, especially on the early stages. Acquisition of word order, negation, question and certain aspects of grammatical morphemes are discussed. Some of these features are unknown in English (e.g. sentence final particles, classifiers, and the grammatical morpheme "de"), while others are more widely encountered (e.g. word order). The existing data revealed many interesting language-specific developmental features. For example, in almost all aspects of syntactic development discussed in this article, the course of development is characterized by very early control of correct grammatical forms with subsequent development generally consisting of fine tuning. This is quite unlike English, whose development (e.g. negation and question) often involves an incorrect early form that gradually aligns with adult form only with long development. This general phenomenon in the development of Chinese syntax is most likely a consequence of the simplicity (in forms at least) of Chinese syntax in areas discussed in this article.

Mandarin Chinese

Modern day China consists of the ethnic Han majority and a number of ethnic minorities spread over China's northern, western, southwestern and southern border areas. The various dialects spoken by the Han people, despite their substantial variations, can be regarded as belonging to a single language family--the Chinese language family. The distribution of Chinese dialects is intimately related to China's topography. Over the northern and northwestern plains, where communication is less hindered by mountains, people can understand each other despite various accents. In the mountainous southern and southeastern China, speech from one county may be totally unintelligible to people from a neighbouring county.

Mandarin Chinese refers to the dialect spoken in Beijing. This dialect (and its variants) is widely spoken in northern, northwestern and southwestern China. Mandarin acquired its high status primarily due to the importance of Beijing which has been China's capital city since the Yuan dynasty (late 13th to 14th centuries). Beijing's political prominence has made her dialect the standard speech among high officials for centuries. Thus, both because of its high status, and its use throughout much of China, Mandarin Chinese has been the most important Chinese dialect for the last several centuries.

In this century, both the Nationalist government, and the Communist government promoted a "national language" to unify spoken Chinese. Both governments chose Mandarin for this purpose; therefore, Mandarin became even more important in modern China. It is estimated that more than 70% of today's Chinese, as well as most the educated young Chinese, speak this dialect.

Gramatical Sketch of Mandarin Chinese

Mandarin Chinese has many interesting features unlike those in European languages. First of all, the basic linguistic unit "word", as used in English, does not have an easy counterpart in Mandarin. In written Chinese, the "character" is the basic independent unit. Each character is a single syllable consisting of a single morpheme. This single, monosyllabic unit is called "tzyh" in Chinese. Chao (1968: 130), a prominent Chinese linguist, called this unit the "sociological word" by which he meant that the common non-linguist Chinese would take this unit to be a word in the English sense. However, whether this sociological word can be regarded as linguistic word is questionable, since many Chinese "tzyh" are bound morphemes, and many syntactically unitary words in Chinese are multisyllabic. Nevertheless, morphological change within "tzyh" does not exist, although various compounding processes can yield compound words and hence provide flexibility in word invention. Related to morphological simplicity, Mandarin does not require the verb of a sentence to agree with the subject, nor do verbs mark tense or voice. In short, the Chinese "tzyh" is an independent written character; as a single monosyllabic morpheme, there is no morphological change involving this unit in Mandarin grammar.

A second interesting feature of Mandarin is its sentence structure. Since no agreement between subject and verb is required, the relationship between subject and predicate is often in the topic-comment mode rather than actor-action. Chao (1968: 70) estimated that in ordinary discourse, about half of spoken sentences are of topic-comment construction. Although one may regard actor-action structure as a special case of the topic-comment mode, in general, the topic of the sentence need not be the actor of the action verb. Furthermore, many Mandarin sentences do not need a subject. This is not simply to say that the Mandarin subject may be ellipted like many other languages. In fact, under certain conditions, Mandarin sentences would sound odd if there were a subject. In other words, subjectless sentences are the norm under certain conditions. These conditions are (1) when concerned with climatic phenomenon (e.g. thunder, rain, cloud, and wind etc.), (2) when concerned with existence of an object or event (in English, "there" is used as subject), (3) truisms, and (4) when the subject is unknown or unimportant (in English, a truncated passive, or subject complement is used) (Wang, 1987: 64). As can be seen, all conditions stated above involved situations where the subject is unknown or where there is simply no logical subject (e.g. climatic phenomena).

When analyzing a Mandarin sentence, pressing it into the pattern of NP + VP is sometimes a futile exercise. When confronting a child's utterances, one must judge the correctness of the output in terms of what is acceptable under the circumstances rather than against a set of rules based on European languages.

A final feature of interest concerns Mandarin word-order typology. In Mandarin, word-order is the single most important syntactic device for sentence interpretation. Since inflection is almost non-existant in Mandarin, to identify the semantic role of various constituents one relies heavily on word-order. Yet, when one looks at features that characterize word-order typology (Greenberg, 1963), it becomes apparent that Mandarin contains features indicative of SOV as well as SVO language (Li and Thompson, 1981). For example, Mandarin has prepositions, auxiliaries preceding the verb, and the surface structure of SVO for simple declarative sentences (all are SVO features). It also has postpositions, modifier/head arrangement, sentence final particles, and SOV surface structure (all are SOV features).

Therefore Mandarin can not be easily classified either as an SOV or as an SVO language. This may be the result of a gradual transition of Mandarin from an SVO to an SOV language in the last thousand years or so. Several facts can be cited to support this contention. For example, northern China where Mandarin is spoken, was invaded and occupied by nomadic tribes for long periods of time after the disintegration (in early 3rd century) of the Han (dynasty) Empire. These nomadic peoples spoke languages of the Altaic language family (typical SOV language) and had significant impact on the languages of northern China. Significantly, dialects in southern China (e.g. southern Min spoken in Taiwan) where nomadic influence was minimal, show less SOV features than Mandarin. Furthermore, substantial evidence indicates that SOV sentences were much less common before the Tang dynasty (early 7th to early 10th century), reflecting that pre-Tang Chinese spoke a purer form of SVO language.

Word-order occupies a pivotal position in Chinese syntax. The acquisition of Mandarin syntax can not begin without knowledge of word order. Therefore, any discussion of syntactic acquisition of Mandarin must begin with word-order.

The Acquisition of Word-Order

1. The early stages

Two-word utterances mark the beginning of possible word-order knowledge. A longitudinal project involving 8 children undertaken by this author and Chen Shall-Way provided the data base for Cheng's (1986) analysis of early sentence structures during the period of $1.0 < MLU < 1.75$. With one exception (a child who reached MLU of 1.75 at 16 month), all other children reached MLU of 1.02 at around 20 monthw, and further development of 4 or 5 months was needed to reach MLU of 1.75. This rate of development approximates closely data reported for English (Wells, 1985: 124).

When one examines natural utterances by young children with an eye for word-order acquisition, two issues must be addressed. The first concerns the nature of the syntactic form (i.e. word-order) used to express various semantic content, and whether any consistent syntactic error is evident. The second issue concerns the nature of syntactic growth. Neither issue can be resolved without adequate knowledge of the semantic intention of the early utterances. As in many other research projects, semantic content was determined by contextual information recorded during data gathering sessions in our project. According to Cheng (1986), the semantic content of 2 to 3 word utterances may be classified into 12 patterns as follows: (1) actor + action, (2) patterns related to refusal, (3) patterns related to request, (4) more + x, (5) more + action, (6) patterns related to nonexistence, (7) location of entity, (8) location of action, (9) patterns that draw attention to something, (10) possessor + possessed, (11) property, function, and experience + entity, (12) big/small/much + x. This list contains many semantic categories familiar in the acquisition data of different languages at a comparable age. Of the patterns listed above, actor + action emerged early and had the highest rate of expansion for all children. Of the 245 actual verbs found in the data, the greatest majority were transitive verbs (135). Intransitive verbs (47), stative verbs (36) and descriptive verbs (27) were comparatively less frequent.

Regarding syntax, the most interesting question is whether the early patterns followed the typical word-order of Mandarin for the intended meaning. It seems that correct Mandarin word-order is always followed in the actor-action patterns; this is also the case for the possessor-possessed relationship, although many early utterances omitted the obligatory possessive marker "de". For entity and attribute, there are many examples of both 'entity + attribute' and "attribute + entity" order. In Mandarin, a modifier normally precedes head, so the attribute + entity pattern corresponds to the correct word-order of adjective/noun. The entity + attribute pattern is also correct, if the entity is the subject of a sentence with an adjective verb (Li & Thompson, 1981: 142). Examination of individual patterns revealed that (1) different words were used in these patterns (i.e. for any particular pair of words, their positional order was constant), (2) in light of contextual information both "entity + attribute" and "attribute + entity" patterns can be regarded as having the correct word order.

The most serious violation of Mandarin word-order in the data was found in utterances of "nominal + action" where the nominals (animate or inanimate) were direct objects of the verb (i.e. action). This pattern is in serious violation of normal Mandarin word-order. However, as mentioned earlier, OV construction is sometimes acceptable in Mandarin. Usually verbs implied in active disposal toward the object are used in OV construction (i.e. "ba" construction). In addition, OV construction is acceptable when O is the topic in a topic-comment mode. Based on contextual information, most of the OV patterns found in our data were incorrect. This type of word-order error seems to be the only significant error at this stage. What could be the reason(s) for this error? Several possibilities may be entertained. The easiest explanation is that these are simply occassional speech errors that might occur even in adult speech. However, this explanation is unlikely to be true, since 5 of the 8 children were observed to produce this erroneous pattern and the frequency (in utterance type) ranged from 20 to more than 50 per child. Furthermore, if two words, N and A, were observed to form a N+A pattern, then the reverse order (A+N) was seldom observed. Therefore, we can rule out the speech error explanation.

The second possibility is that at this point in development, children have acquired the "actor + action" pattern, but have not yet acquired "action + object". When forced to express the latter semantic relation, they overgeneralize the actor action pattern to the new situation. Cheng (1986) favoured this explanation. However, concurrent with the OV pattern, there were even more instances of correct action + object pattern by the same child (Note: the same verb did not seem to appear both ways). Thus it is difficult to argue that the child had not acquired the correct VO pattern.

An alternative explanation would be to regard these OV construction as topic + comment, and therefore no longer erroneous. The problem with this proposal becomes evident when one realizes that topic and comment are syntactically ill-defined terms. Some people (Li & Thompson, 1981: 15) would define topic as always occurring at the beginning of a sentence. If this position is followed, then topic + comment can legitimize all 2-word utterances. On the other hand, if one takes the position that the topic of an utterance must be determined semantically, and syntactically speaking, the topic can be found any where in the sentence, then one must decide whether O is indeed the topic in the OV construction. Unfortunately, for two word utterances, it is almost impossible to determine the topic on semantic grounds. In short, there is no easy way to determine whether OV construction corresponds to topic + comment in two word utterances.

Before leaving this topic, it is interesting to note that in another order prominent language, English, erroneous OV pattern also occurs frequently (Braine, 1976). Braine called these order errors "groping patterns". He also argued that patients of action should develop after the contrasting agent is firmly established. If this is the case, then one naturally expects OV to develop somewhat later than SV.

2. Canonical schemas and word-order.

When developed beyond two or three-word sentences, sentence structures naturally become more complicated. How do children expand their utterances to these more complicated structures? At least for word-order languages, a natural strategy would be to establish sentence interpretation on the basis of certain canonical word-order schemas. Several specific proposals, such as Bever's NVN strategy (1970), Chomsky's MDP (1969), and Slobin's canonical form (1985), made just such claims. Naturally, children also use semantic strategies based on contextual information and/or their knowledge of the world to interpret sentence meaning, but these are not our present focus.

An often used method to check whether something like a canonical schema is used to interpret simple declarative sentences relies on children's responses to passive sentences. Since passive sentences reverse the normal order of subject and object, any reliances on normal word-order to interpret the semantic role of the noun phrase would show up as consistent errors. In fact, Bever's original proposal of the NVN (word-order) strategy is based on precisely this kind of data. Chang (1986) ran a study on this issue based on this method. As mentioned earlier, Chinese does not have a formal passive voice, since there is no verbal change in Mandarin. However, in Mandarin, there is a construction (the "bei" construction) that functions in an analogous way to the passive voice in English. In the "bei" construction, the order of subject and object is reversed. The purpose of this construction, like the passive voice, is to emphasize the semantic object. The contrasting canonical form to the "bei" construction is the "ba" construction which occurs much more frequently than "bei". To make this point more clearly, the contrasting forms are listed below:

1. word-order of "ba" form: S   "ba"   O   V

2. word-order of "bei" form: O   "bei"   S   V

(note: S and O refer to the semantic subject and semantic object, V is the verb, and "ba", "bei" are two Mandarin grammatical morphemes.)

In the study by Chang (1986), 3 to 5 year-old children were tested on "bei" and "ba" construction. Comprehension of these sentences were tested by an acting-out method. To minimize the use of semantic strategy, only reversible sentences were employed. Results of this study are presented in table 1.

Table 1
Percentage of responses under each category (from Chang, 1986).
(100% = 72 Responses)

Sentence Type	N1 ba N2 V			N1 bei N2 V			N bei V			N1 N2 V		
Response Type	N1A*	N2A	0	N1A	N2*	0	NA	Npatient	0	N1A	N2A	0
Age 3	75.0	23.6	1.4	54.2	44.4	1.4	33.3	61.1	5.6	38.9	51.4	9.7
Age 4	88.9	11.1	0.0	43.1	56.9	0.0	29.2	69.4	1.4	51.4	45.8	2.8
Age 5	90.3	5.6	4.1	25.0	75.0	0.0	16.7	83.8	0.0	45.8	48.7	5.4

*N1A: N1 as agent

As expected, the "ba" construction is easier than the "bei" construction in that the 75% correct response rate on "ba" at 3 years of age is comparable to 5-year-old children's responses to "bei". Furthermore, similar to English data, the truncated passive is easier than the full passive.

With regard to the crucial issue of canonical schema, one must look at the consistent reversal error of the "bei" sentence. None of 4-year-olds showed reversal, and only 2 of the 19 3-year-old children showed consistent reversal. The rest of the mistakes were more or less random. This result would not be strong enough to conclusively support the canonical schema hypothesis. However, the issue is not closed. Since the study was a cross-sectional study, we simply do not know whether our sample of 3-year-old subjects captured the children at just the moment when they would have reversed the "bei" construction. The weakness of cross-sectional design in language acquisition study is amply demonstrated here. Only a longitudinal study can give us a clear picture of the developmental pattern of each child.

Another study concerned with word-order strategy in sentence interpretation involving three-and-a-half- to five-and-a-half-year old children was conducted by Jeng (1991). She used sets of normal and deviant sentences to test children's interpretations. As a comparison, adults' reactions were also tested.

The sentences have three basic structures, NVN, NNV and VNN; N refers to nouns (animate and inanimate), and V refers to verbs (all transitive). In Mandarin syntax, NVN sentences are the normal structure. NNV, without the grammatical morpheme "bei" or "ba" or other phonological markings such as pause or stress, are considered deviant. VNN sentences are all deviant. Even in the correct NVN structure, one may still obtain semantic deviation (e.g. the cracker ate the baby). In general, semantic deviation in our test sentences is the result of an irreversible sentence with inanimate subject. In short, the study looks into the influence on comprehension of sentence structure, animacy, and reversibility. The last factor could generate semantic deviation under normal syntax.

Again, an acting-out method was used. For NVN sentences, when the semantic information was consistent with syntactic structure (i.e. reversible sentences), the first noun was always taken as the actor, as it should be in Mandarin. Three-and-a-half-year old subjects had a slightly lower correct response rate (88%) than four- and five-year-old subjects (over 90%) and adults (100%). However, when semantic information contradicts syntactic structure (i.e. irreversible sentences with an inanimate noun as the first N), children tended to follow word-order (syntactic) interpretation at a higher rate (63% for 3-and-a-half-year-olds and 75% for four-and-a-half-year-olds) than adults (44%) who preferred semantic interpretations (56%). This result does not agree with English data (Macwhinney, Bates & Kliegl, 1984). In English, the syntactic interpretation becomes stronger as subjects become older. Therefore, in previous studies concerned with word-order languages, it is generally assumed that semantic strategy is less mature than syntactic strategy (Bates & Macwhinney, 1982; Slobin & Bever, 1982; Sinclair & Bronckart, 1972).

For the NNV sentences, since for NNV to correspond to SOV one normally has the word "ba" which was absent from our test sentences, subjects' interpretation of NNV became rather diverse. When semantic information constrained interpretation, subjects preferred the semantic interpretation over more than 80% of the responses regardless of age. However, when semantic information did not indicate a clear actor (i.e. in reversible sentences), most children preferred to interpret NNV as SOV (75% for three and half year-old, 50% and 53% for four-and-a-half- and five-and-a-half-year olds respectively), but adults preferred the SV subunit at a rate of 78%, with only 16% using the SOV interpretation. When one contrasts the children's average response rate of around 60% for the SOV interpretation with adults' rate of less than 20%, the difference is quite remarkable. It seems that children had a much greater tendency to use the canonical SOV structure in the absence of "ba" than adults.

VNN sentences do not correspond to any known structure in Mandarin; therefore, the response was even less consistent. In general, when semantic clues are clear, semantic interpretation is strong. When semantic information was unreliable, the tendency to use VO as a subunit became strong. Furthermore, the older the subjects the stronger this tendency became.

The overall nature of the interpretation strategy can be summarized as follows: (1) when semantic information was clear, and consistent with word-order information, interpretation was highly consistent (2) when syntax (word-order) contradicted semantic information, children were more likely to follow word-order strategy than adults. The fact that adults are less constrained by word-order, although contradicting expectations, is nevertheless supported by another study with Chinese college students (Mio, 1981). It is rather hard to explain why in a language where word order is the only important syntactic device, adults are even less likely than children to use this information to interpret sentences when word-order conflicts with semantic information. This is true even in totally grammatical sentences of SVO construction. Miao (1981) suggested that the fact that word-order is less powerful in Mandarin sentence interpretation than in English can be explained by the many types of word-order in Mandarin. Not only SVO, but also SOV ('ba'), OSV ('bei'), SV, and OV are commonly encountered. Thus, it is difficult to rely on word-order to determine the semantic subject. This explanation fails to consider that in each of the cases mentioned above, the subject is either marked by an explicit marker (e.g.,"ba" or "bei") or by a pause in conversation. The issue is not whether word-order varies, but how clearly the subject is marked. The fact that adults do not rely on word-order to determine the subject has more to do with the topic-comment structure of many Mandarin sentences in which the subject is determined semantically rather than by word-order. Consequently, when adults are required to determine the subject of a sentence, they do not exclusively rely on word-order to make their choice. But when children are required to do the same, they rely on word-order to a greater extent, because word-order is more explicit than non-syntactic information, especially in an experiment where efforts are made to eliminate non-syntactic information.

In general, the studies on word-order acquisition seem to support the idea that children initially adopt canonical schemas for sentence interpretation. This strategy relaxes later on, when they grow older and become more adapted to using non-linguistic information to interpret Mandarin, which has a much looser structure than English.

The Acquisition of Questions and Negation

1. Questions

Compared to English, the syntactic structure of Mandarin interrogative sentence is vastly simpler. Since there is no requirement of subject-verb agreement, morphological changes related to verbs in Mandarin questions are totally absent. Li and Thompson (1981) listed four grammatical devices that may be used to pose questions. One may turn a declarative statement into a question by adding a sentence final particle (such as "ma" or "ne"). This type of question may be called the particle question. A second device uses a question word whose information is requested. For example, if the declarative sentence is "John went to school"; replacing the word "school" by a question word relating to place, the sentence is changed into the English equivalent of "Where did John go". If one replaces "John" in the declarative sentence by a question word relating to a person, then the sentence becomes something like "Who went to school" in English. Many question words in Mandarin function similarly to English words like "What", "Where", "When", "How" and so forth.

Another question-making device in Mandarin is generally known as the V-not-V question. One may pose a question by listing the two alternatives of choice. For example, the English question "Do you want to come?" would have the form "you want-not-want come" in Mandarin. Obviously, answers to this type of question can simply be one of the two alternatives listed(somewhat similar to English yes/no answer). This type of question can be expanded to a general disjunctive form where the two alternatives may be two full sentences joined by the disjunctive word "or".

The fourth interrogative device is related to the V-not-V form. It is a form of tag question that tags the A-not-A form onto a declarative sentence. The tagged part usually consists of the phrase "right not right", "be not be" or something similar.

Regarding the development of Mandarin questions, the most detailed and reliable data were reported by Cheng (1991). The data base is indentical to the one used in her analysis of two-word utterances reported in this article. The earliest form of Mandarin question to emerge is the sentence-final particle (or the particle question). Despite substantial variation in the MLU value at which the first question emerges, there is complete uniformity in form among the seven children whose data were analyzed (see Table 2). At the first stage of interrogative development (1.0 <= MLU <= 1.75) all questions (37 different questions among 7 children) were of this type. This is quite different from English data (Brown, 1973; Ervin-Tripp, 1970). Since the initial stage of English questions relies on intonation or fixed routines (what date? where ball? etc.) to indicate interrogative intent, there is ample room for developmental change later on. Mandarin questions, on the other hand, because of syntactic simplicity are fully grammatical even at the initial stage. Furthermore, no intonational question was ever discerned in our data. Perhaps the early control of a linguistic device to pose questions eliminated the necessity of intonation. However, the early maturity of particle questions does not imply that no development takes place in Mandarin questions. Development takes place first on the types of question-device mastered, and secondly, on the semantic content of childrens' queries.

Table 2

Emergence of first questions (from Cheng, 1991).

Subject	D	E	F	G	H	I	J
Age	17,20	21,12	23,11	24,7	21,12	23	25,1
MLU	1.06	1.64	1.55	1.53	1.12	1.29	1.64
Longest Utterance	3	4	4	5	2	3	6

In the second stage (1.75 <= MLU <= 2.25), roughly half of our subjects began to use certain question-words (such as "schenme" or what) to pose questions. Even at this stage, the great majority of questions were still in the particle form. V-not-V disjunctive question were observed. The syntactic structures of their questions, though simple, were mostly correct. Some question words were still absent at this stage. They were words similar to English "why" and "when". "Who", "which" and "how" were all used occasionally by some children in our sample. The "where" question was posed by sentence final particle, instead of the actual question word "where".

The last type of question to emerge was the V-not-V type, which began to appear at $2.25 <= \text{MLU} <= 2.75$. It is interesting to note that there was an apparent "decalage" between answering the V-not-V question and the use of this form to pose questions, since the earliest correct responses by children to other's queries involved V-not-V questions. In fact, most children can respond correctly to V-not-V question even at the single word stage. Children understood the query-answer exchange fairly early, and furthermore, the answer to V-not-V question was almost a routine (either V, or not-V). This may account for the early emergence of their ability to answer V-not-V questions. In an informal test, this author found that young children would answer clearly nonsensical questions in V-not-V form (for example using nouns instead of verbs in the form) by saying V (or not-V). Thus, children can perform in a syntactically correct manner without proper semantic content. The late appearance of posing V-not-V questions may be due to the cognitive difficulties of formulating two alternatives in a single sentence.

The order of development of different wh-questions appears to be similar in Mandarin and English. This could reflect universal cognitive order concerning childrens' understanding about places, objects, people, reason, time, number...,etc. Both English and Mandarin appear to have the highest rate of development of questions in stage 3 (around $2.25 <= \text{MLU} <= 2.75$), in content as well as in form. Perhaps because of its structural simplicity, fully grammatical Mandarin questions developed earlier than English, but there may not be much difference by way of semantic content.

When one examines the development of questions in Mandarin in light of known data in other languages (e.g. Slobin, 1985), one sees an interesting interplay between communicative intent, communicative devices to express the intent, and the cognitive foundations of these expressions. Children clearly understand the question-answer interplay as early as the one-word stage. This can be seen not only in our data, but in other languages where the syntactic form of questioning is simple (e.g. Japanese). At this point children also show a clear intention to question others; however, when the proper form for this objective is too complicated, they would find informal devices (e.g. intonation) to achieve this objective. Whether they are in full control of the grammatical device or not, the content of their questions and the order of development of the content are quite similar across different languages.

2. *Negation*

Mandarin negation makes several distinctions that are not explicit in English. For example, rejection ("bu"), denial ("mei"), non-existence ("meiyou"), and an imperative form of prohibition ("mei" or "buyao"), are expressed by different negative particles. In the acquisition of Mandarin negation, a child must acquire the distinction as well as the appropriate application of these words. Syntactically, he must also learn the proper place in a sentence for the negative particles. In Mandarin negation, the negative particle generally precedes whatever it negates. Thus the serial position of a negative particle in a sentence can vary substantially. In general, a negation tends to be applied to an action, attribute of object or event, experience, manner, or aspect of an action. Therefore, the negation is intimately related to a verb, adverb or adjective. For example, the sentence "I "bu" (no) surely come", means that I may or may not come, since the negative particle is placed before the adverb "surely". If the negative particle is placed before the verb "I surely "bu" (no) come", then it means that I will surely not come. For negating the attribute of an object or event, again the negative particle must immediately precede the adjective, wherever it may be in the sentence. Therefore, the placement of the negative particle depends on the scope of application of the negation (Li and Thompson, 1981: 417). In more complicated cases, the same rule still holds. For example, the English sentence "It is not that I would not come, I could not come." would have the equivalent Mandarin as follows:

      bu shi wo bu lai, shi wo bu neng lai
      no be I no come, be I no able come.

The three "bu" particles precede three verbs (one is actually an auxiliary verb).

The difference between the particle "bu" and "mei" in Mandarin constitutes an important aspect of negation acquisition. According to Li and Thompson (1981: 421), the distinction is functional, in that "mei" negates the completion of an event, while "bu" is a neutral negation. Therefore, when one wishes to negate an attribute, or the state of an object, or an auxiliary verb, "bu" is used. On the other hand, to deny that something has ever happened, been completed, or been experienced, "mei" is required. Sometimes, however, the difference can be rather arbitrary. For example, "there is not a book on the shelf", would require "meiyou", but "books are not on the shelf" would require "bu" as the appropriate negative particle. Granted, there is a difference in shades of meaning; nevertheless, the difference is quite subtle. It would seem that mistaken use of the negative particles should be frequent in children.

Cheng (1988) analyzed the same set of data she used in her previous reports for the development of questions in Mandarin. She focuses on the acquisition of (1) rejection and prohibition ("bu"), (2) non-existence and denying possession ("meiyou"), and (3) other more complicated constructions. Although both forms of negation (" buyao" and "meiyou") can be found in single-word utterances, among two-word utterances, rejections developed slightly ahead of the non-existence usage. This is different from the English data reported by Bloom (1970).

With respect to the negative particle "buyao", the earliest appearance in the single word stage took the form "buyao" (not want) to signal rejection and refusal. It also functioned as an imperative prohibition to others in the early utterances. Judging from context, both ways were used correctly. A little later, in the two-word stage, the construction "person + buyao" began to appear. In addition, patterns of "action + buyao", "object + buyao" would also appear. It should be noted that in "action + buyao", the proper word-order should be "buyao + action", if it is meant to negate the action. Therefore, the observed pattern contains a word-order error. Some children quickly corrected themselves and adopted the correct word-order. There were two children who persisted with the wrong order for quite a while. Cheng (1988) believed that these children had a clear tendency (i.e. by a pause between the two words) to use the "action + buyao" pattern to emphasize the action. Three-word patterns usually came in the form of "person + buyao + action" (e.g. mother buyao hold, auntie buyao come... etc.). After MLU greater than 1.75, negations became more varied. Expansion of the negative sentences tended to occur at the verb phrase. For example, longer negations such as "person + buyao

+ action + object ", "person + buyao + action + location", and more complicated sentences using expansion of the noun phrase as object of the action appeared. At the end of the project, two children even constructed negative questions in the form of a negative sentence plus a sentence final particle to form a negative particle question.

Overall, the development of negation with "buyao" as the negative particle seemed to follow the process of combining existing segments of a full sentence to form more complicated sentences. For example, in the single-word stage, we have "buyao"; then this negative particle was combined with an action word or subject (agent) to form a two-word pattern. At this point, both "action + object" and "buyao + action" were observed. In the three-word utterances, we saw "person (agent) + buyao + action ". Since none of these progressively longer sentences required movement of constituents, or verbal morphological change, word-order of these longer sentences were mostly correct (Cheng, 1988).

Compared to "buyao", the other negative particle, "meiyou", had a slower evolution. Even though both "buyao" and "meiyou" were heard during the single-word stage, some children used "gone" or "no see" (with " bu " as the negative particle) to indicate non-existence, instead of " meiyou ". Later on, during the two-word stage, the patterns of both " meiyou + entity " and "entity + meiyou" began to appear. Similar to other modifier/head structures, the proper word-order should be "meiyou + entity". This correct pattern soon became the dominant combination. Further expansion of meiyou included (1) expanding entities to phenomena, states of entity, and non-occurrences of events, (2) slightly later, "meiyou" became a negative particle to indicate the non-possession of objects by animate beings (e.g. cat "meiyou" ears, doll "meiyou" hands...etc.) or the non-existence of an entity at a specific location (e.g. here "meiyou", chair "meiyou" cat...etc.).

Cheng (1988) listed all other negations besides "buyao" and "meiyou" in Table 3. In this table, only four older subjects' data were presented since the other subjects were too young to produce many negations other than "buyao" and "meiyou". From the data presented in Table 3, it is apparent that more complicated negations appeared after a MLU value of 1.50, and most did not appear before MLU = 2.00. The most frequent occurrences of negations involved negating the completion of an event, negating compound verbs, and negating adjectives. Frequency of occurrence did not seem related to the order of appearance. Negations listed in Table 3 can be regarded as further extensions to the earlier development of "buyao" used in rejection, and "meiyou" applied to an entity to signal non-existence. The actual negative particles used in the later-appearing negations were either "bu", or "meiyou" applied to verbs, auxiliary verbs, or stative verbs. This is different from the earlier use of "meiyou" that applied mostly to nouns(i.e. entities, people...etc.). The use of "mei" alone is extremely rare, even though it is permissible in Mandarin.

Table 3

Frequency of occurrence (in type) of different categories of negation (from Cheng, 1988).

Negation category subject	G	H	I	J
negating completion of an event	35(1.48)*	11(2.37)	16(1.49)	9(2.06)
negating experiencing	2(2.27)	0	0	0
negating of progressive aspect	5(2.24)	2(2.08)	1(1.53)	3(2.59)
negating change of state	5(1.46)	0	0	0
negating adjectives	22(1.53)	5(2.00)	11(1.53)	5(2.19)
negating auxiliary	10(2.24)	1(2.58)	13(1.45)	14(2.29)
negating stative verb	1(2.47)	3(2.37)	4(2.28)	23(2.19)
negating compound verb	9(2.24)	14(2.37)	12(2.28)	23(2.19)
expecting non-repetition of an event	7(2.06)	2(2.37)	1(1.53)	7(2.06)
action has stopped	5(2.06)	1(2.08)	1(2.20)	5(2.06)
negating with Shi (be)	5(2.24)	5(2.58)	2(2.22)	9(2.59)

* Numbers in parenthesis indicate the MLU value of the first observation of this type of negation

The general course of development of Mandarin negation did not involve movement of the negating element from outside a declarative sentence to an appropriate position inside the sentence, as proposed by Bellugi (1967) and McNeil (1970). It is more a matter of the child learning how the negative particle in Mandarin is applied to the appropriate segment of the sentence, and how the different senses of negation are expressed by different negative particles. There were some consistent errors in applying inappropriate negative particles. Most of these errors consisted of using "meiyou" to deny a simple fact, that should have had a simple "bu". For example, to deny a simple state (e.g. fat, dirty, cold, good looking...etc), one should use a simple "bu". But many children used "meiyou" instead. This type of mistake occurs even in adult speech. The semantic implication of "meiyou" under this condition is different from "bu". With "meiyou", one implies that an expected state did not occur (e.g.if you ate a great deal and did not get fat, then "meiyou" is more appropriate to deny being fat), where "bu" would be a simple denial of a fact. Given that the mistake is unidirectional (using "meiyou" when "bu" is more appropriate), one may say that a natural tendency exists in Mandarin to extend the sense of non-existence to that of denying the state of being. This is most apparent in children's usage, but can sometimes be found in careless utterances from adults as well.

The Acquisition of Grammatical Morphemes

Grammatical morphemes discussed in this section are all bound morphemes, thus excluding some of the common function words which have already appeared in previous discussions. Common grammatical morphemes in Mandarin include various affixes, the particle de, sentence-final particles, various classifiers, quantifiers, co-verbs, prepositions...etc. The acquisition of these morphemes is surely a complex story. However, since relevant data are not readily available, only three types of grammatical morphemes will be discussed. They are, sentence final particles, de, and classifiers. All three classes of morphemes emerge early in the development of Mandarin, and are very important in sentence construction.

1. Sentence final particles.

Sentence final particles occur at the end of Mandarin sentences. The exact number of these particles vary according to dialects, and changing habits of speakers in a community, but at least two dozen can be easily identified Chao,1968: 797). The semantic and pragmatic functions of these particles are very elusive. Although one may identify some aspects of some particles' function, no one ever claimed to have an exhaustive list of their functions.

To an observant Mandarin speaker, the following facts about these particles should be quite apparent: (1) they occur much more frequently in conversation than in writing, unless the writing is a direct quotation of conversation, (2) children use them more than adults, and (3) they occur more in informal and intimate conversations than in formal conversations. It may be argued that sentence final particles in Mandarin have a somewhat analogous function to stress and intonation in other languages.

Yang (1987) conducted a detailed study on three aspects of sentence final particles. She looked into the development and semantic functions of some early-appearing particles as well as the production and comprehension of a specific particle"le". "Le" deserved special attention for reasons that will be discussed later. There were 16 subjects in Yang's study, eight of which had an average age of 20 months at the beginning of the study. They were observed for about 10 months. The other eight subjects had begun their observation session at different ages varying from 24 to 44 months, and each subject was observed for 4 months.

Five particles seemed to emerge early and were the focus of Yang's analysis. Their phonetic and semantic descriptions are listed below:

ya/a : impatience (used in high pitch), reduced forcefulness, to emphasize negation (with negative particle)

ne : question particle

le : currently relevant state, new information and state

ou : concern, friendly warning

la : combining le and ya (with corresponding meaning), impatience (stronger than ya alone)

Two points concerning this list must be made clear. First, no one claims that the list provides all semantic functions of these particles. Second, the semantic functions of these particles apply to the entire sentence preceding the particle. Particles by themselves do not have much meaning, which makes their orthography in written Chinese somewhat uncertain.

The age at which these particles were first observed to emerge by eight children is presented in Table 4. Data from other children (N=8) were not presented due to the advanced age of these children, who used a number of particles from the beginning of the observation sessions. From table 4, it seems that children used some particles in their two or three-word utterances as young as 18 months. By the age of 27 to 30 months all children controlled three or more particles. This is truly a remarkable feat, given the elusiveness of the semantic functions of sentence final particles. However, perhaps the same can be said about stress and intonation.

If one adopts the age at which 50% of the children in this study acquired the particle as the age of general emergence, then "a/ya", "le", "ou", "la", and "ne" have the respective age of emergence at 20, 21, 22, 25, and 28 months. This order of development does not fit well with individual patterns. For each individual, different particles seemed to emerge quite closely to each other.

Since most particles have more than one semantic function, it is interesting to note the order of their acquisition. For "a/ya", the earliest function acquired is impatience. For example, when children are repeatedly asked to identify a familiar object in a picture book, they may respond with this particle to express their impatience. Later on, "ya" was used to signal reconfirmation, when the child was uncertain about

Table 4
Emergence of the 5 sentence final particles (adapted from Yang, 1987).

final particle	1	2	3	4	subject 5	6	7	8
Ya	18	20	16	21	28	20	22	26
Le	-	14	21	21	21	20	24	-
La	18	-	-	20	-	21	30	-
Ou	21	-	20	22	-	20	27	29
Ne	22	-	18	-	28	-	25	-
Other	21	23	18	21	21	21	25	26

something (e.g. names of objects). Negating functions came even later. No clear case of reduced forcefulness was observed in connection with the use of "ya". As for "la", its function of impatience also appeared early. Most of its other functions can be described as combined functions of "le" and "ya". ("Le" will be described below) "Ne" usually appeared with the single function of questioning. Finally, with "ou", children first used it as an implied surprise (e.g. more stones than expected, taller than expected,...etc); only later did the function of friendly warning become evident.

Finally, we come to "le", which can function as an aspect marker (completion) as well as a sentence final particle . Normally, these separate functions of "le" can be easily distinguished by its position in the sentence (as an aspect marker, it follows the verb; as sentence final particle, it appears at the end of a sentence). However, when a sentence ends with a verb, one would need other means to determine "le's" function. Another special feature of "le" concerns its frequent co-occurrence with other sentence final particles. When this happens,"le" invariably precedes the other particle and modifies the semantic function of the other particle with "le's" own function. The main function of "le", as characterized by Li and Thompson (1981), is to signal a state of current relevance in a particular situation. For example, a simple question may be posed by using the particle "ma", however, when "le-ma" is used, the question may imply an immediate relevance to a preceding statement. For example, when we are discussing the whereabouts of a friend, we may use " he went to China "le-ma" ?" as a way of expressing the unexpected information (that he went to China) about this friend. Li and Thompson (1981) listed five separate situations that reflect this implication of "le". They are (1) change of current state, (2) correcting a wrong assumption, (3) progress so far, (4) what happens next, and (5) closing a statement. Yang's data revealed that the earliest usage of "le" appeared around 25 months (when 50% of her subjects controlled this usage), with the semantic function of change of current state. The next two functions- what happens next, and progress so far- appeared almost together around 30 months. The last observed function (correcting a wrong assumption) appeared around 47 months. The case of closing a statement is somewhat complex, mainly because "le" can be used as a closing statement as well as a closing for an entire conversation. Yang did not attempt to analyze this function of "le".

To obtain more consistent data on the comprehension and production of "le", Yang also conducted an experimental investigation. In production, she constructed play sessions in which to elicit specific statements that would include "le". In comprehension, she used two puppets in a contrived situation where one puppet would say a sentence with "le"; the other puppet would say the same thing without "le". The child was asked to judge which puppet was more correct. There were four trials for each of the four semantic functions (i.e. I=change of current state, II=progress so far, III= what may happen next, IV= negating an incorrect assumption). Thus the maximum score for each condition is 4. Mean scores for both comprehension and production are presented in Table 5. It is clear that results from this experimental investigation are quite similar to observational data discussed earlier in that function category I is the easiest, and IV the hardest. This is true for both production and comprehension.

In general, the semantic functions of "le" vary greatly, and their acquisitions seem to develop over a long time. Even at age 5, the average performance on "le" as a negation to an incorrect assumption is still fairly low.

Table 5

Mean performance on production and comprehension (in parenthesis). (Date from Yang, 1987.)

age	semantic function I	II	III	IV
3	2.94 (1.17)	1.50 (0.72)	0.67 (1.00)	0.11 (0.44)
4	3.83 (2.72)	2.94 (1.56)	1.78 (1.61)	0.33 (0.78)
5	3.89 (3.33)	3.44 (2.67)	3.00 (1.94)	1.89 (1.56)

2. Classifiers

Li and Tompson (1981) wrote "To a speaker of English, one of the most striking features of the Mandarin noun phrase is the classifier. A classifier is a word that must occur with a number (e.g."yi" one, "ban" half, "shi" ten) and /or a demonstrative (e.g. "zhei" whole, "nei" that, "nei" which), or certain quantifiers (such as "zheng" whole, "ji" how many/a few, "mou yi" a certain and "mei" every) before the noun." (p.104). In fact the use of classifiers under similar conditions is fairly common in many East Asian language (e.g. Burmese, Japanese, Laotian, Thai and Vietnamese). In English, something analogous to a classifier is used when a mass noun is quantified (e.g., a cup of milk, a truck load of dirt, etc.), but in Chinese a classifier is obligatory for all nouns when a number occurs before a noun. Thus instead of saying "three houses" as in English, in Chinese one would say "san don fangzi" (i.e., inserting the classifier "don" between the number "san" and the noun "fangzi").

There are dozens of classifiers in modern Chinese (Chao,1968), but their range of application varies. Some classifiers have very restricted use. For example, "chu" can only be used with 'stage play' or 'opera', "feng" with 'letter' and "ben" with 'book' or other bound volumes. At the other extreme, the classifier "ge" can be used with almost any noun. For most classifiers, however, their use is loosely determined by the shared perceptual or conceptual dimensions of a collection of nouns. For instance, "jang" is used with nouns referring to objects with an extended surface(e.g. papers, desks, chairs, beds, etc.), "ba" with nouns referring to objects that can be handled and grasped (e.g. axes, fans, knives, scissors, etc...). Since most classifiers are bound morphemes with little referential meaning, there are few cues in the classifiers themselves which would reveal the common dimension of the associated noun category.

From our own data and an early report by Chao (1951), it seems certain that the most common Chinese classifier "ge" appears in the spontaneous speech of children around 24 months of age. By the middle of the third year, "ge" would rank as the fourth most frequently occurring word in children's speech (Yang, Yang & Shou, 1973). The acquisition of the full range of these words certainly continues for many years, since even some adults have difficulty deciding on the proper use of some rare classifiers. The nature of the acquisition process may depend on the range of application of the classifiers. For the very restrictive classifiers, rote learning would seem the right way to proceed, much like the learning of irregular verbs in English. On the other hand, for the more widely applied classifiers, learning by extension or generalization may be more likely. Clark and Clark (1977) have noted that many dimensions underlying the applicability of classifiers are the very ones used by children in their overextension of early nouns.

Chang (1987) conducted a study to determine whether children can extend appropriate classifiers to new objects, and whether a regular order of acquisition exists for 12 commonly-used classifiers. Three groups of children with mean ages of 4, 5, and 6 years participated in the study. To test their ability for generalization, four objects of different shape were given a single pseudo-name (a non-sense word). Children were asked to pick up one of the objects on the basis of the classifier. If the child can do this, then he demonstrates his knowledge that the classifier is somehow related to the specific shape of an object. All together, 4 classifiers- "lih", "tyau", "jang" and "kyau"- were tested. Table 6 presents the data on generalization of these 4 classifiers. An age trend of improvement is quite apparent, but even the youngest group (4 year-old) had 3 children who generalized all classifiers correctly. In the oldest group, almost all children were able to generalize these classifiers. There was also an orderly trend among the classifiers acquired. The easiest one to generalize was "lih", followed by "tyau", "jang", and "kyau". This trend was fairly uniform among our subjects.

Table 6

Number of subjects correctly generalized classifiers (from Chang, 1987).

number of classifiers correctly generalized	4	3	2	1	0	total N
age group						
6:01	9	1	0	0	0	10
5:03	5	2	3	0	0	10
4:00	3	0	1	2	4	10

The important point of this experiment has been the demonstration that children did not have to rely on rote memory to learn the appropriate application of classifiers to novel items. Another experiment in the same study attempted to determine the order of acquisition of 12 classifiers. The procedure for the second experiment was fairly simple. A child was shown a picture of an object (e.g. a box), then he was asked the question "there is one _____ box?" the blank space contained the Mandarin question word that means "what". The child's answer would have to be a classifier under the condition. Results from this study are presented in Table 7. From this table, it is clear that an orderly process of acquisition of these classifiers can be easily discerned.

As expected, children's ability to use classifiers improved with age. It is interesting to note that even 6-year-old children still had substantial difficulty with many common classifiers. This difficulty involved the choice of an appropriate classifier for a given noun rather than the failure to insert a classifier between a number and a noun. In fact even the 3-year-olds rarely failed to use classifiers when they were obligatory. Thus, there appears to be a protracted acquisition process. Children first acquire the general knowledge concerning situations that require classifiers for individual nouns. Then they learn the appropriate classifier to use in any given situation.

When one examines the order of acquisition of classifiers, "ge" is the first one to be mastered. This is consistent with Chao's (1951) observation. "Ge" is a very special classifier in Chinese, since it is the only 'general classifier' (Chao, 1968) that can be applied to all nouns. This is not to say that in common adult usage, one would use "ge" and the proper classifier interchangably; rather, if one substitutes "ge" for other classifiers, the resulting combination , although odd, would not be judged as totally incorrect by native speakers. Data from this study show that for the youngest group, out of 120 total responses, 75 were "ge" (only 10 "ge" responses are called for) resulting in high hits and high false positives. The number of false positives decreased substantially as children got older. Many of the "ge" substitutions found in the youngest group cannot be direct reflections of what they hear in the environment, since no adult would use "ge" for some of the nouns in this study (e.g., leaf, book, milk, shirt, scissors.). These mistakes can only be the result of rule-governed errors. One may speculate on the nature of this rule. One possibility would involve the following strategy: (1) a classifier is needed between a numeral and a noun, (2) different classifiers may be needed for different nouns, and (3) when you are not sure of the proper classifier, use "ge". A child following this strategy would have produced the kind of error found in the present study.

In contrast to "ge", "ben" is the most restrictive classifier of those tested. It can be used only in connection with books or other bound volumes. However, it is acquired right after "ge". So the most general, and, perhaps, the most restrictive classifiers are the earliest ones to be acquired.

In general, children's acquisition of classifiers can take diverse routes. For some classifiers, generalization from known to unknown is possible; for others, it requires specific learning and memorization. Finally, if a child is uncertain about the correct classifier to use in any situation, he used the general classifier "ge" as a catch-all.

3. de

In many ways, the particle "de" is unique to Mandarin Chinese. It is the most frequently occurring word in Mandarin (Liu, Chung, & Wang, 1975), and it is one of a few Chinese characters that have no homophone. Its grammatical function is exceeding versatile. Although linguists do not completely agree with each other in the analysis of "de's" function (Chao, 1968; Chu, 1961; Li & Thompson, 1981; Tang, 1979), we may summarize some of its more important functions as follows:

a: genitive marker: a possessive phrase can be constructed by NP + de

b: association relation: a general association relation between NP's may be expressed by NP1 de NP2 (e.g. the roof of the stadium = stadium de roof)

c: prepositional phrase: when NP1 of the above construction is a place word, it usually becomes a prepositional phrase (e.g. people in the stadium = stadium de people)

d: noun modifier: it usually takes the form of Adj. de N, while Adj.+de functions as a modifier to N. (e.g. red barn = red de barn)

e: relativization: a relative clause modifies a head noun, so a relative clause is also a noun modifier. In Mandarin, relativization is marked by "de". The general construction takes the form: relative clause + de + head noun, where "de" functions to nominalize the clause

f: nominalization: In addition to nominalizing clauses, "de" can nominalize verb phrases by V de NP (e.g. things to eat = eat de things)

Table 7
Order of acquisition of 12 classifiers (from Chang, 1987).

classifiers age (year:month)	ge	ben	jang	pian	tyau	liang	jy	baa	juan	kuay	herl	ke
4:00	0	1	0	0	0	0	0	0	0	0	0	0
4:02	0	0	1	0	0	0	1	0	0	0	0	0
3:05	1	0	0	0	0	0	0	0	0	0	0	0
3:10	1	1	0	0	0	0	0	0	0	0	0	0
4:00	1	0	0	0	0	0	1	0	0	0	0	0
4:05	1	0	0	0	0	0	0	0	0	0	0	0
5:05	1	0	0	0	0	0	1	1	0	0	0	0
4:10	1	0	1	0	1	1	0	0	0	0	0	0
3:07	0	1	0	0	0	0	1	1	0	0	0	0
5:03	1	1	1	0	1	1	0	0	0	0	0	0
5:01	0	1	0	1	0	1	1	0	0	0	0	0
6:02	1	1	0	1	0	0	1	0	0	0	0	0
5:08	1	1	0	1	1	0	0	0	1	0	1	0
6:04	1	1	1	0	0	0	1	0	0	0	0	0
3:01	1	1	1	0	0	0	1	0	1	0	0	0
5:05	1	1	1	0	0	1	0	0	0	0	0	0
5:01	1	1	1	1	0	0	1	0	1	0	0	0
4:08	1	1	1	1	1	0	0	0	0	0	0	0
5:03	1	1	1	1	1	1	0	0	0	0	0	0
6:00	1	1	0	1	1	1	1	0	0	0	0	0
6:01	1	1	1	1	0	1	1	0	1	0	0	0
6:00	1	1	1	0	0	1	1	1	0	0	1	0
5:00	0	1	1	1	0	1	1	1	0	0	0	0
6:00	1	1	0	1	1	0	0	1	1	0	0	0
6:05	1	1	1	1	0	1	1	1	0	0	0	0
6:02	1	1	1	1	0	1	1	1	1	1	0	0
5:01	0	1	1	1	1	1	1	1	1	1	0	0
5:04	1	1	1	1	1	0	1	1	1	1	0	0
6:03	1	1	1	1	1	1	1	1	1	1	0	0
5:10	1	1	1	1	1	1	1	1	0	1	1	0

N=30
Note: 1 refers to correct responses, 0 incorrect responses

g: verb modifier: Adj + de can function as a manner adverb to modify verbs. The adjective in this construction is usually reduplicated.(e.g. walk slowly = slow-slow de walk)

h: shi....de construction: this is a special construction in Mandarin that emphasizes a particular action, state, situation...etc. The complete sentence usually consists of a subject followed by "shi" (be), then a nominalization by "de" (e.g. This is from ancient Egypt = This "shi" from Egypt <u>come-de</u>)
Nom.

i: complex stative construction: according to Li and Thompson (1981:621), the complex stative construction takes the form:

clause + de + stative { clause }
{ verb phrase }

and the function of this construction relates to inferred meanings, which can either be the manner of the verb phrase or the resultant state when the event in the first clause has been carried to such an extent that an unusual state has resulted. (e.g. He laughed so hard that his hat fell off = He laughed de hat fell off)

j: sentence linking: "de" can be used as one of the many ways that sentences are linked to one another in Mandarin. For example, conditional sentences (if.....then) in Mandarin can be constructed with "de-hua" or "de-shihou". (e.g. if you wish, I'll go with you = you wish de-hua, I with you go.)

In addition to the functions listed above, there are other less frequent constructions with de (Chao , 1968; 285-301). However, even without those lesser functions, de's grammatical functions are sufficiently complex to occupy an unique status in Mandarin syntax.

The emergence and development of various functions of "de" was reported in Chang and Huang (1986) is presented here in Table 8. In this table, de's functions are classified as follows: 1 incomplete associative phrase (function a,b,and c discussed above), 2 complete associative phrase, 3 manner adverb(function g), 4 incomplete modifier phrase, 5 complete modifier phrase,6 nominalization (function f), 7 shi...de construction, 8 relativization, 9 complex stative construction, and 10 sentence linking.

Table 8

Emergence and development of de's functions (from Chang & Huang, 1986).

subject	recording sessions	1	2	3	4	5	6	7	8
A								2(1)[a]	2(1)
		14,28*	15,25	16,23	17,20	18,27	19,17	20,14	21,6
B								1(5)	
		16,20	17,17	18,15	19,24	20,16	21,4	22,6	23,11
C				1(4)	1(2)	1(2)	1(5)		1(28)
				2(3)		2(2)	2(2)		2(14)
				4(1)		6(1)	4(1)		4(2)
								6(7)	5(2)
								8(2)	6(9)
									8(2)
		19,19	20,7	21,4	22,17	23,3	24,7		26,26
D				6(1)		1(2)	1(1)	1(1)	1(2)
								4(1)	
		20,11	21,12	22,4	23,4	24,9	25,1	26,4	26,26
E		1(2)			1(7)	1(2)	1(18)	1(4)	1(14)
						4(1)	2(1)	4(3)	2(2)
						6(1)	4(1)	6(2)	4(15)
							6(1)		
		21,19	22,16	23,14	24,11	25,1	26,8	27,5	28,3

Table 8 (continued)

F	1(4)	1(2)	1(3)	1(3)	1(2)	1(1)	1(1)	1(1)
	4(2)	4(2)	4(10)	4(5)	4(5)	2(2)	2(3)	2(2)
	6(6)	6(11)	5(1)	6(9)	6(2)	3(2)	4(9)	4(4)
		7(1)	6(7)	7(1)	8(1)	4(6)	6(2)	5(2)
			7(2)			6(7)	7(1)	6(11)
			8(1)			7(1)		7(1)
						8(2)		
	22,22	23,26	24,17	25,14	26,14	27,12	28,9	29,7
G	1(1)	1(1)	1(1)			1(1)	1(2)	1(6)
	2(1)	2(1)				2(1)	2(11)	2(3)
						7(1)	3(1)	6(2)
							6(1)	7(2)
							8(1)	9(1)
	23,29	24,16	24,27	25,6	25,20	26,5	26,18	27,1
H	1(1)	1(1)	2(3)	6(1)	1(1)	1(1)	1(2)	2(1)
			6(1)		2(1)	5(2)	6(1)	4(4)
					6(5)	6(2)		6(2)
					8(1)			
	26,18	27,1	27,14	27,21	28,12	28,27	29,10	29,24
I	1(1)	1(1)	2(4)	2(3)	1(7)	1(3)	1(6)	1(1)
	2(1)	2(2)	4(2)	6(2)	2(5)	2(10)	2(5)	2(23)
	8(1)	4(3)	6(2)		4(1)	3(1)	4(5)	4(9)
	9(2)	5(1)			6(3)	4(2)	6(2)	5(2)
		6(2)			7(2)	6(1)		6(1)
		7(1)			8(1)	7(3)		7(2)
						9(1)		8(3)
	30,11	30,26	31,10	31,23	32,8	32,23	33,4	33,20

* age in month, day.
[a] numbers in parenthesis represent frequency of occurrence and numbers outside represent classification of de's function.

From Table 8, it is apparent that the first use of "de" emerged around 20 to 22 month in the form of incomplete associative phrase (i.e. NP + de). Many of these incomplete phrases were genitive phrases (i.e. possessor + de), and concurrent with this form, there were also other incomplete genitive phrases of the "possessor + possessed " form, with the obligatory "de" missing. Furthermore, by using a simple z test [$z^2 = (x-y)^2 / (x+y)$, where x = number of children developed x before y; y = number of children developed y before x, for any pairs of function x and y], Chang and Huang (1986) found the following developmental order (at $p<.05$); $1=2=4=6<7=5=8<3=9=10$ (Where A=B means no significant difference between A and B, A<B means A developed before B)

When one looks at this order of development, two factors seem to be at work. One is the complexity of sentence construction; the other relates to cognitive development. For example, the late appearance of complex stative constructions (type 9) and sentence linking(type 10)is perhaps a consequence of the complexity of these constructions (except, in sentence linking, the cognitive complexity of conditional sentences may also play a role). The late appearance of manner adverbs (type 3) seems unrelated to sentence complexity, since manner adverbs, on the surface, are no more complex then nominalization. However, the late development of adverbs of time and manner is not unique in Mandarin (de Villiers and de Villiers, 1978), and is probably determined by the underlying cognitive requirement.

Nominalization (type 6) is involved in both relativization (type 8) and shi...de construction (type 7), and its development prior to 7 and 8 is quite logical. The early
appearance of NP de NP, (type 1, 2), Adj de NP, (type 4, 5), and V de NP (type 6) seems to indicate that although theoretically one can distinguish many different phrasal structures, children in the process of acquiring them do not seem to make such distinctions. One is even tempted to hypothesize that as far as constructions 1,2,4,5 and 6 are concerned, children may be following a simple rule of "word de word" subjected only to semantic restrictions.

If this is the case, one should see phrases that are meaningful (or semantically sound) but are not conventionally acceptable. Since Chang and Huang (1986) did not present any error analysis, there is no hard data to confirm the above hypothesis.

Concluding Remarks

After our bird's-eye view of Mandarin syntax acquisition, several aspects of this area of research might be apparent. First of all, there is an urgent need to accumulate more data. Although we have covered many important aspects of Mandarin syntax development, there are many more aspects of this development which have few available data. For example, little data exist on aspect and coverb development, the development of noun and verb phrases, pronouns, and auxilliary verbs. Even with topics covered in this review, the amount (and often quality) of data needs a substantial boost before a more reliable and comprehensive picture can emerge.

One important reason to look into Mandarin syntactic development has to do with the continuing search for language universals and particulars. In this regard, the present research effort has already yielded some interesting results. For example, the development of Mandarin negation and questions presents very interesting contrasts, as well as similarities, to English development. Naturally, the important question is where these discoveries lead us in terms of theories of language acquisition. In some respects, (for example, see the chapter by Chien in this volume) research on Mandarin acquisition has already forced rethinking in theory, but the majority of the Mandarin data still have not been widely known and consequently have not had any impact on theory formulation.

The future course of research in Mandarin syntax development must follow two distinct, and seemingly contradictory, courses to become more significant. On the one hand, for Mandarin syntactic development to be more meaningfully described, the data based on linguistic models characteristic of Mandarin must be analyzed. For example, there is general agreement that the Mandarin sentence is best described by topic-comment structure, yet few people have actually used this structure to analyze Mandarin developmental data. Whether better results can be obtained by this alternative analysis is uncertain, but it is more than likely that using linguistic models based on European languages to analyze Mandarin data in general could blind us to many interesting features unique to Mandarin.

On the other hand, Mandarin acquisition data need to be further integrated into the main stream of language development research. Current theoretical formulations, although largely based on European data, have on occassions attempted to integrate data of non-European languages (e.g. Turkish, Japanese, & Hebrew). Nevertheless, data on Mandarin Chinese have seldom been considered. This is primarily due to the lack of availability of the data in English. As more Mandarin data are known, the situation should change quickly.

In short, to contribute more to our comprehensive understanding of language development and its theorization, developmental researchers must look more closely at Mandarins own unique features as well as better integrate it into the main stream of current research.

References

Bates, E. and MacWhinney, B.(1982) Functionalist approach to grammar.In E. Wanner and L. Gleitman (eds.) *Language acquisition*: The state of the art. Cambridge, Ma, Cambridge University Press.

Bellugi, U.(1967) *The acquisition of negation*. Unpublished Ph. D. dissertation, Harvard University.

Bever,T.G. (1970) The cognitive basis for linguistic structures. In J. R. Hays (ed.) *Cognition and the development of language*. New York , Wiley.

Bloom,L. (1970) *Language Development: Form and Function in Emerging Grammar*. Cambridge, MA: MIT Press.

Braine, M. (1976) *Children's first word combinations*. SRCD Monographs, serial No. 164.

Brown, R. (1973) *A First Language: The Early Stages*. Cambridge, MA: Harvard University Press.

Chang, H.W. (1986) Young children's comprehension of the Chinese passive. In H. Kao and R. Hoosain (eds.), *Linguistic, Psychology, and the Chinese Language Hong Kong*. University of Hong Kong Press.

Chang, H.W. (1987) *Preschooler's use of Classifiers in Mandarin Chinese*. unpublished manuscript.

Chang, H.W. and Huang, H.L. (1986): *The development of production and comprehension of "de" in Mandarin*. Report NSC-74-0301-H002-16 National Science Council, Taipei, Taiwan. (in Chinese)

Chao, Y.R. (1951) The Cantian idiolect: An analysis of the Chinese spoken by a twenty-eight month-old child. *Semitic Philology, 11*, 27-44.

Chao, Y.R. (1968) *A Grammar of Spoken Chinese*. Berkeley, CA: University of California Press.

Cheng, S.W. (1986) The earliest grammatical rules in Chinese toddlers and their probable development. *Chinese Journal of Psychology, 28*,93-122.(In Chinese)

Cheng, S.W. (1988) Beginning negative sentences among Mandarin-speaking toddlers. *Chinese Journal of Psychology, 30*,47-63.(In Chinese)

Cheng,S.W. (1991) The development of questions in Mandarin. *Chinese Journal of Psychology.*(in Press, in Chinese)

Chomsky,C. (1969) *The acquisition of syntax in children from 5 to 10.* Cambridge, Mass. MIT press.

Chu, D.S.(1961): Talking about "de". *Chinese language, 12*,1-15.(in Chinese)

Clark, H.H, and Clark,E.V. (1977) *Psychology and Language.* New York. Harcourt Brace Jovanorich, Inc.

de Villiers, J.G. and de Villiers, P.A. (1978): *Language Acquisition.* Cambridge, Ma. Harvard University Press.

Ervin-Tripp, S. (1970) Discourse agreement: How children answer questions.In J.R. Hayes(ed.), *Cognition and the Development of Language.* New York: Wiley.

Greenberg, J.H. (1963) *Universals of Language.* Cambridge, MA: MIT Press.

Jeng, L.Y. (1991) Young children's comprehension of canonical Mandarin sentence. *Chinese Journal of Psychology.* (in Press, in Chinese)

Li, C. and Thompson, S. (1981) *Mandarin Chinese: A Functional Reference Grammar.* Berkeley, CA: University of California Press.

Liu, Y.M., Chung,C.Y. and Wang, S.C. (1975): *Frequency table for common Chinese words*, Taipei, Liu-kou Press (in Chinese)

MacWhinney, B., Bates, E. and Kliegl, R. (1984): Cue validity and sentence interpretation in English, German and Italian. *Journal of Verbal Learning and Verbal Behavior,23*, 127-150.

McNeil, D. (1970) *The Acquisition of Language.* New York: Harper and Row.

Miao, X.C. (1981) Word order and semantic strategies in Chinese sentence comprehension.*International Journal of psycholinguistics, 8*, 109-122.

Sinclair, H. and Bronckart, J. (1972): SVO--a linguistic universal? A study in developmental psycholinguistics. *Journal of Experimental Child Psychology, 14*, 329-48.

Slobin, D.I. and Bever, T. (1982): Children use canonical sentence schemas: A cross linguistic study of word order inflections. *Cognition, 12*, 229-65.

Slobin, D. (1985) *The Crosslinguistic Study of Language Acquisition. Vol.2.* Hillsdale: New Jersey. LEA.

Tang, T.C.(1979): "de" in Mandarin Chinese. In Collected papers on Mandarin Grammar by T.C. Tang (ed.). Taipei: Student Press.

Wang, L. (1987) *A History of Chinese Linguistics.* Taipei: Blue Light Press. (In Chinese)

Wells, G. (1985) *Language Development in the Preschool Years.* Cambridge: Cambridge University Press.

Yang, K.S., Yang, Y.W. and Shou, Y.F. (1973) *The development of spoken vocabulary in young children* .Taipei, Taiwan Huan- Chu press. (In Chinese)

Yang, L.Y. (1987) *The development of sentence final Particles in Mandarin Chinese.* Unpublished M.A. thesis, National Taiwan University. (In Chinese)

Theoretical Implications of the Principles and Parameters Model for Language Acquisition in Chinese

Yu-Chin Chien
California State University, San Bernardino

In this chapter, we review the essentials of one of the most prominent linguistic models, namely Chomsky's "Principles and Parameters" model. Several unique arguments regarding issues of language acquisition and the implications for language acquisition in Chinese are discussed. We also review various experimental studies in Chinese acquisition which were devised under the framework of the Principles and Parameters approach. Empirical evidence supporting some of the essential predictions made in the Principles and Parameters model are discussed.

The study of language acquisition from the cross-linguistic perspective has two ultimate goals. One is to describe the similarities and differences between children's knowledge of language at various stages of development across different languages. The second is to explain how a child, based on a limited set of data, can acquire any human language in a relatively short period of time if he or she is placed in an appropriate speech environment -- the 'logical problem of language acquisition' which has often been discussed in the fields of theoretical linguistics and language acquisition (cf. Chomsky, 1981, 1986, 1988; Hornstein & Lightfoot, 1981;

Hornstein, 1984; Pinker, 1984, 1989; Wexler, 1982). Ideally, the first goal is not too difficult to achieve; if one can provide reliable and valid empirical assessments of children's language competence at various points of development, then a cross-linguistic comparison of these empirical data can be done. The second goal, however, is not as easy as the first one. To grasp the fact that any normal child who is exposed to just a set of deficient data can acquire any human language in a relatively short period of time, one must postulate a mental mechanism which satisfies the following two constraints: on the one hand, the mental mechanism must be broad enough in order to accommodate the diversity of different possible human languages and, at the same time, it must be narrow enough so that the child who encounters only a limited set of linguistic evidence can make relevant hypotheses about the language that he or she is acquiring without too many false steps (cf. Chomsky, 1981, 1988).

In organizing this chapter, we have two related objectives. The first objective is to review and discuss the essentials of one of the most prominent linguistic models, namely the "Principles and Parameters" model (hereafter, the PP model), which has given an insightful account for the logical problem of language acquisition specified above. The second objective is to look at the implications of the PP model for language acquisition in Chinese and to review some experimental studies in Chinese acquisition which were devised under the framework of the PP approach. One of the major attempts for this chapter is, thus, to enumerate empirical evidence to justify some of the essential predictions made in the PP model. The discussions made in this chapter regarding the PP model will only focus on issues related to syntactic acquisition. Other kinds of language development, such as the development of the pragmatic or semantic concepts or principles will be mentioned when necessary.

The Essentials of the Principles and Parameters Model

In the "Principles and Parameters" model, language acquisition is considered to be an interactive process: a constant interaction that occurs between the child's a priori knowledge of language and the data that the child is receiving from his or her speech environment. This process of language acquisition is characterized by Chomsky as the schema given in (1) (Chomsky, 1988:35).

(1) data --> language faculty --> language --> structured expressions

The "language faculty," as argued by Chomsky (1986, 1988), is one of the interacting components of the human mind; it is a part of the human biological endowment that is specific for language related activities. This language faculty is distinct from other components of the human mind that are responsible for general cognitive activities such as problem solving or artistic creativity. Through interacting with data from a particular speech environment, the language faculty develops from its initial state, progresses through a sequence of intermediate states, and ends with its steady state. According to Chomsky (1988), the initial state of the language faculty, before any experience, is accounted for by "Universal Grammar (UG)," which, in essence, is presented in the child's mind as a system of principles and parameters. The final state of the language faculty, after it has been presented with data of experience, is accounted for by the grammar of a particular language. Given the schema specified in (1), Chomsky outlines the language acquisition process in the following way: "presented with data, the language faculty determines a particular language: [Chinese], English, etc. This language in turn determines a wide range of potential phenomena going far beyond the presented data (1988: 35)." As an example, if a child is placed in a Chinese-speaking environment, then the child's innate language faculty will select pertinent data from this Chinese environment, make use of these data in a way predetermined by the internal structure of the language faculty, and construct Chinese. Chinese is thus incorporated into the child's mind which will then enable the child to produce and comprehend Chinese utterances that extend beyond the set of input data that he or she has received.

The language acquisition process outlined above does not imply that the concept of "learning" is an irrelevant notion in the Principles and Parameters model. Rather, one of the most fundamental tasks within this model is to determine what particular aspects of linguistic structure are given and what must be learned on the basis of exposure to a particular language (cf. Chien & Wexler, 1990; Chomsky, 1981, 1988; Gleitman, Landau, & Wanner, 1988; Hyams, 1986; Lust, 1986, 1987, in press; Pinker, 1984; Roeper & Williams, 1987; Valian, 1990). There is an agreed-on assumption that if a linguistic principle is operating universally across different languages, or if it carries abstract linguistic concepts which are not clearly presented in the input data and thus not accessible to the language learner, then this principle must be unlearned (or genetically preprogrammed). For example, the abstract principle of structure-dependency that enters into rule operations is universally true for most human languages; this principle is assumed to be innate. The Binding principles that govern the interpretations of proforms (e.g., the reflexive *ziji* "self" or the pronoun *ta* "he/she") which have carried many inaccessible abstract concepts, such as "binding," "c-commanding," "coindexing," and "governing categories," are also assumed to be innate. What have to be learned, then, are the linguistic properties that vary across different languages and the linguistic notions that can be clearly conveyed through the input data to the language learners. For example, the enormous set of vocabulary items employed by a particular language, each with its own meaning, phonological and grammatical properties, is assumed to be learned. The specific values of various UG parameters associated with a particular language are also considered to be learned on the basis of exposure to the linguistic data of that language.

By assuming that children are born with a set of intricate UG principles and parameters, the process of language acquisition can be reduced to a process including learning lexical items and fixing values for the UG parameters (cf. Borer, 1984; Wexler & Chien, 1985; Wexler & Manzini, 1987). (For discussions of other comprehensive models, see Gleitman, Landau, & Wanner, 1988; Lust, in press; and Valian, 1990.) As pointed out by Chomsky (1986, 1988), Universal Grammar that constitutes the initial state of the language faculty is only partially 'wired-up'. It can be viewed as a system which is analogous to a switchboard with its switches being set to a neutral position (also see Aitchison, 1989; Cook, 1988). The principles of UG are the built-in structure of the language faculty. They are analogous to the preprogrammed electrical circuits that underlie the switchboard. The parameters of UG-- each consists of a set of values compatible with language specific properties-- are the open variables of the language faculty. They are analogous to the switches of the switchboard that can be turned on and off or be set to a particular value. With genetically predetermined UG, children know in advance what possible paths and available options that human languages can take. With data of experience, children learn lexical items, discover the parameter values corresponding to the language they are acquiring, and fix the parameters. This parameterized approach of language acquisition can be demonstrated by the illustration given in (2). We simplify this illustration by omitting the lexical learning process and including only one intermediate state, one

(2)

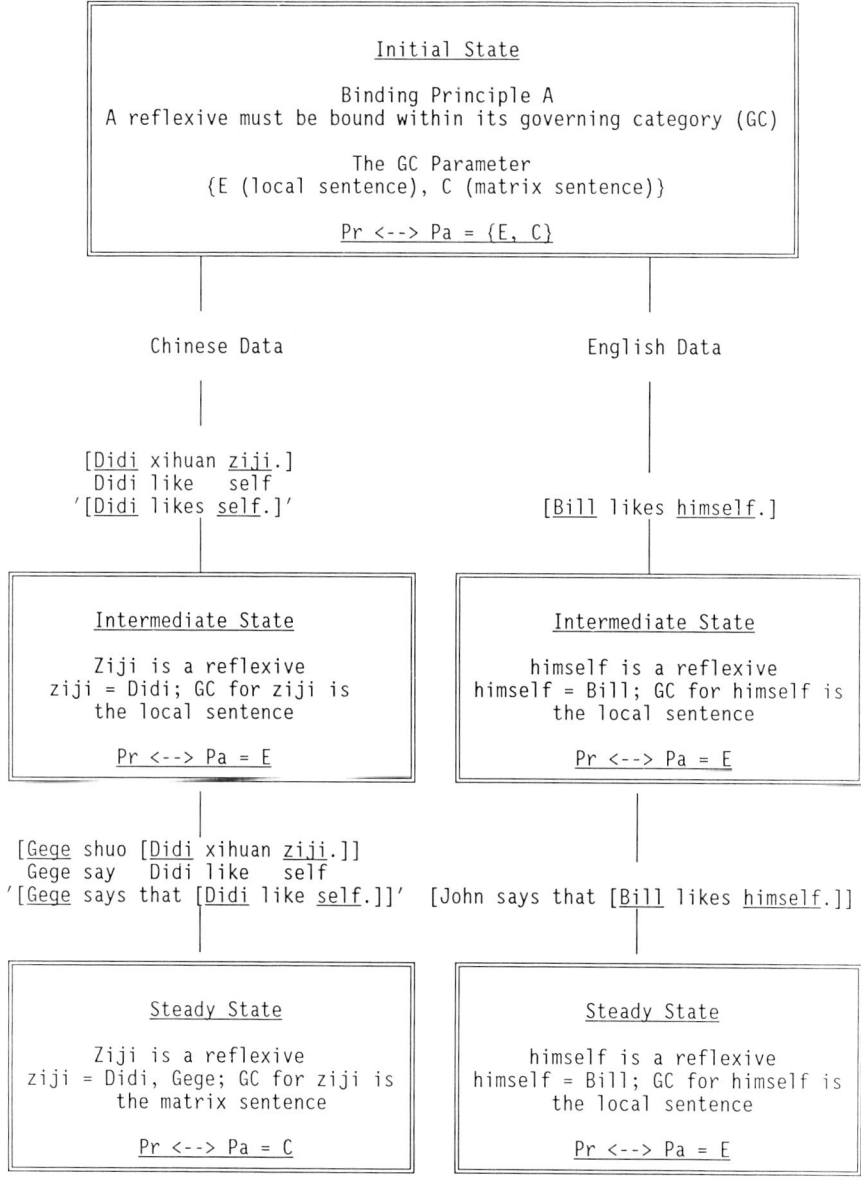

principle (Pr), and one parameter (Pa) with two values (i.e., the Chinese value "C" and the English value "E").

As can be seen in the preceding illustration (2), Chinese and English have many linguistic principles in common (cf. Huang, 1982 and Li, 1990). One of them is Binding Principle A stated in the first box of the illustration. Binding Principle A deals with the interpretation of a reflexive (e.g., *ziji* or "himself") which, in contrast to a name (e.g., John) does not carry its own independent referential features. Informally speaking, Binding Principle A tells us that a reflexive must be coreferential with another constituent in a sentence, and that constituent must bear a certain structural relationship with the reflexive. Similar to other language universal principles, Binding Principle A is assumed to be genetically preprogrammed; it belongs to the initial state of the language faculty. Associated with Principle A, there is a structure-dependent concept, namely "governing category". It defines the domain within which the reference of a reflexive must be identified. In English, it is required that the reflexive "himself" has an antecedent inside the local sentence (i.e., the smallest clause that contains the reflexive and a subject). In Chinese, the antecedent of the reflexive *ziji* does not have to obey this "locality" requirement. As long as it is inside the matrix sentence, the antecedent for *ziji* can either be local or long-distant. For example, in the English sentence given in (3), "himself" can only refer to the local antecedent "Bill," but not the long-distance antecedent "John." In the Chinese equivalent given in (4), *ziji* can be coreferential with either the local antecedent *Didi* or the long-distance antecedent *Gege*.

(3) [John says that [Bill likes himself]].

(4) [Gege shuo [Didi xihuan ziji]].
    Gege say Didi like   self
    '[Gege says that [Didi likes self]].'

As indicated in the examples given in (3) and (4), the "governing category (GC)" for reflexives is varied across different languages (Manzini & Wexler, 1987). It is a parameter with several values, two of which being the "Chinese (C)" and "English (E)" values corresponding to the matrix sentence and the local sentence, respectively. (For a more detailed discussion of the parametric approach and the parameter of "governing category," see Manzini & Wexler, 1987 and Wexler & Manzini, 1987.) In the initial state of the language faculty, the GC parameter is not fixed. In the process of language acquisition, children fix the parameter to a certain value according to the input data available to them. This first-set value can be revised if there is sufficient data to suggest so, otherwise the value will stay the same. For example, a child who is raised in a Chinese-speaking environment, after hearing simple sentences like "Didi xihuan ziji (Didi likes self) in a fitting context, may first set the GC parameter to the "E" position and allow only the local coreferential relationship between *ziji* and its antecedent. Later, the child receives complex sentences such as (4) in other fitting contexts. These data will be sufficient to trigger the reset of the GC parameter from the "E" position to the "C" position, which in turn will enable the child to accept both the local and the long-distance antecedents for the reflexive *ziji*. A child who is raised in an English-speaking environment will go through a parameter-setting procedure very similar to the one just described, but he or she will not reset the GC parameter for "himself," because there is no data to suggest the change. Since the parameters corresponding to the principles are not fixed at the initial state (i.e., they are open to any value), the child's mind is, thus, capable of acquiring any language. When all parameters are fixed, the child will reach the final stage of language acquisition, that is, to arrive at the steady state of the language faculty and completely learn a particular language. If all parameters are set to the "C" value, the child is said to have acquired Chinese. On the other hand, if all parameters are fixed on the "E" value, then the child is said to have acquired English. This illustration points out that as long as a child is raised in an appropriate speech environment, no matter what racial background the child has, he or she will be able to learn any human language. A Chinese child who is raised in an English-speaking community can learn perfect English and an American child who is raised in a Chinese-speaking community can learn perfect Chinese.

To summarize, the Principles and Parameters model has presented several unique arguments regarding issues of language acquisition. These arguments are summarized as follows:

(A) Language acquisition is an interactive process: a constant interaction that occurs between the child's a priori knowledge of language and the data that the child is receiving from his or her speech environment.

(B) Language acquisition does not solely depend upon general cognitive development. Rather, it depends on the development of a formal autonomous system, namely, the language faculty.

(C) The two major ingredients that constitute the initial state of the language faculty (i.e., the UG principles and the UG parameters) are genetically predetermined; they are unlearned.

(D) By assuming that principles and parameters of UG are innate, the process of language acquisition can be naturally reduced to a process including learning lexical items and fixing values for the parameters on the basis of exposure to a particular language.

(E) In the initial state of language acquisition, the child's language faculty is open for acquiring any language, and acquiring a particular language is to fix all the parameters of Universal Grammar appropriately.

In the following section, we will discuss the implications of the PP model for language acquisition in Chinese and review some experimental studies in Chinese acquisition which were devised under the framework of the PP approach. By doing this, we seek to enumerate empirical evidence to justify some essential predictions made in the PP model which we have just discussed. The first two sets of studies concern children's acquisition of language concepts and children's early sentence organization. These studies demonstrate some of the spirit of the PP approach by showing that children are sensitive to the structure-dependent nature of language. The final set of studies is concerned with parametric variations and children's knowledge of binding principles. The Subset principle related to parameter-setting and other alternative explanations concerning children's acquisition of binding are discussed.

The Implications of the PP Model for Language Acquisition in Chinese

There are many interrelated implications that can be drawn from the

Principles and Parameters model for language acquisition studies. The most general one has to do with the issue concerning the "autonomy of the language faculty." As mentioned in the previous section, one of the major arguments made in the PP model is that language acquisition does not solely depend upon general cognitive development, rather, it depends upon the development of a formal autonomous system, namely, the language faculty. This "formal autonomous system" in the study of early childhood language implies that children's early language concepts and early sentence constructions should manifest a "structure-dependent" (or grammatical) nature which, in essence, cannot simply be derived from semantic or pragmatic notions or be defined over simple sentence properties such as linear word order. Does this implication receive any support from empirical studies of Chinese language acquisition? Our answer is a positive one. As can be seen from the following experiments, not only have these studies provided several interesting facts regarding Chinese children's early language concepts and constructions, but they also constitute a necessary basis for comparison, disentangling some questions which obviously cannot be answered by studying English acquisition alone.

Chinese Children's Early Language Concepts

Much first language acquisition research has centred on defining the nature of children's concepts in early child language. Some researchers have argued that there is evidence for children's early access of grammatical concepts such as "subject" (e.g., Bloom, 1970; Bloom, Lightbown, & Hood, 1975; Gleitman & Wanner, 1982; McNeil, 1966; Valian, 1981a, 1981b). Other researchers, however, have argued that concepts which function as grammatical subjects in child language are in fact based on semantic or pragmatic concepts such as "agency" or "topic" which do not actually manifest any "structure-dependent" nature (e.g., Bowerman, 1973; deVilliers, 1980; Bates & MacWhinney, 1982; Bates, McNew, MacWhinney, Devescovi, & Smith, 1982; Gruber, 1967). In order to clear away the controversies, Chien and Lust (1983; 1985; also Chien, Lust, & Mangione, 1983) have devised several experimental studies to investigate Chinese children's early language concepts, including the grammatical concept "subject" and the pragmatic (nongrammatical) concept "topic." They have argued that a critical test of whether children do access the grammatical concept of "subject" requires that the grammatical concept (i.e., "subject") and the related nongrammatical concept (i.e., "topic") be clearly distinguishable and equivalently available in the language. Previous studies have dealt mainly with English, a "subject-prominent" language, with the word order of subject-verb-object (SVO), in which a topic of a sentence is usually introduced by the grammatical subject (Reinhart, 1981). Thus, in English the two concepts "topic" and "subject" are often confused with each other. As a result, based on the English data alone, no clear-cut conclusion regarding the nature of children's early concepts can be achieved. In Chinese, as can be seen in the following discussion, concepts of "subject" and "topic" in many cases are clearly distinguishable; "topic," as well as "subject," are equally accessible in the language. Chinese, thus, constitutes a critical language for evaluating children's early concepts.

In contrast to English, Chinese has been characterized as a "topic-prominent" language (Li & Thompson, 1976). It makes productive use of sentences with both topics and distinct subjects (e.g., [5]). The topic in Chinese is sentence initial and can be separated from the rest of the sentence by a pause or by a pause particle (e.g., "ya"). The topic generally sets a semantic or pragmatic framework within which a main predication holds (Chafe, 1976; Li, 1976; Li & Thompson, 1976, 1981; Tsao, 1977). It is seldom repeated in a sentence, but can be coreferential with gaps or pronouns. The subject, on the other hand, is immediately related to the verb in the main predication and controls grammatical processes related to the verb. For example, in "control sentences" such as (6), it is "subject" but not "topic" that obligatorily controls the gap (0). (Note, languages often have embedded clauses which lack a subject. The phenomenon of "control" governs how the missing subject is interpreted.) In (6), the topic is *xiaogou* (puppy) and the subject is *yanjing* (the eyes). It is the subject, "eyes," that like to move around, not the topic "puppy." In other words,

(5) <u>Nei-ke shu</u> (ya), yezi hen da, suoyi wo hen xihuan <u>0</u>.

That-CL tree (topic), leaf (subject) very big, so I very like
'That tree, (its) leaves are very big, so I like (it).'

(6) Xiaogou, <u>yanjing</u> xihuan <u>0</u> dong-lai-dong-qu.

Puppy (topic), eye (subject) like 0 (subject gap) move around.
'The puppy, (its) eyes like to move around.'

yanjing (eyes) is interpreted as the subject of both *xihuan* (like) and *dong-lai-dong-qu* (move around).

In addition to sentences like (5) and (6) where "subject" is clearly distinct from "topic", Chinese also makes productive use of sentences such as (7). As can be seen from (7), Chinese does not always require a structurally distinct topic and subject. Similar to English, the unmarked word order for Chinese is SVO (Huang, 1982); therefore, in many cases, the sentence initial topic overlaps with the grammatical subject.

(7) a. Nainai dapo huaping le.
Grandma (subject) break vase Asp.
'Grandma broke the vase.'

b. <u>Nainai</u>, *0* dapo huaping le.

Grandma (topic), break vase Asp.
'Grandma, (she) broke the vase.'

The facts revealed in (7) lead to an important question in Chinese acquisition, namely, do Chinese children, in early stages of first language acquisition, access both the concepts of "topic" and grammatical "subject"? Since simple sentences such as (7)-- which are common structures in the natural speech of Chinese children-- can be analyzed as organized either around the topic or the subject, it is possible to argue that young Chinese children could achieve early sentence organization on the basis of the concept of "topic" alone, without any access to the concept of grammatical "subject". Thus, this can be used to argue against the "autonomy of language faculty" assumption. In order to answer the question, Chien and Lust (1985) tested 95 Chinese-speaking children between the ages of 2-and-a-half and 5, using an "elicited imitation task." Each child was asked to imitate a set of coordinate constructions (e.g., [8a] & [9a]) and a set of control constructions (e.g., [10a] & [11a]) with either topic or subject redundancy as indicated by the underscoring. Sentences (8a) and (10a) have topic redundancy, that is, the topic is repeated. Sentences (9a) and (11a) have subject redundancy, that is, the subject is repeated.

(8) a. *Coordinate construction with redundant topic:*

<u>Baobao</u>, jiao hen xiao; <u>baobao</u> ye hen keai.

Baby (topic), feet (subject) very small; *baby* (redundant topic) also very cute
'*The baby*, (her) feet (are) very small; *the baby*, (is) also very cute.'

b. *Baobao*, jiao hen xiao; *0* ye hen keai.

Baby (topic), feet (subject) very small;
0 (a gap resulting from topic reduction) also very cute.
'The baby, (her) feet (are) very small; (she is) also very cute.'

(9) a. *Coordinate construction with redundant subject*:

Gonggong, *huzi* hen bai *huzi* ye hen chang.
Grandfather (topic), beard (subject) very white beard (redundant subject) also very long.
'Grandfather, (his) beard (is) very white (and his) beard (is) also very long.'

b. Gonggong, *huzi* hen bai *0* ye hen chang.

Grandfather (topic), beard (subject) very white
0 (a gap resulting from subject reduction) also very long.
'Grandfather, (his) beard (is) very white (and) also very long.'

(10) a. *Control construction with redundant topic*:

Xiaohua, jiejie xihuan *Xiaohua* dai maozi.
Xiaohua (topic), older sister (subject) like Xiaohua (redundant topic) wear hat.
'Xiaohua, (her) older sister like Xiaohua (to) wear a hat.'

b. *Xiaohua*, jiejie xihuan *0* dai maozi.

Xiaohua (topic), older sister (subject) like
0 (a gap resulting from topic reduction) wear hat.
'Xiaohua, (her) older sister likes (to) wear (a) hat.'

(11) a. *Control construction with redundant subject*:

Xiaohua, *baba* xihuan *baba* kan dianshi.
Xiaohua (topic), father (subject) like father (redundant subject) watch TV.
'Xiaohua, (her) father like (her) father (to) watch TV.'

b. Xiaohua, *baba* xihuan *0* kan dianshi.

Xiaohua (topic), father (subject) like 0 (a gap resulting from subject reduction) watch TV.
'Xiaohua, (her) father likes (to) watch TV.'

As can be seen from the coordinate constructions such as the one given in (12) below, in contrast to the control constructions such as (6), coordinate constructions (with no redundant topic or subject) do not obligatorily require reference to the grammatical subject. Both "topic" and "subject" can be coindexed with empty positions. In other words, both meanings indicated in (12b) and (12c) are possible for sentence (12a).

(12) a. *Wawa, yanjing* hen da, *0* ye hen keai.

Doll (topic), eyes (subject) very big, 0 (gap) also very cute.

b. 'The doll, (her) eyes are very big, (and she is) also very cute.'

c. 'The doll, (her) eyes are very big (and her eyes are) also very cute.'

In imitation, children tend to eliminate redundancy. In Chien and Lust's study, there are two options for reducing redundancy by creating a gap. One possible gap would result from forward topic reduction (e.g., 8a-->8b & 10a-->10b). Another possible gap would result from forward subject reduction (e.g., 9a-->9b & 11a-->11b). Considering the control constructions, both types of reduction produce similarly derived structures (10b & 11b). They both have a gap in the complement subject position. Neither is ungrammatical in itself. However, in control sentences, only subject reduction leaves a gap with a correct anaphoric relation; that is, only subject can control. In other words, in control sentences, reduction of subject redundancy (such as 11a-->11b) maintains the meaning of the original sentence (11a); reduction of topic redundancy (such as 10a-->10b) changes the meaning of the original sentence (as denoted by *). On the other hand, since coordinate constructions do not require grammatical subjects to control for gaps, reduction of either the redundant topic (8a-->8b) or the redundant subject (9a-->9b) is grammatically well-formed regarding the anaphoric relation. That is, in both cases, the meaning of the original sentence can be maintained.

The rationale for Chien and Lust's study is quite simple. If Chinese children know that in control sentences such as (6), it is "subject," but not "topic," that obligatorily controls the gap (while in coordinate sentences such as [12], the gap can be coreferential with either the "topic" or the "subject"), then this will constitute evidence that Chinese children distinguish the structural differences across these sentence types, and that they can and do access the grammatical category "subject" when the structure requires it. In other words, if children do access the concept of "subject" and can differentiate this grammatical category from the pragmatic category of "topic," they should not allow forward topic reduction in the control sentences that require an obligatory control relation between the subject and the gap. Therefore, the transformation of (10a) to (10b), that is, the transformation that changes the meaning of the original sentence, should be blocked. For the remaining three constructions, however, redundancy reduction should occur. That is, the same children should produce the transformations of (8a) to (8b), (9a) to (9b), and (11a) to (11b). These transformations maintain the meaning of the original sentences.

The results confirm the predictions. Reduction of redundancy is structurally constrained. Critically, Chinese children consistently blocked the reduction of the redundant topic in the control constructions (10a-->10b), although they frequently reduced the redundant topic in the coordinate constructions (8a-->8b). On the average, only 3.36% of the time did children transform (10a) to (10b), while 25.74% of the time they transformed (8a) to (8b). In addition, when imitating the control constructions, children made significantly more forward subject reductions than forward topic reductions. About 15% of the time, children did reduce the redundant subject that followed the control verb (11a-->11b). Children also reduced the redundant subject 29.63% of the time when imitating subject redundant coordinate sentences (9a-->9b). These results indicate that Chinese children do distinguish the concepts of "topic" and "subject", and they do access the grammatical category of "subject" when the structure requires it. The general implication of this study is that even in highly topic-oriented languages such as Chinese, it is necessary to attribute some sensitivity concerning "structure-dependent" concepts as well as semantic or pragmatic ones to young children acquiring their first language. The results confirm this conclusion for children as young as 2-and-a-half, who were shown to be at early stages of syntax and semantics necessary for complex sentence formation. In essence, these experimental results significantly lower the age or language level at which a unique and independent nonlinguistic pragmatic or semantic concept base, such as "topic", may sufficiently define the nature of children's grammatical categories like "subject", if it does so at all.

Chinese Children's Early Sentence Constructions

One obvious fact about human sentence organization is that sentences are strings of words with linear order. As mentioned in the previous section, Chinese is an SVO language in which the subject precedes the verb and the object follows the verb in the unmarked cases. English is also an SVO language, while Japanese is an SOV language. In the process of language acquisition, children seem to notice this obvious fact of linear word order at a very young age (cf. Lust & Wakayama, 1981 among others). However, most regularities of language are formulated by hierarchically arranged structures which are not reducible to linear word orders. The question is, thus, in early stages of language acquisition, are children mainly guided by highly abstract structure-dependent principles or are they guided by simple linear word orders? To answer this question properly, one needs to examine languages in which structural principles do not correlate with linear word orders. As can be seen from the following discussions, Chinese is an ideal language for this test.

The "principal branching direction" is a fundamental parameter which is closely related to the "head-direction" parameter. In most languages, the principal branching direction of phrase structures matches the linear word order of sentence constructions. For example, in English, the verb precedes the object and the unmarked branching direction is to the right. In Japanese, the verb follows the object and the unmarked branching direction is to the left. With regard to the relationship between word order and branching direction, Chinese is considered to be an atypical language. According to Huang (1982), in Chinese, the unmarked word order is SVO like English and unlike Japanese, yet, the unmarked branching direction is to the left like Japanese and unlike English. We illustrate the property of branching direction using complex sentences with a relative clause such as the one given in (13). Chinese places relative clauses (e.g., zhui ai chi bisabing de) before head nouns (e.g., renzhegui) and is thus left-branching. As can be seen from the English translation given in (13), English places relative clauses (e.g., who loves pizza the most) after head nouns (e.g., the ninja turtle) and is thus right-branching.

(13) [[zhui ai chi bisabing de] renzhegui] jiaozuo lioudinghua.
[[Most love eat Pizza Rel.] ninja turtle] name Michaelangelo
'The ninja turtle who loves Pizza the most is Michaelangelo.'

By examining children's acquisition of coordinate constructions, Lust and her collaborators suggested that there is a strong relationship between the type of coordinate constructions that young children preferred and the property of branching direction of a particular language (Lust, Flynn, Chien, & Clifford, 1980; Lust, Wakayama, Snyder, & Bergmann, 1980; Lust & Chien, 1984; Lust, 1986, 1987). For example, children acquiring English, an SVO right-branching language, have found it easier to imitate coordinate constructions with forward reductions (e.g., 14) than those with backward reductions (e.g., 15). On the other hand, children acquiring Japanese, an SOV left-branching language, have found it easier to imitate coordinate constructions with backward reductions (e.g., 16) than forward reductions (e.g., 17).

(14) *Eat* the crackers and *0* the cake.
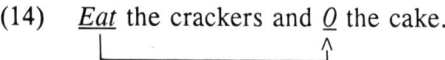

(15) Push *0* and hug *the kitty-cat*.
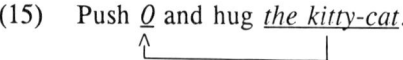

(16) Zubon-to *0* seetaa-o *kiru*.

Pants-and 0 sweater put-on.
'Put on pants and sweater.'

(17) *Booru-o* nageru-shi *0* tsukamaeru.

Ball throw-and 0 catch.
'Throw and catch the ball.'

How about children acquiring Chinese, an SVO but left-branching language? Are they guided by the abstract principle of branching direction, or are they guided by the more accessible notion of linear word order? Lust and Chien (1984) discovered that, similar to Japanese children but unlike the American children, when VO sentences (i.e., sentences with only verbs and objects) were considered, Chinese children (between the ages of 2 and 5) preferred coordinate constructions with backward reductions to those with forward reductions. They found it easier to imitate sentences like (18) than sentences like (19) (75.5% correct vs. 51.5% correct).

(18) Xi-yi-xi *0* ye ca-yi-ca *wawa*.

Wash 0 also dry doll
'Wash *0* and dry *the doll*.'

(19) *Wanwan* xiao-gouxiong han *0* xiao-huoche.

Play little-bear and 0 little-train
'*Play with* teddy-bear and *0* choo-choo train.'

However, an interesting and apparently paradoxical result concerning Chinese children's acquisition of coordinate constructions should be mentioned. Chinese children exhibited a very different response pattern when dealing with the SV coordinate constructions compared to their responses to the VO sentences. They frequently reduced redundant subjects in a forward direction and did not prefer backward reduction (e.g., 20) over forward reduction (e.g., 21) in these SV sentences (forward vs. backward: 80% correct vs. 77% correct).

(20) Mama *0* han baobao dou *shuijiao-le*.

Mother 0 and baby all sleep-Asp.
'Mommy *0* and baby *slept.*'

(21) <u>Xiao baobao</u> ye kuku *0* ye xiaoxiao.

Little baby also cry 0 also laugh
'*The baby* cries and *0* laughs.'

The results concerning the VO coordinate constructions clearly indicate that Chinese children, in their early stages of language acquisition, are sensitive to the abstract structure-dependent principle, namely, principal branching direction, which cannot simply be defined over the more accessible properties of linear word order. How about the results concerning the SV coordinate constructions? How can we explain the apparent paradox that exists between children's responses to these SV sentences and their responses to the VO sentences? Lust and Chien suggest that in early language acquisition, children are sensitive to the interaction between a predominant Chinese "topic-comment" structure (in SV) and the abstract structure-dependent concept of "principal branching direction." When the concept of "topic" is involved in the sentence, both types of reduced constructions (forward and backward) are equally acceptable to the children. Even though both English and Chinese are characterized as SVO languages, unlike the English-speaking children, in all cases Chinese children do not prefer forward over backward coordinate constructions. This result clearly indicates that the abstract principle of branching direction plays a significant role in children's acquisition of their first language. Children's early language concepts and early sentence constructions do manifest a "structure-dependent" nature which, in essence, cannot simply be derived from semantic or pragmatic notions or be defined over simple sentence properties such as linear word order.

Parametric Variations and Chinese Children's Knowledge of Binding Principles

Another "structure-dependent" concept that appears to affect first language acquisition is that of "c-command." As defined by Reinhart (1981, also see Chomsky, 1981), in a phrase-marker, node A c-commands node B if and only if the first branching node which dominates A also dominates B, and A does not dominate B, nor does B dominate A. (Note: a branching node is a node which branches into two or more immediate constituents.) Accordingly, in (22) and the corresponding phrase structure, NP1 "Snoopy" c-commands NP4 "him/himself," NP3 "Garfield's friend" also c-commands NP4 "him/himself," yet NP2 "Garfield" does not c-command NP4 "him/himself."

(22)

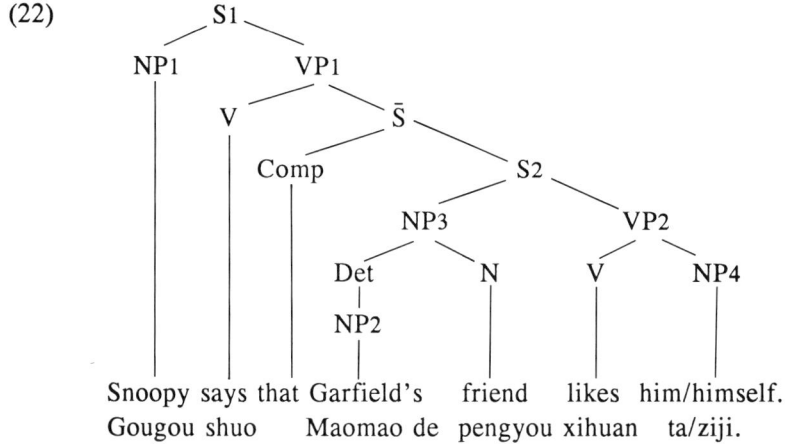

Snoopy says that Garfield's friend likes him/himself.
Gougou shuo Maomao de pengyou xihuan ta/ziji.

The structural notion of "c-command" constitutes an important element of many linguistic principles, such as Chomsky's (1981) Binding Principles. Binding principles deal with the relations between different kinds of elements in sentences, for example, empty categories (e.g., traces and null pronouns), reflexives (e.g., *taziji* "himself" and *ziji* "self"), and pronouns (e.g., *ta* "him"). In (23), we give the definitions of two Binding Principles (i.e., Principle A and Principle B).

(23) *Binding Principle A*: A reflexive must be bound in its governing category, where bound means c-commanded and coindexed with an antecedent.

Binding Principle B: A pronoun must be free in its governing category, where free means not bound.

Binding Principle A is relevant to the determination of possible antecedents for reflexives. (We have already discussed this briefly in Section 2.) Binding Principle B is relevant to the determination of possible antecedents for pronouns. The interaction of the structural notion of "c-command" and the parameter of "governing category" in Principles A and B determines the antecedents for reflexives and pronouns. As discussed in Huang (1982), these two principles are both observed in Chinese. Like "himself," *ziji* is a reflexive that requires a c-commanding antecedent. (See Huang & Tang, 1991 for the discussion of the exceptional cases.) However, differing from "himself," *ziji* is a long-distance reflexive, that is, the antecedent for *ziji* does not have to be local. As in (20), there are two correct antecedents for *ziji*, that is, the long-distance c-commanding antecedent *Gougou* and the local c-commanding antecedent *Maomao de pengyou*. The non-c-commanding NP *Maomao* cannot serve as an antecedent for *ziji*. Chinese has another reflexive, *taziji*. Similar to "himself" but different from *ziji*, *tajizi* is a local reflexive. It requires a local c-commanding antecedent. *Ta* is a pronoun, and like English "him" or "her," it may refer to the long-distance c-commanding NP, the local non-c-commanding NP, but not the local c-commanding NP. (Due to the space constraint, we will not discuss *tajizi* and *ta* in detail. For further discussion, see Huang & Tang, 1991, and Aoun & Li, 1990.)

There is another fact concerning the Chinese reflexive *ziji*, that is, it may only have a subject, but not an object, as its antecedent. In other words, *ziji* is subject-oriented. This subject-only property regarding Chinese reflexives is illustrated by the example given in (24). In (24), only the subject NP *Gougou* may serve as the antecedent for *ziji*. This is different from English in which the reflexive "himself" may have either a subject or an object as its antecedent.

(24) Gougou gei Maomao yi-zhang ziji-de zhaopian.
Snoopy give Garfield one-CL self's picture
'Snoopy gives Garfield a picture of himself.'

Various theories have been proposed to account for the long-distance attribute of *ziji* together with its subject-orientation property. For example, one important class of theories, namely, the movement-to-INFL approach has viewed subject-orientation and long-distance *ziji* as two coherent outcomes of LF-movement (cf., Battistella, 1987, 1989; Cole, Hermon, & Sung, 1990). Also see Huang & Tang, 1991, for a slightly different approach concerning LF-movement of *ziji*. LF stands for Logical Form, one major level of UG representations; INFL (inflection) is a "mood-indicator," a clausal element at LF. S-->NP INFL VP.) In this account, the relationship between *ziji* and its antecedent is argued to be covertly local in nature. *Ziji*, in Logical Form, is raised into INFL (25b), and since INFL is locally c-commanded by the subject (not the object), *ziji* can only take a subject antecedent. Additionally, since INFL-to-INFL movement is possible, *ziji* can be moved successively from a lower INFL to a higher INFL (25c); thus, it can be long-distance. Example (25) illustrates the LF-movement of *ziji* (from "a" to "b," then "b" to "c"). In (25b), *ziji* is locally c-commanded by *Gougou* "Snoopy." In (25c), *ziji* is locally c-commanded by *Xiaohu* "Tigger." As a result, sentence (25) is ambiguous in two ways, that is, *ziji-de zhaopian* "self's picture" can be interpreted as either Snoopy's picture or Tigger's picture, but not Garfield's.

(25) a. Xiaohu shuo Gougou gei Maomao yi-zhang ziji-de zhao pian.
Tigger say Snoopy give Garfield one-CL self's picture
'Tigger says that Snoopy gives Garfield a picture of himself.'

b. Xiaohu shuo [Gougou [yi-chang ziji-de zhaopian [gei Maomao t]]].
Tigger say [Snoopy [one-CL self's picture [give Garfield trace]]]

c. Xiaohu [yi-chang ziji-de zhaopian [shuo [Gougou t gei Maomaot]]]
Tigger [one-CL self's picture [say [Snoopy trace give Garfield trace]]]

The *ziji*-movement analysis described above does not provide information concerning the acquisition issue. However, as will be seen from later discussions, based on this analysis one may develop some interesting hypotheses regarding Chinese children's acquisition of long-distance *ziji* and subject-oriented *ziji*.

A second account of the subject-orientation property and the long-distance property of *ziji* is implied in Manzini and Wexler's (1987) specification of the "proper antecedent (PA)" parameter and the "governing category (GC)" parameter. The PA parameter consists of two values: the subject-only value (related to the Chinese reflexive *ziji*) and the any-antecedent value (related to the English reflexive "himself"). The GC parameter, as mentioned earlier in section 2, consists of several values, two of which being the "Chinese" value (that allows both local binding and long-distance binding) and the "English" value (that allows only local binding). In the parametric account, Manzini and Wexler (1987) argued that there are some parameters within which different values define different languages which yield subset relationships. For example, with respect to the PA parameter, English can be viewed as a larger language when compared to Chinese, because sentences with subject antecedents are found in both Chinese and English, while sentences with object antecedents are only found in English. Thus, Chinese is a subset of English when the PA parameter is considered. With respect to the GC parameter of reflexives, Chinese can be viewed as a larger language compared to English. This is due to the fact that sentences with local antecedents are grammatical in both English and Chinese, while, sentences with long-distance antecedents are only grammatical in Chinese. Therefore, English is a sub-set of Chinese when the GC parameter of reflexives is considered.

According to the PP model discussed in Section 2, the values of these parameters have to be learned by the child. For example, children acquiring Chinese as their first language have to learn the "subject-only" value and the "C" value for *ziji*. This will allow them to correctly reject object antecedents and accept subject antecedents, no matter whether they are long-distance or local. Children acquiring English as their first language, on the other hand, have to learn the "E" value and the "any-antecedent" value for "himself." This will allow them to reject long-distance antecedents and accept local antecedents, no matter whether they are subjects or objects. A learnability problem seems to have been created (Wexler & Manzini, 1987). Considering the PA parameter, Chinese is a subset of English. Thus, if a Chinese-speaking child ever incorrectly selects the "any-antecedent" value for the PA parameter, then, from positive data alone, there will be no way to ever change back to the correct "subject-only" value (cf. Brown & Hanlon, 1970; Baker, 1979; Wexler & Hamburger, 1973; Wexler & Culicover, 1980; Wexler, 1982). Similarly, considering the GC parameter, English is a subset of Chinese. If an English-speaking child ever mistakenly selects the "C" value for the GC parameter, then, from positive data alone, there will be no way to change back to the correct "E" value which allows only local antecedents. To solve this learnability issue, Wexler and Manzini (1987) proposed a learning principle, namely, the Subset principle (given in [26]) to account for the parameter-setting process. (See also Berwick & Weinberg, 1984; Berwick, 1985; and Manzini & Wexler, 1987 for more discussions concerning the Subset principle.)

(26) *Subset Principle*: Select the value of a parameter which yields the smallest language consistent with the input data.

According to the Subset Principle, the parameter-setting process is simply to "map the input data to that value of a parameter which defines the smallest of the language compatible with the data" (Wexler & Manzini, 1987:61). It predicts that the subject-only value (which allows only the subject antecedent) and the "E" value (which allows only the local antecedent) should be the child's first attempt in the process of setting the PA parameter and the GC parameter, respectively. Thus, one should not expect Chinese-speaking children to mistakenly select object antecedents for *ziji*, although English speaking children might go through a stage in which only subjects could be antecedents. On the other hand, one should not expect the English-speaking children to incorrectly choose long-distance antecedents for "himself," while one may expect the Chinese-speaking children to go through a stage that allows only local binding of *ziji* before reaching the stage that allows both local binding and long-distance binding.

Is there any empirical support of Wexler and Manzini's parametric approach? Can the Subset Principle explain acquisition orders of parametric values in Binding regarding *ziji*? Do young Chinese children exhibit any response patterns indicating that they know the abstract structural concept of "c-command?" Currently, there are several experimental studies which were especially designed to answer these empirical questions. For example, by using several different research methodologies including the act-out tasks (e.g., the "Simon-says" game and the "Party" game), the picture-identification task, and the grammaticality judgment task (i.e., the Yes/No judgment task), Chien and Wexler (1987, also Chien, Wexler, & Chang, 1990) have found that the basic binding results for English also held for Chinese. Chinese children steadily progressed toward almost 100% accuracy (around age 5) on the question of c-command of a reflexive by its antecedent. For example, when children were presented with sentences such as (27) as well as the two corresponding pictures (A and B), and asked to select a picture that goes well with the sentence, on the average, they selected Picture A more than 90% of the time. This result indicates that Chinese children know the abstract structural notion of "c-command" which, to a large degree, is not reducible in any obvious way to semantic, pragmatic, or cognitive-based concepts.

With regard to the setting of the GC parameter for *ziji*, Chien and Wexler (1987, also see Chien, Wexler, & Chang, 1990, in preparation)

(27) Xiao-xiangxiang-de mama bang ziji xizao.
    Little elephant's mother help self take a bath
    'The little elephant's mother helps herself take a bath.'

Picture A   Picture B

reported that many children strongly rejected (i.e., 5 or 6 items out of 6) long-distance antecedents for *ziji*. They consistently preferred local binding to long-distance binding, even for those children as old as 7. The response pattern exhibited by the children is consistent with the Subset Principle, because it is predicted that the "C" value of the GC parameter, which allows both local and long-distance binding of *ziji*, is the most marked one; thus, the "C" value should be acquired later. However, since adult subjects tested by the same methodologies also preferred the local antecedent almost as much, despite the fact that the long-distance antecedent is grammatically correct, one may speculate that Chinese children may have knowledge of long-distance binding but for some reason do not exhibit this knowledge due to some task-specific factors. Obviously, more clear-cut data are required before any further conclusions can be made. Suppose that the Chinese-speaking children at age 7 still do not exhibit knowledge of long-distance binding as Chien and Wexler suggested. A follow-up question one may ask is "why should it take so long for a child to set the GC parameter for *ziji*?" Children by this age should have had plenty of opportunities to hear sentences with long-distance anaphora in the appropriate contexts. Why weren't these data enough for the children to set the GC parameter? The Subset Principle does not deal with these issues. In essence, as suggested by Wexler and Manzini (1987), the Subset principle predicts that any input that is not allowed by the smaller language will cause the learner to switch the parameter setting. One could envision that it might require a few exposures; the child might not pay attention to the input data or the input data might not be meaningful to the child. But why such a long delay in development? This is still an open question. Let us put aside this question for a moment and take a look at the experimental results concerning Chinese children's knowledge of the subject-only property of *ziji*.

By using the yes/no judgment task, Chien, Wexler, and Chang (in preparation) found that Chinese-speaking children, unlike adults, were willing to accept an object NP as the antecedent for *ziji*. For example, in one experiment the experimenter presented each subject with a picture consisting of the following basic layout: a cartoon character, Donald Duck, is blindfolded, a second cartoon character, Mickey Mouse, is telling Donald Duck about something, and a third cartoon character, Goofy, is not doing anything in particular. Besides the basic layout, there is a big tree, and clearly shown in the picture, only one of the three above mentioned cartoon characters is standing underneath the big tree. After the subject has a chance to carefully inspect the picture, the experimenter presented a test sentence like (28) and asked the subject to make a judgment about the match or mismatch between the picture and the sentence presented to him or her.

(28) Milaoshu gaoshu Tanglaoya shuo ziji zhanzai yi-ke da shu xiamian.
Mickey Mouse tell Donald Duck say self stand one-CL tree under
'Mickey Mouse tells Donald Duck that he is standing underneath a big tree.'

Adult subjects ($n = 16$) gave quite consistent results. About 92% of the time, they answered "yes" to a picture depicting the "matrix subject" as the antecedent (i.e., Mickey Mouse is standing underneath the big tree). About 91% of the time, they replied "no" to a picture indicating the "matrix object" as the antecedent (i.e., Donald Duck is standing underneath the big tree). In other words, they only very rarely allowed *ziji* (i.e., about 9% of the time) to have an object antecedent. The Chinese child subjects ($n = 80$) exhibited a quite different response pattern from the adults. For example, children between the ages of 4 and 5 accepted the subject antecedent about 62.5% of the time, and only rejected the object antecedent about 45% of the time. Their acceptance rate for the object antecedent was not much less than their acceptance rate for the subject antecedent (55% vs. 62%). These results suggest that Chinese children make some nonadult-like mistakes; they do not always select the presumably less marked subject-only value when setting the PA parameter for the reflexive *ziji*. To them, sentence (28) is ambiguous; *ziji* can refer to either the subject antecedent *Milaoshu* or the object antecedent *Tanglaoya*. This set of data, to a large degree, has disconfirmed the Subset principle prediction which suggests that Chinese children would not go through a stage in which the PA parameter is mistakenly set to the "any-antecedent" value. In order to explain this set of results concerning Chinese children's knowledge of *ziji*, one may have to adopt acquisition theories other than the Subset approach. However, it should be pointed out that since the Subset Principle is an UG-external learning principle, the disconfirmation of this Subset principle does not invalidate the PP model in general. (See Kapur, Lust, Harbert, & Martohardjono, in press, for other related discussions about the Subset principle). Currently, several experiments and approaches under the general framework of the PP model have sought to find out whether it is actually the case that Chinese children do not have knowledge of long-distance *ziji*. If so, what can explain the lack of long-distance binding? And, why does it take so long for Chinese children to acquire this knowledge of long-distance binding? Moreover, why is it the case that Chinese children do not reject object antecedents for *ziji* in the beginning? What makes them later learn the fact that *ziji* can only take subject antecedents rather than any antecedents? Is there any relationship between children's rejection of long-distance *ziji* and their acceptance of object antecedents for *ziji*?

For example, Chien, Wexler, and Chang (in preparation) have proposed a working hypothesis based on the analysis that *ziji* moves in LF (cf., Battistella 1987, 1989; Cole, Hermon, & Sung, 1990; Huang & Tang, 1991). The working hypothesis can be stated as follows: what is missing from Chinese children's early grammar is the movement of *ziji* at the level of Logical Form. In other words, when children encounter sentences such as (25a), they do not automatically move *ziji* in Logical Form and generate the corresponding LF representations (e.g., [25b] and [25c]). Children take *ziji* as bound at surface structure. Since, at surface structure, both the subject and the object NPs c-command *ziji*, as long as these two NPs are local to *ziji*, they can be taken as the antecedents for *ziji*. Thus, for Chinese children both local subjects and local objects can be antecedents for *ziji*. (See Reinhart and Reuland, 1991 for related discussions such as the concept of "logophoric" anaphor.) Moreover, since *ziji* is covertly "local" in nature, if *ziji* does not move at LF (overtly at surface structure), *ziji* may not be "locally" bound by the long-distance NP. Thus, for Chinese children *ziji* can only have the local NP as its antecedent but not the long-distance one. This hypothesis treats children's rejection of long-distance *ziji* and their acceptance of object antecedents for *ziji* as two coherent consequences of the inability to move *ziji* at LF. If this working hypothesis is a correct one, we would expect children to exhibit knowledge of long-distance *ziji* and knowledge of subject-orientation of *ziji* in a concurrent manner. In other words, when children indicate their acceptance of long-distance antecedents for *ziji*, they should, at the same time, reject object antecedents for *ziji*. A preliminary analysis of some available data seems to suggest that this might be a conceivable proposal. However, one important task after obtaining more supporting data for this hypothesis is to find out what are the determining factors which make Chinese children realize that *ziji* moves in Logical Form. Obviously, no information concerning LF-movement can be conveyed through the input data to the language learners. If UG-external learning principles cannot explain the development, then, we may have to postulate that these determining factors are essentially UG-internal. (For some related discussions concerning this point, see Kapur, Lust, Harbert, & Martohardjono, in press). To explain why it takes so long for children to learn LF-movement of *ziji*, the theory of syntactic maturation may constitute a good candidate (See Gleitman, 1981 for an important early statement of the logic of maturation, and Borer & Wexler, 1988a, 1988b for discussions concerning the idea of UG-constrained maturation.)

Summary and Conclusion

In summary, the Principles and Parameters model presents several unique arguments regarding issues of language acquisition. It also provides several interrelated implications for language acquisition studies. In this chapter, we have discussed various Chinese studies which were devised under the framework of the PP model and have enumerated empirical evidence to support some of the essential predictions made in the PP model. For example, we have shown that Chinese children's early language concepts and early sentence constructions manifest a "structure-dependent" nature which, in essence, cannot simply be derived from semantic or pragmatic notions, or be defined as simple sentence properties such as linear word order. Moreover, we have indicated that Chinese children's knowledge of "c-command," an abstract structural notion, is not reducible in any obvious way to semantic, pragmatic, or cognitive-based concepts or principles. With regard to the setting of the GC parameter and the PA parameter, we have demonstrated that the UG-external learning principle (namely, the Subset principle) may not be the right approach in accounting for the process of parameter-setting. Without following the Subset prediction, Chinese children allow object antecedents as well as subject antecedents for the reflexive *ziji*. Moreover, for a long period of time, Chinese children do not indicate a knowledge of long-distance binding of *ziji*. Under the general framework of the PP model, we have proposed an alternative account in which we have tried to treat Chinese children's lack of long-distance binding of *ziji* and their acceptance of object antecedents for *ziji* as two coherent outcomes of their ignorance of *ziji*-movement in Logical Form. To what degree this account is correct, of course, must be determined by further theoretical and empirical investigation. A series of experiments adopting this approach is now being conducted in our language acquisition laboratory. In these experiments, we use different research methods and different linguistic materials and hope to obtain more convergent data to support and extend our current findings. There have been several other Chinese experiments which we have not discussed in this paper, due to their complexity and our lack of space. These studies were designed to test Chinese children's knowledge of empty categories. The results have shown that Chinese children do make reference to configuration in the determination of empty categories even in the absence of surface cues. They differentiated bound anaphora from free anaphora which reflect deeper principles of Universal Grammar. (For those who are interested in these studies, see Lust, Mangione, & Chien, 1984 and Lust and Chien, in preparation). The results discussed in Section 3 and the results concerning children's acquisition of empty categories have all pointed to the conclusion that children are sensitive to UG principles.

Putting aside some particulars still being debated concerning UG principles and parameters and the question of how exactly parameters are set, we can tentatively conclude that the PP model has provided us with an insightful explanation concerning the logical problem of language acquisition. From this model we understand why a child can come to master apparently unlearnable linguistic principles and constraints and why a normal child, based on just a limited set of data, can learn any human language (an abstract and intricate system of linguistic knowledge) in just a short period of time.

Acknowledgments

Some studies discussed in this article were supported by the NSF Grant BNS-88-20439 and the Taiwan National Science Council Grant (NSC80-0301-H-002-41). I would like to thank the two editors of this book for providing me with the chance to write this article, Dr. Barbara Lust for invaluable comments and constant support, and Dr. Ken Wexler for stimulating discussions. I would also like to thank Dr. James Huang and Dr. Yen-Hui Audrey Li for their insightful remarks regarding our research on Chinese and the anonymous reviewer for several valuable comments regarding this paper. Moreover, I would like to thank my research collaborators in Taiwan, Dr. Hsing-Wu Chang and Dr. Bonnie Chen for conducting some of the Chinese experiments. Finally, I would like to thank Joyce Mochizuki for proofreading this article.

References

Aitchison, J. (1989). *The articulate mammal: an introduction to psycholinguistics*. London: Unwin Hyman.
Aoun, J., & Li, Y.-H. A. (1990). Minimal disjointness. *Linguistics, 28*, 189-204.
Baker, C. L. (1979). Syntactic theory and the projection problem. *Linguistic Inquiry, 10(4)*.
Bates, E., & MacWhinney, B. (1982). Functionalist approaches to grammar. In E. Wanner & L. R. Gleitman (Eds.), *Language acquisition: The state of the art* (pp. 173-218). Cambridge: Cambridge University Press.
Bates, E., McNew, S., MacWhinney, B., Devescovi, A., & Smith, S. (1982). Functional constraints on sentence processing: A cross-linguistic study. *Cognition, II*, 245-299.
Battistella, E. (1987). *Chinese reflexivization*. Paper presented at the 2nd Harbin Conference on Generative Grammar, Heilongjiang University, Harbin, People's Republic of China; ms., University of Alabama at Birmingham.
Battistella, E. (1989). Chinese reflexivization: A movement to INFL approach.

Linguistics, 27, 987-1012.
Berwick, R. (1985). *The acquisition of syntactic knowledge.* Cambridge, MA: MIT Press.
Berwick, R., & Weinberg, A. (1984). *The grammatical basis of linguistic performance.* Cambridge, MA: MIT Press.
Bloom, L. (1970). *Language development: Form and function in emerging grammar.* Cambridge, MA: MIT Press.
Bloom, L., Lightbown, P., & Hood, L. (1975). Structure and variation in child language. *Monographs of the Society for Research in Child Development, 40(2, Serial No. 160).*
Borer, H. (1984). *Parametric syntax.* Dordrecht, The Netherlands: Foris.
Borer, H., & Wexler, K. (1988a, March). *On the acquisition of agreements.* Paper presented in the 11th GLOW Colloquium, Hungary.
Borer, H., & Wexler, K. (1988b). *On the development of agreement and the uniqueness of external arguments.* Paper in preparation, U. Mass. at Amherst and MIT.
Bowerman, M. (1973). Structural relationships in children's utterances: Syntactic or semantic? In T. Moore (Ed.), *Cognitive development and the acquisition of language* (pp. 197-213). New York: Academic Press.
Brown, R., & Hanlon, C. (1970). Derivational complexity and the order of acquisition of child speech. In J. R. Hayes (Ed.), *Cognition and the development of language,* Wiley, New York.
Chafe, W. L. (1976). Giveness, contrastiveness, definiteness, subjects, topics, and point of view. In C. Li (Ed.) *Subject and topic.* New York: Academic Press.
Chien, Y.-C., & Lust, B. (1983). Topic-comment structure and grammatical subject in first language acquisition of Mandarin Chinese: A study of equi-constructions. *Papers and reports of child language development, 22,* 74-82.
Chien, Y.-C., & Lust, B. (1985). The concepts of topic and subject in first language acquisition of Mandarin Chinese. *Child Development, 56(6),* 1359-1375.
Chien, Y.-C., & Lust, B., & Mangione, L. (1983, April). *The concepts of topic and subject in first language acquisition of Mandarin Chinese: A study of coordinate structures.* Paper presented at the meetings of the Society for Research in Child Development, Detroit.
Chien, Y.-C., & Wexler, K. (1987, Oct.). *A comparison between Chinese-speaking and English-speaking children's acquisition of reflexives and pronouns.* Paper presented in the 12th Annual Boston University Conference on Language Development.
Chien, Y.-C, & Wexler, K. (1990). Children's knowledge of locality conditions in binding as evidence for the modularity of syntax and pragmatics. *Language Acquisition, 1(3),* 225-295.
Chien, Y.-C, Wexler, K., & Chang, H.-W. (1990, October). *The development of long-distance Binding in Chinese.* Paper presented at the 15th Annual Boston University Conference on Language Development, Boston.
Chien, Y.-C, Wexler, K., & Chang, H.-W. (in preparation). *Chinese children's acquisition of long-distance binding and subject orientation of ziji.*
Chomsky, N. (1981). *Lectures on government and binding.* Dordrecht, The Nether-

lands: Foris.
Chomsky, N. (1986). *Knowledge of language: Its nature, origin and use.* New York: Praeger.
Chomsky, N. (1988). *Language and problems of knowledge.* Cambridge, MA: MIT Press.
Cole, P., Hermon, G., & Sung, L.-M. (1990). Principles and parameters of long-distance reflexives. *Linguistic Inquiry, 21(1),* 1-22.
Cook, V. J. (1988). *Chomsky's Universal Grammar: An Introduction.* Cambridge, MA: Basil Blackwell.
deVilliers, J. G. (1980). The process of rule learning in child speech: A new look. In K. E. Nelson (Ed.), *Children's language* (pp. 1-44). New York: Gardner.
Gleitman, L. (1981). Maturational determinants of language growth. *Cognition, 10,* 103-114.
Gleitman, L., Landau, B., & Wanner, E. (1988). Where hearing begins: Initial representation of language learning. In F. Newmyer (Ed.), *The Cambridge Linguistic Survey,* Cambridge, MA: Cambridge University Press.
Gleitman, L., & Wanner, E. (1982). Language acquisition: The state of the art. In E. Wanner & L. Gleitman (Eds.), *Language acquisition: The state of the art* (pp. 3-50). Cambridge: Cambridge University Press.
Gruber, J. S. (1967). Topicalization in child language. *Foundations of language, 3,* 37-65.
Hornstein, N., & Lightfoot, D. (1981). *Explanations in linguistics.* London: Longman.
Hornstein, D. (1984). *Logic as grammar: An approach to meaning in natural language.* Cambridge, MA: MIT Press.
Huang, C.-T. J. (1982). *Logical relations in Chinese and the theory of grammar.* Ph.D. Dissertation, MIT.
Huang, C.-T. J., & Tang, C.-C. J. (1991). The local nature of the long-distance reflexive in Chinese. In J. Koster & E. Reuland (Eds.), *Long-distance anaphora* (pp. 263-282). Cambridge: Cambridge University Press.
Hyams, N. (1986). *Language acquisition and the theory of parameters.* Dordrecht, The Netherlands: Reidel.
Kapur, S., Lust, B., Harbert, W., & Martohardjono, G. (In press). On relating Universal Grammar and learnability theory: The case of binding domains and the 'Subset Principle'. In E. Reuland, & W. Abraham (Eds.), *Knowledge and Language: Issues in representation and acquisition.* Dordrecht: Kluwer Academic Publishers.
Li, C., (Ed.). (1976). *Subject and topic.* New York: Academic Press.
Li, C., & Thompson, S. (1976). Subject and topic: A new typology of language. In C. Li (Ed.), *Subject and topic* (pp. 457-490). New York: Academic Press.
Li, C., & Thompson, S. (1981). *Mandarin Chinese: A functional reference grammar.* Berkeley: University of California Press.
Li, Y.-H. A. (1990). *Order and constituency in Mandarin Chinese.* Dordrecht, The Netherlands: Kluwer Academic Publishers.
Lust, B. (Ed.). (1986). *Studies in the acquisition of anaphora: Volume I. Defining the constraints.* Dordrecht, The Netherlands: Reidel.

Lust, B. (Ed.). (1987). *Studies in the acquisition of anaphora: Volume II. Applying the constraints.* Dordrecht, The Netherlands: Reidel.

Lust, B. (In press). *Universal grammar as a model of initial state.* Cambridge, MA: Bradford Book.

Lust, B., & Chien, Y.-C. (1984). The structure of coordination in first language acquisition of Mandarin Chinese: Evidence for a universal. *Cognition, 17,* 49-83.

Lust, B., & Chien, Y.-C. (In preparation). *Chinese-speaking children's interpretation of pronouns.*

Lust, B., Flynn, S., Chien, Y.-C., & Clifford, T. (1980). Coordination: The role of syntactic, pragmatic, and processing factors in its first language acquisition. *Paper and reports on Child Language Development, 19,* Stanford University, 79-87.

Lust, B., Mangione, L., & Chien, Y.-C. (1984). The determination of empty categories in first language acquisition of Chinese. In W. Harbert (Ed.), *Cornell Working Papers in Linguistics, 6,* 151-165.

Lust, B., & Wakayama, T. (1981). Word order in first language acquisition of Japanese. In P.S. Dale and D. Ingram (Eds.), *Child language: an international perspective.* Baltimore: University Park Press.

Lust, B., Wakayama, T., Snyder, W., & Bergman, H. (1980). *The development of coordination in the natural speech of young Japanese children.* Paper presented at Boston University Child Language Conference, Fall. Extended version submitted for publication.

Manzini, R., & Wexler, K. (1987). Parameters, Binding theory, and learnability. *Linguistic Inquiry, 18,* 413-444.

McNeil, D. (1966). Developmental psycholinguistics. In F. Smith & G. Miller (Eds.), *The genesis of language: A psycholinguistic approach* (pp. 15-84). Cambridge, MA: MIT Press.

Pinker, S. (1984). *Language learnability and language development.* Cambridge, MA: Harvard University Press.

Pinker, S. (1989). Language acquisition. In M. I. Posner (Ed.), *Foundations of cognitive science* (pp. 359-400). Cambridge, MA: MIT Press.

Reinhart, T. (1981). Pragmatics and linguistics: An analysis of sentence topics [Special Issue]. *Philosophica, 27(1).* (Also distributed by Indiana University Linguistics Club, Bloomington.)

Reinhart, T., Reuland, E. (1991). Anaphoric territories. In J. Koster & E. Reuland (Eds.), *Long-distance anaphora.* Cambridge: Cambridge University Press.

Roeper, T., & Williams, E. (Eds.). (1987). *Parameter setting.* Dordrecht, The Netherlands: Reidel.

Tsao, F.-F. (1977). *A functional study of topic in Chinese: The first step toward discourse analysis.* Unpublished doctoral dissertation, University of Southern California.

Valian, V. (1981a). *Syntactic categories in the speech of young children.* Unpublished manuscript, Columbia University.

Valian, V. (1981b). Linguistic knowledge and language acquisition. *Cognition, 10,* 323-329.

Valian, V. (1990). Null subjects: a problem for parameter setting models of language acquisition. *Cognition, 35,* 105-122.

Wexler, K. (1982). A principle theory for language acquisition. In E. Wanner, & L. R. Gleitman (Eds.), *Language acquisition: The state of the art* (pp. 288-315). Cambridge, MA: Cambridge University Press.

Wexler, K., & Chien, Y.-C. (1985). The development of lexical anaphors and pronouns. *Papers and reports of child language development, 24,* 138-149.

Wexler, K., & Culicover, P. (1980). *Formal principles of language acquisition.* Cambridge, MA: MIT Press.

Wexler, K., & Hamburger, H. (1973). On the insufficiency of surface data for the learning of transformational languages. In K. J. Hintikka, J. M. E. Moravcsik & P. Suppes (Eds.), *Approaches to natural language,* Dordrecht, The Netherlands: Reidel.

Wexler, K., & Manzini, R. (1987). Parameters and learnability in Binding theory. In T. Roeper, & E. Williams (Eds.). *Parameter setting.* Dordrecht, The Netherlands: Reidel.

Part V

NEUROPSYCHOLOGICAL AND METHODOLOGICAL ISSUES

Deep and Surface Dyslexia in Chinese

Wengang Yin and Brian Butterworth
University College London

A study of 11 Chinese brain-damaged patients with reading disorders indicates that reading aloud a nonalphabetic script, like reading alphabetic scripts, can be accomplished using two distinct routines: one which associates a whole written word with its complete pronunciation, and one which utilises parts of the written word. Each routine can be selectively impaired by brain-damage, resulting in different patterns of reading disability, i.e. "deep" and "surface" dyslexia. These data are consistent with the independent neural organisation of each routine, and the generality of the two-routine model for reading alphabetic and nonalphabetic scripts.

Studies of acquired disorders of reading Chinese have been the subject of intermittent reports since Lyman's pioneering paper in 1938 (Lyman, Kwan, & Chao, 1938). These studies have been confined to issues of the neural anatomy of Chinese reading disorders (Lyman, et al., 1938; Wang & Li, 1959; Tang, 1978; Hu, Zhu, & Wu, 1983; Li, Hu, Zhu, & Sun, 1984; Hu, Zhu, & Liu, 1986); clinical classification - for example, whether dyslexia is accompanied by dysgraphia (Wang & Tang, 1959; Tang, 1978; Wang & Li, 1981; Li, et al., 1984; Hu, et al., 1986); the relationship between speaking ability and reading capacity (Hu et al., 1983); and whether the reading impairment was at the level of words or at the level of sentences (Hu, et al., 1986). Little attention has been paid to specific *types* of dyslexia, and the potential functional dissociations these might reveal.

Recent studies of acquired disorders of alphabetic reading have revealed distinct types of dyslexia, which are held to be the consequences of selective deficits to components of the reading process. These findings support models of reading incorporating at least two, functionally and neurally separable, routines: a lexical routine that maps whole written words onto their pronunciations, or a sublexical routine that maps letters onto phonemes. (Marshall & Newcombe, 1973; Patterson, 1981). However, since both models and data are based on alphabetic readers and it is unclear which aspects of the reading process are common to all scripts and which are script-dependent. In this study, we describe for the first time the types of dyslexia found in Chinese readers using modern neuropsychological techniques. Although Chinese script is based on characters standing for words rather than on letters standing for sounds, evidence is presented that one group of patients suffer a selective deficit to a routine that maps whole characters onto pronunciations, and that a second group suffer an impairment to a sublexical routine that utilises the phonetic radicals that make up characters.

Recent models claim that skilled adults can read words aloud in two fundamentally distinct ways. (1) By means of a lexical procedure that associates a letter string as a whole with a meaning and a whole-word pronunciation. This is the fast preferred routine for skilled adult readers. (2) By means of a sublexical procedure, that associates single letters, or small groups of letters, with separate syllables or phonemes (the component sounds of a word), which then have to be assembled to yield the pronunciation of the whole word. This routine is used for reading new words and novel letter strings in adults, and is held to be a necessary stage in the development of reading skills in children (Coltheart, 1982; Frith, 1985; Seymour & MacGregor, 1984).

The precise operation of the sublexical routine is disputed. Mapping by rule from one or two letters onto single phonemes has been advocated (Coltheart, Besner, Jonasson, & Davelaar, 1979); while Shallice and McCarthy (1985) prefer sets of correspondences among units of various sizes. A single, lexical analogy procedure, backed up by grapheme-phoneme correspondences, has been suggested by Marcel (1980) and Kay and Marcel (1981); while a single procedure for reading both words and non-words has been advocated by Seidenberg and McClelland (1989).

Support for the model has been adduced from selective impairments of reading performance consistent with a deficit to one or other reading routine (Marshall & Newcombe, 1973; Patterson, 1981; Coltheart, 1982; etc). One class of patient makes characteristic regularisation errors in reading. For example, the patient HTR (Shallice, Warrington, & McCarthy, 1983) read GAUGE as "gorge"; other reported patients read GONE with a long "o" (as in BONE) and PINT with a short "i" (as in HINT). However, these patients are able to read aloud correctly both regularly spelled words and novel letter strings (pseudo-words) (Shallice, et al., 1983; Howard & Franklin, 1987), though they have particular difficulty with irregularly spelled words like PINT, (Coltheart, 1982), and in general, accurate reading depends on the degree of regularity, so that words with exceptional spellings, like COLONEL and YACHT, are hardest (Shallice, et al., 1983). This pattern of impairments is called "surface dyslexia" (Marshall & Newcombe, 1973) and is predictable from a deficit to the whole word routine, but where the routine for mapping letters onto phonemes is intact. The two critical indicators of this impairment are thus (1) regularisation of irregularly-spelled words and (2) poorer performance reading irregular words. [However, it should be noted that Shallice and his colleagues (see Shallice 1988, Chapter 5, for a review) have identified a further class of patients, who are able to read at least mildly irregular words, especially if these words are also familiar - like HAVE and GIVE. These patients, called "phonological readers" by Shallice, are often unable to give the meaning of words they have read correctly. The patient M.P., reported by Bub, Cancelliere, and Kertesz (1985), is such a case].

A second class of patient, by contrast, does not make regularisation errors, and reads irregularly-spelled words as well as regularly-spelled ones; however, these patients are unable to read novel letter strings (Marshall & Newcombe, 1973). These patients fall into two distinct subclasses. In the first, termed "phonological" alexia or dyslexia (Beauvois & Derouesne, 1979), the reader will read real words accurately, and indeed may have very good reading skills for real words (Campbell & Butterworth, 1985). This pattern of impairments is taken as evidence that the sublexical routine has been impaired, while mapping from whole words is relatively intact.

A second subclass has been termed "deep dyslexia" (Marshall & Newcombe, 1973). These patients are also unable to read novel letter strings, but whereas phonological alexics read real words accurately, these patients misread a word as one with a similar meaning. For example, the patient GR read DINNER as "food", and UNCLE as "cousin" (Coltheart, 1982). While spelling regularity is not a critical variable in determining reading accuracy for these patients, word meaning is: thus deep dyslexics are poorer at reading abstract than concrete words, and function words than nouns, verbs or adjectives (Coltheart, 1980). For deep dyslexic patients, although the sublexical routine is seriously impaired, the lexical routine has not been entirely spared: the presence of meaning-related errors, and the effects of meaning variables on reading accuracy, have suggested to Marshall and Newcombe (1973) and others that the lexical routine involves the mediation of the semantic system, rather than a "direct routine" from lexical orthography to whole word pronunciation. The presence of semantic errors and poor abstract word reading may therefore indicate additional deficits in the semantic system itself. Newcombe and Marshall (1980a,b) further speculate that in normal readers the sublexical routine may act as a check on the output of the lexical routine. That is, the lexical routine produces "food" for DINNER, while the sublexical routine will produce the phonologically incompatible output, "dinner", and thus the reader will know that "food" cannot therefore be correct. Since the deep dyslexic patient cannot use the sublexical routine, this error will go through unchallenged.

Attempts to test the generalizability of the two-routine model to readers of nonalphabetic scripts has been limited to studies of Japanese patients. These studies show a selective deficit of the ability to read Kana, a script that represents syllables, while the ability to read Kanji, a script based on Chinese logographs, is preserved (Sasanuma, 1980). It was believed that reading Kanji is basically a lexical process, and the details of reading impairment of Kanji have not been analyzed further in terms of the two-routine model. Nevertheless, it is important to note that Kanji is different from the characters used by Chinese readers. A character used by Chinese usually has one pronunciation (with some exceptions), while a Japanese Kanji usually has two pronunciations: an On-reading which is based on Chinese sound, and a Japanese Kun-reading, but sometimes several On-readings. A Japanese reader has to decide which reading should be employed against the background where the particular character is set. As far as the phonetic component in Kanji (the structural element which may provides the reader with the clue of how the character is to be pronounced) is concerned, it is not as reliable as that in Chinese characters.

Because Chinese script is nonalphabetic, it is widely assumed that characters contain no sublexical information as to their pronunciation. This is not the case. Most characters, including the vast majority of common characters, contain a "phonetic radical" which can indicate how the character is to be pronounced. A phonetic radical, in isolation, is like a normal character that stands for a word or morpheme (Sampson, 1985). Phonetic radicals are used in the creation of new characters for loan words and can be used to construct pronounceable pseudo-words. For historical reasons, these radicals are often an unreliable guide to phonology: some ("*regular*") characters are pronounced like the radical in isolation, other ("*irregular*") characters are not (see Table 1). The reliability and accuracy of representing sound through the phonetic radical has been examined (Yin, 1991). Thirty-six percent of phonetic radicals completely represent the characters' sound. Forty-eight percent of phonetic radicals partially represent the sound. Sixteen percent of phonetic radicals do not represent the sound at all. Clearly, this representation of the characters' sound through phonetic radical can not be neglected, but the accuracy of this representation should also be taken into consideration when thinking about how reading is achieved.

Although this way of encoding the spoken language is very different from alphabetic scripts, it is nevertheless possible that a sublexical routine to phonology is available to normal Chinese which makes use of clues from phonetic radicals. If this is so, then one should find analogues of the dyslexias that result from the selective impairment of either the lexical or the sublexical routines to phonology.

A series of reading tests were therefore devised to examine the possibility that Chinese dyslexics (1) made errors analogous to alphabetic dyslexics, and (2) were sensitive to the analogous critical variables of regularity and of lexicality (that is, real words vs. pseudo-words). If the two routines are employed by Chinese readers, and each routine can be selectively impaired, then the following patterns of reading disturbance should be observed.

Analogue of Deep Dyslexia[1]
1. Many semantic errors
2. No regularisation errors
3. Comparable accuracy for regular and irregular characters
4. Pseudo-words unreadable

Analogue of Surface Dyslexia
1. No or few semantic errors
2. Many regularisation errors
3. Regular characters read more accurately
4. Pseudo-words readable

Table 1
Example of regularization.

Regular character	Irregular character
評	秤
Pronunciation: [Píng]	Pronunciation: [Chèng]
Meaning: comment	Meaning: steelyard

Phonetic radical

平

Pronunciation: [Píng]

Regularization

秤 [Chèng] --- pronounced as [Píng]

Method

Subjects

Eleven brain-damaged right-handed patients were examined from the Tiantan Hospital in Beijing and the First Hospital of the Beijing Medical University. All were native speakers of Mandarin Chinese. The basic conditions of these patients are as follows:

QXS: He had been an engineer with a university degree. He suffered cerebral arteriosclerosis for years. Since symptoms such as bad memory had been become more and more severe, he went to hospital for treatment in 1987. The CT scan showed that the ventricles and sulci were enlarged. Meanwhile, SPECT (Single Photon Emission Computed Tomography) demonstrated RCBF (Regional Cerebral Blood Flow) decreased in the area of MCA (Middle Cerebral Artery) in the left hemisphere. He was diagnosed as having encephalatrophy with more severe condition in the left hemisphere.

LWY: He was a cadre of a company with a secondary school education. In June of 1988, he suffered cerebral vascular occlusion in the left hemisphere. The CT scan showed that there was a low-density region in the conjunctive area of the temporal, parietal and occipital lobes. The lesion extended backwards to the pole of the occipital lobe.

LYM: Before retirement, he was a statistician. He also had a secondary school education. He suffered a meningioma in the left hemisphere. In 1986, he went to Beijing medical hospital to have the brain tumour removed. The CT scan showed a 6 x 4 cm size tumour in the left temporal lobe.

LSH: He was a technician who had graduated from a polytechnic. In February of 1988, he suffered cerebrovascular occlusion in the left hemisphere. The CT scan showed a low-density area in the conjunctive area of the temporal, parietal and occipital lobes in the left hemisphere.

LQF: Before retirement, he was an accountant with a secondary school education. In 1986, he had cerebrovascular occlusion in the left hemisphere. The CT scan showed that around the left basal ganglia there was a low-density area. Outside of the left corona radiata there was a spot of occlusion.

LZY: He was a worker with a secondary school education. In January of 1988, he suffered cerebrovascular occlusion in the left hemisphere. The CT scan showed there was a lesion in the conjunctive area of the temporal, parietal and occipital lobes in the left hemisphere. Meanwhile, SPECT (Single Photon Emission Computed Tomography) demonstrated CBF (Cerebral Blood Flow) had decreased in the area of the temporal and occipital lobes in the left hemisphere.

WBY: He was a professor in a university. In 1985, he suffered cerebrovascular occlusion in the left hemisphere. The CT scan showed some lesions located in the conjunctive area of the temporal, parietal and occipital lobes. At the time he was examined in 1989, he had recovered a lot of his language ability.

LSJ: He used to be a secondary school teacher with a degree from a polytechnic. In 1988, he suffered a cerebrovascular occlusion in the left hemisphere. The CT scan showed there was a large low-density region on the junction of the temporal, parietal and occipital lobes.

LLH: He was a professor at a university. In 1986, when visiting Italy his brain was badly damaged in a car accident. The CT scan showed that there was a destruction on the left frontal and temporal part of the skull, and the cerebral cortex underneath had also been damaged.

LDJ: She was a secondary school teacher with a university degree. In June of 1988, she suffered cerebrovascular occlusion in the left hemisphere. The CT scan showed there were lesions in the left ganglia area and the left parietal and occipital area. Meanwhile, a MRI (Magnetic Resonance Imaging) scan showed that there were lesions in the post-parietal branch and angular gurus branch of MCA of the left hemisphere.

ZZG: He was a student at elementary school. He suffered from a kind of cerebral vascular malformation disease, called Moya Moya's disease. The CT scan made in August of 1988 showed that there was a lesion in the frontal lobe of the right hemisphere. Meanwhile angiography proved the diagnosis of Moya Moya's disease.

These eleven patients were found to have various degrees of language dysfunction. In addition to reading tests, their speaking, listening and writing abilities were also assessed. A variety of associations between disorders in reading and impairment of other language functions.

A brief summary of these patients are given in Table 2(a and b).

The neuroanatomy of these patients show the importance of the left hemisphere in reading Chinese. All of these eleven patients except one child had left hemisphere damage. Within the left hemisphere the lesions were mostly localized in conjunctive areas of the temporal, parietal and occipital lobes. These findings are consistent with previous studies on Chinese reading disorders (Lyman, et al., 1938; Wang, et al., 1959; Tang, 1978; Hu, et al., 1983; Li, et al., 1984; Hu, et al., 1986). There is thus no evidence that the supposedly pictorial nature of Chinese characters leads to localisation of function in the right hemisphere, where picture and visual object recognition is carried out.

An examination of the patients' comprehension, speaking, writing and reading abilities reveals 4 distinct clinical categories:

(1) *Pure alexia* - a reading disorder not accompanied by writing impairment, sometimes called alexia without agraphia. Patients LYM, QXS, WBY and LLH fell into this category.

(2) *Alexia with agraphia* - a reading disorder which is accompanied by writing disorder - manifested by patients LWY, LSH and LZY.

(3) *Alexia with agraphia and aphasia*. Patients ZZG, LDJ, LSJ and LQF showed language problems in addition to their reading and writing deficits.

It should be noted that the reading deficits accompanied a wide range of abilities in listening comprehension, speaking and writing, ranging from normal to very severely impaired.

Table 2(a)
Patient Summary.

Name	Age	Sex	Onset	Etiology	Hemisphere	Location
QXS	64	M	Unknown	Cerebral arteriosclerosis	left	MCA* area
LWY	53	M	1988	Cerebrovascular occlusion	left	temporal occipital
LYM	73	M	Unknown	Meningioma	left	temporal
LSH	55	M	1988	Cerebrovascular occlusion	left	parietal, temporal occipital
LQF	76	M	1986	Cerebrovascular occlusion	left	BG* area CR* area
LZY	28	M	1988	Cerebrovascular occlusion	left	parietal, temporal occipital
WBY	58	M	1985	Cerebrovascular occlusion	left	parietal, temporal occipital
LSJ	65	M	1988	Cerebrovascular occlusion	left	parietal, temporal occipital
LLH	62	M	1986	Trauma	left	frontal, temporal
LDJ	57	F	1988	Cerebrovascular occlusion	left	parietal, occipital
ZZG	12	M	Unknown	Moya Moya's disease	right	frontal, parietal

MCA: middle cerebral artery. BG: basal ganglia. CR: corona radiata.

Table 2(b)
Patient Summary.

Name	Education level	Writing	Listening	Speaking
QXS	University	+	+	+
LWY	Secondary school	-	+	+
LYM	Secondary school	+	+	+
LSH	Polytechnic	- -	+	+
LQF	Secondary school	- -	+	+ -
LZY	Secondary school	+ -	+	+
WBY	University	+	+	+
LSJ	Polytechnic	-	+ -	+
LLH	University	+	+	+
LDJ	Secondary school	-	+	- -
ZZG	Elementary school	- -	+	-

Notes:
Writing
 +: could write sentences without difficulty
 +-: unable to write some common characters
 -: unable to write many common characters, but able to write their own names and addresses
 --: able to write few or no characters

Listening
 +: able to understand all questions asked by the examiner
 +-: patient could follow simple commands, but failed to understand some questions

Speaking
+: could describe common objects, and could express him or herself freely
+-: unable to name some common objects with abnormal hesitancy
-: great word finding difficulty
--: only a few words correctly produced, speech often incomprehensible

Reading tests

Each patient was asked to read aloud 40 common regular characters, 21 common irregular characters, 12 common phonetic radicals and 14 pseudo-words. Pseudo-words were invented pictophonetic (two component) characters constructed from phonetic radicals in legal positions. Phonetic radicals typically take the same position in all the characters; such as, for example, 里 [lǐ], always appears on the right (理 "reason", pronounced [lǐ], 鲤 "carp" [lǐ], and 俚 "vulgar" [lǐ]). In the pseudo-words of this study, all the radicals appeared in their normal position on the right.

Regularisation errors were identified according to the principle described above. Errors were classified as semantic, if they were similar in meaning or related in meaning to the target; e.g. in 别 "leave" [bié] read as 分 "separate" (verb) [fēn], the errors were similar in meaning; while for 子 "child" [zǐ] read as 小 "little" [xiǎo], the error was related in meaning.

Patients making regularisation errors were classified as "surface" dyslexics, while the remainder were classified as "deep" dyslexics. The presence of semantic errors was not sufficient to identify deep dyslexics, since all Chinese readers make semantic errors. This unusual phenomenon may be due to the unavailability of a sublexical phonemic check on output for many characters. In an experiment with normal subjects, Yin (1991) found that the presence of a phonetic radical is usually sufficient to suppress a semantic error. The frequency of these errors was recorded and analyzed.

Results

The proportions of each type of error are give in Table 3. The percentage correct for each type of character is given in Figure 1. The patients classified as surface dyslexics made a high proportion of regularisation errors (25% to 75%). Both groups made semantic errors, but a significantly higher proportion were made by the deep dyslexics ($t=5.28$, $df=7$, $p<.005$). There were further differences between the semantic errors made by each groups. The "deep" dyslexic group made semantic errors no matter the target character (the character they were required to read aloud) had a phonetic radical or not. While the "surface" group made semantic errors only when the target character had no phonetic radical.

Table 3
Reading errors.

Types	Patients	Semantic Errors	Regularization
DEEP DYSLEXIA	QXS	24 %	0
	LYM	45 %	0
	LLH	54 %	0
	ZZG	57 %	0
	LDJ	50 %	0
	LWY	47 %	0
	LSJ	41 %	0
SURFACE DYSLEXIA	LSH	17 %	46 %
	LZY	21 %	53 %
	LQF	14 %	25 %
	WBY	0	75 %

(PERCENTAGE OF TOTAL ERRORS)

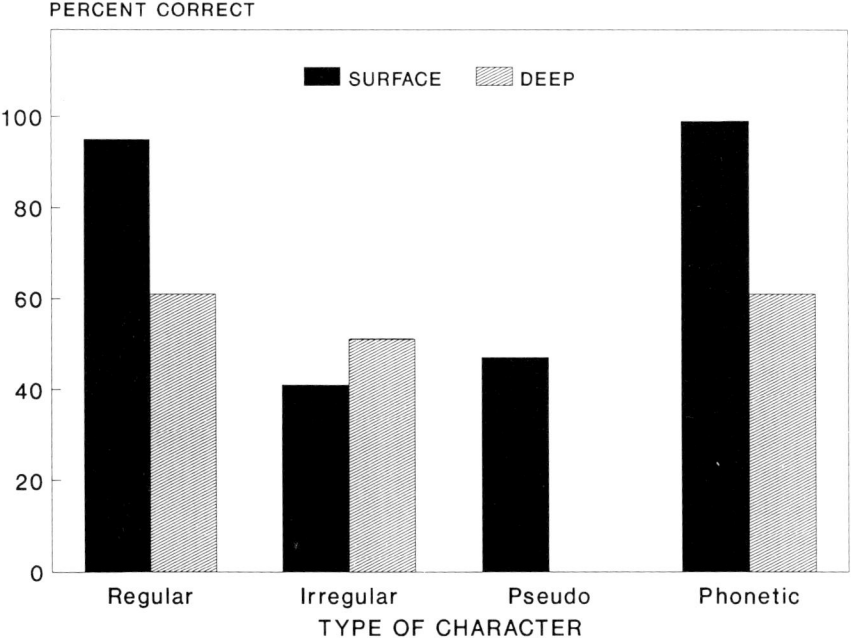

Figure 1.

Because many Chinese characters have a component or "signific" (Sampson, 1985) which has the function of indicating or implying the category of meaning of the character. Therefore a question is raised here: do the semantic errors made by patients have some relationships with the significs of the characters they read?

It was found that most semantic errors happened with the single-graph characters which have not got a signific in their construction (75 percent of all characters which produced semantic errors were single-graph characters). However, 62 percent of all the characters which had a signific in the structure produced semantic errors. On the whole, there were only 12 percent of all semantic errors which had a relationship to the signific of the characters. Some examples of the relationship between semantic errors and significs are as follows: 秧 "seedling", [yāng], was read as 苗 "young plant", [miáo]. 禾 is a signific which indicates something relevant to grain, especially rice. The meaning of 禾 is grain. It's pronunciation is [hé]. 軀 "trunk", [qū], was read as 体 "body", [tǐ]. 身 is a signific which indicates something relevant to a body. The meaning of 身 is human body. It's pronunciation is [shēn]. 锯 "saw", [jù] was read as 锤 "hammer", [chuí]. 钅 is a signific which indicates something is made from metal. 钅 is no longer a single-graph character as many significs are. 钅 is evolved from a single-graph character 金 [jīn] which means "gold" or "metal".

All deep dyslexic patients were completely unable to read pseudowords aloud. On the other hand, the surface dyslexics were able to read better than 40% of them on average. This difference is partly explained by reading performance on phonetic radicals in isolation.

The deep dyslexics showed comparable performance on regular and irregular characters, while the surface dyslexics were significantly better on regular characters ($t=3.06$, $df=3$, $p<.05$).

One case of deep dyslexia provided a unique opportunity to study the word by word extent of an acquired reading problem. Patient LSJ was an active learner. When he left hospital, he did not rest passively waiting for recovery, rather he adopted an active strategy to help his recovery by learning. He spent much of his time at home reading a dictionary (Xin Hua Zi Dian, 1971) to see how many characters he failed to read, and how many characters he still retained the ability to read. Each character on every page of the dictionary was marked by him according to his reading results. The marks he used included circles, ticks and underlinings. Red circles indicated the characters which he could still correctly read, i.e. he knew both the meaning and the sound of them; the black circles marked the characters which he felt looked strange. The ticks were used to stand for the characters whose meanings he knew (either precisely or roughly) but which he could not read aloud; the underlinings were used to signify the characters for which knew neither the meaning nor the pronunciation.

The dictionary used by LSJ has a vocabulary of about 11,000 characters. There were 490 characters which were marked with red circles, indicating that he knew both meaning and pronunciation. One hundred and three characters, marked by black circles, looked strange to him. However, he felt he knew the meaning of 5,570 characters marked by ticks, which he failed to pronounce. Apparently, LSJ retained in his vocabulary 6,060 characters whose meaning he still knew (though not all precisely). Thus, only for 8 % of his total reading vocabulary could LSJ get the correct pronunciation (490 / 6060 = 0.08). This showed that knowledge of the sound of characters could be dissociated from knowledge of meaning.

Further analysis performed on LSJ's data revealed an interesting double dissociation. LSJ could read some 18 characters when they were in combination-forms, but he failed to read them as single graphs, even though those single-graphs were used in combination-forms which he could successfully pronounce, and moreover, the pronunciation of those single-graphs and combination-forms were the same. On the other hand, LSJ could read 82 characters as single-graphs, but failed to read them in combination-forms, again despite their having the same pronunciation.

This double dissociation suggests that LSJ always read characters as wholes, and could not exploit the phonetic radicals in attempts to pronounce combination-forms. That is to say, if a combination-form which he could pronounce, contained a phonetic radical, he was not necessarily able to use this fact to read aloud the isolated radical; on the other hand, if he could pronounce a phonetic radical, he could not always make this information available to attempt a pronunciation of a form he did not recognise. Thus this patient provides us with remarkable evidence of a relatively preserved lexical routine in the absence of a sublexical routine. As would be expected from the dictionary study, this patient falls squarely into our classification of Deep Dyslexia, making a high proportion of semantic errors, and no regularisation errors (Yin, 1991).

Discussion

The results of the present study demonstrate that patterns of impairment quite analogous to those of alphabetic dyslexics can be found in readers of a nonalphabetic script. Seven of the patients showed symptoms consistent with a selective disorder in the use of sublexical information in reading, but relatively spared ability to read real words as a whole. At the same time, four patients were able to use sublexical information, and indeed appeared to rely on it even where inappropriate: that is, those characters where only an intact lexical routine would have yielded a correct pronunciation were read sublexically.

Regularisation and semantic errors turned out to be highly reliable predictors of overall performance on the four types of character.

However, these data do not mean that readers of nonalphabetic scripts use precisely the same processes as alphabetic readers. With respect to the sublexical routine, they clearly cannot employ grapheme-phoneme rules, at single phoneme or higher levels: phonetic radicals provide clues to the pronunciation of the whole word, rather than to a part of it. Moreover, it is not clear from these data how similar the Chinese lexical routine is to its alphabetic counterpart. Marhsall and Newcombe (1973) assumed that the alphabetic lexical routine necessarily involves a semantic interpretation of the written word; a more direct mapping from whole words to pronunciation, without the involvement of meaning (which would support, for example, the ability to read correctly irregular words without understanding them) is still controversial (See Bub, et al., 1985; Howard and Franklin, 1987; for discussion). It still needs to be established whether the lexical routine for Chinese readers necessarily involves semantic recoding.

Newcombe and Marshall (1980a,b) have further suggested that the independent availability of a phonological representation of the written word can serve as a check on the output of a lexical routine that utilises the semantic system. They claim that the semantic system in deep dyslexics has become unstable, and because the nonlexical routine is unable to deliver an independent check, semantic errors are likely to be produced. This study provided evidence that the presence of a phonetic radical in a character can prevent or reduce the likelihood of semantic error, because surface dyslexics who have a demonstrable capacity to make use of phonetic radicals in reading characters aloud made no semantic errors when there was a phonetic radical in the character.

Despite the very different ways in which Chinese and alphabetic writing systems represent their languages, the reading processes that decode them appear to have the same broad underlying cognitive architecture.

Acknowledgments

The research reported here was carried out mainly at the Beijing Tian-Tan Hospital, and the authors wish to record their thanks to Li Yi and Zhang Xiaoying of the Neurology Department. We also thank Gao Surong and the Neurology Department of the First Hospital of Beijing Medical University for their help.

Yin Wengang was supported when this research was conducted by a scholarship from the Academica Sinica, People's Republic of China.

Some of the material in this paper was previously published in *The Proceedings of the Royal Society Series B, 245, 91-95 (1991)*. We are grateful for permission to reproduce Figure 1.

Footnote

1. Two further symptoms of alphabetic deep dyslexia, noted above, were not tested: the effects of concreteness and the effects of grammatical category.

References

Beauvois, M-F. & Derouesne, J. (1979) Phonological alexia: Three dissociations. *Journal of Neurology, Neurosurgery and Psychiatry, 42*, 1115-1124

Bub, D., Cancelliere, A. & Kertesz, A. (1985) Whole-word and analytic translation of spelling-to-sound in a non-semantic reader. In Patterson, K. E., Marshall, J. C. & Coltheart M. (eds), *Surface Dyslexia: Neuropsychological and Cognitive Studies of Phonological Reading*. London, Erlbaum.

Campbell, R. & Butterworth, B. (1985) Phonological dyslexia and dysgraphia in a highly literate subject: A development case with associated deficits of phonemic processing and awareness. *Quarterly Journal of Experimental Psychology, 37A*, 435-475

Coltheart, M. (1980) Deep dyslexia: A review of the syndrome. In Coltheart, M., Patterson, K. E. & Marshall, J. C. (Eds), *Deep Dyslexia*. London, Routledge & Kegan Paul. 22-47

Coltheart, M. (1982) The psycholinguistic analysis of the acquired dyslexias: Some illustrations. *The Philosophical transactions of the Royal Society of London, B298*, 151-164

Coltheart, M., Besner, D., Jonasson, J. & Davelaar, E. (1979) *Quarterly Journal of Experimental Psychology, 31*, 489-507

Frith, U. (1985) Beneath the surface of developmental dyslexia. In Patterson, K. E., Marshall, J. C. & Coltheart M. (eds), *Surface Dyslexia: Neuropsychological and Cognitive Studies of Phonological Reading*. London, Erlbaum. 301-327

Howard, D. & Franklin, S. (1987) Three ways for understanding written words and their use in contrasting cases of surface dyslexia. In Allport, D.A., Mackay, D., Prinz, W. & Scheerer, E. (eds), *Language Perception and Production: Common processes in listening, speaking, reading and writing*. London, Academic Press. 340-366

Hu, C.Q., Zhu, Y.L. & Liu, A.L. (1986) A neurolinguistic study on reading disorders after brain damage. *Chinese Journal of Neurology and Psychiatry, 19*, 26-29.

Hu, C.Q., Zhu, Y.L. & Wu, W.Z. (1983) The supporting effect of spoken language to written language -- A neurolinguistic analysis through cases of brain damage. *Acta Psychologia Sinica, 3*, 349-353.

Kay, J. & Marcel, A. (1981) One process not two in reading aloud: Lexical analogies do the work of non-lexical rules. *Quarterly Journal of Experimental Psychology, 33A*, 397-413.

Li, X. T., Hu, C. Q., Zhu, Y. L. & Sun, B. (1984) Neurolinguistic analysis of Chinese alexia and agraphia. In Kao, H. S. R & Hoosain, R. (eds),

Psychological Studies of the Chinese Language. Chinese Language Society of Hong Kong. 151-166.

Lyman, R. S., Kwan, S. T. & Chao, W. H. (1938) Left occipito-parietal brain tumour with observations on alexia and agraphia in Chinese and English. *The Chinese Medical Journal*, 54, 491-515

Marcel, T. (1980) Surface dyslexia and beginning reading: a revised hypothesis of the pronunciation of print and its impairments. In Coltheart, M., Patterson, K. E. & Marshall, J. C. (Eds), *Deep Dyslexia*. London, Routledge & Kegan Paul. 227-258

Marshall, J. C. & Newcombe, F. (1973) Patterns of paralexia: A psycholinguistic approach. *Journal of Psycholinguistic Research*, 2, 175-199

Newcombe, F. & Marshall, J. C. (1980a) Response monitoring and response blocking in deep dyslexia. In Coltheart, M., Patterson, K. E. & Marshall, J. C. (Eds), *Deep Dyslexia*. London, Routledge & Kegan Paul. 160-175

Newcombe, F. & Marshall, J. C. (1980b) Transcoding and lexical stabilisation in deep dyslexia. In Coltheart, M., Patterson, K. E. & Marshall, J. C. (Eds), *Deep Dyslexia*. London, Routledge & Kegan Paul. 176-188

Patterson, K. E. (1981) Neuropsychological approaches to the study of reading. *British Journal of Psychology*, 72, 151-174

Sampson, G. (1985) *Writing Systems*. Hutchinson Education, London.

Sasanuma, S. (1980) Acquired dyslexia in Japanese: Clinical features and underlying mechanisms. In Coltheart, M., Patterson, K. E. & Marshall, J. C. (Eds), *Deep Dyslexia*. London, Routledge & Kegan Paul. 48-90.

Seidenberg, M. S. & McClelland, J. (1989) A distributed, developmental model of word recognition and naming. *Psychological Review*, 96, 523-586

Seymour, P. H. K. & McGregor, C. J. (1984) Developmental dyslexia: A cognitive experimental analysis of phonological, morphemic and visual impairments. *Cognitive Neuropsychology*, 1, 43-82 .

Shallice, T. *From Neuropsychology to Mental Structure*. Cambridge, Cambridge University Press, 1988.

Shallice, T. & McCarthy, R. (1985) Phonological reading: From patterns of impairment to possible procedures. In Patterson, K. E., Marshall, J. C. & Coltheart, M. (eds), *Surface Dyslexia*. London, Erlbaum. 361-397.

Shallice, T., Warrington, E. K. & McCarthy, R. (1983) Reading without semantics. *Quarterly Journal of Experimental Psychology*, 35A, 111-138.

Tang, C.M. (1978) Alexia. *The Progress of disease in Nervous system*, 1, 113-117.

Wang, X. D. & Li, J. (1981). Agraphia. *Chinese Journal of Neurology and Psychiatry*, 14, 148-151

Wang, X. D. & Tang, X. J. (1959). Alexia. *Chinese Journal of Neurology and Psychiatry*, 5, 180-187

Xin Hua Zi Dian (Chinese Dictionary), (1971). Shang-Wu Publishing House, Beijing.

Yin, W. (1991). *On reading Chinese characters -- an experimental and neuropsychological study*. Unpublished Ph.D. thesis. University of London.

Cross-Linguistic Research on Language and Cognition: Methodological Challenges

Terry Kit-fong Au
University of California, Los Angeles

This essay discusses several methodological challenges and possible solutions in cross-linguistic research on the relation between language and cognition. Some are rather common concerns in cross-linguistic research; others are specific to research on language processing in Chinese. This essay will focus on four basic ingredients of research: hypotheses, stimulus materials, evaluation of previous findings, and subject populations.

In studying the relation between language and cognition, I and other researchers face a number of methodological challenges. Some are rather common concerns in cross-linguistic research; others are specific to research on language processing in Chinese. This essay will discuss several such challenges--illustrated with actual research stories--and some possible solutions. It will focus on several basic ingredients of research, namely, hypotheses, stimulus materials, evaluation of previous findings, and subject populations.

Hypotheses

Human beings seem to be forever curious about differences among cultures and how such differences came about. Cross-cultural differences in how people perceive and reason about the world are often intriguing. Trying to understand the origins of such differences can be quite an adventure--intellectual and otherwise. One of the best known hypotheses about the origins of cross-cultural differences in thinking is the Sapir-Whorf hypothesis (Sapir, 1949; Whorf, 1956). It has two main tenets: (1) *Linguistic Relativity*--Structural differences between two languages are generally paralleled by non-linguistic cognitive differences in the native speakers of the two languages; (2) *Linguistic Determinism*--The structure of a language strongly influences or fully determines the way its speakers perceive and reason about the world.

One reason why this view is fascinating has to do with the kind of thought that Sapir and Whorf focused on. They were interested in how the structure of language might shape fundamental and pervasive aspects of thinking such as perception of social reality, concept of time, causality, the ontological distinction between object and event, and so forth. Does language look like a good candidate for what organizes and shapes our thinking? This possibility is intuitively appealing because we typically do think in words (see e.g., Bickerton, 1990). It seems possible that arbitrary differences between languages could lead to parallel differences in fundamental and pervasive ways of thinking. On the other hand, one cannot help but be skeptical that something truly basic in human thinking could be pushed around by different linguistic structures. How can one reconcile these two views on this major hypothesis about the origins of cross-cultural differences?

Consider a recent investigation of counterfactual reasoning in Chinese and English (Bloom, 1981, 1984; Au 1983, 1984). Bloom (1981) noticed that there is a distinct counterfactual marker in English (i.e., the subjunctive) but not in Chinese, and speculated that Chinese speakers should have more difficulty and be therefore less inclined to reason counterfactually. Like the kind of thought Sapir and Whorf were interested in, counterfactual reasoning is very fundamental and pervasive in human thinking. For instance, if regret is a universal emotion, then counterfactual reasoning must also be universal. Imagine that a mother sent her child to run an errand, and the child was killed in an accident. The mother would no doubt wish she had not asked her child to run that errand. More generally, when one regrets some past action and wishes things had out otherwise, one has to engage in counterfactual reasoning.

One does not have to look far to see that counterfactual reasoning is an integral part of everyday life. For instance, in order to feel frustrated, we have to be able to imagine that we could have accomplished what we almost managed to--but did not--accomplish; to feel grateful to someone, we have to be able to imagine that things would probably not have worked out so well without that person's help; to feel lucky (or unlucky), we have to be able to imagine that things could have turned out worse (or better), otherwise we would be simply blessed (or cursed). In order to fantasize, to enjoy pretense play, fictions, and dramas, we need to enter some counterfactual worlds. In order to learn from past mistakes, we need to consider what might have been and should have been. These many and varied aspects of everyday thinking all seem to require counterfactual reasoning, and importantly, seem to be pervasive across cultures. How can something so fundamental in human thinking be at the mercy of the presence or absence of a distinct counterfactual marker in our languages? One way or the other, each language must have some way or ways to mark counterfactuality and to allow its speakers to think and talk counterfactually. Given these conclusions about counterfactual reasoning, what should one do with a hypothesis such as Bloom's?

The story of Bloom's investigation will be told later in this chapter; for now, a point can nonetheless be made. If Bloom's hypothesis turned out to be valid, the findings would be very compelling support for the Sapir-Whorf hypothesis, which states that language structure shapes thought. On the other hand, it is also important to be realistic about the plausibility of such a hypothesis. That is, if the kind of thinking in question is truly fundamental and seems universal in human thinking--and counterfactual reasoning seems to fall into this category--it is probably not the best domain to look for cross-cultural differences. (Such caution can be valuable even beyond the stage of hypothesis formulation. For instance, if one finds cross-cultural differences in something that is very fundamental in human thinking, it would be worth taking a hard look at the findings to see if the evidence is indeed compelling and sound.)

In formulating hypotheses, researchers doing cross-linguistic studies have more to worry about than just the danger of unchecked enthusiasm in finding cross-cultural differences. We also have to worry about how well we know the foreign languages that we are working with. When we do not speak those languages, it seems reasonable to turn to informants who speak the languages or to secondary sources such as published linguistic analyses; but such secondhand information is often inadequate and at times misleading.

Consider, for example, some work reported by Aaronson and Ferres. They were interested in how the linguistic differences between English and Chinese may lead to associated cognitive performance differences between [Chinese-English] bilinguals and monolinguals in processing the meaning and structure of sentences (Aaronson & Ferres, 1987). When they compared these two languages, they had to rely on their Chinese informants and some published analyses of the Chinese language. This research strategy unfortunately resulted in a rather problematic analysis of the differences between Chinese and English. For instance, these researchers noted that there are a considerable number of lexical categories in English. They then asserted, "Sinologists have divided morphemes into 'full' words...and 'empty' words.... These differences between languages are..." (p. 78). The logic of their analysis goes like this: Some linguists thought that Chinese words could be put into two or three categories, and we know that English words can be put into many more categories, so Chinese and English are different. One obvious problem with this analysis is that the "full-empty" distinction comes from an ancient linguistic theory. According to more current linguistic analyses, the lexical categories in Chinese are quite comparable to those in English (e.g., Chao, 1968). Indeed, it is rather easy for a native Chinese speaker with some training in linguistics to see such similarities between English and Chinese. More generally, equating languages with theories about them can be dangerous. For example, theories about the English syntax have undergone major transformations in the past three decades, whereas English syntax has stayed more or less the same. Because Aaronson and Ferres' hypothesis was based on a problematic analysis of one of the two languages being compared, it is not clear what to make of their empirical findings.

Inadequate knowledge of the Chinese language also may have hurt Bloom's hypothesis formulation. As noted earlier, Bloom assumed that there is no distinct counterfactual marker in Chinese. If language could shape thought, he speculated, the presence of the subjunctive should help English speakers reason counterfactually. But there are in fact a number of ways to mark counterfactuality in Chinese. The one Bloom focused on (*A not being the case. If A being the case, then B will be the case*) is only one of them. Some examples in Classical Chinese are *wei, shi,* and *jie* (e.g., Eifring, 1988; Garrett, 1983-85; Wu, 1987; Yen, 1977). Some examples in Modern Chinese are *hai yiwei, yaobushi*, and *yaoshi...zao jiu* [or *zeme hiu*]...*le* (Eifring, 1988; Ramsey, 1987; Wu, 1987). No doubt, it remains an open question whether there might be subtle and specific differences between English and Chinese speakers in counterfactual reasoning because the counterfactual markers are somewhat different between the two languages. Nonetheless, it is probably safe to say that Bloom's hypothesis oversimplifies the differences between English and Chinese in terms of counterfactual markers. He thought that there is a distinct counterfactual marker in English but not in Chinese and predicted that Chinese speakers generally would be less inclined to reason counterfactually. But he did not seem to realize that there are actually several counterfactual markers in Chinese. Better knowledge of the Chinese language might have helped him come up with a more sophisticated and more plausible hypothesis.

Stimulus Materials

Bloom set out to test his hypothesis in several studies by asking some Chinese and English speakers in Hong Kong, Taiwan, and the United States to read a counterfactual story. The subjects were then asked whether the implications discussed were true (Bloom, 1981, 1984). His most dramatic findings were that, in one study, 98% of the native English speakers appreciated that the implications of the story were contrary to fact, whereas only 6% of the Chinese speakers in Hong Kong and Taiwan did so when asked to read a Chinese version of the story (Bloom, 1981). If Bloom's surprising findings turned out to be valid, they would be very compelling support for the Sapir-Whorf hypothesis.

The problem with these findings is that the counterfactual in the Chinese version of this story was not expressed properly because some of the hypothetical markers were missing. Recall that one way to express a counterfactual in Chinese is to use the construction *A not being the case. If A being the case, then B will/may/can be the case.* *Then* can be translated into Chinese as *jiu*; however, *jiu* has two rather different senses. When *jiu* is followed by a hypothetical marker such as *will, may,* or *can*, it means "then," as in "If A, then B." But when *jiu* is followed by *is* or *are* (*shi* in Chinese), it means "precisely." In Bloom's story, *what would have most influenced him would have been...* was rendered in Chinese as something that means "what influenced him most was precisely...."

Another mistake in expressing the if-then conditional in Bloom's Chinese version was that *once influenced by that Chinese perspective, Bier would then have synthesized...* was rendered in Chinese as "Therefore, it was not until after Bier had been influenced by the Chinese perspective that he synthesized...." The problem in this case has to do with the Chinese word *cai*, which also has two senses. Bloom did not seem to realize that when followed by a hypothetical marker such as *will, may,* or *can, cai* is an adverb of contingency as in "only if A, then B." Without a hypothetical marker, it is an adverb of time as in "not until then" or "just then" (see Chao, 1968 for an in depth analysis of if-then conditionals in Chinese). Hypothetical markers are also missing in several other place in Bloom's Chinese Version of the story. The overall result is that the story was told in the factual mode rather than the counterfactual mode in Chinese. To evaluate the importance of hypothetical markers in Chinese counterfactuals, I created another version of the story by adding appropriate hypothetical markers to Bloom's Chinese version (Au, 1984). I then randomly assigned my revised version and Bloom's version to a group of Chinese speakers in Hong Kong. The results were straightforward. When the hypothetical markers were present in the story, over 80% of the Chinese speakers gave a counterfactual interpretation to the story. By contrast, when hypothetical markers were absent, less than a quarter of the subjects did so. These results suggest that the low counterfactual response rate for Bloom's Chinese version clearly cannot be taken as evidence for language having profound effects on thought. Several other studies have likewise revealed that when the counterfactuals are expressed correctly in Chinese, Chinese speakers seem to have little difficulty in thinking counterfactually (Au, 1983, 1984, 1988, in press; Liu, 1985; see also Cheng, 1985; Takano, 1989; Vorster & Schuring, 1989 for critiques of Bloom's methodology).

How can a researcher be sure that the stimulus materials in a cross-linguistic study are comparable in all of the languages if the researcher is not fluent in those languages? One solution is to collaborate with other researchers who are native speakers of the languages. This strategy should be safer than getting free or paid advice from informants who speak those languages but have little or no research training because, for one thing, co-investigators would know more about research methods. Co-investigators should also be more willing to speak up when they have concerns or reservations about the stimulus materials and research methods. By contrast, a paid or volunteer informant might be too shy or intimidated or simply might not care enough about the research to disagree openly with a researcher.

Another way to help ensure that the stimulus materials are comparable across languages is to prepare them in several steps. For instance, in my work on counterfactual reasoning (Au, 1983), I first wrote the stimulus story in English (my second language), showed it to several native English speakers in the U.S. for comments, and then revised it accordingly to make sure that the English was idiomatic. I then translated the story into Chinese (my native language) and then showed it to a native Chinese speaker who teaches Chinese in Hong Kong. I then revised the Chinese version according to her suggestions to make sure that the Chinese was idiomatic.
 Then I went back to modify the English version slightly so that it would better match the revised Chinese version. And finally, I checked with a native English speaker to make sure that the final English version was good. Going back and forth between two (or more) languages can certainly be time-consuming. But in the long run, it should be worthwhile because it can help protect researchers from wasting valuable research resources on problematic stimulus materials.

Evaluation of Previous Findings

Researchers' inadequate knowledge about the languages of interest in cross-linguistic studies can cause problems not only in the stimulus materials, but also in the researchers' evaluation of potentially pertinent findings in the literature. For instance, Aaronson and Ferres' (1987) reliance on secondhand knowledge of the Chinese language led them to contradict themselves unknowingly. They wanted to compare Chinese morphemes and English words in terms of how much information is carried by these linguistic units. They were aware that this comparison was unfair because an average word carries more information than a morpheme. For instance, the word *walked* is made up of two morphemes (*walk* + *ed*) so that *walked* carries more information than just *-ed* alone. These researchers nevertheless went ahead to compare Chinese morphemes with English words because Chinese morphemes are separated by space in written Chinese, just as English words are separated by space in written English. This decision would probably have been somewhat more defensible if they had focused on written Chinese in their conclusions. But they later contradicted this decision--apparently unknowingly--when they cited Kratochvil's (1968) analysis of the Chinese morpheme *de* to support their claim that the meaning of a Chinese morpheme is often ambiguous. But the morpheme *de* is ambiguous only in spoken Chinese, not in written Chinese. If Aaronson and Ferres had known more about the Chinese language, they could have made a more informed evaluation of Kratochvil's analysis. They probably could also have avoided the unfortunate situation of focusing on written Chinese in their empirical work and trying to support their claims with an example that works in spoken but not written Chinese.

Subject Populations

The most commonly used design in cross-linguistic research is the between-subject design. Typically, native speakers of two different languages are asked to respond to stimulus materials in their own native language. A difference between the two groups of speakers' responses is often interpreted as something associated with, or caused by, the structural differences between the two languages. This kind of conclusion is problematic because there can be many other plausible explanations for such a group difference (see also Chen & Tsoi, 1990).

One example of this kind of methodological problem can be found in Lenneberg and Roberts' (1956) test of linguistic relativity in the domain of colour terms. They reasoned that if there is a parallel between language and thought, people should be better at remembering things that can be readily named in their language than things that have no simple names. They noticed that monolingual speakers of Zuni, an American Indian language, had a colour term (*lhupz?inna*) that covers both yellow and orange. Bilingual Zunis who spoke English as a second language typically would render this word as "yellow," and often used a loan-word (*?olenchi* from *orange* in English) or its more common derivative (*?olenchinanne*) for the orange colour. When Lenneberg and Roberts tested the recognition memory of Zunis for yellow and orange, all four of their monolingual Zuni subjects failed miserably. Their eight bilingual Zuni subjects remembered the colours better than the monolingual Zunis, but not as well as a group of native English speakers in a study conducted by Brown and Lenneberg (1954). These findings were interpreted as evidence for a parallel between language (colour names) and cognition (colour memory) and, hence, were taken as support for linguistic relativity.

These findings were, however, confounded with the subjects' age, schooling, test-taking experience, and familiarity with Western culture. According to Lenneberg and Roberts (1956, p. 31), "Unfortunately the monolingual subjects were elderly and on this basis alone were not representative of the general adult population." The monolingual Zunis' poor performance may have resulted from their poor memory of arbitrary items (such as the colours of Munsell colour chips) due to old age, rather than their not having distinct colour terms for yellow and orange. Furthermore, Lenneberg and Roberts (1956, p. 23) also noted, "Many [Zuni subjects] were somewhat apprehensive about participating in an unfamiliar test situation." By contrast, the native English speakers used as a comparison group were test-wise students at Harvard and Radcliffe Colleges. The Zunis' relatively poor performance, then, could have reflected their feeling uneasy in the testing situation (cf. Cole, Gay, Glick, & Sharp, 1971; Price-Williams, 1962).

Another well-known attempt to test the Sapir-Whorf hypothesis had similar problems. Whorf (1956) suggested that covert grammatical categories in a language may affect how its speakers perceive the world. For instance, whenever Navaho speakers talk about handling an object, they have to add a suffix called a classifier to the verb corresponding to the shape or some other important attribute of the object. So, they use one classifier for long flexible objects such as a piece of rope, another for long rigid objects such as a stick, and so forth. Carroll and Casagrande (1958) reasoned that the obligatory use of shape classifiers for verbs might make Navaho speakers more likely to group objects by shape than by, say, colour and size. They tested this hypothesis with Navaho children who spoke only or predominantly Navaho, Navaho children who spoke only or predominantly English, and Caucasian children who spoke only English. The children saw ten pairs of objects, one pair at a time. The pair members differed from each other in two of the following aspects: shape, colour, size. For each pair, the children had to decide which member went best with a third object that was similar to each pair member in one of two contrasting features but that matched neither member exactly. For instance, children saw a yellow stick and a blue rectangular block. Then they were asked which of these two objects went best with a blue stick. The findings with the Navaho children were exactly as Carroll and Casagrande had predicted. The Navaho-dominant children favored shape over colour in grouping objects; the English-dominant Navaho children favored colour over shape. Moreover, while in both groups the preference for shape increased with age, the former began to prefer shape to colour around three to four years of age; the later did not until nine years of age.

These results would be straightforward support for a weak form of linguistic relativity if they were not complicated by the findings with the Caucasian English-speaking children. By age four, these English-speaking children began to favor shape over colour in grouping objects. This finding is consistent with the results of other studies examining young children's colour and shape preference in classifying objects (e.g., Baldwin, 1989; Melkman, Tversky, & Baratz, 1981). This finding raises the question why these English-speaking children showed a shape preference as early on as the Navaho-dominant children. One other result further erodes the support for linguistic relativity initially offered by the findings with the Navaho children. Namely, the shape preference of the Caucasian children was even stronger than that of the Navaho-dominant children from around age four on, despite the obligatory use of shape classifiers in Navaho but not in English.

Carroll and Casagrande tried to explain these unexpected results by attributing the Caucasian children's preference to their experience with toys of various shapes. They argued that the shape-colour preference could be affected by experience in handling many objects of varied shapes as well as by covert shape-class in language. They were probably correct about the role of experience in handling objects of different shapes. In the 1950's, in an attempt to integrate American Indian children with the Caucasian community, some American Indian children were sent to boarding schools far away from their homes. Many of those schools were poorly equipped and had strict disciplines. As a result, children attending such schools probably had little time and few opportunities to play with many toys and objects of varied shapes. By contrast, the Navaho-dominant children probably spent most of their time on the reservation, and as a result had ample experience in handling objects of various shapes from their outdoor activities. Carroll and Casagrande did not report the home and school environments of the Navaho and Caucasian children. It is now impossible to find out whether the English-dominant Navaho children indeed attended schools that offered few opportunities to play with a variety of toys.

Because of the potential confound of different experiences in handling objects of various shapes, the difference in colour-shape preference between the English-dominant Navaho children and the Navaho-Dominant Navaho children is difficult to interpret. While Carroll and Casagrande could still be correct in their claim that the covert shape-classes in Navaho verbs would lead to shape preference in classifying object, their findings were inconclusive. There are other differences between the English-dominant and Navaho-dominant Navaho children that could also account for the findings in this study.

With 20/20 hindsight, one may find the confounding factors in Lenneberg and Roberts' and Carroll and Casagrande's studies painfully obvious. But these two studies are by no means unique. In fact, potential confounds such as educational level, home and school environments, and familiarity with Western culture are quite common in cross-linguistic studies. One way of dealing with this kind of problem is to look at the patterns of subjects' responses rather than their absolute performance. This is exactly what Heider (1972) did in her work on colour naming and colour memory of Dani--an Indonesian New Guinea language--and English speakers. She noticed that Some Dani speakers had only two basic colour terms (*mili* for "dark" and *mola* for "light"). By contrast, English speakers had eleven basic colour terms: *black, white, red, green, yellow, blue, brown, purple, pink, orange, grey*. She found that both English and Dani speaker remembered focal colours (e.g., red, green, yellow, blue) more accurately than non-focal colour colours (e.g., reddish brown, olive green, peach colour). Note that the Dani speakers did so even though they did not have colour terms for either the focal colours or the non-focal colours. Therefore, colour naming seems to be quite tangential to colour memory.

Interestingly, as in Lenneberg and Roberts' (1956) study, the English-speaking Americans in Heider's study remembered colour stimuli more accurately than speakers of a language with fewer basic colour terms. But this should be hardly surprising. Here again, the superior performance of the test-wise American subjects was completely confounded with the subjects' experience in test-taking. If Heider had only compared the absolute performance of the Dani speakers with that of the English speakers, she would probably have come to the same conclusion as Lenneberg and Roberts (1956). That is, better colour memory is associated with richer colour vocabularies. But by comparing instead the response patterns of the two subject populations, Heider was able to reveal that colour naming can be quite tangential to colour memory--just the opposite of Lenneberg and Roberts' conclusion.

While Heider's study provides rather compelling evidence for cultural universality and linguistic insignificance in colour memory, it remains an open question whether support for linguistic relativity can be uncovered in other domains (cf. Bloom, 1981). Researchers who are interested in finding support for linguistic relativity may wonder what kind of evidence would be good enough to silence skeptical critics of the Sapir-Whorf hypothesis. Here are two suggestions.

One strategy is to use bilingual speakers and randomly assign each subject to stimulus materials in either language. Because all of the subjects come from the same population, and the random assignment of subjects ensures that the subjects in the two language conditions will be comparable as long as the sample size is reasonably large (see also Au, 1983, 1984; Brown, 1986). This research design, however, does have two drawbacks. First, the subjects' mastery of the languages constitutes a potential experimental confound. For instance, suppose Bloom had found some native English speakers who also spoke Chinese as a second language and randomly assigned either the Chinese or the English version of a counterfactual story to each bilingual subject. Now suppose he found that the counterfactual response rate was higher for the English version than the Chinese version. Such a (hypothetical) finding affords at least two explanations. First, it is easier to reason counterfactually in English than in Chinese. Second, the bilinguals performed better in their native language than in a second language. Fortunately, this problem can be rather easily overcome by testing another type of bilinguals--native Chinese speakers who speak English as a second language. If the stimulus materials are genuinely comparable in the two languages, and if the bilinguals still perform better in English (their second language) than in Chinese (their native language), proponents of the Sapir-Whorf hypothesis might stand a better chance to convince their critics.

But this design may not provide a fair test of linguistic relativity because it may underestimate the effects of language on thought. For instance, if language indeed shapes the way we perceive and reason about the world, learning a second language might irreversibly alter a person's world view. So, the absence of language effect in an experiment done with only bilingual speakers could be due to the bilinguals' similar world views--views that are shaped by the same two languages. On the other hand, if this kind of design yields a language effect, even though the cards are stacked somewhat against revealing such effect, the results will be all the more compelling evidence of a robust language effect.

Another research strategy for finding convincing language effects is to look at patterns of responses rather than absolute performance. For instance, if one can find a linguistic marker that favors certain kind of thinking in one language, and another linguistic marker that favors another kind of thinking in another language, one can test both kinds of thinking in native speakers of such two languages. If language indeed shapes thinking, native speakers of one language should do better in one kind of thinking and worse in the other kind of thinking than native speakers of the other language. This kind of cross-over interaction pattern should give a boost to the view of language shaping thought.

Concluding Remarks

This essay set out to discuss some methodological issues in cross-linguistic study of language and cognition. Several research stories were recounted to illustrate and exemplify various methodological problems. Some are specific to language processing in Chinese, and other are relevant to cross-linguistic research in general. I have proposed some possible solutions to invite further discussion on, and proposed solutions for, these and other methodological problems in cross-linguistic research on language and thought. Do consider this a standing invitation.

References

Aaronson, D., & Ferres, S. (1987). The impact of language differences on language processing: An example from Chinese-English Bilingualism. In P. Homel, M. Palij, & D. Aaronson (Eds.), *Childhood bilingualism: Aspects of linguistic, cognitive, and social development* (pp. 75-119). Hillsdale, NJ: Erlbaum.

Au, T. K. (1983). Chinese and English counterfactuals: The Sapir-Whorf hypothesis revisited. *Cognition, 15*, 155-187.

Au, T. K. (1984). Counterfactuals: In reply to Alfred Bloom. *Cognition, 17*, 289-302.

Au, T. K. (1988). Language and cognition. In R. L. Schiefelbusch and L. L. Lloyd (Eds), *Language perspectives: Acquisition, retardation, and intervention* (125-146), second edition. Austin, TX: Pro-ed.

Au, T. K. (in press). Counterfactual reasoning. In G. R. Semin & K. Fiedler (Eds.), *Toward a social psychology of powerful linguistic devices*. London: Sage.

Baldwin, D. A. (1989). Priorities in children's expectations about object label reference: Form over color. *Child Development, 60*, 1291-1306.

Bickerton, D. (1990). *Language and Species*. Chicago: The University of Chicago Press.

Bloom, A. H. (1981). *The linguistic shaping of thought: A study in the impact of language on thinking in China and the West*. Hillsdale, NJ: Lawrence Erlbaum.

Bloom, A. H. (1984). Caution--the words you use may affect what you say: a

response to Au, *Cognition, 17,* 275-287.
Brown, R. (1986). *Social Psychology* (2nd Edition). New York: The Free Press.
Brown, R. W., & Lenneberg, E. H. (1954). A study in language and cognition. *Journal of Abnormal and Social Psychology, 49,* 454-462.
Carroll, J. B., & Casagrande, J. B. (1958). The function of language classifications in behavior. In E. E. Maccoby, T. M. Newcomb, & E. L. Hartley (Eds.), *Readings in social psychology* (pp. 18-31). New York: Holt, Rinehart and Winston.
Chao, Y. R. (1968). *A grammar of spoken Chinese.* Berkeley: University of California Press.
Chen, H.-C., & Tsoi, K.-C. (1990). Symbol-world interference in Chinese and English. *Acta Psychologica, 75,* 123-138.
Cheng, P. W. (1985). Pictures of ghosts: A critique of Alfred Bloom's *The linguistic shaping of thought. American Anthropologist, 87,* 917-922.
Cole, M., Gay, J., Glick, J. A., & Sharp, D. W. (1971). *The cultural context of learning and thinking.* New York: Basic Books.
Eifring, H. (1988). The Chinese counterfactual. *Journal of Chinese Linguistics, 16,* 193-217.
Garrett, M. (1983-85). Theoretical buffalo, conceptual kangaroos, and counterfactual fish: A review of Alfred Bloom's *The linguistic shaping of thought. Early China, 9-10,* 220-236.
Heider, E. R. (1972). Universals in color naming and memory. *Journal of Experimental Psychology, 93,* 10-20.
Kratochvil, P. (1968). *The Chinese language today.* London: Hutchinson University Press.
Lenneberg, E. H., & Roberts, J. M. (1956). The language of experience: A study in methodology. *International Journal of American Linguistics* (Memoir No. 13, Suppl. 22), 1-33.
Liu, L. G. (1985). Reasoning counterfactually in Chinese: Are there any obstacles? *Cognition, 21,* 239-270.
Melkman, R., Tversky, B., & Baratz, D. (1981). Developmental trends in the use of perceptual and conceptual attributes in grouping, clustering, and retrieval. *Journal of Experimental Child Psychology, 31,* 470-486.
Price-Williams, D. R. (1962). Abstract and concrete modes of classification in a primitive society. *British Journal of Educational Psychology, 32,* 50-61.
Ramsey, S. R. (1987). *The languages of China.* Princeton: Princeton University Press.
Sapir, E. (1949). In D. G. Mandelbaum (Ed.), *Selected writings of Edward Sapir in language, culture and personality.* Berkeley and Los Angeles: University of California Press.
Takano, Y. (1989). Methodological problems in cross-cultural studies of linguistic relativity, *Cognition, 31, 141-162.*
Vorster, J., & Schuring, G. (1989). Language and thought: Developmental perspectives on counterfactual conditionals. *South African Journal of Psychology, 19,* 34-38.
Whorf, B. L. (1956). In J. B. Carroll (Ed.), *Language, thought and reality: Selected*

writings of Benjamin Lee Whorf. Cambridge, MA: MIT Press.

Wu, K.-M. (1987). Counterfactuals, universals, and Chinese thinking--A review of The linguistic shaping of thought: A study in the impact of language on thinking in China and the West. *Philosophy East and West, 37,* 84-94.

Yen, S. L. (1977). On the negative wei in Classical Chinese. *Journal of the American Oriental Society, 97,* 469-481.

Author Index

A

Aaronson, D. 179,182,190,370,373, 374
Abbate, M. 220
Aitchison, J. 126,127,316
Allen, P.A. 27,29
Alva, L. 46
Aoun, J. 332
Arbib, M.A. 5
Arnoult, M.D. 5
Atkinson, R.C. 48
Attneave, F. 5
Au, T.K. 193,367-378,368,372,373

B

Baddeley, A. 124,168
Baker, C.L. 334
Baldwin, D. A. 376
Balota, D.A. 39,97
Baratz, D. 376
Bargh, K. 69
Barnes, M. 69,96
Baron, J. 48,68,69,166
Bates, E. 180,200,207-234,208,209, 210,212,214,216,227,230,231,285, 321
Battistella, E. 332,338
Bauer, D. 69
Beattie, G. 180
Beauvillain, C. 147

Beauvois, M-F. 351
Becker, G.A. 131
Beijing Language College 132,133, 134
Beilin, H. 243
Bell, L. 49
Bellugi, U. 293
Bentin, S. 93
Bergman, H. 328
Berwick, R. 334
Besner, D. 160,350,365
Bethell-Fox, C.E. 5
Bever, T.G. 262,283,285
Bias, R. G. 68
Bickerton, D. 368
Biederman, I. 7,8,9,24,25,27,31,46
Bloom, A. H. 368,369,370,371,372, 377,378
Bloom, L. 271,291,321
Bohn, L. 192
Borer, H. 316,339
Bourne, L.E. 184
Bowerman, M. 321
Bradley, D. 133
Braine, M. 282
Bronckart, J. 285
Brown, G. 97
Brown, G.D.A. 105
Brown, R. 271,288,334,374,378
Bruck. M. 96
Bub, D. 351
Buchanan, M. 124

Burani, C. 143
Butterworth, B. 126,349-366,351

C

Cairns, H. 258
Campbell, R. 351
Cancelliere, A. 351
Cao, F. 245
Cao, H. 16
Caramazza, A. 132,133,137,142, 143
Carpenter, P.A. 132,181,182,183, 185,186,187
Carroll, J. B. 375,376,377
Casagrande, J. B. 375,376,377
Chafe, W.L. 322
Chambers, S.M. 68,95
Chan, K.-T. 182,187
Chang, H.W. 180,213,247,248,260, 263,277-311,283,284,300,303,304, 305,307,308,335,337,338,341
Chang, L.H. 24
Chang, S.W. 30
Chang, Y.K. 112,113,117,118,119, 127
Chao, W. H. 349
Chao, Y.R. 121,180,195,210,211, 213,230,231,278,279,294,299, 301,302,304,370,372
Charney, R. 247
Chen, G. 210
Chen, G.P. 248,262,263
Chen, H.-C. 17,18,46,151-172,165, 171,175-207,177,178,182,184, 187,193,199,200,202,374,377
Chen, J.W. 11
Chen, M.J. 187
Chen, S. 43,210,217,227,228
Cheng, C.-M. 7,25,29,67-92,75,85, 90,97,112,115,179
Cheng, G.P. 246
Cheng, P.W. 372

Cheng, R.L. 153,156
Cheng, S.W. 280,281,282,288,291
Chien, Y.-C. 313-345,315,316,321, 323,325,326,328,329,330,335,336, 337,338,340
Chomsky, C. 283
Chomsky, N. 313,314,315,316,330
Chu, D.S. 302
Chuang, C.J. 4,123,179
Chumbley, J.I. 94,95,96,104
Chung, C.Y. 302
Clark, E. 244,248,251,299
Clark, H. 244,248,299
Clifford, T. 328
Cole, M. 375
Cole, P. 133,141,142,145,332,338
Collins, A. M. 71
Coltheart, M. 47,69,350,351
Comrie, B. 213,231
Conboy, G.L. 18
Conrad, R. 48
Cook, V.J. 316
Corrigan, R. 214
Cotton, B. 4,42
Cromer, R. 262
Culicover, P. 334
Cutler, A. 141

D

Danks, J.H. 180,184,185,192,199, 200
Davelaar, E. 160,350
de Villiers, P.A. 307
de Villiers, J.G. 307,321
Derouesne, J. 351
Deutsch, W. 247
Devescovi, A. 208,321
Ding, S-S. 213
Drewnowski, A. 18,27,178

E

Eifring, H. 370,371
Ellis, A. 180
Elman, J.L. 42
Emerson, P.L. 29
Endo, M. 42
Erickson, D. 49
Erickson, J.R. 26
Eriksen, B.A. 54
Eriksen, C.W. 54
Ervin-Tripp, S. 288

F

Fang, F.X. 249,272
Fang, S.P. 7,17,18,27,46,96
Fears, R. 192
Feng, L. 16
Ferres, S. 179,182,190,370,373,374
Feustel, T. 46
Flores d'Arcais, G.B. 41,52,53,55, 56,60,61
Flynn, S. 328
Fodor, J.D. 48
Forster, K.I. 68,96,132,137,141
Fowler, C. A. 70
Francis, W. 7
Francis, W.N. 179
Franklin, S. 351,364
Frazier, L. 48
Freeman, R.H. 131
Freyd, J.J. 166
Friedmann, R.B. 41
Frith, U. 350
Frost, R. 93,94
Fujimura, O. 48
Furlin, K.R. 113,128

G

Garner, W.R. 24
Garrett, M. 370
Gass, S. 214
Gay, J. 375

Gelade, G. 16,17
Geschwind, H. 41
Gibson, E.J. 8
Gilligan, G. 147
Givon, T. 211
Gleitman, L. 315,316,321,339
Glick, J. A. 375
Glucksberg, S. 185
Glushko, R.J. 69,94,95,104
Gough, P. 48
Graesser, A.C. 182,183,186,190, 192
Green, D.W. 182
Greenberg, J.H. 113,128,279
Gruber, J.S. 321
Guo, D.J. 148
Guo, X.C. 253,269,272
Guo, Y. 248

H

Haber, L.R. 123
Haber, R.N. 123
Haberlandt, K.F. 182,183,186,190, 192
Hagiwara, H. 38,43
Hakamura, I. 42
Hamburger, H. 334
Hankamer, J. 131,132
Hanlon, C. 334
Hannen, P. 42
Hanson, V. L. 70
Harbert, W. 338,339
Hardyck, C. 42
Hartje, W. 42
Hatta, T. 41,42,46
Hawkins, J.A. 147
He, L. 148
Healy, A.F. 18,27,178,184
Heider, E. R. 377
Henderson, L. 38,97,131,142
Hermon, G. 332,338
Hildebrandt, N. 38,42

Hillinger, M. L. 68,70,71,72,89
Hirata, K. 41
Hiscock, M. 42
Ho, C. 187,199
Honjon, Y. 42
Hood, L. 321
Hoosain, R. 38,111-130,112,121, 123,125,168,179,200
Hopcroft, J.E. 5
Hori, T. 42
Hornak, R. 70
Horng, R.Y. 94
Hornstein, D. 313
Hornstein, N. 313
Howard, D. 351,364
Hsi, M.S. 43
Hsieh, N.-M. 70,71,72,73,89
Hsu, C-C. 45
Hsu, J. 258
Hu, C.Q. 349,356
Hua, H.Q. 265
Huang, C.-T.J. 317,323,327,332, 338,341
Huang, H.L. 304,305,307
Huang, J.T. 4,7,9,10,11,15,16,17, 19,21,22,25,26,28,112,115,124, 125
Huang, S.F. 180
Hue, C.W. 26,93-108,105
Huey, E.B. 176
Hung, D.L. 3,4,38,42,43,49,93,200,
Hyams, N. 315

I

Ingram, D. 258
Inhelder, B. 268
Itoh, M. 41

J

Jakobson, R. 240
Jared, D. 97,104,105

Jeng, L.Y. 285
Jensen, C. R. 74
Jerg, A.G-J. 42
Ji, G.P. 20
Jing, Q. 123
Johnson, N.F. 27
Jonasson, J. 350
Juola, J.F. 165,177,184,200
Just, M.A. 132,133,181,182,183, 184,185,186,187,190,192

K

Kapur, S. 338,339
Katz, L. 93
Kawakami, M. 60,61
Kay, J. 350
Kerlinger, F.N. 186
Kershner, J.R. 42
Kertesz, A. 351
Kfoury, A.J. 5
Kiely, J. 186
Kieras, D.E. 186
Kimura, Y. 48
Kintsch, W. 185
Kirsner, K. 46
Kitamura, S. 45
Kliegl, R. 180,285
Kobayashi, Y. 41
Kong, L.D. 255
Kratochvil, P. 373,374
Krueger, L.E. 48
Kucera, H. 7,179
Kuczaj, S. 244
Kuo, W.F. 44
Kurcz, I. 180,192,200
Kwan, S.T. 349

L

LaChappelle, N. 220
Lai, C. 17
Lam, A. 49

Landau, B. 315,316
Laudanna,A. 132,143
Lee, S-Y. 45
Lees, R.B. 114
Lenneberg, E. H. 374,375,377
Leong, C.K. 42
Leung, Y.-S. 189
Levin, H. 8
Lewis, S.S. 48,69
Li, C. 180,185,211,212,279,281, 282,287,290,291,297,298,302,304, 322
Li, H.-T. 72
Li, J. 349
Li, P. 180,190,207-234,211,213, 214,217,230,231
Li, W. 16
Li, X.N. 255
Li, X.T. 349,356
Li, Y.-H.A. 317,332,341
Li, Y.M. 238,239
Lightbown, P. 321
Lightfoot, D. 313
Lin, J. 265
Lin, Y.T. 113
Liou, S.N. 25,26
Liu, A.L. 349
Liu, H. 180,207-234,214,230
Liu, I.M. 4,24,26,112,115,117,121, 122,179
Liu, L.G. 372
Liu, Y.M. 302
Loftus, E. F. 71
Lu, J-M. 212
Lucker, G.W. 45
Luo, C.R. 20
Lust, B. 315,316,321,323,325,326, 327,328,329,330,338,339,340,341
Lyman, R.S. 349,366

M

MacWhinney, B. 180,200,207,208, 209,212,214,216,227,231,285,321
Madden, D.J. 27,29
Makita, K. 44,45
Manelis, L. 131
Mangione, L. 321,339
Manzini, R. 316,318,333,334,335, 336
Maratsos, M. 244
Marcel, A. 350
Marcel, T. 350
Marr, D. 10
Marshall, J.C. 350,351,352,364
Martin, R. C. 74
Martohardjono, G. 338,339
Mattingly, I.G. 49
McCann, R. S. 160
McCarthy, R. 350,351
McClelland, J.L. 8,17,28,29,31,96, 350
McCusker, L. X. 69
McGregor, C.J. 350
McNamara, T.P. 18,184
McNeil, D. 293,321
McNew, S. 208,321
McRae, K. 97,98
Melkman, R. 376
Meyer, D. 94
Meyer, D. E. 68,69,70,72,73,74,81, 88,89
Miao, X.C. 180,286,237-275,252, 253,258,260,262,209,210,214, 217,227,228
Miceli, G. 132
Miller, G.A. 111
Millis-Wright, M. 17
Min, R.F. 246,272
Miron, M.S. 125
Mitchell, D.C. 182
Mito, H. 42
Moll, R.N. 5
Monoi, H. 43
Mori, K. 41
Morita, M. 122,177

Mozer, M.C. 17
Muise, J.G. 97
Murphy, G.L. 126

N

Naremore, R. 244
Neely, J. M. 80
Nelson, K. 262
Newcombe, F. 350,351,352,364
Ng, M.-L. 199
Norris, D. 97

O

O'Regan, J.K. 177
Ohnishi, H. 42
Oliver, W. 18
Orchard, L.N. 122,177
Osaka, R. 41
Osgood, C.E. 121,125

P

Paradis, H. 38,43
Patterson, K.E. 350
Pechmann, T. 247
Pedhazur, E.J. 186
Peng, D.L. 122,131-150,177
Peng, R.X. 24
Peng, Z.Z. 253,256
Perfetti, C.A. 44,49
Perfetti, C.A. 185
Piaget, J. 268
Pinker, S. 313,314
Podgorny, P. 5
Poggio, T. 10
Polkowska, A. 192
Pollatsek, A. 177,178,181,184,185
Pomerantz, J. 24
Ponitzky, S. 44
Posner, M. I. 74,81

Potter, M.C. 41
Price-Williams, D. R. 375
Prinzmetal, W. 17

R

Ramsey, S. R. 371
Rayner, K. 177,178,181,184,185
Reicher, G. 121
Reinhart, T. 322,330,339
Reuland, E. 339
Riha, J.R. 182,186
Roberts, J. M. 374,375,377
Roeper, T. 315
Romani 132
Rozin, P. 44,45
Rubenstein, H.R. 48,69
Rubenstein, M.A. 48,69
Rubin, G.S. 131
Ruddy, M.G. 68,94
Rumelhart, D.E. 9,28,29,31

S

Saito, H. 52,53,60,61
Sakurai, S. 9,10,11
Salili, F. 168
Sampson, G. 352,361
Sanders, E. 70
Sapir, E. 368
Sasanuma, S. 41,43,48,352
Scarborough, H.S. 182
Schneider, N.J. 182,186
Schreuder, R. 41
Schuring, G. 372
Schvaneveldt, R.W. 68,94
Segui, J.
Seidenberg, M.S. 49,68,69,94,96,
  97,99,101,104,105,350
Sergent, J. 121
Seymour, P. H.K. 350
Shallice, T. 350,351
Shao, W.M. 248

Sharp, D. W. 375
Shen, E. 177
Shepard, R.N. 5
Shiffrin, R.M. 48
Shimamura, A.P. 46
Shimizu, A. 42
Shou, Y.F. 299
Shulman, H. G. 70
Silveri, M.C. 132
Sima, H.A. 123
Simon, H.A. 123,124
Sinclair, H. 285
Slobin, D. 262,268,271,283,285,289
Smith, M.C. 46
Smith., S. 208,321
Snyder, C. R. R. 74,81
Snyder, W. 328
So, K.F. 41
Song, Z.G. 248
Sotsky, R. 44
Souther, J. 17
Stanovich, K. E. 69
Stark, L.W. 122,177
Stern, J.A. 122,177
Stevenson, H.W. 45
Stigler, J.W. 45
Strand, T.L. 27
Strawson, C. 68,69
Strohner, H. 262
Sun, B. 349
Sun, C.-F. 211,228
Sun, C.W. 9
Sun, F. 177,179
Sun, F.C. 122
Sung, L.-M. 332,338

T

Taft, M. 132,133,136,137,140,141,
  145,151-172,152,160,161,164,165,
  166
Tai, C.J. 245,247
Tai, J. 211

Takahashi, K. 42
Takano, Y. 372
Tanenhaus, M.K. 69,96
Tang, C.-C.J. 332,338
Tang, C.M. 349,356
Tang, J. 260,267
Tang, T.C. 180,280,302
Tang, X.J. 349
Taylor, I. 5,180
Taylor, M.M. 5,180
Taylor, S.E. 177
Tharp, D. 131
Theios. J. 97
Thompson, S. 180,195,211,222,279,
  281,282,287,290,291,297,302,304,
  322
Thomson, N. 124
Tohsaku, Y.H. 42
Treiman, R. 166
Treisman, A. 16,17
Tsao, F.-F. 322
Tsao, Y-C. 46,57
Tseng, S.C. 24
Tsoi, K.-C. 46,177,193,199,200,374
Tsou, S.L. 9,23
Turvey, N.T. 49
Tversky, B. 376
Tyack, D. 258
Tzeng, C.-H. 85
Tzeng, O.C.S. 125
Tzeng, O.J.L. 3,4,38,42,43,46,49,
  93,94,200,210

U

Ullman, J.D. 5
Underwood, G. 69

V

Valian, V. 315,316,321
Van Dijk, T.A. 185
Vorster, J. 372

W

Wakayama, T. 337,338
Wang, C.C. 24
Wang, L. 223,231,279
Wang, L.H. 117
Wang, M.Y. 25,26
Wang, S.C. 4,112,179,302
Wang, W.S.-Y. 4,42,49,57,95,153, 180
Wang, X.D. 349,356
Wang, Y.M. 263
Wanner, E. 315,316,321
Ward, N. 184
Warrington, E.K. 351
Washington, D. 244
Waters, G.S. 69,96
Weinberg, A. 334
Wells, G. 280
Wexler, K. 314,315,316,318,333, 334,335,336,337,338,339,341
Whorf, B. L. 368,375
Willems, K. 42
Williams, E. 315
Wolfe, S. 125
Wong, A. 42
Wong, S. 42
Woolley, J.D. 182
Wu, C.J. 13,14,15,25
Wu, H.Y. 241
Wu, J. 43
Wu, J.Z. 242,252,253,255,256,259, 260,264,267,268,269,270
Wu, K.-M. 370,371
Wu, M.F. 46
Wu, P. 7,17,18,27
Wu, R. 132
Wu, T.M. 238,241,253,256,272
Wu, W.Z. 349

X

Xin Hua Zi Dian (Chinese Dictionary) 362
Xu, H.H. 259
Xu, Y. 168,171
Xu, Z.Y. 238,239,246,252,253,256, 272

Y

Yang, K.S. 299
Yang, L.Y. 295,296,297,298,299
Yang, W.C. 30
Yang, Y.W. 299
Yeh, J.S. 26,115
Yen, S. L. 370
Yin, W. 349-366,353,359,363,364
Ying, H. 210
Ying, H.C. 242,248,249,262
Yu, B. 16,123

Z

Zajonc, R.B. 125
Zhang, B.Y. 131-159,145
Zhang, G. 123,124
Zhang, J.G. 245,246,265
Zhang, R.J. 238,239,243,272
Zhang, S. 49
Zhou, G.G. 255
Zhou,Y.G. 95
Zhu, J.Q. 241
Zhu, L.M. 242
Zhu, M.S. 237-275,238,239,242, 245,246,252,253,257,259,260,261, 264,267,268,269,270,272
Zhu, Y.L. 349
Zhuang, X.J. 242

Subject Index

A

Abstract phonological representation 156
Activation-synthesis model 95-96, 104
Animacy 180,207-211,213-215,217-218,221-229,231,277
Aphasia 37,43,210,356

B

Bilingual processing 199
Binding 316,320,333-336,338,340
Binding principles 316,320,330-331

C

C-command 316,330-333,335,338, 340
Character boundary 151-170,176, 178
Character complexity 27,42,154, 158,176-178,180,186,189-191
Character inferiority effect 20,178
Character network 145-146
Character recognition 5-6,8-10,14, 20,25-33,37-61,67,104,178
Character vs. word 111-130,176-181,349-353,359,362-364
Chinese aphasia 37,210
Chinese bigram 18

Chinese-English bilingual 46,122, 193,199,230,370
Classical Chinese 118-119,370
Coindexing 316
Competition Model 208-209,229
Complexity effect 25-28,30
Component processes in reading 185-192
Components parsing 14,48
Compound character 7,9,19,29
Comprehension processes 48,185, 192-200
Confounds 377
Context effect 30-31,33,38
Context-oriented language 229
Cooperative algorithm 12
Counterfactual reasoning 368-369, 371,373
Cross-cultural differences 368-369
Cross-linguistic research 367,374, 379
Crosslinguistic comparison 208
Cue strength 208,227
Cue validity 208

D

Decomposed storage 131
Deep dyslexia 43,59,351,353,360, 362-363,365
Definiteness 228
Dyslexia 37,41,43-45,58,349-351,

353,360,362-363,365

E

Emergent features 27,28,30
Eye movements 111,122-123,177, 181
Eye-voice span (EVS) 32

F

Face recognition 33
Fixation position 177

G

Governing category 316,318,331-333
Graphemic activation process 37,54-56,165-166

H

Homophony 151,153,157-159,161, 163,166-167
Horizontally-structured characters 7,14,18,20,26
Horse-racing model 5,29,30
Human thinking 368-369

I

Illusory conjunction 19-21
INFL (inflection) 11,126,176,180, 193,195,279,332-333
Inflectional morphology 211,229
Inflectional markings 176,180,193, 195,229
Inhibitory link 143-144
Interactive activation model 31,33, 208

L

Language acquisition/development 37,41,44-45,208,237-275,277-311, 313-316,319-330,339-340
Language faculty 315-316,318-321, 333
Language structure 193,200-201,369
Lateralization 6,37,41-43,50
Learnability 334
Left-branching 328-329
Lexical access 6,37-39,44,47-48,51-54,61,67-91,93,95,97-99,132, 137,142,185,193
Lexical procedure 350,
Lexical structure 111-130,131-150, 152-153,169
Lexical violation 151,159-160,166, 169,171,195-199
Lexicon 30,38-39,43,47-48,50, 53,67-69,79,94,104,111,120,126-128,131-133,137,139-146,166
LF (Logical Form) 332-333,338-340
Linguistic determinism 368
Linguistic relativity 368,374,376-378
Linguistic variation 209
Local binding 333-336
Logical problem of language acquisition 313-314,340
Long-distance binding 334-336,338, 340

M

Mandarin Chinese 49,214,229,277-278,302,308
Mandarin vs. Cantonese 49
Marginal frequency 9
Memory access 25-28,30
Methodological Challenges 367
Morpheme 111-120,125-128,131-133,137,139,141-146,152,176-178,211,213,253,277-279,283, 285,294,309,352,370,373

Subject Index

Morphological complexity 180
Morphologically decomposed form 131,142-143,145

N

Naming 6,9,18,27,29,33,37,40-41,46-47,49,56,59-62,68-69,87,93-101,103-104,377
Nominal compound 6,114-115,120
Nonaccidental property 5,9,11-12,21

O

Object marker 207,211-212,218,226-230
Object recognition 9,11,26-27,29-30
On-line methods of studying reading
   eye-monitoring 181-183
   moving-window 175-176,181-185,187,192,199,201
   multiple-word display 182
   single-word display 182
Orthographic depth Model 96,101,104
Orthography 41-43,45-46,49,62,72,75,89,93-94,104,132,141,165-167,295,352

P

Parameter-setting 319-320,319-320,334-340
Parameters 315-316,319-320,334,340
Passive marker 207,211,213,218,226-229
Perceptual cohesiveness 19-20
Perceptual separability 14-15,18,29
Phonological activation process 37-40,42-44,47-51,57-61,67-91,153,156,161,164-165,167,169-170
Phonological dyslexia 351

Principal branching direction 313,327,329-330
Principles and parameters Model 313-315,319,321,339
Psychological reality 29,111,115

R

Reading 37-40,43-45,47-51,62
Reading comprehension 175-205
Reading strategies 175,177,181,185-200
Recognition-by-components (RBC) 9,26,30,38,61
Recursive structure 7
Regressions 184
Right-branching 328

S

Saccade length 122,177
Sapir-Whorf hypothesis 368-369,371,375,377-378
Semantic activation process 37,39,42,48-61,175,180-181,185,188,192-195,197-199
Semantic errors 352-353,359-361,363-364
Semantic violation 185,193-194,197-199
Sentence interpretation 185,200,208-210,212,214,216-218,226,228,230,279,283-284,286-287
Stem compound 7,9,14,19-21,29,39,57
Stroop effect 37,46-47,50
Structure-dependent nature 320-321,330,339
Subitizing 15
Subject-orientation 332-333,339
Subject-prominent 322
Subset principle 320,334-338,340
Surface dyslexia 43,349,351,353,360

Syntactic boundary 188,190
Syntactic violation 196-197
Syntax acquisition 308

T

Task demand in reading 190,200
Tones 151,153,156-164,167-170, 239,266
Topic 112,151,185,271,279,281-282,308,321-327,330
Topic-prominent 255,322

U

UG (Universal grammar) 315-316, 330,332,338-340
Unique compound 19
Unit frequency 9,19-21,29

V

Vertically-structured characters 7,18,26
Visual gluing 22,25

W

Word boundary 111-115,117-118, 120,122,128,152-154,158,160-161, 164-167,169-171,176-179
Word inferiority effect 178
Word length 177-178,183,186-191, 195
Word order 133,180,196,207-212, 214-215,217-218,221-229,254-255, 263-264,277,279-286,291-294,321-323,327,329-330,340
Word recognition 5,6,11,25,29,32, 33,68,93-95,105,132-134,140-141, 144-146,200
Word superiority effect 6,31